Seeming Knowledge

Studies in Christianity and Literature 1

Seeming Knowledge

Shakespeare and Skeptical Faith

JOHN D. COX

BAYLOR UNIVERSITY PRESS

Cover Design: Cynthia Dunne, Blue Farm Graphics
Cover Image: Aristotle (384–322 BC) with a Bust of Homer, 1653 (oil on can-
vas), Rembrandt Harmensz. van Rijn (1606–69) / , Metropolitan Museum of
Art, New York, USA / The Bridgeman Art Library. Used by permission.

Library of Congress Cataloging-in-Publication Data

Cox, John D., 1945-
  Seeming knowledge : Shakespeare and skeptical faith / John D. Cox.
     p. cm. -- (Studies in Christianity and literature ; 1)
  Includes bibliographical references and index.
  ISBN 978-1-932792-95-9 (cloth/hardcover : acid-free paper)
  1. Shakespeare, William, 1564-1616--Philosophy. 2. Shakespeare, William,
1564-1616--Religion. 3. Skepticism in literature. 4. Knowledge, Theory of,
in literature. I. Title.

  PR3001.C67 2007
  822.3'3--dc22

                                   2007022393

Printed in the United States of America on acid-free paper with a minimum
of 30% pcw recycled content.

To Hope

CONTENTS

Rembrandt's portrait of Aristotle with a bust of Homer is an artist's interpretation of a philosopher thinking about a poet, and the painting is therefore a fitting icon for a book that endeavors to interpret how a playwright thought about various philosophical problems in his plays and poems—including the problem of his own art. Rembrandt imagines Aristotle not as a fourth-century Greek but in a fantastic costume, apparently of the artist's own devising (it has no identifiable historical model), and since Rembrandt knew a good deal about ancient fashion, this sartorial invention would seem to be deliberate and meaningful. Perhaps it acknowledges that at least in some part of him, the ancient philosopher thinks like Rembrandt, because this is Rembrandt's Aristotle.[1]

Rembrandt's version of Aristotle's contemplation offers other hints as to how the artist imagines the philosopher's thinking. From the chain around Aristotle's neck hangs a medallion that bears the image of Alexander, the philosopher's former pupil who, however, preferred to model himself on Achilles, the greatest of warrior heroes imagined by Homer, the poet whose bust Aristotle touches with his right hand, while his left touches the chain from which the medallion hangs. This implicit positioning of the philosopher between the poet and the hero is suggested also in Aristotle's gaze, which focuses reflectively on the middle distance between the bust and the chain. The painting thus seems to contrast the contemplative solitude of the moral philosopher in his study with the action of godlike heroes, yet only the philosopher is alive in the painting, while both the poet and the hero are present only in artistic remembrances—a marble bust and a medallion. Yet Aristotle too is alive in Rembrandt's portrait only in artistic remembrance. This is very much an artist's way of imagining certain philosophical problems that the painting implicitly addresses in its distinctive medium, and it therefore offers parallels to what I am suggesting about the thinking in Shakespeare's plays and poems[2]

Many of the puzzles of Rembrandt's painting are also puzzles in Shakespeare's writing. Both dress the past in a complex and ambiguous vision of the artist's own imagining; both contrast action and contemplation; for both, the quality of artistic representation is fictive and illusory; both challenge the viewer's ability to know and describe just what we are seeing as we contemplate what the artist imagines; both raise the difficulty of interpreting ideas in an artistic medium that has made them its own, and for Shakespeare this difficulty is compounded by the theatrical medium, because it adds words to visual presentation, so that what we see is not stationary and permanent, like a painting, but active and momentary and capable of remarkable interpretive variety each time it is theatrically realized.

In approaching Shakespeare's plays and poems, this book foregrounds ideas—as Rembrandt's painting implicitly does in its central figure—while keeping the poetic and theatrical medium always in mind. The book focuses on skepticism, the primary philosophical innovation of the sixteenth century, because skepticism has come to be Shakespeare's assumed position. I agree with this assessment, but I argue that skepticism in the sixteenth century is too often read as a direct counterpart to what it became in the heyday of the Enlightenment. In contrast, I describe an outlook that I call skeptical faith, which I argue is represented most influentially in the sixteenth century by More and Erasmus, as a result of their discovery of the skeptical dialogues of the Greek satirist, Lucian, translated and published by them in the interest of reforming church and society. Skeptical faith also, however, describes the reaction to the translation of Sextus Empiricus in 1562, as each side of the Reformation divide appropriated Pyrrhonist arguments to demolish what it took to be the rational underpinnings of the heretical other. As an example of skeptical faith, Shakespeare is closer to the early humanists than to the Reformation combatants, and his response to the human situation might better be described, I suggest, as suspicion than skepticism, because he is more doubtful about those who know than he is about what they know. In this, Shakespeare is closely akin to More and Erasmus, though his affinity with them may have more to do with his debt to medieval religious drama than to direct or even indirect borrowing from early sixteenth-century humanist writing.

The book is divided into two parts, in the first of which I examine the influence of skeptical faith on Shakespeare's sense of dramatic genre; in the second, on the shape of his thinking with regard to particular philosophical problems. Where genre is concerned, I devote a chapter apiece to the three kinds of plays that John Heminge and Henry Condell identified when they compiled the 1623 First Folio: comedy, history, and tragedy. Comedy and tragedy were familiar, because they derived from classical theory and practice, and Shakespeare was certainly acquainted with Plautus and Seneca, the ancient playwrights who were thought to be the best in each kind by Renaissance critical theorists. Yet Shakespeare increasingly puts his own distinctive stamp on each of these genres as his writing matures, and I argue that what makes them most distinctive is Shakespeare's continuing reflection on the narrative of salvation history and its way of imagining the human situation. This reflection is rendered allusively, not allegorically, and it does not fully reveal meaning in either comedy or tragedy, because the plays consistently imagine human beings in the fallen world, well short of the apocalypse ("revelation") and therefore encumbered by imperfection, both in themselves and in what they know. This burden, I argue, is the best explanation of Shakespeare's suspicion. The resolution that marks the end of comedy thus comes well short of perfection, while the end of tragedy emphasizes the mystery of suffering, not its meaning, by confronting us with the need to acknowledge another's pain, not to explain it, because its meaning is not revealed.

The history play is Shakespeare's most original genre, because it has no classical precedent, but it too derives from the narrative of salvation history, which offered Elizabethan playwrights the only precedent for treating history dramatically. Shakespeare's debt to medieval religious drama of all kinds is evident in the early history plays, and I argue that *2 Henry VI* in particular (possibly the earliest of them) may be inspired by Skelton's *Magnificence*. Yet the debt is not allegorical, and the meaning of history in Shakespeare's history plays is not providential, as in the mystery plays. Shakespeare's characters create their own destiny, as they struggle to acquire and maintain political power, and in that respect the plays are secular. Their secularity is marked by their open-endedness, which is a structural characteristic of the plays themselves, and by their thematic attention to time, the essence of secular history.

The second part of the book turns from dramatic genre to ideas. Here the strategy is to focus on five philosophical problems, in light of which the plays and poems can be usefully discussed with skeptical faith in mind: politics, ethics, esthetics, ontology, and epistemology. In chapter 5 I consider politics, in order to maintain continuity with chapter 4, on the history play as a genre, and to address what Shakespeare seems to be doing politically in the mature history plays, the so-called second tetralogy. I argue that his focus on the struggle for political power is skeptical, topical, and original. It is skeptical because it implicitly challenges Tudor commonplaces about the clarity of divine right. It is topical because Shakespeare makes monarchical succession the implicit source of tension and conflict in all nine of his Elizabethan history plays, and the question of who would succeed Elizabeth I was perhaps the most urgent issue of her regime, though discussion of it was forbidden. As a question of what we now call political science, monarchical succession is an original topic for Shakespeare, because Machiavelli—the early modern thinker who has the best claim to be called a political scientist—shows little or no interest in it. I argue further that mere rationalizing in the interest of power is limited in Shakespeare's histories by the moral limitations of the monarch as a human being before God. This is explicit in *Richard II* and brilliantly implicit in other, more successful, seekers after power, like Henry IV and V.

Chapter 6 takes up the question of ethics by focusing on stoicism in the Roman plays, from *Titus Andronicus* to *Cymbeline*. In most of Shakespeare's plays, moral recognition is inseparable from faith, so ethical questions are addressed by addressing religious ones, but Shakespeare consistently identifies stoic thinking about ethics with ancient Rome, as if that were Rome's most distinctive quality, and his stoics pursue virtue as if it were an achievable goal of autonomous human effort, distinct from religious belief. After *Titus Andronicus*, Shakespeare imagines with increasing perceptiveness and skepticism how characters live according to a stoic model. The gap between affirmation and action is central, as it is in Christian ethics, but the stoic quest for virtuous perfection yields other ambiguities, which Shakespeare depicts sometimes in isolation, as in *Julius Caesar* and *Coriolanus*, and sometimes in implicit conjunction with Christian virtue, as in *Antony and Cleopatra* and *Cymbeline*.

I treat esthetics, epistemology, and ontology together in chapter 7, because they were not distinguished as separate philosophical questions before the Enlightenment, and I argue that Shakespeare's blending of them is therefore characteristic of thinking in his own day—an example of his being very much of an age in some things, rather than for all time. Shakespeare's esthetic self-consciousness has long been recognized, admired, and explicated, but its deep immersion in religious questions of his day makes it inseparable from questions of knowledge and the nature of being. Sidney's *Defense of Poesie* implicitly defends the English church's compromise on religious signs, and Shakespeare's frequent references to his own fictive art imply a similar position, with the difference that Shakespeare is more receptive to the medieval theater of signs than Sidney is, and Shakespeare's dramatic art is therefore more richly informed by medieval dramatic art than neoclassical strictures allowed.

The concluding chapter situates Shakespeare's epistemology in the context of contemporary thinking, especially in France. The history of modern epistemology is usually traced to Descartes, and Richard Strier has recently followed Stanley Cavell in arguing that Shakespeare's skepticism is analogous to Descartes's, even though Shakespeare was thirty years older than Descartes and died twenty years before Descartes first published. With Stuart Clark's comments about Descartes's "evil genius" in mind, however, Strier's incisive observation can be taken in the opposite direction: not to confirm Shakespeare as a nascent rationalist skeptic but to show that he was equally uncertain (along with Descartes and virtually everyone else in the early seventeenth century) about the precise borders between visible reality and demonological illusion. Montaigne's influence on Shakespeare is certain, judging from Shakespeare's paraphrase of Montaigne's essay "On the Cannibals" in *The Tempest*. Montaigne's skepticism relates principally to self-knowledge, as Geoffrey Miles has recently argued, and insofar as it is directed to motive and behavior, it might be identified more accurately with suspicion than with skepticism. Looked at this way, Shakespeare's affinity with Montaigne puts Shakespeare closer to Pascal than to Descartes. Pascal was even younger than Descartes, of course, so the issue is not one of influence but of affinity. Pascal was more strongly influenced by Montaigne than by any other writer, and Pascal's celebrated Christian skepticism makes Pascal a more illuminating parallel to Shakespeare than Descartes among seventeenth-century French thinkers.

Anyone who writes a book is aware of how much it owes to others, and I want to acknowledge, as best I can, those who have helped to make this book possible. The National Endowment for the Humanities supported me during a year's leave of absence in 2004–2005, when I was capably assisted by the hard-working, conscientious, and expert staff of the Folger Shakespeare Library in Washington, D.C. I received constant encouragement, especially in the form of critical questions, from Patricia Parker, who was in residence at the Folger during the same year. She invited several other readers to her flat for a discussion of chapter 3 in April 2005. I am grateful to Peter Erickson, Mariko Ichikawa, Kate Narveson (and her visiting husband, Eric Crump), and Virginia Vaughan for their time and ideas on that occasion. Debora Shuger read the entire book twice in various forms and had valuable suggestions for improving it both times. Her meticulous penciled comments on the typescripts have saved me from many errors and pointed me in many helpful new directions. Others who have read part or all of this book and offered invaluable assistance in improving it include Sarah Beckwith, Michael Bristol, Curtis Gruenler, Alan Jacobs, Anthony Low, Richard Strier, and Merold Westphal. I am grateful to Patrick Henry for inviting me to contribute an essay about Shakespeare and philosophy to *Philosophy and Literature*; the resulting essay eventually became part of chapter 5. A version of chapter 1 appeared in *Religion and Literature*, of chapter 2 in *International Shakespearean Yearbook*, and of chapter 8 in *Cythera*. I am thankful to the editors of all four journals for their permission to publish material in altered form that first appeared in their pages. I was kindly hosted by Maurice Hunt and members of the Department of English at Baylor University in the spring of 2004, when I delivered the John P. Reesing Lecture, based on material I wrote for this book. Beatrice Batson invited me to read part of chapter 3 at Wheaton College's Shakespeare Institute in June 2005, and I offered another part of the same chapter at the Elizabethan Theatre Conference, organized at Waterloo University later the same month by Kenneth Graham and Phillip Collington.

Unless otherwise noted, quotations from Shakespeare throughout the book are from David Bevington's fifth edition of the *Complete Works*, published by Pearson Longman of New York in 2004. Quotations of the Bible are from *The Geneva Bible* (1560) as prepared in facsimile and introduced by Lloyd E. Berry (Madison: University of Wisconsin Press, 1969).

This book is dedicated not to a person but to an institution, Hope College, where I have taught for almost thirty years. Such a name for a college lends itself to many uses. The development office likes to appropriate the name for fund drives—"Hope in the Future" and "Campaign for Hope," for example. The college's internal Web page is facetiously called "KnowHope," and the student newspaper, *The Anchor*, was long ago named for the college's symbol, which is drawn from Hebrews 6:19: "Which hope we have as an anchor of the soul." As befits any institution, but especially a liberal arts college, the tradition associated with the name is multifaceted, complex, and contested. Acknowledging all these factors, two colleagues recently used the title, *Can Hope Endure?* for a history of the college's relation with its founding religious tradition.[3]

Hope College has supported me as a teacher and scholar, and I wish to record my gratitude to President James Bultman, Provost James Boelkins, Dean William Reynolds, and then Chair of the Department of English, Peter Schakel, for granting me a leave of absence in 2004-2005 to write this book. Liberal arts colleges emphasize teaching before research, and I have enjoyed the stimulation of good students and the challenge of indifferent ones in working out my ideas in the classroom as well as the library. I am particularly grateful to several students who read all ten of Shakespeare's comedies with me in an upper-division seminar during the spring semester of 2004, when I began seriously thinking about the interrelationship between skepticism and suspicion in early drama.

Colleges are more than pedagogical machines with bureaucracies and budgets, however, in that they exist to nourish the life of the mind, and my dedication is meant to recognize what Hope College has offered as a community named for one of the three theological virtues. I have already mentioned complexity and contest, without which the life of the mind must inevitably wither, as Milton long since recognized and affirmed. The very distinction between cardinal and theological virtues was contested when Thomas Aquinas first formulated the difference, as he frankly acknowledged in the way he framed the issue in *Summa Theologica*. Transcending mere contest, however, was the spirit of the three virtues Thomas thought were infused by grace: faith, hope, and love. My effort to trace the influence of these virtues (or the effect of their absence) on the works of Shakespeare has been inspired by conversations with colleagues from many different disciplines at Hope College, which takes the virtues seriously while understanding and practicing them variously, and this book would not be what it is without those conversations.

1

SKEPTICISM AND SUSPICION
IN SIXTEENTH-CENTURY ENGLAND

They say miracles are past, and we have our philosophical persons to make modern and familiar things supernatural and causeless. Hence is it that we make trifles of terrors, ensconcing ourselves into seeming knowledge when we should submit ourselves to an unknown fear.

All's Well That Ends Well, 2.3.1–6

SKEPTICISM

The reception of skepticism in the sixteenth century can be made to support a narrative about a deluge of disbelief: "the sources of a commonly shared sense of the sacred were rapidly running dry and floods of unbelief rising torrentially."[1] The publication of two first-time translations of ancient skeptical texts from Greek to Latin helps to define this story: Lucian's *Dialogues* in the first decade of the century and Sextus Empiricus' *Outlines of Pyrrhonism* in 1562. Taken in conjunction with increasing interest in Cicero's *Academica*, another ancient treatise on skepticism, these translations can be seen as flood markers in the surging tide of doubt from Machiavelli, through Erasmus, Rabelais, Montaigne, Shakespeare, and Bacon to Descartes. Where Shakespeare in particular is concerned, this narrative has been especially influential. Stanley Cavell, one of Shakespeare's best interpreters in the second half of the twentieth century, identifies his own thinking as "a late stage in the process of skepticism in the West, that history (assuming there is such a thing, or one thing) that begins no later than Descartes and Shakespeare."[2] Cavell's conjunction of Descartes with Shakespeare as key authors in the history of skepticism points to the narrative in question. Descartes' attempt to find a dependable and rational foundation for reflection began in methodological skepticism and came to define the philosophical enterprise over the next two centuries. Linking

Shakespeare with Descartes thus enhances Shakespeare's authority in a story of emerging secularism, in which skepticism is a key indicator.

The advent of skepticism, however, is more complex than this story of a great flood suggests, and Shakespeare's skepticism is anything but a straightforward drowning in unbelief. For one thing, Shakespeare does not use the word "skeptic" or its derivatives, whereas Descartes formulated his rationalism with the challenge of contemporary skepticism specifically in mind.[3] It seems unlikely that a poet so sensitive to words would have ignored "skeptic," had he known it and understood its import.[4] Moreover, careful analysis of Shakespeare's skepticism takes one in some unexpected directions. Robert B. Pierce, for example, finds instances of each of Sextus Empiricus' ten modes of skeptical "therapy" in Shakespeare, and Pierce's instance for the third mode comes from Duke Humphrey's exposure of religious fraud in *2 Henry VI*.[5] This mode holds that "we dare not assume that what is apprehensible to our five senses constitutes the reality of what we perceive" (150). Duke Humphrey illustrates this mode by asking Simpcox to identify various colors, after Simpcox claims to have just regained his sight miraculously, though born blind. When Simpcox naïvely identifies the colors accurately, Humphrey points out that he is lying, because Humphrey has just used common knowledge that in the case of sight, four senses cannot make up for the loss of one. Pierce's analysis is incisive, and the example is apt, but the conclusions one can draw are many and ambiguous. For present purposes, the incident does not prove that Shakespeare was skeptical of religious faith, because his source for the Humphrey episode was John Foxe's *Acts and Monument of the Christian Church*, more commonly known as "Foxe's book of martyrs." Shakespeare could be using Foxe as a cover for his own skepticism of course, but Houston Diehl points out that Foxe himself deliberately "empowered the skeptic," in her phrase, in order to attack what he saw as abuses in belief.[6] How Shakespeare is using skepticism in this case needs to be evaluated not just from the episode itself but also from the whole of the play in which it appears, from Shakespeare's writing in the early history plays, and from what was happening around the playwright in the early 1590s.[7]

Foxe himself is extremely unlikely to have known Sextus Empiricus, but he did not need to. His most immediate inspiration was probably the former Carmelite friar, John Bale, who popularized a style of scoffing disbelief regarding traditional religion in the name of reformed faith long before Sextus was translated—at the time Thomas Cromwell was promoting the Henrician reformation of the 1530s.[8] Bale, however, almost certainly imbibed his polemical skepticism from traditional believers themselves, like Erasmus and Thomas More. They in turn were inspired by the ancient Greek satirist, Lucian, whose *Dialogues* they both translated, and whom Erasmus imitated closely in his *Colloquies*, while both *The Praise of Folly* and More's *Utopia* are Lucianic in spirit. Their motive in turning to Lucian in this way was to excoriate abuses in early sixteenth-century church and society, continuing a late-medieval tradition of anti-clerical satire that Bale adapted and used for his own purpose (or the purpose of Thomas Cromwell). The part that skepticism played in religious reform throughout the sixteenth century has been too little studied and understood, but it points to a combination of skepticism and belief that needs to be kept in mind as a possibility for Shakespeare as well.

The point can be illustrated from one of Erasmus' colloquies, *Exorcism, or The Specter*, first published in 1524. In this dialogue, the primary speaker, Anselm, describes an elaborate hoax that Anselm had heard about from one Polus, who was "the author of this play as well as an actor in it."[9] Polus initiated the prank because he wished to gull a self-important local parish priest named Faunus, who "looked upon himself as uncommonly wise, especially in divinity." Polus therefore proceeded to convince Faunus that the region was haunted by "the soul of someone suffering frightful torments" (231). Pretending to be the soul himself, Polus identified the sufferer to Faunus as "the soul of a Christian" (235), who needed to make restitution for money it had gained by fraud when alive. Anselm laughingly describes the elaborate devices that Polus used to deceive Faunus: the wailing and instructions of the supposedly tormented soul, strange lights at night, staying outside a circle Faunus drew to exclude the soul, letting another and cleverer priest into the secret in order to increase its credibility to Faunus, mentioning that the defrauded money is buried somewhere in order to play on Faunus's greed. All this was designed to trick Faunus into performing an exorcism, which Polus led him to believe was successful in order to enjoy the spectacle of pride and insufferable self-aggrandizement that Faunus predictably presented as a consequence. Polus brought the charade to a close by writing a letter in which the suffering soul purportedly assured Faunus that "God has regarded the righteous intention of your heart and as a reward has freed me from torture. Now I live in bliss with the angels" (237).

Several points about this colloquy deserve attention for their place in the history of religious skepticism in the sixteenth century. For one thing, Polus's trick is presented in theatrical metaphors from first to last: Anselm says, "you'd swear it was comic fiction" if it had not actually happened; Polus started the rumor of the haunting "as a prologue to his play," "an actor for the play was found," and so on (231). In other words, insofar as exorcism involves an encounter with the supernatural, Erasmus' colloquy reduces it to a theatrical trick. This kind of iconoclastic reduction became a favorite device of Protestant reformers, but to find it in Erasmus, especially as late as 1524 (seven years after Luther nailed his theses to the door of Wittenberg church) is worth notice, because Erasmus eventually took issue with Luther, refusing to sanction the Protestant reformers' break with Rome. Samuel Harsnett's later equation of exorcism with theater in *Declaration of Egregious Popish Impostures* (1603) has been identified by Stephen Greenblatt as a skeptical "emptying out" of traditional ritual, replacing belief with unbelief.[10] What then are we to say about its appearance in Erasmus, eighty years earlier? Is Erasmus also emptying out traditional ritual, even as a traditional believer? If so, at what point, and where, do we find the putative "filled up" ritual of traditional religion? The answer would appear to be offered in a history like Eamon Duffy's *Stripping of the Altars*, with its compelling "thick description" of pre-Reformation faith.[11] But Duffy's picture needs to be complemented by Erasmus' colloquies, which are also part of pre-Reformation faith. At least one traditional believer clearly thought the picture needed correction, and he used Lucianic skepticism to achieve his purpose.

Moreover, Erasmus was not alone in resorting to Lucian to correct what he saw as religious abuses. As early as 1506, Thomas More also published translations of the Greek satirist's dialogues, *Menippus siue Necromantia* and *Philopseudes* ["lover of lies"] *siue Incredulus* among them, satirizing necromancy and exorcism, respectively.[12] There is evidence, moreover, that Erasmus' *Exorcism* is based on an actual trick that More and a relative had played on a gullible local priest, making Erasmus' colloquy an inside joke between himself and More.[13] Anselm's interlocutor in the colloquy is called "Thomas," suggesting that More appears both as Polus, who executes the trick, and as Thomas, who listens to Anselm describe the trick and responds to Anselm's narrative. When "Thomas" describes Polus as "the author of this play as well as an actor in it," he is not only clarifying the theatrical nature of this exorcism; he is also describing Thomas More's part in it. This is the same Thomas More, however, who would later write (though certainly in very different circumstances) *The Supplication of Souls* (1529) in immediate retort to Simon Fish's *Supplication of the Beggars*, an early reformation attack on the doctrine of purgatory. The soul in Erasmus' colloquy is clearly imagined to be in purgatory, because Faunus's efforts enable the soul to move from suffering to "bliss." Somehow, therefore, it must have been possible for More to reconcile in his own mind his trick on a parish priest involving the exorcism of a soul in purgatory and his ardent defense of purgatory against a reformer's attack, only five years after Erasmus published *Exorcism*. Such a reconciliation might well be called skeptical faith.

More is not the only one whose writing complements Erasmus' colloquy, for its later influence may have been greater than has been recognized. If anyone would have known both *Exorcism* and its origin in Lucian, it would be Ben Jonson, whose familiarity with literary sources was recognized as formidable in his own day.[14] It is therefore hard to imagine that Erasmus and Lucian do not somehow figure in Jonson's 1616 play, *The Devil Is an Ass*, which includes a fake exorcism in a play. Jonson was certainly mocking religious excesses in his own day (one of his characters mentions "little Darrel's tricks," referring to John Darrel, a well-known contemporary Puritan controller of demons[15]), but his play has several elements in common with Erasmus' tale: a fake demonic possession, a fake exorcism, a willing participant to help in the deception, and a naïve, self-important, and greedy gull, who is the object of the trick. Certifiable indebtedness is not the point; what is important is the strong possibility that for Jonson, as for Erasmus, depicting an exorcism as a theatrical trick was a way to reform moral and religious thinking and practice rather than to express religious doubt. Direct spectacular contact with the supernatural was a source of personal charisma for the one who made the contact in the early seventeenth century, as in the early sixteenth, and it was therefore subject to abuse, as both Erasmus and Jonson were well aware; indeed, the English church eventually decided that merely to claim this kind of contact was inherently abusive and legislated against such claims in the canons of 1604. If reform was indeed Jonson's motive, could it not have been some part of Shakespeare's motive as well? In *The Comedy of Errors, Twelfth Night,* and *King Lear,* Shakespeare also staged fake demonic possession or fake exorcism in circumstances that are even more complex than those in *The Devil Is an Ass*—complex, that is, in their precise import. Perhaps, as Greenblatt avers, these staged manifestations of supernatural power "empty out" the supernatural, but with the example of Erasmus in mind, it is not clear that that is the only possibility or even the most likely one.

Erasmus himself defended *Exorcism* as an attack on "the tricks of imposters accustomed to play upon the credulous minds of simple folk by feigning apparitions of demons, souls, and heavenly voices." [16] This is an ironic misreading of his own colloquy, however, as Erasmus indicates in a reminder that "Pope Celestine was similarly imposed upon," for this comment turns Erasmus' supposed explanation into yet another opportunity to poke fun at the credulity of fallible churchmen. [17] Erasmus was certainly capable of mocking popes, as he makes clear in *The Praise of Folly*, but his satire of greed, self-importance, corruption, hypocrisy, and general moral laxity in Folly's oration, which was strongly influenced by Lucian, concludes with his most brilliantly ironic meditation, which is completely foreign to Lucian: an affirmation of Paul's admonition that Christians must be "fools for Christ's sake." [18] This is the standard by which Erasmus evaluates the folly of church and society in *The Praise of Folly*, as he asserts in defending the work in his letter to Martin Dorp (1515), and it is presumably the standard by which he evaluates the folly and greed of Faunus in *Exorcism* as well. [19] A revealing passage in another oration, this time spoken by Lady Peace, rather than Lady Folly, suggests that the pervasive metaphor of the theater in *Exorcism* may be linked to the charade that Erasmus thinks Christians routinely make of their faith:

If Christ achieved nothing, what is the need of so many ceremonies today? If he achieved something which matters, *why is he so neglected today, as if all he did was to stage some foolish farce?* Does any man dare to approach that sacred table, the symbol of friendship, the communion sacrament of peace, if he intends to make war on Christians, and prepares to destroy those whom Christ died to save and to drink the blood of men for whom Christ shed his own blood?[20]

In effect, Polus fights fire with fire in *Exorcism*: faced with theatrical displays of false virtue, he stages a false supernatural effect in order to expose the folly of those who are taken in by it. The theatrical metaphors of *The Praise of Folly* work similarly to put human achievement into divine perspective, thus revealing both human pretension and human limitations.[21] The satire in *Exorcism* is much like Jonson's in its exposure of human vanity, but Erasmus undergirds his satire with moral and spiritual idealism that Jonson never quite manages, even in his masques' allegorical celebration of Jacobean kingship.

The first wave of humanist skepticism in the early sixteenth century eventually gave way to a related but distinct form of skepticism that was encouraged by the translation of Sextus Empiricus' *Outlines of Pyrrhonism* in 1562. As Richard Popkin has shown, throughout the remainder of the sixteenth century and the beginning of the seventeenth, Pyrrhonism became a weapon in controversy between Catholics and Protestants, because Sextus's argument against the reliability of criteria for truth was useful in Catholic attacks on Protestant belief in the individual conscience informed by the Bible, and in Protestant attacks on Catholic belief in the authority of tradition as interpreted by the church.[22] Both sides could (and did) retreat from reason into faith in the face of attacks by the other, because faith is not founded on a rational criterion for truth. Augustine's *credo ut intellegam* ("I believe in order that I may understand") thus became useful to both sides as a bulwark against skeptical attack by religious opponents. The long habit in the West of appropriating pagan authorities for Christian belief (arguably operating in Erasmus' and More's embrace of Lucian) continued with Sextus, whose skepticism was baptized, so to speak, by both sides of the religious divide as a way of attacking heresy.[23] The first historical effect of Pyrrhonist skepticism's advent in the sixteenth century therefore seems paradoxical and improbable in view of what skepticism eventually became: initially, it was used to defend faith on both sides of the religious divide, and it can therefore be accurately identified as a new form of skeptical faith.[24]

This effect is evident in England, as well as on the continent. Thomas Nashe had access to an English translation of Sextus as early as 1590, likely in manuscript, and he refers to it frequently.[25] One of his longest allusions is in *Pierce Pennilesse His Supplication to the Divell* (1592), a satirical attack on the seven deadly sins, enumerating contemporary social ills, especially in London. Nashe's rhetoric is exuberant, as always, but his moral thinking is traditional, as the device of the seven deadly sins makes clear: it had been used satirically as early as *Piers Plowman*, had been revived for the same purpose as recently as book I of Spenser's *Faerie Queene* (1590), which Nashe praises in the final section of *Pierce Pennilesse*, and was soon to provide the basis for social satire in a play called *The Seven Deadly Sins*, performed by the Chamberlain's Men (Shakespeare's acting company) as late as 1597–1598.[26] Moreover, Nashe explicitly defends the Elizabethan regime, with its unique fusion of church and crown. Just before alluding to Sextus, he mocks those who "take occasion to deride our Ecclesiastical State, and all Ceremonies of Divine worship" in their advocacy of simplified ecclesiastical vestments (1:172). Among others, he mentions "Anabaptists," "Familists," and "Martinists."[27] These objects of his satirical jibing are lumped together as "Atheists" who "triumph and rejoice, and talk as profanely of the Bible, as of Bevis of Hampton. I hear say there be Mathematicians abroad that will prove men before *Adam*; and they are harbored in high places, who will maintain it to the death, that there be no devils." Nashe thus follows the contemporary pattern of using the prevailing skeptical authority, Sextus, in defense of (Elizabethan Protestant) faith—a faith whose expression seems remarkably naïve, if one views it from the perspective of Enlightenment skepticism.[28]

In short, Shakespeare inherited a long tradition of combining faith and skepticism in the cause of religious reform, and he seems to have been untouched by the *crise pyhrronienne*, as Popkin calls it—that is, the crisis brought on when skepticism was applied to knowledge of the natural world, as well as the criteria for faith. This crisis, which arose for the first time in the early seventeenth century, evoked such a decisive response from Descartes that he deflected the skeptical attack in the second half of the seventeenth century away from religious controversy, scholasticism, or Platonism and redirected it to his own ideas in particular.[29] The results have long been recognized in the history of philosophy, eventually including a sophisticated skeptical argument that demolished Descartes' rational proof for God's existence. This carefully argued philosophical atheism, however, was a product of the eighteenth century, and it therefore needs to be distinguished from the naïve "atheism" of Shakespeare's contemporaries, which belonged for the most part to vituperation and rhetorical abuse rather than rational religious doubt.[30]

The most sophisticated application of Sextus's skepticism in Shakespeare's lifetime was by Montaigne, and it is an application that Shakespeare certainly knew by the time he wrote *The Tempest*.[31] Montaigne is an unusually imaginative example of the initial response to Sextus. Montaigne's skepticism applies to rational certainty, including rational certainty of doubt, because Pyrrhonian skepticism denies the rational demonstrability of doubt itself: "they [the Pyrrhonians] seek to be contradicted, so as to create doubt and suspension of judgment, which is their goal."[32] Without a rational basis for doubting the laws and customs of his community, Montaigne provisionally accepted them—an acceptance that extended perforce to religious laws and customs: "As for the actions of life, they [the Pyrrhonians] are of the common fashion in that. They lend and accommodate themselves to natural inclinations, to the impulsion and constraint of passions, to the constitutions of laws and customs, and to the tradition of the arts."[33] Montaigne seems to have been read initially as a faithful Catholic, for his books were placed on the Index for the first time only in 1676, by which time skepticism had taken a new turn, making Montaigne appear to be a threat to faith rather than a defender of it.[34]

SUSPICION

The verity of it is in strong suspicion.

Winter's Tale, 5.2.29–30

The consistent application of skepticism in the sixteenth century to the cause of religious reform suggests that skepticism as a category of doubt might be less helpful in assessing Shakespeare's thinking than suspicion. This may seem an odd claim on the face of it, because in philosophical parlance suspicion describes an innovative nineteenth-century application of doubt to the knower, rather than what is known. Paul Ricoeur argues that the most important point in common between Marx, Freud, and Nietzsche is their recognition, in various ways, of a disjunction between conscious intention and unconscious motivation. This disjunction is the origin of what Ricoeur calls "suspicion," and he distinguishes it from skepticism, because skepticism applies to doubt about rational certainty, which is not the concern of "the school of suspicion." [35] All three "masters of suspicion" in the nineteenth century, he points out, responded to consciousness in a similar way, in that all of them made "the decision to look upon the whole consciousness primarily as a 'false' consciousness" (33). The "modern" thinker or rationalist, inspired by Descartes' "Cogito"—that is, his confidence in rational consciousness—"triumphed over doubt as to things by the evidence of consciousness." In contrast, the nineteenth-century "postmodern" thinkers "triumph over the doubt as to consciousness by an exegesis of meaning. Beginning with them, understanding is hermeneutics: henceforward, to seek meaning is no longer to spell out the consciousness of meaning, but to *decipher its expressions*." [36] Though "false consciousness" is a term Marx coined to describe in particular how people imagine and believe in their world in ways that deny or even contradict their socio-economic conditions, Ricoeur employs the term more broadly to describe any situation in which people deceive themselves, whether socio-economically, as for Marx; psychologically, as Freud argues; or "genealogically," to use Nietzsche's term for getting at what he proposed was the historical construction of ethics in particular.

It may seem perverse to suggest that a postmodern way of thinking is more applicable to Shakespeare than a modern one, but I want to urge that the point makes sense historically as well as hermeneutically, because of the deep mistrust of human nature that gave rise to early modern skepticism in the first place. In other words, while the development of skepticism remained primitive by Enlightenment standards in Shakespeare's lifetime, the suspicion of human nature was very old and highly developed, and it touches postmodern suspicion in some important ways. Take, for example, the issue of self-deception, which Ricoeur identifies as fundamental to the postmodern perception of false consciousness. Describing self- deception philosophically is harder than might be supposed. Herbert Fingarette argues that it is best grasped by imagining the self as a community of subselves, and he acknowledges that "the metaphor of the self as a community rather than a collection" derives ultimately from Plato and was modified by Christian thinking about the "Spirit" and the "Flesh." [37] Mike Martin argues that evading "self-acknowledgment" is a better explanation for self-deception than Fingarette's notion of self-division, but Martin's understanding of the tradition is more reminiscent of the Enlightenment than of philosophical suspicion, in that he seems to assume that self-knowledge involves perfect rational self-acknowledgment. [38] The opposite assumption is basic to Christian thinking, which asserts the non-perfectibility of the self, including the impossibility of perfect self-acknowledgment, as Augustine recognizes throughout the *Confessions*.

Fingarette's suggestion that self-deception originates in a notion of the self as a community of subselves found its most influential expression historically in personified abstraction and eventually in the morality play, which has long been recognized as basic to the repertory of the traveling acting companies who are credited with establishing the first permanent commercial theaters in London during Shakespeare's lifetime. From well before the Reformation, the English morality play had enacted divided consciousness by staging the parts of the soul as separate characters (in other words, a community of subselves) in a drama of temptation through self-deception, fall, and recovery. In the morality play called *Wisdom*, for example, from the second half of the fifteenth century, the self is imagined as a character called Anima (the soul), who is composed of the traditional five wits and three "mights" or powers (Mind, Will, and Understanding), all eight of whom are represented as characters in the play apart from Anima herself. In effect, the interior of the self (the soul) is thus rendered in exterior terms, in keeping with allegorical tradition since Prudentius. [39] Satan tempts Anima first through the mights, whom he proceeds to deceive and corrupt, so that the soul is, in effect, divided against itself through self-deception. [40] Much closer in time to Shakespeare, the division of the self is explicit in Apius's comment about himself in *Apius and Virginia*: "But

out I am wounded, how am I deuided? / Two states of my life, from
me are now glided," and the accompanying marginal stage direction
specifies: "Here let him make as [t]hogh he went out and let Con-
si[e]nce and Iustice come out of him."[41] In the course of the play, Apius
thus literally divides into three and confronts two parts of himself,
Conscience and Justice, as if they were characters external to him. This
is an instance where self-division has little or nothing to do with self-
deception, but Fingarette's point nonetheless stands: one cannot
deceive oneself without being divided.

Marlowe's *Dr. Faustus* (1588) may be the first morality play to imagine a drama of divided consciousness without staging the soul's parts
externally, but that kind of staging remained conventional until late in
the tradition. In Nathaniel Woodes's *The Conflict of Conscience* (1581),
for example, the divided self is enacted by the title character, Philologus, at the moment when he decides to recant his Protestant allegiance: "To say truth, I do not care, what to my soul betide, / So long
as this prosperity and wealth by me abide."[42] "Prosperity" and
"Wealth" would be separate characters from Philologus in some other
morality plays (*Everyman*, for instance), but Philologus is actually
defeated by a character called "Sensual Suggestion," who stands for
something like "imagination," because this character/mental faculty
persuades Philologus to picture himself as the possessor of wealth and
social prominence that the tempter (a Cardinal in Woodes's play) offers
to Philologus if he will recant. Sensual Suggestion, in other words, is a
part of Philologus that is divided against the rest of him and eventually corrupts the whole in a drama of what might well be called half-
knowing self-deception or, in other words, moral false consciousness.

In short, numerous English morality plays suggest that in deceiving oneself, one is divided against oneself in specifically moral terms,
and the criteria for knowing that one has fooled oneself (or that others have fooled themselves) are drawn from traditional moral insight
regarding the position of the self before God. The same idea of self-
division was also available to Shakespeare in book 1 of *The Faerie
Queene*, a narrative allegory of Christian salvation that has many
points in common with morality plays. The spirit that Archimago
summons to deceive the Redcrosse Knight in canto 1 is an aspect of
the knight himself, insofar as it appears in an erotic dream, and its
deception of him is therefore a way of imagining self-deception.

Moreover, the three pagan knights that Redcrosse keeps meeting throughout book 1, Sans Foy, Sans Loy, and Sans Joy are also, in some sense, aspects of the Redcrosse Knight himself—a community of sub-selves that he must recognize and defeat, because they are corrupt, in order to incorporate their opposites into himself: faith, law (that is, the Pauline "new law" of love), and hope, the three principal virtues of the Christian life, whom Redcrosse meets in the House of Holiness. This way of understanding the Sans brothers helps to explain why, as the champion of faith, Redcrosse has the easiest time defeating Sans Foy and the hardest time defeating Sans Joy, or the error of despair. For despair confronts Redcrosse again in the personification allegory of canto 9, even after Redcrosse has defeated Sans Joy, and the repeated confrontation is a way of imagining human nature's proneness to error in the process of personal moral reformation known as sanctification. To put the allegorical point in abstract terms: Redcrosse is self-deceived about his success after his first encounter with Error.

Though Shakespeare does not use terms derived from "self-deceived," he clearly knew what the process involved, as is evident from the very beginning of his career.[43] Moreover, the concept of self-deception (without the term itself) was articulated by both Montaigne and by Sir John Davies' *Nosce Teipsum*, which was influenced by Montaigne.[44] Terms associated with "self-deceived" were first used by a Calvinist theologian, Daniel Dyke, whose last book, *The Mystery of Self-Deceiving*, was published in 1614, two years before Shakespeare's death.[45] Not surprisingly, Dyke's chief authority is Augustine, whose meditations on the divided self in *The Confessions* are the *locus classicus* for the psychology of moral self-reflection.[46]

Suspicion and moral self-deception were available to Shakespeare not only in the morality play and moral poetry like *The Faerie Queene* and *Nosce Teipsum* but also in Erasmus and More. In Erasmus' *Exorcism*, Polus informs the gullible priest, Faunus, that the tormented spirit, played by Polus himself, bears Faunus's name. " 'Why, that's my name,' says Faunus. Now, because of their common name, he becomes very eager for Faunus to free Faunus."[47] Erasmus thus sati-rizes the self-importance of the exorcist, which enables him to be deceived more easily: flattery and self-deception make him vulnerable to the deception that Polus practices at his expense. Malvolio in *Twelfth Night* again comes to mind, since he appears in a play not only where others pretend to exorcise his madness but also where he is gulled through self-deception that originates in overweening ambition. Erasmus' fondness for the *theatrum mundi* metaphor appears in *Twelfth Night* as well: "If this were played upon a stage, now," remarks Fabian, when Malvolio makes a fool of himself, "I could condemn it as an improbable fiction" (3.4.129–30).

Thomas More's division of himself in *Utopia* between character More and Hythlodaeus is a way of staging a debate in the author's mind about the best way a thoughtful and well-intended person should proceed in a corrupt kingdom. In effect, More and Hythlodaeus are a community of subselves of author More, as the latter explored a question in his own mind that he had not yet settled: whether he should accept service with Henry VIII. Though self-deception is not a function of the strategically divided self in *Utopia*, More imagined moral self-deception in another character he created, King Richard III, who may well be inspired in part by personified vices in morality plays written by More's contemporaries, Henry Medwall and John Skelton.[48] Though they wrote before the advent of the Vice as a single dominant character in the morality play, they invented many memorable and influential personified vices. More's Richard frequently recalls these vices, not only in his association with hell but in his self-deceived confidence that he can triumph by means of demonic methods, and More's fascination with actual morality plays—not only seeing them but performing in them—is well known.

Given the long history of moral suspicion they inherited, it makes sense that Erasmus and More turned to Lucian the Greek satirist and thus promoted a fruitful vein of skepticism in English thinking. It also makes sense that their adoption of Lucian should have coexisted with their continuing commitment to traditional religion, since that commitment gave rise to their interest in Lucianic satire in the first place. Skepticism for these two did not supplant their faith; rather, skepticism and faith complemented one another as essential aspects of the same vision of the human situation. They were skeptical of the human pretension to rational knowledge, because they regarded human beings as too fallible to achieve anything certain, perfect, or complete on their own, and this view of human incapacity derived not from reason itself but from scripture and ecclesiastical tradition— in other words, from faith.

Suspicion and Self-Deception in Two Early Comedies

O father Abram, what these Christians are,
Whose own hard dealings teaches them suspect
The thoughts of others.

The Merchant of Venice, 1.3.159–61

Shakespeare's suspicion of human perfectibility as an expression of skeptical faith is evident from the beginning of his career, as we can see in two of his earliest comedies: *Love's Labor's Lost* and *The Comedy of Errors*. Though both plays are heavily indebted to dramatic models that were authoritative or fashionable in the early 1590s—John Lyly's court comedy and Roman comedy, respectively—they are not merely imitative. Both take the traditions they represent remarkably lightly, especially for plays written by a novice author, and their bemused or ironic distance might well be described as skeptical. This is a skepticism, however, that not only emphasizes human imperfection but that also might well be said to originate in moral suspicion of the kind that animates *Utopia* or *The Praise of Folly*.

It is not hard to guess that the pact made by four young noblemen and sealed with an oath is doomed to comic failure from the outset in *Love's Labor's Lost*. Their solemn agreement to live in perfect asceticism in the name of "philosophy" (1.1.32) inevitably unravels in 4.3, when each of them enters in sequence with a rationalizing and ambivalent lament about having violated his oath by falling in love, though each is judgmental about the others' failure at the same time. The first to acknowledge his failing in soliloquy is Berowne, who then "stands aside" (4.3.18SD) and thus overhears the confessional soliloquy of the second, who is no less than the King who had bound them all to their oath in the first place. The King likewise "steps aside" (40SD), setting up a pattern by which each overhears the next to enter, with Berowne overhearing all three. The pattern is then reversed, when the third steps out of concealment to berate the fourth; the second emerges to berate the third and fourth, and finally Berowne reveals himself to scold them all: "Now step I forth to whip hypocrisy" (147). Addressing the third, he summarizes the situation with a telling allusion: "You found his mote; the King your mote did see; / But I a beam do find

in each of three" (157–58). He is alluding to a saying of Jesus in
Matthew 7:3-5:

> And why seest thou the mote, that is in thy brothers eye, and perceivest
> not the beam that is in thine own eye? Or how sayest thou to thy
> brother, Suffer me to cast out the mote out of thine eye, and behold a
> beam is in thine owne eye? Hypocrite, first cast out the beam out of
> thine own eye, and then shalt thou see clearly to cast out the mote out
> of thy brothers eye.[49]

I want to urge that this allusion is not merely decorative (though
Love's Labor's Lost is infamous for its decorative allusions) but that it
suggests something about self-ignorance and self-deception that is so
consistent in Shakespeare as to constitute a basic assumption. To be
sure, the "philosophy" the young men subscribe to at the beginning
is a generalized stoicism, and their obviously self-deceived oath to live
in perfect ascetic virtue derives in part from the critique of the stoic
who cannot live up to his own affirmations. This critique was
indebted historically to skepticism and cynicism, as Lyly implicitly
acknowledges in his court play, *Campaspe* (1584), when Diogenes the
cynic berates Alexander the Great for inconsistency. Lyly is the
strongest influence on the young playwright who penned *Love's Labor's
Lost*, but Lyly does not refer the motif of self-ignorance to a saying
from the gospels, whereas Shakespeare does.

In keeping with the biblical reference, Berowne is himself the
greatest hypocrite (or to put it less moralistically, the least self-
knowing), because he conceals his own fault while invoking the gospel
to berate the faults of others:

> I, that am honest, I, that hold it sin
> To break the vow I am engagèd in,
> I am betrayed by keeping company
> With men like you, men of inconstancy. (173–76)

Shakespeare does not allow Berowne to enjoy his falsely-assumed
moral superiority for long, because Berowne's secret is revealed
almost immediately by coincidence—in other words, by a turn of the
plot that Shakespeare invented. No sooner has Berowne scolded his
companions than a dairymaid enters to give a letter to the King in
loyal duty, because she has been told the letter is treasonous. It is in
fact, however, Berowne's love letter to Rosaline, and Berowne is thus
compelled to admit that he is as fallible as his companions: "Guilty,

my lord, guilty! I confess, I confess" (201). Another saying from Matthew's gospel is thus evoked implicitly by the fact that the first to accuse the others is the last to be exposed, and that as a nobleman he is exposed by a laboring female commoner: "But many that are first, shall be last, and the last shall be first" (19:30). Patricia Parker has pointed to a rhetorical pattern of *hysteron proteron* ("the latter put as the former") in this play, occurring throughout in its highly decorative language, as well as in scenes like 4.3, with its over-determined patterning.[50] The motif may have an erotic motive, as Parker suggests, but the biblical saying seems at least as germane.

This is particularly true in light of the way the play ends. Unlike most of Shakespeare's romantic comedies, this one suspends the pairing off for at least a year (5.2.800) and perhaps indefinitely. The reason for this suspension seems closely related to the young men's too easy verbal facility—the very quality that made it possible for them to take their oath in the first place, without reckoning what it might really mean. Marcade's news of the French king's death is the most serious passage in the play—long admired for the way it suddenly changes the bantering and lighthearted mood—and the French princess's response is the play's most honest pronouncement: "Dead, for my life" (5.2.716).[51] After this, Berowne's declaration that "Honest plain words best pierce the ear of grief" (749) seems to be just more self-deceiving rhetoric, especially since the eloquent speech that immediately follows it (750–72) appears designed to impress Rosaline rather than to express honest commiseration with the newly-bereaved Princess or even to acknowledge her grief in any but the most perfunctory way.

In short, the young men have learned very little, including Berowne, who is the cleverest and apparently the most self-aware of all the courtiers (1.1.33–48). Faced with death (one of the "Four Last Things" in medieval and Elizabethan spirituality), he carries on as if he had forever to live.[52] *Respice finem*, "remember the end," is the traditional advice with respect to death, in light of which one was supposed to order one's priorities in such a way as to *live well*. That is why the ladies advise their would-be lovers to spend a year getting serious by withdrawing from the world and helping "the speechless sick" and "groaning wretches"—pointed allusions to the *lack* of verbal facility in those who are ill (5.4.790–808, 840–44). The Princess seems to think the young courtiers have something to learn from those who suffer.

Respice finem is also suggested in an exchange between the King and the Princess, after she has been informed of her father's death. "Now, at the latest minute of the hour, / Grant us your loves," he urges, again pressing his suit. But she replies, "A time, methinks, too short / To make a world-without-end bargain in" (5.4.783–85). The bargain she alludes to is presumably the marriage vow, "till death us depart," in the archaic phrasing of the Elizabethan prayer book.[53] But the Princess's phrase also glances at the end of the world, the Last Judgment, another of the Four Last Things (the other two being heaven and hell) in light of which Christians were advised to live well. One way of understanding *Love's Labor's Lost* is that it is about young people whose class pretensions, hormones ("your own affections / And the huge army of the world's desires" [1.1.9–10]), high-mindedness, and general myopia all combine to prevent them from living well—that is, from living either truthfully or troth-fully ("and thereto I give thee my troth," concludes the Elizabethan marriage vow), with equal regard for one's neighbor as for oneself.[54] The young lords' high-minded commitment to idealizing self-denial falls apart in 4.3, when they acknowledge their inability to measure up to it, with explicit allusions to the "mote" and the "beam," one of the classic biblical sayings about the difficulty of knowing oneself. With assistance from Berowne's facile rationalization, however, they replace their first idealizing intention with another, in which they make their own erotic desire absolute and comically misidentify sexual attraction with charity:

> Let us once lose our oaths to find ourselves,
> Or else we lose ourselves to keep our oaths.
> It is religion to be thus forsworn,
> For charity itself fulfills the law,
> And who can sever love from charity? (4.3.335–39)

At no point in this play do they ever find themselves, despite Berowne's confidence that they can do so in the wake of their mutual self-revelations. In three successive scenes (4.3, 5.1, and 5.2), characters observe other characters from a point of view the observers think to be superior without realizing their own deficiencies, and Costard's comment about Nathaniel in the part of Alexander the Great therefore applies to all the observers: "alas, you see how 'tis—a little o'erparted," i.e., cast in a part that is too demanding for his abilities (5.2.580–81).[55] In a way that no character recognizes, the Play of the Nine Worthies is a comment on those who watch it: the more they mock its inept performance, the more they reveal how o'erparted they are themselves. Even after the intervention of death, the King will-fully pursues his suit to the Princess, and Berowne launches into still another self-deceived flight of rhetorical fancy ("Honest plain words best pierce the ear of grief").

What is comically doubted in *Love's Labor's Lost*, then, is not knowl-edge itself, as in skepticism, but human beings' (especially young men's) ability to know themselves—that is, to understand their fallibility, the restrictions of their social perspective (especially where social class is concerned), and "troth" or their obligation to others. Berowne blames the Princess for spoiling the play: "these ladies' courtesy / Might well have made our sport a comedy" (5.2.865–66), but his comment makes clear that he still does not see that he has done more to prevent a com-edy than she has. This oversight reproduces his earlier accusation of his fellows for "inconstancy" (4.3.176), while concealing his own, mak-ing himself the first of several such characters in Shakespeare. "Were man / But constant, he were perfect," opines the aptly named Proteus in *Two Gentlemen of Verona* (5.4.9–10), and Balthasar's song in *Much Ado about Nothing* follows suit:

> Men were deceivers ever,
> One foot in sea and one on shore,
> To one thing constant never. (2.3.62–64)

The point is not simply that such characters are untrustworthy—find-ing "troth" very difficult—but that they deceive themselves about this very feature, thinking and speaking as if they were "constant," as Berowne does, even when they are least so. Shakespeare's wry obser-vation of this dismal fact undoubtedly owes a good deal to age-old critiques of stoicism, as Geoffrey Miles has argued for the Roman plays, but its presence in *Love's Labor's Lost* suggests that it was not nec-essarily associated with Rome in Shakespeare's thinking but was also deeply involved with distinctly Christian assumptions that appear allusively but all-importantly in this early comedy[56]

Moreover, when the same assumptions emerge in *The Comedy of Errors*, they offer a fuller sense of what they mean, both for the play in which they appear and for Shakespearean comedy more generally.

The biblical allusions in this play have been thoroughly explicated by Patricia Parker,[57] and they are all the more striking in that they occur in a play that is closely dependent on the Roman playwright, Plautus, and that meets the strict neoclassical expectations for unity in time, place, and action. The play's multitudinous allusions to the Bible are thus juxtaposed incongruously with its highly conscious classicism. The effect, I would argue, is to qualify implicit classical values, just as the passing biblical references in *Love's Labor's Lost* help to qualify aristocratic and rhetorical values in that play[58]

The failure of self-knowing is even more central to *The Comedy of Errors* than to *Love's Labor's Lost*, since it is enacted symbolically in the farcical inability of two pairs of identical twins to recognize each other—literally to recognize themselves in someone else.[59] But the motif extends beyond this obvious application, which is at the heart of the play's farce, for it also appears in Luciana, a character Shakespeare invented to express Christian moral directives about marriage incongruously in a Roman play. Paraphrasing Paul's letter to the Ephesian church, Luciana lectures her sister, Adriana, on the duties of wifely submission, and she generalizes this duty to encompass the whole of created order:

> There's nothing situate under heaven's eye
> But hath his bound, in earth, in sea, in sky.
> The beasts, the fishes, and the wingèd fowls
> Are their males' subjects and at their controls.
> Man, more divine, the master of all these,
> Lord of the wide world and wild wat'ry seas,
> Endued with intellectual sense and souls,
> Of more preeminence than fish and fowls,
> Are masters to their females, and their lords. (2.1.16–24)[60]

Luciana may be right in principle, according to Elizabethan expectation, but her moralism prevents her from acknowledging the problems of her beleaguered sister, who retorts sharply: "This servitude makes you to keep unwed," eliciting a more honest response from Luciana: "Not this, but troubles of the marriage bed" (2.1.26–27). That Luciana's cosmic idealism is inappropriate in these circumstances is evident in her assertion that the human male is "lord of the wide world and wild wat'ry seas," for the frame story of Egeon says just the opposite. Egeon describes the wild sea that separated his family in the first place as the "always-wind-obeying deep" (1.1.63)—hardly responsive to human male lordship; and the men folks' subsequent ventures into the wide world have produced nothing but calamity, misunderstanding, and imminent tragedy (the anticipated execution of an innocent traveler). To a man, this father and his sons are not the masters of sea and world, but their hapless victims.

More importantly, in light of her moral idealism, Luciana is no more perceptive about the cause of the confusion in Ephesus than her sister and brother-in-law, and she becomes just as compromised by it. When Adriana and Luciana mistake Antipholus of Syracuse for Adriana's husband, Luciana resists her supposed brother-in-law's romantic attention, though it originates not in adulterous passion, as she imagines, but in a stranger's honest affection (3.2.1–70). Yet her resistance is expressed in stichomythia and word play, common signs of social banter with erotic undertones in Shakespeare's early comedies, so that she appears to be flirting at the same time she is resisting. When she breaks off the conversation, her confused expression emphasizes her ambivalent resistance: "I'll fetch my sister, to get her good will" (3.2.70). How Luciana thinks Adriana would ever grant her good will to her sister in these circumstances is unclear, and the confusion is clearly inconsistent with Luciana's earlier moral idealism about marriage—but perhaps that is precisely the point. Like the four young noblemen in *Love's Labor's Lost*, Luciana is less able to live up to expressed high ideals than she believes she (or her sister) should be, and the resulting difference between word and action suggests a lack of self-knowledge on her part that complements the more obvious failure of the twins to recognize themselves in their doubles.

The solution to the problems in *The Comedy of Errors* is more complete and satisfying than in *Love's Labor's Lost*, because self-knowledge is based on the simple recognition that everyone has confused two pairs of twins. But the solution in *The Comedy of Errors* is not simple. On one hand, it reunites the family, results in two sets of brothers finding each other after a lifetime's absence, preserves Egeon's life, restores his and Emilia's marriage, reunites them with their long-lost sons, makes possible the fulfillment of Luciana's and Antipholus of Syracuse's innocent romance, eliminates the immediate source of misunderstanding between Adriana and Antipholus of Ephesus, and concludes with a winsome image of fraternal affection and respect between the two slave twins. A brewing dispute between these two as to precedence is resolved when one of them offers a way to clear the stage with a gesture of concord and mutual affirmation: "We came into the world like brother and brother, / And now let's go hand in hand, not one before another" (5.1.426–27).

This solution is so delightful and so complete that it seems to respond to the play's many apocalyptic references. Arguably these amount, in the end, to a reflection of eschatological perfection—to an image of heaven in human community. Such an end is explicitly evoked in comical allusions to "the world's end" (2.2.106) and "doomsday" (3.2.99). Moreover, the implicit advice *"respice finem,"* which is crucial to the end of *Love's Labor's Lost*, appears explicitly in *The Comedy of Errors*, when Dromio of Ephesus puns cleverly on being beaten: "Mistress, respice finem, respect your end; or rather, to prophesy like the parrot, 'Beware the rope's end'" (4.4.41–43).[61] Moving from "the doom of death" and a harshly imposed law (1.1.2ff.) at the outset, through hopeless muddle and misunderstanding, *The Comedy of Errors* eventually yields a world in which the harsh law is simply set aside (5.1.391) and a miraculous "birth" reunites a family and a community: "After so long grief, such nativity" (5.1.407).[62]

As Patricia Parker points out, however, the seeming perfection of the play's conclusion is called into question by the very arbitrariness and enormity of human error that precedes it. If so many mistakes can spring from the simple failure to recognize that two sets of twins have appeared in the same city for the first time in many years, then how satisfactory is any settlement of the difficulties? More fundamentally, why do people in this play make such exaggerated assumptions and treat each other so badly in light of such an obvious and trivial mix-up? Assumptions of adultery, theft, lying, even demon possession, the beating of slaves, the hasty recourse to angry and dismissive words—all spring from the same palpable misconception. Lack of self-knowledge in *The Comedy of Errors*, symbolized in the failure of twins to recognize each other and enacted in Luciana's (the best of characters) inability to understand her own motives, seems to indicate such remarkable fragility in human nature that the upbeat ending seems merely arbitrary. As a reflection of eschatological perfection, it is all too temporary.

Far from skeptically undercutting the play's religious allusions, however, this tension between the hope for perfection and manifest human imperfectibility arguably points to moral suspicion with a distinctive Christian origin. The repeated motif of delay applies not only to the plays' muddled middle acts, as Parker points out, but also to its end.[63] No matter how satisfying the end might be, it is still not "the promised end"—the eschatological end of time—that Kent refers to fearfully in *King Lear* (5.3.268). "Apocalypse" means "revelation," as the Geneva translators make clear in titling the last book of the Bible, "The Revelation of John the Divine." But if the end of comedy is not apocalyptic, then it is not perfectly revelatory: the full truth remains hidden, and comedy offers only at best a glimpse of it. The situation as *The Comedy of Errors* concludes is undoubtedly better than it was as the play began, and the improvement gestures definitively toward Christian assumptions, rather than classical ones, but "better" is neither "best" nor "perfect," and the principal difficulty is the ineradicable human proneness to error, evident in the way people fail to understand themselves and each other.

One quality that nearly everyone lacks is patience, as James Sanderson points out,[64] and patience is a virtue advocated principally in the New Testament as a quality of those waiting for the End. "Patients" and "patience" is one of the play's many puns, evident for example in the farcical suffering of Antipholus of Ephesus as the impatient patient of the officious Dr. Pinch, in contrast to the patient Emilia, mother of the Antipholus twins, who maintains her hope through three decades of delay:

> Thirty-three years have I but gone in travail
> Of you, my sons, and till this present hour
> My heavy burden ne'er delivered. (5.1.401–3)

The virtue exemplified by Emilia is described by the apostle Paul in his letter to the Roman church: "Neither do we so [rejoice under the hope of the glory of God] only, but also we rejoice in tribulations, knowing that tribulation bringeth forth patience, And patience experience, and experience hope, And hope maketh not ashamed, because the love of God is shed abroad in our hearts by the Holy Ghost, which is given unto us" (Rom 5:3-5). Paul's point is that patience and eschatological hope are closely linked, because both are virtues produced by the coming of Christ and are therefore signs of Christ's return—promises of the kingdom which Christ established in his coming, though it will not be fully realized until his second coming. This eschatological hope, enabled by grace in light of eschatological delay, is peculiarly suited to the "already-but-not-yet" quality of the ending in *The Comedy of Errors*. The only character who embodies patience and hope is the abbess, who is also the longest-suffering character, because she has been in "labor" for thirty-three years by the end of the play. While the comic rebirth of her family echoes the divine comedy, however ("After so long grief, such nativity"), especially in renewed relationships and self-understanding, it is merely a rest in human affairs, not the all-revealing (apocalyptic) finale—a gratifying and promising pause but not "the promised end" itself.

This tonal ambiguity of *The Comedy of Errors* is, I would argue, the play's most important debt to Christian thinking, as well as the most characteristic quality of Shakespearean comedy in general.[65] Nearly always, his comic characters discover something about themselves that enables an improvement in their relationship with others, and the end of their story is therefore better than its beginning, but the end is always temporary, a meaningful but fragile product of limited self-discovery in circumstances that the playwright contrives to look like providence—in part, by having characters occasionally acknowledge it as such.[66] As theology, moreover, the eschatological tentativeness of Shakespeare's comic endings is neither abstruse nor controversial, despite the contentions that marked theology in his day. Deeply embedded in the Pauline epistles, the idea that present virtue is, at its best, a mere promise of future perfection is also the principal distinction between Augustine's City of God and City of Humankind; it is ubiquitous in medieval theology; and it was reaffirmed by the Reformers.[67] As Bryan Ball summarizes Reformation thought on this subject, "eschatological hope was held to have a direct bearing on the present life of the believer."[68]

For Shakespeare in the early 1590s, when he likely wrote *The Comedy of Errors*, the most impressive literary embodiment of ambivalent eschatological hope ("already, but not yet") was book 1 of Spenser's *The Faerie Queene*, published in 1590. In this, the most explicitly Christian of the six books Spenser completed, the knight who allegorically symbolizes the title virtue (holiness) is both a representa-

tive Christian in general and St. George in particular, champion of
the true church, which for Spenser was the Church of England with
Queen Elizabeth at its head, figured in some sense as *The Faerie Queene*
in Spenser's narrative. St. George's task is therefore both to achieve
salvation for himself (a process called "sanctification," from *sanctitas*,
"holiness") and to defend the church. Perhaps significantly for *The
Comedy of Errors*, this knight's first encounter is with a monster called
Error, yet the subduing of that monster is not the end of error for the
Redcrosse knight—either in his mistakes (sometimes literally produced by demonic illusion, as some characters in Shakespeare's play
fear is the case) or his wandering. Moreover, the perfecting (i.e., the
ideal completion) of his task is delayed not only by repeated error on
his part but also by the very nature of the task itself. This is because
the task is time-bound, and time is open-ended, so a respite like the
one St. George enjoys in the House of Holiness is necessarily temporary, and his task, no matter how necessary and glorious, cannot be
completed short of the end of all things, as he acknowledges after
defeating the dragon, which in some sense is Satan himself.[69] This
point comes home to him for the first time when he has a vision of the
New Jerusalem from atop the Mount of Contemplation in the House
of Holiness, and he recognizes the contrast between a revelation of
eschatological perfection and the essential imperfection (marked by
error and mistaken appearances) of his present existence:

> Till now, said then the knight, I weened well
> That great *Cleopolis* where I haue beene,
> In which that fairest *Faerie Queene* doth dwell,
> The fairest Citie was, that might be seene;
> And that bright towre all built of christall cleene,
> *Panthea*, seemd the brightest thing, that was:
> But now by proofe all otherwise I weene;
> For this great Citie that does far surpas,
> And this bright Angels towre quite dims that towre of glas. (I.x.58)

My point is not that *The Comedy of Errors* and book 1 of *The Faerie
Queene* are the same or even similar, but that they draw on the same
set of assumptions that illuminates what they do in fact have in
common. This includes a characteristic "comic" shape that implies
contingent hope (both stories end in the solving of substantial problems facing the principals at the outset), common suspicion about

human nature, and a common ambivalence that derives from a specifically Christian sense of how human beings acquire virtue while never becoming perfectly virtuous in themselves.[70]

The origin of early modern skepticism in moral suspicion suggests that "suspicion," might more accurately describe Stanley Cavell's hermeneutic, with which this chapter began, than "skepticism," though Cavell repeatedly affirms the latter, both in his own philosophy and in his criticism of Shakespeare. Connecting his discussion of J. L. Austin on speech acts to Descartes, for example, Cavell takes Descartes as a point of origin, without considering where Descartes' reaction to skepticism came from—that is, what skepticism looked like before Descartes, and especially that it looked very different in England in the 1590s from the way it looked in France in the 1630s.[71] Cavell assumes a similar historically absolute identity for skepticism in his reading of Shakespeare, which typically understands the plays as allegories of skepticism. Cavell theorizes his interpretation of *Othello*, for example, this way: "this means that I claim my text on Shakespeare's text as an enactment of (illustration of? evidence for? instance of? model for? image of? allegory of?) the theoretical movement of *The Claim of Reason* at large, but to no greater extent, and to no smaller, than the convincingness of the reading of *Othello* in its own terms."[72] The convincingness of Cavell's readings speak for themselves, as every reader of his famous essay on *King Lear* well knows,[73] but his perceptiveness about self-deception in general and his frequent recourse to Freud in particular suggest again that "suspicion" is a more accurate term for what Cavell sees in Shakespeare than "skepticism."

The point is not to quarrel with Cavell's terms but to clarify his understanding of Shakespeare, since skepticism was not only new and strange in Elizabethan culture (Shakespeare seems not to have known the word, as we have seen) but also served principally to abet religious controversy, whereas something very like "suspicion," or awareness of moral false consciousness, was as old as the Bible on both sides of the sixteenth-century religious divide. (Berowne's saying about the mote and the beam is only one of many biblical examples of this kind of suspicion.[74])

Distinguishing skepticism and suspicion is even more important in approaching the work of another Shakespearean critic, Harry Berger, who has been strongly influenced by Cavell.[75] Berger titles his book

from the same passage in *All's Well* (quoted at the head of this chapter)
that titles this one, but he reads Lafew's statement not as a rejection of
a philosophy (like skepticism, perhaps?) that makes "modern and
familiar things supernatural and causeless," as Lafew seems to intend,
but rather as a description of postmodern suspicion: the "terrors" and
"unknown fear" that Lafew describes are, for Berger, the unstated and
therefore mysterious motives that animate Shakespeare's characters,
despite their apparent conscious intentions, so their "seeming knowledge" is the failure of conscious self-understanding.[76] Berger is closest
to Freud in his explication of what he calls unconscious "complicities"
among characters, whose language he closely analyzes, because he
assumes that "the unconscious is a discourse network" (xix). Berger
acknowledges that this strategy involves the risk of being drawn into
"the vertiginous vortex of Lacanian conundrums," but a more profound influence would seem to be Nietzsche, through Marcel Mauss's
The Gift, to which Berger frequently refers. If the most generous of
human words and gestures are necessarily tainted with self-deception
and self-interest, then suspicion, like Bottom's dream in *A Midsummer
Night's Dream*, has no bottom. Harry Berger's playful choice to refer to
Henry V with his own name is a case in point, yielding sentences like
the following that looks both at its ostensible subject (Henry V) and at
Berger himself: "Obscure motives and unruly impulses lurking under
the probable intentional surface of Harry's language makes its bottom
hard to discern, cloud it with uncertainties that resist penetration now
and may possibly resist it later" (308).

Bottomless suspicion is problematic, however, as a way of understanding Shakespeare. Its power derives from the critic's ability to
uncover layers of self-deception in infinite reaches of bad faith—the
"complicities" Berger's subtitle alludes to—among Shakespeare's
characters, especially those who are apparently most self-knowing.
Bad faith thus necessarily rules out any possibility of good faith, no
matter how tentative or limited it might be. One consequence is that
Berger's way of reading offers no means of distinguishing one kind of
play from another or even of distinguishing one play from another.[77]
Every play becomes, in effect, the same play in its relentless uncovering of duplicity, self-ignorance, and ingenious manipulation of others
through guilt and blame. A critical strategy that does not discern *The
Merchant of Venice* from *King Lear* (and seemingly provides no way to do

so) is a limited strategy, no matter how incisive its individual readings might be.[78] The problem, I would argue, is that while Berger's suspicion is extraordinarily attentive—and always repays careful reading—it consistently occludes the derivation of suspicion in Shakespeare, namely, faith, and therefore omits the possibility of hope and love that the plays repeatedly affirm, albeit in limited and imperfect ways. We have seen an example of this affirmation in *The Comedy of Errors*, where suspicion of human nature is strong but contained. The hope that pervades the ending of that play is qualified by the fragility of human understanding, but it is hope nonetheless, and its relation to the faith that all baptized Christians shared in Elizabethan England (regardless of their position on the religious spectrum) is latent in the play's biblical allusions, which provide the context for understanding not only the qualified hope of the play's ending but also its profound but comic mistrust of human nature.

This ambivalence marks the end of even the happiest Shakespearean comedies, and Berger brilliantly analyzes its impact on the end of *Much Ado about Nothing* in particular. But to imply that nothing has changed in that play because the social infrastructure has not been transformed is to push ambivalence into a pessimistic perfectionism that falsifies the play.[79] It is hopeful, for one thing, that Benedick has proved his trust of Beatrice, when he accepts her challenge to confront Claudio with the wrong he has done to Hero (4.1.288), and the issue on which Beatrice asks Benedick to stand with her is Hero's innocence. Hero is less interesting than the socially unconventional Beatrice, and Hero's commitment to social expectation indeed requires at least a qualified affirmation of that expectation if one is to affirm the play's ending, but the ending is not perfect, and the moral perfectionism that is the other side of limitless suspicion therefore requires one to reject the limited hope the play offers. The parties to "conventional reconciliation," Berger asserts, "would have to be reborn in a new heaven and earth, a new Messina, before they could enter into a relationship free of the assumptions of their community" (24). This is an acute observation, but it is not apparent that the assumptions of their community are irredeemably suspicious—merely that they are limiting, as are the conventions of any community, and that they indeed come well short of the New Jerusalem in some of the ways Berger describes. Shakespearean comedy never offers a new heaven and a new earth, but it nearly always gestures in that direction, and the gesture is a hopeful one, as in *The Comedy of Errors* and Spenser's *Faerie Queene*. Things can be better, the ending of Shakespeare's comedies usually imply, even if they cannot be perfect.

Whether Shakespeare himself was a Christian believer or not, and if so, what kind of believer he may have been (secret recusant? church papist? Catholic Pyrrhonist? nominal adherent to the English church?) is impossible to say for certain, because he left no letters, diaries, testimonials, or even records of conversations to tell us.[80] What we can know, as Jeffrey Knapp argues, is that he offered his audience in late Elizabethan and early Jacobean England a genial but unusually thoughtful version of what they believed in common.[81] Perhaps he was indeed a skeptic in the vein of Montaigne, as many suspect, but if he was, he followed Montaigne in provisionally but critically accepting in his writing the beliefs of the community in which he found himself, including widespread religious belief, as his ubiquitous biblical allusions make clear—a point in which he contrasts with Montaigne, who would choose Horace every time, given a choice between Horace and the gospels.[82] Such a position might well be described as skeptical faith, and at the very least it gave Shakespeare's audience the world thoughtfully "as they liked it," in the phrase that Alfred Harbage used many years ago, and the plays continue to give that world to us.[83]

PART I

GENRE

2

COMIC FAITH

The web of our life is of a mingled yarn, good and ill together. Our virtues would be proud if our faults whipped them not, and our crimes would despair if they were not cherished by our virtues.

All's Well That Ends Well, 4.3.70–73

I am for the house with the narrow gate, which I take to be too little for pomp to enter. Some that humble themselves may, but the many will be too chill and tender, and they'll be for the flowery way that leads to the broad gate and the great fire.

All's Well That Ends Well, 4.5.49–55

The editors of the First Folio of 1623 divided Shakespeare's plays into three genres: comedy, history, and tragedy. We do not know whether the playwright authorized this division, and we have no evidence beyond this text that he thought in terms of it himself. John Heminge and Henry Condell, who compiled the First Folio, undoubtedly recognized the authority of classical tradition as precedent for tragedy and comedy, as Ben Jonson did in his commendatory poem, "To the memory of my beloued, the Author Mr. William Shakespeare." Shakespeare's first editors ignored another prestigious precedent, however: the Italian neo-classical invention of a new genre, tragi-comedy, introduced to England during Shakespeare's active writing career, that might conceivably have described four or five of Shakespeare's late plays, now called "romances." Heminge and Condell included two of these among the comedies and one each among the histories and tragedies, while omitting the fifth (*Pericles*) entirely. Where the history plays are concerned, though Shakespeare started writing them very early—possibly as early as he wrote anything for the stage—no critical authorization existed for them (Jonson's poem pointedly omits them), so Heminge and Condell either knew something we do not, or they were using their own critical intuition in this case.

With no critical commentary to tell us what impelled the generic divisions chosen by the First Folio's editors, I want to suggest that the principal precedent was salvation history, and the next three chapters explore the relationship between sacred history and each of the Folio's three genres in turn. In no case is the relationship direct, allegorical, or systematic. That is, Shakespeare did not stage biblical stories; the comedies he wrote do not involve an allegory of Christian salvation, like book I of *The Faerie Queene*; and they do not assume a systematic theology. The relationship between the divine comedy and Shakespearean comedy is more complex and less distinct than in Spenser, and it manifests itself in assumptions about the human situation that appear in all the comedies. Shakespeare's characteristic suspicion of individuals and their communities—whether family, city, or kingdom—is the principal source of comic difficulties in the first place, and those difficulties are usually more or less resolved, though never entirely removed, through the renewal of individuals and the consequent possibility of sociable reconciliation. What makes this comic pattern Christian are frequent biblical allusions, of the kind we have seen in *Love's Labor's Lost* and *The Comedy of Errors*, the pervasive insistence on human imperfection, and the possibility of tentative renewal by means of specifically Christian virtues. In other words, though Shakespeare had many sources for comedy, the most comprehensive and informative inspiration for them suggests that they are skeptical but affirmative derivatives of the best-known and most pervasive narrative he shared with his audience.

SUSPICION AND COMEDY

Comedy is the genre Shakespeare most favored, and it is the genre that arguably best represents his characteristic way of thinking. Though his tragedies are commonly regarded as his most profound works, he had moved beyond early experimentation to write some of his best comedies (*A Midsummer Night's Dream*, *The Merchant of Venice*, *Much Ado about Nothing*) well before his first major tragedy (*Hamlet*, 1599–1601), and he wrote eighteen comedies (if one includes *Henry VIII*), as opposed to just ten tragedies over the course of his roughly twenty-year career. Moreover, he wrote the last of his tragedies, *Coriolanus* (1608), before the best of the late comedies that have come to be called "romances": *Cymbeline* (1608–1610), *The Winter's Tale* (1609–1611), and *The Tempest* (1611).[1] He is also famous for his English histories, a genre he perfected, if he did not invent it, but he wrote just nine history plays (if one excludes *Henry VIII*), and he wrote all of those in the first ten years of his career —before *As You Like It* and *Twelfth Night*, two of his most sophisticated and best-loved romantic comedies. Though the chronology cannot be determined with absolute accuracy, the continuity of comedy in Shakespeare's career is unmistakable—from beginning to end, before, during, and after his best achievements in tragedy and history.[2]

As a young playwright, Shakespeare seems to have been impressed by the humanist advice to imitate the two classical genres that had become fixed in critical commentary, judging from his earliest efforts in comedy and tragedy, respectively[3] *The Comedy of Errors* closely imitates Plautus' *Menaechmi*, and his first attempt at tragedy, *Titus Andronicus*, is no less imitative of Senecan tragedy. Moreover, *The Comedy of Errors* adheres very closely to neoclassical theory about the well-made play in its perfect unity of time, place, and action—the "three unities" that would shortly thereafter be influentially advocated for the first time in English by Sir Philip Sidney in his *Apology for Poetry*.[4] Even in his early, imitative, neoclassical experiment, however, Shakespeare already acknowledges nonclassical models of comedy, both in the frame plot he added to Plautus and in the many biblical allusions that run throughout the play, giving it a texture that is quite different from Plautus and suggesting a context for the comic action that is distinctively Christian.

This distinctive element in Shakespearean comedy is the most important clue, I would suggest, to his sense of genre. On one hand, comedy is deeply suspicious in its thoughtful exploration of the human capacity for self-deception, misperception, and the destruction of relationships. On the other hand, Shakespeare's comedies also strongly affirm the possibility of repairing and renewing individuals and communities. Repair and renewal, however, are always qualified, because, while human nature and circumstances are improvable, they are not perfectible, at least on this side of "the promised end," which no comedy ever depicts, though some allude to it in suggestive ways. No Shakespearean comedy is an allegory of this quintessentially Christian pattern, but particular assumptions nonetheless consistently underlie and ultimately animate human action in Shakespearean comedy, making this genre a good example of what I am calling skeptical faith.

As Elizabethans read the Bible, moreover, this pattern was not exclusive to the New Testament nor innovative in it. The story of King David is a case in point, especially in its bleak portrayal of kingly behavior and its frankness about the failings of its principal subject, who is nonetheless introduced, in the words of the prophet Samuel, as "a man after [the Lord's] own heart" (1 Sam 13:14). David's story seems "secular" in contrast to the stories of the patriarchs and the judges, because the hand of God is seldom evident in it, and the issues are decidedly this-worldly. David's shabby treatment of Uriah the Hittite and his wife Bathsheba is a narrative of greed, abusive power, lying, deceit, treachery, and political murder on the part of Israel's greatest king (2 Sam 11). Self-deception is a particular feature that this story shares with Shakespearean comedy, and it is rendered most compellingly in the king's response to Nathan the prophet after Uriah's death. Nathan tells David a parable about injustice, which elicits the king's indignation: "Then David was exceeding wroth with the man [who acted unjustly in the parable], and said to Nathan, As the Lord liveth, the man that hath done this thing, shall surely die" (2 Sam 12:5). Having behaved much more oppressively than the man in the parable, David nonetheless condemns him out of hand, deceiving himself about the disparity between his own actions and his indignation with someone else. Nathan boldly springs the rhetorical and moral trap he has carefully set: "Then Nathan said to David, Thou art the man" (12:7).

This story is noteworthy in its recognition not only of self-deception but also of restorative faith—David's instant recognition of what he has done and his repentant response to Nathan's admonition: "Then David said unto Nathan, I have sinned against the Lord. And Nathan said unto David, The Lord also hath put away thy sin, thou shalt not die" (12:13). A story that spares nothing in its examination of self-deception about wretched motives and worse actions thus includes also the possibility of restoration and hope, as the official Elizabethan homily pointed out: "afterwards he fell horribly, committing most detestable adultery and murder: and yet, as soon as he cried, *Peccavi, I have sinned* unto the Lord, his sin being forgiven he was received into favor again."[5]

The story of David and Bathsheba is particularly illuminating as a parallel to Shakespearean comedy, because George Peele turned it into drama in about 1590, and it was published in 1599, when Shakespeare had been active in the London theater world for perhaps ten years.[6] Peele unsurprisingly interprets David as Adam-like in his fall and a proto-Christian in his repentance, because that is how the Christian tradition had long understood the story.[7] But Peele adds political realism as a gloss on human evil in the story itself. Inspired only by the biblical narrator's remark, "Then David sent messengers" (2 Sam 11:4), Peele invents a royal servant called Cusay, who coerces Bethsabe by mouthing the truths of state:

> David (thou knowest fair dame) is wise and just,
> Elected to the heart of Israel's God,
> Then do not thou expostulate with him
> For any action that contents his soul.[8]

Cusay is a political hatchet man—almost certainly based on what Peele knew of Elizabethan court politics—who resourcefully translates royal commands into coercive actions without questioning their implications. One of Peele's most effective additions to his source is a scene in which Cusay and Absalon follow David's orders to make Urias drunk so that he will sleep with Bethsabe, in case David has made her pregnant (495–551). Their sniggering asides, laden with irony at Urias' expense, effectively evoke the smug hypocrisy of abusive power.

Monstrous human actions and the potential for renewal and redemption are emphasized in sayings and stories in the New Testament as well. Both Matthew and Luke report the saying of Jesus that Shakespeare alludes to in *Love's Labor's Lost* (discussed in chapter 1)—the reproof of those who ignore the "beam" in their own eye while pointing out the "mote" in their neighbor's eye (Matt 7:3-4 and Luke 6:41-42). In Matthew this saying immediately follows, and is linked thematically to, the saying that provided the title of *Measure for Measure*, one of Shakespeare's most thoughtful explorations of self-deception in comedy, as we shall see. Matthew also reports a parable of abusive power on the part of a servant who begged to be forgiven a debt of ten thousand talents (identified as "three score pound" in the Geneva gloss), and barely escaped being sold into slavery with his entire family when his master forgave the debt (18:23-27). Yet the servant's response was to find "one of his fellows, which ought him an hundred pence [Geneva gloss: "Which amounteth of our money to the sum of 25 shillings, or very near"], and he laid hands on him, and took him by the throat, saying, Pay me that thou owest." When the second debtor begged for mercy, the first would not listen but had him imprisoned till the debt was paid. Hearing of his servant's duplicity, his master imposed the same penalty on his servant that the servant had imposed on another, "till he should pay all that was due to him." The point of the story, according to Matthew, is not only that people impose intolerable burdens on one another but that a potential solution exists in willingness to acknowledge one's own failure on one hand and to forgive on the other: "So likewise shall mine heavenly Father do unto you, except ye forgive from your hearts, each one to his brother their trespasses" (Matt 18:35). Even a desultory Elizabethan churchgoer would have heard in this story, and especially in its conclusion, an echo of the frequently recited "Lord's prayer," as translated in the *Book of Common Prayer*: "And forgive us our trespasses, as we forgive them that trespass against us."[9]

This brief survey suggests that the religious narratives Shakespeare's culture offered for suspecting human motives and actions were more pervasive, incisive, and compelling than contemporary skepticism, which was used principally in the 1590s to bolster attacks on opposing religious positions, as we have seen. Moreover, the source of suspicion was not contemporary skepticism but faith—the very faith into which every Christian was baptized. Machiavelli was infamous in Elizabethan England for his godless suspicion, but political suspicion just as profound and very closely akin to Hobbes's was available in no less respected an authority than St. Augustine.[10] Though the English theologian Richard Hooker has often been cited as a parallel to Shakespeare's recognition of an ideal hierarchy in human affairs and the cosmos, Hooker's way of reading the Bible, as Debora Shuger has pointed out, was so suspicious of "emotional delusion" and "subjective projection" that it effectively demystified "spiritual" interpretation of the kind that had prevailed at least since St. Augustine.[11] Hooker developed this kind of exegesis as a polemical move to resist pressure from Puritan reformers, and his demystification of biblical exegesis therefore parallels (and may well have been inspired by) the kind of skepticism that early reformers showed in their attacks on transubstantiation and other miracles of traditional religion.[12] That satirical skepticism derived in turn from the Lucianic satire of Erasmus and More, who were deeply suspicious of motives and actions in the interest of reform before the Protestant reformers (above, chap. 1). Hooker's biblical exegesis thus fits a cultural pattern that was common among defenders of the Elizabethan church.

Where moral suspicion is concerned, Shakespeare is closest to the biblical paradigm in his "comedies of forgiveness," as R. G. Hunter called them, which recur throughout his career, from beginning to end, but self-division and the division of oneself from others is complemented by self-recognition, reconciliation, and renewed community in nearly all of his comedies, whether they conclude with forgiveness or not.[13] In chapter 1 we have seen an example in the recognition of identical twins and the reunited family in *The Comedy of Errors*, and more examples appear in comedies from the middle and end of Shakespeare's career that do not depend on forgiveness for their resolution.

As You Like It

In *As You Like It*, for example, written in mid-career (1598–1600) as one of the latest of Shakespeare's festive comedies, self-deception is central to romantic confusion, while self-knowledge is the key to mutual understanding in the most promising relationships by the end. Moreover, self-knowledge is twice identified with "conversion" (4.3.137, 5.1.160). The first of these allusions is made by Oliver, Orlando's oppressive older brother, who exults in his change in terms that might have come straight from Augustine's *Confessions*:

> 'Twas I, but 'tis not I. I do not shame
> To tell you what I was, since my conversion
> So sweetly tastes, being the thing I am. (4.3.136–38)

A clearer description is hard to imagine of the self once divided but now restored to itself, so to speak—the common situation at the end of innumerable morality plays, where a community of subselves is eventually reconciled.

Oliver's description of himself to Orlando late in the play recalls Orlando's admonition to Oliver in the play's opening lines, which explicitly evoke the theme of mutual knowing: "I know you are my eldest brother, and in the gentle condition of blood you should so know me" (1.1.43–44). Oliver in fact does know Orlando at the beginning, as he reveals in spite of himself, in his ambivalent ruminations to himself about his younger brother:

> I hope I shall see an end of him; for my soul, yet I know not why, hates
> nothing more than he. Yet he's gentle, never schooled and yet learned,
> full of noble device, of all sorts enchantingly beloved, and indeed so
> much in the heart of the world and especially of my own people, who
> best know him, that I am altogether misprized. (1.1.156–61)

Oliver is clearly divided against himself in a way that involves self-
deception: he is unable to acknowledge, even to himself, that he knows
Orlando (that is, he is unable to know he knows) until he "repents," and
he does that only after Orlando unexpectedly (for both of them) risks
his life for him (4.3.128ff.), manifesting a level of charity that has a specific biblical description: "Greater love than this hath no man, when any
man bestoweth his life for his friends" (John 15:13). Orlando's loving gift
to his hate-filled and murderous brother does as much as anything in
this play to make it a comedy of atonement, as Hymen's song suggests,
even though Hymen, the god of marriage, is actually referring to wed-
dings, not to fraternal reconciliation:

> Then is there mirth in heaven,
> When earthly things made even
> Atone together. (5.1.107–9)[14]

Oliver knows himself, and becomes at one with himself for the first time,
when he sees Orlando act toward him in "kindness, nobler even than
revenge" (4.3.129), which seems to enable Oliver to love himself as
Orlando loves him (i.e., in charity, despite Oliver's hatefulness), and for
the first time Oliver can acknowledge (both to himself and to his brother)
that he knows Orlando, thus setting the two brothers at one as well.[15]

Oliver is not the only self-deceived character in *As You Like It*, for the
condition is endemic. The melancholy Jaques is the play's most consistent skeptic, repeatedly calling into question the motives of everyone
except Touchstone the Fool, whom he admires because the Fool is, if
anything, more reductive in his outlook than Jaques himself. Jaques
approvingly quotes Touchstone's summary of passing time, "And so
from hour to hour we ripe and ripe, / And then from hour to hour we
rot and rot" (2.7.26–27), which seems to inspire his own meditation on
human vanity: "All the world's a stage, / And all the men and women
merely players" (2.7.138–39), with its famous summary of life's seven
ages (140–65). But Jaques does not know himself. Not only can he not
see how foolish he is in wishing to be a fool and insisting that the courtiers must rid their minds of any notion that he is wise (2.7.45–47), but

as many critics have pointed out, his reductive summary of human life is belied by the circumstances in which he pronounces it, because just as Jaques dismisses old age as nothing but "second childishness and mere oblivion" (2.7.164), the generous aged Adam enters, with Orlando assisting him. Jaques fails as a touchstone for other characters, because his pronouncements about the world are always more sweeping than his real knowledge of the situations he describes, rendering his skepticism abstract, hackneyed, and predictable, and pointing to his own limitations rather than the real limitations of others—a myopia that simply defines him, or that he is at least unable to overcome within the bounds of the play.

The problem of self-deception is a challenge for the play's principal characters, Rosalind and Orlando, as well, but we see them growing in self-awareness throughout the play, in contrast to Oliver and Duke Frederick, who are suddenly "converted" at the end. Rosalind's self-ignorance is made clear when Touchstone mocks her gently for her identification with Silvius's hopeless longing for Phebe (2.4.42–59). Like Jaques, she is identifying with a social and psychological cliché (he with fashionable melancholics, she with unhappy lovers), and Touchstone tries to joke her into awareness of it. Her self-deception is apparent when she says to Touchstone, "Thou speak'st wiser than thou art ware of" (2.4.54), for she is being patronizing to a supposed fool, without recognizing something about herself that he recognizes, i.e., that she is being foolish—more foolish than he, in fact, like Jaques shortly afterwards. By the time she encounters the courtship clichés of Orlando, however, she recognizes not only their bad poetry (3.2.162–64) but also "the quotidian [fever] of love" they represent (357), and her response is to offer a cure for it (409–15) that involves her brilliant disguise of herself as herself in order to enable Orlando to know himself.[16] Rosalind thus increasingly becomes a more effective touchstone for others' follies than Touchstone himself is. By the time she encounters Silvius and Phebe again, she readily discerns their shallowness (3.5), and her encounter with Jaques is wry and incisive, eliciting his self-important description of his melancholy (4.1.1–36), which clearly does not fool her, though it seems to fool Jaques himself. In such situations, Rosalind's discernment of others is so much truer than their discernment of themselves that we see them for what they are because of her. Her perspicacity is thus truer in the end than Touchstone's, because his is so reductive, yet her perception is distinct from Jaques's hectoring moralism, because her wry awareness of her own vulnerability is so manifest and so appealing.

As You Like It is famous for the way it pairs off four couples in the end (Rosalind and Orlando, Celia and Oliver, Silvius and Phebe, Touchstone and Audrey), and audiences have long delighted in this happy spectacle. But like the end of *The Comedy of Errors*—and indeed all of Shakespeare's festive comedies—this ending, no matter how engaging, is far from perfect. It therefore leaves us in the fallen world: hopeful but still far from the New Jerusalem, because Shakespearean comedy is not an apocalyptic form. Unlike Jaques, Touchstone is as self-knowing as Rosalind, but what he knows is that he is irredeemably reductive, as he affirms repeatedly in acknowledging his incongruous attraction to Audrey (3.3, 5.1, 5.4.54–61). He seems to have little hope for this relationship beyond momentary sexual satisfaction (3.3.35–42), though low expectation at least involves the possibility of being pleasantly surprised. Rosalind tricks Phebe into marrying Silvius, and while the trick may be said to parallel faintly the brilliantly loving deception that Rosalind practices on Orlando, neither Phebe nor Silvius ever acknowledges anything about themselves. Oliver's conversion is sudden, as we noticed, and closest to one Christian paradigm for change ("conversion"), but the love between him and Celia is no less sudden, and it is a good deal less credible than the growing awareness of themselves and of each other that develops between Rosalind and Orlando. Moreover, not everyone shares in the renewed community. Like Oliver, Duke Frederick is "converted," but he decides to retire from the world (5.4.160–64), rather than to rejoin it hopefully, and Jaques determines to accompany him (5.4.179–84), seemingly still convinced that he is too good for the wretched society he is so fond of mocking. Things are undoubtedly better at the end of *As You Like It* than they were at the beginning, but they are far from the best they could be, because the fallibility of so many characters is so persistent.

PERICLES

Late in his career, Shakespeare experimented with comedy of a new sort in the so-called romances, in which courtship, if it appears at all, is subordinate to an emphasis on extreme behavior and circumstances, sudden changes of character (for both better and worse), terrible suffering, and miraculous restoration. All four of these late plays (*Pericles, Cymbeline, The Winter's Tale,* and *The Tempest*) also emphasize the pattern I am claiming is central to Shakespearean comedy—a pattern that balances the suffering of self-division, misunderstanding, and injury with restoration and renewal, though the balance is never precise because intractable problems remain, both in individuals and in their society— problems that social science has since learned to call "structural."[17]

The first of the romances, *Pericles* (1606–1608), is different from the rest in that forgiveness plays no part, because Pericles offends no one who needs to forgive him. Still, a particular relationship is ruptured and restored, for after Pericles loses his daughter, Marina, in circumstances beyond his control, he miraculously recovers her again, and this motif parallels other late plays that also explore the father/daughter relationship, from *Othello* to *The Tempest.* Moreover, Pericles' inner life becomes deeply discomposed—a development that brings this play closest to *The Winter's Tale* among the other romances, but also suggests the informing principle of the divided and restored self that we have seen in Shakespearean comedy from the beginning.

Despite the apparent problems of its authorship (the first two acts are in a markedly different style from the last three), *Pericles* is framed, at beginning and end, by two verbal paradoxes that are closely related, both in form and substance, yet they mark the difference between human fallibility and miraculous redeemability.[18] The first is the riddle that Antiochus requires Pericles to solve, if Pericles is to win the hand of Antiochus' daughter:

> I am no viper, yet I feed
> On mother's flesh which did me breed.
> I sought a husband, in which labor
> I found that kindness in a father.
> He's father, son, and husband mild;
> I mother, wife, and yet his child.
> How they may be, and yet in two,
> As you will live, resolve it you. (1.1.65–72)

Like the riddle of the Theban sphinx, this one is not particularly difficult: Pericles realizes at once that the first person singular of the riddle is Antiochus's daughter, and that the riddle describes her incest with her father. The real challenge is therefore not to solve the verbal puzzle but to escape with one's life once one has done so, since Antiochus compels all suitors to submit to immediate death if they cannot answer the riddle correctly (another parallel with the sphinx), but he also plans secretly to murder Pericles when Pericles does solve it (1.1.144–45)—an outcome Pericles avoids only because he guesses rightly that this is the true test and escapes. The grim line of heads of those who preceded Pericles in the trial is thus both literal and symbolic: Antiochus says it literally represents those who failed to meet the challenge successfully (1.1.34–41), but Antiochus's treachery makes the challenge impossible to meet, so the heads also symbolize the paradox that Antiochus has imposed the absolute sterility of death as the inevitable result of his supposed marriage game.[19] Just as Antiochus has dominated his daughter to the point of anonymity, so he dominates her would-be suitors to the point of death. Though the daughter is "clothed like a bride / For th' embracements even of Jove himself" (1.1.7–8), her father has in fact made marriage impossible by dominating and destroying the succeeding generation in every way he can imagine.

The verbal paradox at the end of the play that answers the riddle at the beginning is a single line uttered by Pericles, when he recognizes Marina, his lost daughter: "Thou that begett'st him that did thee beget" (5.4.200). The line echoes allusions to conception and childbirth in Antiochus's riddle, and it could be mistaken for another incest riddle, especially since a father says it to his daughter, but its meaning is very different. Pericles' daughter, whom he physically conceived, "begets" her father spiritually and psychologically by giving him hope after he had abandoned all hope, when she returns to him alive and well years after he had lost her and assumed her to be dead: "Thou that wast born at sea, buried at Tarsus, / And found at sea again!" (201–2). The allusion to conception and rebirth in Pericles' line affirms renewal and rebirth, in contrast to the oppressive sterility imposed by Antiochus.[20] Pericles' line also parallels Emilia's celebratory exclamation in *The Comedy of Errors*, "After so long grief, such nativity" (5.1.407), and Emilia (a mother addressing her sons and therefore a precise counterpart to a father addressing his daughter) also alludes to a paradoxical birth:

> Thirty-three years have I but gone in travail
> Of you, my sons, and till this present hour
> My heavy burden ne'er deliverèd. (5.1.401–403)

Paralleling the threat of death, misunderstanding, and community division that hangs over the first scene of *The Comedy of Errors* is the threat of death and sterility in the first scene of *Pericles*, where the biblical fall is suggested in mythological allusions to a marvelous garden, magical fruit, "deathlike dragons," and a temptation (*Pericles*, 1.1.28–34).[21]

These similarities between *Pericles* and the frame story of *The Comedy of Errors* are traceable to the influence of medieval religious drama, as Howard Felperin has shown in the case of *Pericles*. The evident presence of that tradition in an early neoclassical play and again late in Shakespeare's career confirms his abiding interest not only in writing comedy but also in the way "secular" comedy can imagine human action from the perspective of the divine comedy. In *Pericles* the same interest appears in the contrast between Antiochus' fall and Pericles' "great miracle" (5.3.60), as we have seen, and also in a barely developed but still discernible motif of self-division and self-recovery that recalls the suspicion of human nature implied in self-division and self-deception in the morality play.

When Antiochus first informs Pericles of the riddle's terms, pointing to the row of severed suitors' heads, Pericles responds self-confidently with moral platitudes, thanking Antiochus "who hath taught / My frail mortality to know itself" and therefore to prepare for death (1.1.42–43). Despite his claim, however, Pericles knows neither himself nor the meaning of death as Antiochus has defined it. After reading the riddle, his tone changes, and he turns pale at what he has discovered (1.1.76). By the time he escapes to Tyre, this paleness has turned to "dull-eyed melancholy" that he does not understand (1.2.2). He attributes it principally to fear of Antiochus' reprisal (1.2.7–8 and 16–33), but he also confusedly expresses fear of repeating Antiochus' error:

> the passions of the mind,
> That have their first conception by misdread,
> Have after-nourishment and life by care;
> And what was first but fear what might be done
> Grows elder now, and cares it be not done. (1.2.11–15)

His fear of Antiochus' revenge coexists with a fear of something in himself that he did not know existed and that he has trouble fully acknowledging.

This mysterious melancholy strikes him twice more: once at the court of Simonides (2.3.56 and 92–93) and again most severely after

Cleon and Dionyza tell him that Marina has died (5.1.23–31).[22] In effect, his melancholy is a death-in-life, triggered by Pericles' initial encounter with living death in Antioch. This melancholy recurs at moments of generational crisis because of Pericles' fear of his own capacity for destructive sexuality, which is this play's way of acknowledging doubt about the self.[23] In the second occurrence, Pericles is again competing for a wife, this time in Pentapolis, and again he encounters a possessive father, Simonides, who jokes bawdily (2.3.99–100) in a way that is reminiscent of the frank eroticism expressed by both Pericles and Antiochus in the earlier courtship contest (1.1.21–22 and 31–32). If his own passions aroused fear and care "it be not done" in Antioch, they seem to do so again in Pentapolis. As if Pericles' melancholy were a riddle, Simonides guesses that its cause is Pericles' misfortune and destitution (2.3.56–58 and 92–93), which put him at a disadvantage with other knightly contestants in seeking Thaisa's hand in marriage, but the real reason again seems to lie deeper than Simonides knows or Pericles can acknowledge.

The paradoxical involvement of life with "frail mortality" seems to be confirmed definitively for Pericles when Thaisa dies in childbirth, and it is underscored yet again when he learns that the first and only child Thaisa gave birth to, whom Pericles entrusted to friends, has died. His attempts at generation have produced only premature death, making him—in spite of efforts not to be—a parallel to Antiochus, who wantonly destroyed the generation after him.[24] This time, melancholy overwhelms Pericles, and he sinks into something like a catatonic state, unable to speak or to care for himself (5.1.25–27). Helicanus guesses that the cause is grief (5.1.27), and he is partly right, as Simonides' guess about the cause of Pericles' puzzling melancholy was partly right, but Helicanus did not hear Pericles' expressed fear of his own passions (1.2.9–15), inspired by the example of Antiochus, and Helicanus therefore cannot know the real cause of Pericles' conflict with himself.

Looked at this way, Pericles' melancholy is healed by the restoration of Marina, because she is not only "this great miracle" (5.3.60) but also flesh-and-blood evidence that his efforts at generation have not been deadly after all. The similarity between Antiochus' incest riddle and Pericles' paradoxical exclamation when he recognizes Marina confirms both the cause of Pericles' melancholy (fear that his sexuality is, like that of Antiochus, merely destructive) and its resolution in the "begetting" or rebirth of himself. To be sure, the reunion is "secular," that is, Pericles' rebirth is not literally an instance of Christian conversion, yet the model of salvation is undoubtedly the motive for comedy in this late play, as in earlier ones. The contrast between creation and death is Christian, as are the division and healing of the self and the motif of second birth. "I am great with woe and shall deliver weeping," exclaims Pericles almost as soon as he sees Marina (5.1.109–10), using metaphors of pregnancy and birth that anticipate his imminent delivery yet also recall the wordplay on "labor" in the incest riddle (1.1.67). In the end, his sexuality is innocent and life-giving after all—the male counterpart to Marina's redemptive chastity (4.6.3–10)—despite its ineradicable similarities to the death-dealing of Antiochus, even in the moment of Pericles' restoration.

Those similarities point to another feature of Shakespearean comedy in *Pericles*: the fragility of goodness, even in the climax of unanticipated joy.[25] Pericles has suffered innocently for many years, as saints typically did in hagiographies,[26] and nothing can compensate for this suffering. He and Thaisa have been forcibly separated ever since the birth of their first child, and their capacity for bearing more children in the interim has been wasted (in this regard, part of them has died irrevocably, so that circumstances indeed compel a parallel between Pericles and Antiochus). Most important, perhaps, the courtship and imminent marriage of Marina and Lysimachus are flawed. Lysimachus first met her as her would-be customer in a brothel, and the play gives no indication that she has any romantic interest in him; her father simply proposes that she marry Lysimachus because Lysimachus has "been noble towards her" (5.1.264). The taint of male desire that Pericles met in Antiochus and feared in himself seems just beneath the surface in his patriarchal *dictat* to his daughter that simply brushes aside the same defect in Lysimachus and leaves it unresolved.

EXPERIMENTS IN COMEDY

The view I am putting forward here—that Shakespearean comedy consistently imagines the human situation in light of the divine comedy—raises the question why some of his plays that are apparent comedies do not end well in any way. In two plays, *Love's Labor's Lost* and *Troilus and*

Cressida, very little, if anything, is resolved: characters learn almost nothing about themselves, and the situation at the end is hardly better than it was at the beginning. *Love's Labor's Lost* at least compels its eloquent pageant-makers of romantic longing to acknowledge death, as argued in chapter 2, and death is the first of the Four Last Things, but the point remains that the young noblemen are incapable of acting well in light of death—of taking either their own destiny or that of others with due seriousness—as Christians were urged to do. In two other plays, *All's Well That Ends Well* and *Measure for Measure*, the action is so ambiguous that it seems merely ironic, characters are so troubling that they seem unredeemable, and unbounded suspicion seems the only possible response. If comedy is the defining form for Shakespeare, because comedy most fully celebrates the possibility (however flawed) of charity and grace in human action, what are we to make of these plays?

Where both *Love's Labor's Lost* and *Troilus and Cressida* are concerned, Shakespeare was more than usually indebted to the dramaturgy of another playwright—John Lyly in the first case and Ben Jonson in the second. The irresolution of *Love's Labor's Lost* seems a tribute to Lyly's *débat* style—the elegant posing of intellectual puzzles in suspended dramatic equipoise, as well as in the learned allusions, balanced phrasing, antitheses, parallel constructions, and seemingly infinite *copia* that are the hallmark of Lyly's self-consciously rhetorical style—a style that makes every effort to wear its learning as heavily as possible.[27] If anything, the intrusion of death at the end of the play is a violation of Lylyan decorum—a shattering of the elegant rhetorical surface by an eruption that upsets it, or at least should upset it. Perhaps the insistence of the young courtiers on continuing their romantic quests in elegant phrasing, even in light of death, is as much a comment on Lyly's style as a tribute to it.[28]

Troilus and Cressida has long been recognized as an experiment in Jonson's satirical comedy, and it is an experiment that Shakespeare tried only once.[29] He shows an awareness of Jonson's style in his treatment of characters such as Jaques in *As You Like It* and Malvolio in *Twelfth Night*, but in *Troilus and Cressida* he wrote a whole play in Jonson's manner, though ironically its subject is not common vice in contemporary London (Jonson's favorite satirical target) but unrecoverable human weakness in the classical past that Jonson adulated, and its satirical edge is blunted by the endearing attractiveness of characters—especially

Cressida—even in their weakness. Set during the Trojan war, the play's focus on the romantic courtship of the title characters is played out against the background of Paris's courtship of Helen, which started the war in the first place. Both relationships turn out to be vapid and shallow, just as the best of the war's heroes are bombastic, weak-willed, and opportunistic, and no one in the play learns anything about themselves or improves in their relationships with others, as the principals characteristically do in Shakespeare's other comedies. The broken romance is pointedly set in the midst of a war of attrition, fought on behalf of a faithless couple. The point, as in Jonson's comedies, is simply to expose human weakness, not to suggest a possibility of overcoming it. A mocking commentator, Thersites, bears some resemblance to choric characters such as Touchstone in *As You Like It* and Feste in *Twelfth Night*, but Thersites' foul-mouthed railing and unrelenting bitterness is manifestly different from the gentle, restrained, but piercing irony of Shakespeare's wise fools and much closer to the misanthropic Macilente of Jonson's *Every Man out of His Humor.*

Measure for Measure

In short, *Troilus and Cressida* is an exception that proves the rule for Shakespeare, even where two other experiments in comedy are concerned, *All's Well That Ends Well* and *Measure for Measure.* The second of these has recently earned particularly sharp criticism because of the Duke, who is its presiding authority figure. In this regard, criticism has turned 180 degrees from where it was with earlier critics who read the play as Christian, such as G. Wilson Knight, Roy Battenhouse, and Nevill Coghill.[30] They viewed the action allegorically, agreeing with Angelo that the Duke is "like power divine" (5.1.377)—a manifestation of God in human form; "bound by my charity" (2.3.3); returning measure for measure, as Jesus says God will do in Matthew 7:1; seeing and deploring human evil but responding mercifully and working providentially to alleviate its worst effects. Rejection of this view has turned principally on the Duke's smugness, inconsistency, and manipulative coercion. Recognizing his fallibility has, for many critics, made him anything but godlike and has made the play a prime demonstration of Shakespeare's skepticism and limitless suspicion.

I want to suggest the possibility of taking both sides of this debate seriously, rather than assuming that they are mutually exclusive, because attending to both can clarify how *Measure for Measure* is well within the limits of Shakespearean comedy, not the anomalous "problem play" it has come to be.[31] The key question is whether anything in the end is better than it was in the beginning—that is, whether the situation in Shakespeare's imagined Vienna improves at all over the course of the play. By "improves" I am referring to change neither in social structure nor utilitarian benefit, but rather in self-understanding and neighborly relationships, because that is the consistent standard for improvement in other Shakespearean comedies. Some of the city's inhabitants indeed learn to know themselves better and to treat others with greater regard, and while their motives for doing so are complex, charity and forgiveness are clearly the most important among them.

Let us consider the Duke first, since he has become the play's most controversial character. Though he indeed acts in many ways "like power divine," his fallibility is evident from the outset, and it is arguably tied to self-deception, making him distinctly human in a manner familiar to Shakespearean comedy.[32] In three separate but related instances, the Duke says and does things that circumstances later compel him to modify, and his ability to change is arguably positive. The first of these we encounter is his assertion that he is impervious to passion. When explaining his reason for assuming a friar's disguise, the Duke assures Friar Thomas that he is not planning secret self-indulgence:

> No, holy Father, throw away that thought;
> Believe not that the dribbling dart of love
> Can pierce a complete bosom. Why I desire thee
> To give me secret harbor hath a purpose
> More grave and wrinkled than the aims and ends
> Of burning youth. (1.3.1–6)

His smugness and over confidence are similar to those exhibited by the King of Navarre in *Love's Labor's Lost*, 1.1, and more comically by Benedick in *Much Ado about Nothing*, 2.3. They are the sure rhetorical signs in Shakespearean comedy that characters do not know themselves regarding their own passionate impulses, and when the Duke asks Isabella to marry him at the end of the play, he clearly indicates that he has learned he is not impervious to the dart of love after all. Though he says nothing to acknowledge this change beyond the proposal itself, the contrast between his earlier assertion and his later action reveal the change in him, as well as his similarity to characters in other Shakespearean comedies.[33]

After correcting Friar Thomas's delicate conjecture, the Duke outlines a scheme that he says is his real reason for donning a friar's disguise, and this is the second (and most complex) instance of his speaking and acting in a way he is obliged to change by the play's end. He asserts his belief that he has been too lax in prosecuting the laws of Vienna, and he has therefore appointed a deputy to do the job for him:[34]

> Sith 'twas my fault to give the people scope,
> 'Twould be my tyranny to strike and gall them
> For what I bid them do; for we bid this be done
> When evil deeds have their permissive pass
> And not the punishment. (1.3.35–39)

The Duke's language points to an unmistakably moralistic conception of the laws he is obliged to defend—"my fault," "evil deeds," "punishment"—and this conception reappears regularly in his language, even late in the play, revealing an assumption that strict law enforcement is necessary to prevent moral failings (1.3.19–30; 3.2.32–4, 98; 5.1.326–30).[35]

Given the Duke's reiteration of this conviction in the play's last scene (in effect, its last judgment), it is not clear that he ever abandons it, but circumstances nonetheless challenge it, and most important, he does not live by it. One of the principal ways critics have seen him as godlike is his preference for mercy over strict justice—a preference he exhibits to the full as the play ends, even as he continues to assert that "faults" are "so countenanced that the strong statutes / Stand like the forfeits in a barber's shop, / As much in mock as mark" (5.1.328–30).[36] One way of understanding this contradiction in the Duke is that it reflects an inherent problem in prosecution when laws are conceived primarily to prevent moral failure, as they are in this play. The Duke says that circumstances in Vienna have reached a bad pass because he has not pursued strict justice for fourteen years (1.3.21), but his experiment in appointing someone else to prosecute the laws for him has several ironic consequences: it is too severe in the case of Claudio; it fails to catch parallel cases in Angelo and Lucio; and the Duke himself ameliorates the worst effects of strict enforcement by watching in disguise and ultimately pursuing the same merciful course that he always has.[37] While he continues to iterate his conviction about stern prosecution, he nonetheless maintains a much less severe policy in fact, and what critics have called "the mess in Vienna" therefore never actually changes.[38] Since the Duke's conception of what he has failed to do is moral, he is really endorsing (and lamenting) a familiar conception of the human condition, which the play strongly suggests is not capable of fundamental change. The same conception appears comically in the Provost's frank recognition that "All sects, all ages smack of this vice [i.e., fornication]" (2.2.5), a point also recognized and described more pungently by Pompey (2.1.229–33) and by Lucio (3.2.100–1).

The Duke's moralistic conception of the law helps to clarify how the first two points in which he is mistaken are related. Believing himself to be impervious to passion, he is censorious of those who do not practice the same sexual restraint he does, and he therefore believes the law is necessary to curb others' excess. At the same time, however, he has always understood—and practiced—the need to interpret the law mercifully, even though he finds doing so difficult to the point of being a "fault" in light of the regard he has for his own self-restraint. This way of understanding him explains his moralistic and self-congratulatory soliloquy:

> He who the sword of heaven will bear
> Should be as holy as severe;
> Pattern in himself to know,
> Grace to stand, and virtue go;
> More nor less to others paying
> Than by self-offenses weighing. (3.2.254–59)

The third instance in which the Duke discovers his own fallibility begins with the advice he gives to Claudio in prison (3.1.5–43). Claudio has been caught by Angelo's dragnet for fornicators, and Angelo is determined to enforce the statutory requirement of death for Claudio's offense.[39] Nothing indicates that the Duke disagrees with Angelo on this point, now that he has handed off the responsibility for prosecuting such crimes to Angelo, and the Duke's stoic argument to Claudio that the best preparation for death is to have no regard for life is a strong indication that he is prepared to back his deputy all the way.[40] The Duke changes his mind, however, after he overhears Isabella's report of Angelo's sexual harassment, with its telling revelation of Angelo's hypocrisy. Now, for the first time, the Duke proposes to save Claudio's life: "To the love I have in doing good a remedy presents itself"

(3.1.200–1). The Duke then explains the content of "doing good" to Isabella: to do the "wronged" Mariana "a merited benefit," to "redeem your brother from the angry law," to preserve Isabella herself from threatened harm, and to "please the absent Duke" (3.1.202–5). Since the Duke's decision to do all of these good things (good in his own estimation of them) is a reaction to Angelo's sexual harassment of Isabella, they also depend for their realization on the Duke's hearing Isabella's story, which changes his mind. To his credit, the Duke thus adapts to changing circumstances, but he does so only in violation of his support for the deputy he appointed to prosecute "the angry law." Arguably, his quickness to adapt also offends his self-righteous sense of sexual sin, which, as we have seen, underlies his stated belief that he has been at fault in not prosecuting the laws more strictly. All three of these instances are therefore parallel examples of the Duke's being at odds with himself in ways that resemble self-deception on the part of characters in other Shakespearean comedies.[41]

Recognizing the Duke's fallibility, however, is not the same as asserting that nothing has changed for the better by the end of the play. Though "the mess in Vienna" seems likely to go on pretty much unchanged after the play ends, the Duke has acknowledged his own sexual desire in proposing marriage to Isabella; he has confirmed the preference of mercy over justice, despite his repugnance at the unruly sexual lives of his subjects; and he has "redeemed" Claudio's life, rather than conceding it to "the angry law." Each of these achievements involves increasing self-awareness on the Duke's part, and they are therefore evidence not only that he has learned something but also that he is better for having done so. Moral improvement, however, is not the same as perfection in *Measure for Measure* or in any other Shakespearean comedy. The play's last judgment is not the Last Judgment, and all difficulties are not resolved, despite Wilson Knight's assertion that they are.[42] The Duke is easily nettled by Lucio, for example, who remains irrepressibly funny to the end, and the Duke's forgiveness of Lucio's slander against him one minute, followed by a sentence based on slander against him the next (5.1.530–31, 534), are indications of the Duke's persistent self-importance, as well as of the inherent difficulty of practicing personal virtue in public circumstances. The Duke may be a better man in the end, but he is not necessarily more likable than he was at the beginning.

Recognizing the Duke's fallibility is also important in recognizing Angelo as the Duke's foil in every point. Angelo also denies his sexual desire for self-regarding reasons, but when circumstances urge him to acknowledge it frankly, he is unable to do so, endeavoring to maintain his reputation for stoic abstinence by abusing his power and resorting to concealed sexual harassment. Unlike the Duke, he prosecutes Vienna's laws with vindictive strictness and with no recognition of human frailty, even after he has been compelled to recognize that he is guilty of the same infractions for which he sentences Claudio to death. When he thinks he has forced Isabella to redeem her brother's life by violating her own sexual restraint, Angelo does not release Claudio but treacherously orders that he be executed earlier than had been arranged, thus unknowingly forcing the Duke to scramble for a way to save Claudio's life a second time. The contrast between the two men could not be clearer than in this episode. Whether Angelo learns anything about himself in the end is less clear. His last words express sorrow and penitence, but they also "crave death," which he sees as his "deserving" (5.1.485–88). Though his apology is presumably directed to Isabella, whom he principally offended, he is clearly unable to forgive himself. When Claudio is produced alive, however, the Duke notices a "quick'ning" in Angelo's eye (5.1.506), suggesting hope, especially in the wordplay on "quick" ("alive") in contrast to Angelo's earlier death wish for himself. Whether this is enough to indicate Angelo's transformation is impossible to say.[43]

The play's consistent contrast between the Duke and his deputy makes clear that they face similar problems, both in themselves and in Vienna, but that Lucio is mistaken in his interpretation of how they respond. About Angelo, to be sure, Lucio is pungently perceptive: he describes Angelo as

> a man whose blood
> Is very snow broth; one who never feels
> The wanton stings and motions of the sense,
> But doth rebate and blunt his natural edge
> With profits of the mind, study, and fast. (1.4.57–61)

This description applies precisely to what the young noblemen in *Love's Labor's Lost* attempt to do as well, and it helps to confirm that Angelo is a Shakespearean comic type where self-deception is concerned.[44] The saying of Jesus about the mote and the beam that Berowne uses to chastise his fellows hypocritically in *Love's Labor's Lost* immediately follows the saying in Matthew's gospel that gives *Measure for Measure* its title: "Judge not, that ye be not judged. For with what judgment ye judge, ye shall be judged, and with what measure ye mete, it shall be measured to you again" (Matt 7:1-2).[45] "Go to your bosom," Isabella urges Angelo, "Knock there, and ask your heart what it doth know / That's like my brother's fault" (2.2.141-43). When Angelo finds such a fault in himself, he denies it publicly, as Berowne does, until circumstances compel him to acknowledge otherwise.[46]

No matter how canny his description of Angelo seems to be, Lucio's assessment of the Duke is another matter. For one thing, it moves beyond alleged hypocrisy to include a consistent social bias in Lucio's description: the Duke usurped "the beggary he was never born to" (3.2.92); he consorted with prostitutes, "yes, your beggar of fifty" (122); "The Duke, I say to thee again, would eat mutton on Fridays. He's now past it, yet, and I say to thee, he would mouth with a beggar, though she smelt brown bread and garlic" (174–77). Dramatic irony is strong here, because the Duke is disguised as a mendicant friar while Lucio is describing him to himself, but the class bias is importantly revealing, for Lucio has a strong regard for his social place (he is a "gentleman" [1.2 SD, 1.4.51, 3.2.42]; to use his own terms, "velvet" to another's "list" [1.2.29–30]), yet he assures himself of his status principally by abusing poor prostitutes, whom he repeatedly refers to in colorfully unflattering and socially loaded terms, as in his denigration of the Duke (but cf. "rotten medlar" [4.3.172], "whore" [5.1.526], and "punk" [5.1.533] as well).

But Lucio's social abuse goes beyond language. His intense scorn for those who market the vice that he eagerly pays for is also clear in his cool refusal to offer bail for Pompey, when Pompey is arrested (3.2.42–84)—an action that immediately precedes Lucio's slander of the Duke. Moreover, Lucio himself boastfully admits that when he impregnated Kate Keepdown, he denied paternity in court to avoid being compelled to marry her (4.3.171–72), and another prostitute, Mistress Overdone, claims that Lucio informed on her to the authorities, resulting in her being imprisoned, though she had been keeping his child at her own expense for Kate (3.2.193–98). Graham Bradshaw interprets Lucio's suave treachery as vindictive resentment on his part that Overdone had preserved his unwanted infant, because her imprisonment would leave the child entirely destitute.[47] In short, Lucio's description of the Duke is really a description of Lucio himself, and if anyone is self-deceived in the exchange between Lucio and the Duke, it is surely Lucio, who fails to see how much of himself informs his vicious assessment of the Duke.[48] When the Duke sentences him to marry Kate Keepdown in the play's closing lines, the Duke makes things a little better for at least two victims of "the mess in Vienna," even though one of them is a prostitute and the other is an illegitimate waif, because Kate's being married will presumably give her some legal purchase on Lucio, where support for Lucio's son is concerned. Though rough justice of this kind presumes no improvement in self-knowledge on the part of Lucio and Kate, the example serves to suggest that in at least one instance neighborly relations in Vienna are a little better at the end than they were at the beginning, and that the Duke not only cares about their being better but is personally responsible for their turning out the way they do.

Given the moral standard for improvement in this play, at least one other character may be said to change for the better, and that character is Isabella. Critics have long recognized that she is like Angelo (and I would argue, like the Duke as well) in being self-deceived about her own passions. Desiring "more strict restraint" in a religious order noted for its strictness (1.4.1–5), Isabella warms to the task of pleading for Claudio's life with undeniable forcefulness, after Lucio urges, "You are too cold" (2.2.61), and in her second meeting with the deputy, her words clearly betray her passion, in spite of her inability to comprehend what he is proposing. When he asks what she would do if she were compelled either to "lay down the treasures of your body" or allow Claudio to suffer, she exclaims:

> As much for my poor brother as myself:
> That is, were I under the terms of death,
> Th'impression of keen whips I'd wear as rubies,
> And strip myself to death as to a bed,
> That longing have been sick for, ere I'd yield
> My body up to shame. (2.4.99–104)

Though the lines expressly desire martyrdom, their suppressed sexual energy is unmistakable, but equally important is that in her eager confusion, Isabella avoids Angelo's question (her body or her brother?) and focuses on herself and her wish for her own death, expressed in erotic terms. In this death wish, she echoes Claudio (1.2.128–30 and again, after the Duke has counseled him in prison [3.1.42–43]) and Angelo himself, after the Duke has publicly revealed Angelo's perfidy (5.1.381–82). Repressed or misdirected sexuality is thus identified with a death wish on the part of three major characters: Claudio, Isabella, and Angelo.

Wishing for her own death is one thing for Isabella, but when she visits Claudio in prison, she wishes for his as well, thus effectively siding with Angelo, who has sentenced him to die, whether she intends to or not. Having recovered from the Duke's spell, Claudio expresses his wish to live, thoughtlessly and too eagerly begging Isabella to save him by agreeing to Angelo's proposition (3.1.119–38). Isabella responds with harsh anger, ending with a wish for Claudio's death:

> Die, perish! Might but my bending down
> Reprieve thee from thy fate, it should proceed.
> I'll pray a thousand prayers for thy death,
> No word to save thee. (3.1.146–49)

Though her dilemma is severe, this is not her only possible response to Claudio, and it is a clear instance of her passionate nature getting the better of charitable options. She could show her understanding of Claudio's dilemma (especially since he is her brother), lament the terrible impasse they both face, weep silently in the face of impossible circumstances, pray that God will work things out—but instead, she disowns him as her brother and rejects him. Even before talking to Claudio, she determines that her regard for her own moral purity is more important than her brother's life: "More than our brother is our chastity" (2.4.186), and it is therefore not clear why she goes to him, unless in the unrealistic hope to get his assurance that she has her priorities straight in preferring her chastity to his life. In doing so, however, she has already limited her moral imagination by making chastity a more important virtue than charity, without recognizing that they are not mutually exclusive, and she is therefore very close to Angelo's attitude that imposing deadly restraint on Claudio is more important than mercy. In effect, both Angelo and Isabella are prepared to make Claudio the victim of their visions of sexual purity, and both contrast strongly in this regard with the Duke. As her brother, Claudio is certainly Isabella's "neighbor," but she does not love him as herself, in the spirit of Jesus' saying ("thou shalt love thy neighbor as thyself"[49]), because her demand that he sacrifice his life to preserve her moral ide-alism is made so harshly.[50]

Isabella's passionately self-righteous response to Claudio raises a question about how she responds to Angelo as well. His agonized solilo-quy after he first meets her makes clear that he has never been moved by a woman before (2.2.169–94), and the experience seriously challenges his identity: "What dost thou, or what art thou, Angelo?" (2.2.180). This is because his sense of himself is so closely tied to pride in his reputation for severe restraint. Thus, while asking himself if he "loves" Isabella (184), he also regards his desire as "foul" (181), indicating a struggle between admitting his passion and denying it in the interest of what he later calls "my gravity, / Wherein—let no man hear me—I take pride" (2.4.9–10). In this struggle with himself, it is not clear that he intends all along to coerce Isabella as he finally does, and when he first states his meaning plainly, he simply declares, "I love you" (2.4.142). As in her response to Claudio later, Isabella has several options in reacting to this statement, no matter how much it takes her by surprise: she could thank Angelo for his candor but politely refuse; she could remind him of her religious status and quietly reaffirm her commitment to her vocation; she could say she assumes he is asking to marry her and seek time to con-sider.[51] But as with Claudio, she reacts angrily, construing Angelo's inten-tion as "foul" (147) and threatening to expose him for his hypocrisy (151–52). Faced with this confirmation of what he has most feared about himself (i.e., that his sexual desire is "foul" [2.2.181]) and hearing her threaten his reputation, he reacts viciously, reminding her of the differ-ence in power between them, declaring that his desire is indeed merely foul after all, construing her incomprehension as provocative delay, threatening to torture Claudio if she will not yield (156–71). Clearly he has crossed a line he should not cross, but it is not clear that he crosses it until Isabella angrily rejects him.[52]

Harry Berger notes that in trying to counter Angelo's threat, "the Duke keeps Isabella off balance," but he does so, I would argue, because he sees something better in her than she sees in herself, and he hopes to bring her to awareness of it.[53] One can see this as self-gratify-ing exploitation of her on his part or as a loving test that Isabella even-tually passes so convincingly that the Duke is changed by it and moved to declare his love for her openly.[54] The bed trick is another example of rough justice enacted by the Duke, but in agreeing to it, Isabella does not "compromise herself" to save Claudio, as Berger asserts (363), because she had already compromised her most important principle (charity) in rejecting Claudio harshly—as the Duke knows, because he overheard their conversation. In helping Isabella to understand the solution he outlines, the friar (as she takes him to be) tells her that Angelo not only broke off his engagement with Mariana because her dowry was lost at sea, but that he also *made himself look better* in doing so by "pretending in her discoveries of dishonor" (3.1.228–29). The Duke is thus aware how closely Angelo's identity is tied to his public reputation, and his awareness helps to explain why he decided to test Angelo's "seeming" in the first place (1.3.50–54). Moreover, Angelo reacted heartlessly to Mariana: "he, a marble to her tears, is washed with them but relents not" (3.1.231–32). Hearing this, Isabella at first wishes death on Mariana: "What a merit were it in death to take this poor maid from the world!" (233–34), but when the friar outlines the bed trick, Isabella declares she is "content already" (261). No longer standing self-right-eously on her dignity, and no longer wishing death on every hand, she is prepared to risk herself in admittedly messy circumstances that nonetheless hold out hope for life and rough justice in the long run—though never, as she exclaims in naïve eagerness, "most prosperous per-fection" (262).

Having passed her first test, Isabella faces a more severe one in the play's climactic judgment scene. Here the circumstances are even messier, as she again follows the friar's advice to use deceit in defeating a deceiver.[55] Isabella thinks she is telling something like the truth when she denounces Angelo as a "murderer" (5.1.41), but she knows he is nei-ther "an adulterous thief" (42) nor a "virgin-violator" (43), except, of course, in his own belief about the situation, so her denunciation is strategically duplicitous—virtuous deception, as she conceives of it. In cooperating with the friar as she makes these claims, Isabella cannot know that the Duke has prevented all her charges from being true (except Angelo's being forsworn), but that he allows Isabella to believe them—and to state them openly—both for her own good and possibly for Angelo's good in the long run as well. When the Duke in his own person publicly feigns disbelief and defends Angelo from Isabella's charges, Isabella does not lash out, as she had with Angelo and Claudio, but prays:

> Then, O you blessèd ministers above,
> Keep me in patience, and with ripened time
> Unfold the evil which is here wrapped up
> In countenance. (5.1.120–23)

In reacting this way to the Duke's severe incredulity, she precisely follows the friar's counsel, "Show your wisdom, daughter, in your close patience" (4.3.118), and her growing charity is the "sweet end" that she acknowledges as a consequence of the "bitter physic" of the friar's possibly speaking against her in public (4.6.6–8). Since the friar and the Duke are the same person, he clearly sees the change in her.[56]

Isabella's most difficult test is Mariana's request (with no apparent prompting by the Duke) that she assist Mariana in pleading with the Duke for Angelo's life, after the Duke has uncovered Angelo's perfidy. Since Isabella believes that Angelo indeed forswore himself and indeed treacherously executed Claudio, she has every reason to reject Mariana's request—even to reject it with another angry outburst (her first response on hearing that Angelo executed Claudio had been "Oh, I will to him and pluck out his eyes" [4.3.119])—but instead she joins Mariana in pleading for Angelo's life:

> Most bounteous sir,
> Look, if it please you, on this man condemned
> As if my brother lived. I partly think
> A due sincerity governed his deeds
> Till he did look on me. Since it is so,
> Let him not die. My brother had but justice,
> In that he did the thing for which he died.
> For Angelo,
> His act did not o'ertake his bad intent,
> And must be buried but as an intent
> That perished by the way. Thoughts are no subjects,
> Intents but merely thoughts. (5.1.551–62)

These lines are a remarkable combination of comic irony (Claudio really does live, though Isabella does not know it), less than perfect reasoning, and undeniable charity. Isabella shows mercy to her enemy, Angelo, though he had refused to show mercy to Claudio when Isabella urged a standard that she finally meets herself:

> Why, all the souls that were were forfeit once,
> And He that might the vantage best have took,
> Found out the remedy. (2.2.78–80)

This is the standard of mercy that the Duke also lives by, though he repeatedly deplores the excesses that require him to judge in the first place and condemns himself for not judging more strictly, and the "remedy" Isabella refers to is the divine model for the limited human remedy for fallibility that *Measure for Measure* espouses in the end.

Seeing Isabella's change would be easier if she ever acknowledged it, but aside from her plea for Angelo, she is silent, and her silence has been construed as persistent self-righteousness. Graham Bradshaw faults her for not greeting Juliet warmly (especially since Isabella earlier claimed they were as close as childhood friends [1.4.45–48]) and for not saying something to Claudio after her harsh reaction to him in prison.[57] Shakespeare was certainly capable of writing powerful reconciliation scenes, as he did in other plays, and *Measure for Measure* would be a more profound and moving comedy of forgiveness if Isabella and Claudio were to ask each other's pardon and forgive each other when they meet in 5.1. One possible reading of Isabella's silence is therefore her "total lack of concern," as Bradshaw claims. But Shakespeare's silences are always ambiguous, as Philip McGuire points out, and those at the end of *Measure for Measure* create "a theatrical moment strikingly rich in possibilities."[58] Isabella is not the only silent one in this reunion; so are Claudio and Juliet—even with each other. Moreover, Isabella is famously silent when the Duke asks her to marry him, giving rise to a recent trend in production for her to reject his proposal by turning her back, walking off stage, or simply not taking his proffered hand (5.1.503). While these gestures save her dignity as a woman making choices about her own destiny, they also suggest that she has learned nothing about her passionate nature, even though her earlier choices indicate that she is moving in that direction. Isabella's silences do not prevent her from wordlessly embracing both Claudio and Juliet when they appear, nor from gesturing her acceptance of the Duke's proposal, any more than Claudio's and Juliet's silences prevent them from embracing each other. Silence is anything but univocal, and it gives a director remarkable scope, as John Barton showed in 1970, as the first director to have Isabella reject the Duke's proposal.[59] Moreover, the Duke's offer need not be seen as offensive to Isabella's religious vocation, if she has discovered that commitment to unmarried chastity was not a calling for her after all, and her acceptance of his offer can therefore seal that discovery. In short, her silence does not necessarily imply contempt.

Measure for Measure is the most explicit of Shakespeare's comedies in acknowledging the inspiration of the divine comedy, from the play's allusive title to its knowing references to Christian doctrines of salvation and its characters' struggles to live out what they profess in unusually challenging circumstances. That their struggles reveal their imperfections, even at their best, acknowledges human fallibility in a way that is characteristic of skepticism, though in this play it is clearly expressed through a robust rendering of original sin and the imperfectibility of human nature on this side of the eschaton. In other words, the play's skepticism is the other side of the coin of faith, and it brings *Measure for Measure* into the same generic orbit with other comedies, from *The Comedy of Errors* to *The Tempest*. *Measure for Measure* arguably emphasizes human failing more strongly than any other comedy, at the same time that it more strongly emphasizes the "remedy" (i.e., grace, mercy, charity, and forgiveness) that makes people able to change in themselves and to heal and improve their relationships with others. Change, however, is not perfection. The play's emphasis on death may well derive from the Christian belief that "the wages of sin is death" (Rom 6:23), but it also recalls *Love's Labor's Lost*, where death is one of the Four Last Things in light of which Christians were called to live their lives well. Death is also the opposite of life, however, and the death wish expressed by Claudio, the Duke, Isabella, and Angelo is eventually changed into something more hopeful. The pregnant Juliet complexly symbolizes not only sin and death but also new life, as Lucio affirms:

> Your brother and his lover have embraced.
> As those that feed grow full, as blossoming time
> That from the seedness the bare fallow brings
> To teeming foison, even so her plenteous womb
> Expresseth his full tilth and husbandry. (1.4.40–44)

Lucio no doubt says this sardonically, with salacious relish and evident lack of charity to a novice in a convent, but he says it nonetheless, and the play ultimately bears him out. Juliet enters in the end with Claudio (muffled) and Barnardine: a woman guilty before the law but bearing new life with her thus joins three men (the third being Angelo) whom the law has condemned to die but whom the Duke forgives.

In sum, *Measure for Measure* takes its place along with other comedies as an example of how Shakespeare consistently derived his sense of comic affirmation from the divine comedy. No other comedy erects such formidable barriers to human affirmation. The only news abroad in the world, maintains the Duke at one point, is "that there is so great a fever on goodness that the dissolution of it must cure it" (3.2.217–18). He says this in his judgmental mood, having just heard Lucio slander him and boast about cheating Kate Keepdown and the child she had by him. In short, the play offers plenty of evidence that, as Claudio puts it, "Our natures do pursue, / Like rats that ravin down their proper bane, / A thirsty evil, and when we drink we die" (1.2.128–30). A more eloquent description of original sin is hard to imagine. But that is not all the play offers. Isabella urges on Angelo the Christian standard of redemptive mercy, and though she fails at first to meet that standard herself, she does meet it in the end, reflecting a hopeful pattern of change on an explicitly Christian model that also underlies the other comedies. None of them is an allegory, but all of them construe the human situation as centuries of storytelling had done, both on stage and off—analyzing the problem, proposing the solution, and showing people in action according to an ancient, familiar, and beloved model.

3

TRAGIC GRACE

It easeth some, though none it ever cured,
To think their dolor others have endured.

The Rape of Lucrece, lines 1581–82

Oh, I have suffered
With those that I saw suffer!

The Tempest, 1.2.5–6

In comparison to comedy, the genre that Shakespeare most favored, his efforts at tragedy were fitful. Though he wrote comedies steadily from the beginning to the end of his career, ultimately inscribing almost as many as histories and tragedies combined, after an early effort at tragedy, *Titus Andronicus* (1589–1592), he did not return to this genre for at least two years. His second effort was *Romeo and Juliet* (1594–1596), after which he again set tragedy aside for at least three years before writing *Hamlet* (1599–1601).[1] The difference between *Titus Andronicus* and *Romeo and Juliet* is remarkable, and the difference between *Romeo and Juliet* and *Hamlet* is more remarkable still. It is as if Shakespeare desisted from writing tragedy twice in the 1590s in order to be able to write it with the consummate skill and insight that he eventually achieved. Practice did not make perfect in this case; patience did. *Othello, King Lear, Macbeth, Timon of Athens, Antony and Cleopatra*, and *Coriolanus* were all likely written in the next seven years after *Hamlet*—at the rate of almost one per year. All those plays are not equally accomplished tragedies, as everyone recognizes, but even the least of them bears comparison with the best of what Shakespeare's contemporaries achieved in the same genre. Yet those seven years cannot accurately be called a "tragic period" for Shakespeare, because he likely wrote *All's Well That Ends Well, Measure for Measure*, and *Pericles* during the same years.

What Shakespeare learned about tragedy in the 1590s arguably has something to do with his increasing skill in writing comedy.[2] From the beginning, as we have seen, his comedies imagine human nature in light of Christian destiny—fallen, and therefore indelibly frail; redeemable, and therefore capable of improving in self-knowledge and in sociable relationships; but not perfectible this side of the eschaton, and therefore incapable, even at its best, of acquiring complete self-knowledge or of achieving unreservedly satisfying or permanent relationships. His comedies become increasingly skillful and sophisticated in imagining human beings with these assumptions in mind, and I would argue that his tragedies eventually developed from continuing reflection on the same assumptions and on what they mean. Shakespearean comedy and tragedy share a common vision of human destiny, but they imagine it, so to speak, in different phases.[3] Whereas comedy emphasizes growing self-awareness, resolution, reconciliation, and renewal, with wedding as its typical culminating symbol, Shakespearean tragedy emphasizes misunderstanding, treachery, loss, disastrous accident, and failure, with death as its culminating symbol. Both emphases reflect what actually happens in the continuum of human experience;[4] both, as Shakespeare imagines them, are properly viewed in light of the Last Things, thus emphasizing the fragility of goodness;[5] yet both happen alike to the good and the evil. Indeed, in Shakespearean tragedy, the tragic effect is usually proportionate to the goodness of those who suffer, and the point is not what they do—or fail to do—to bring on their suffering but the enigma of suffering itself.

TITUS ANDRONICUS

The difference comedy makes is especially striking in the contrast between Shakespeare's first effort in tragedy, *Titus Andronicus*, and his second, *Romeo and Juliet*. Written under the strong influence of Seneca, *Titus* attempts to produce in English the same effects that Shakespeare knew well in Latin.[6] Though the play frequently anticipates later tragedies (Hamlet's ambiguous madness in an effort to avenge a loved one's death, Iago's gleeful treachery, Lear's overbearing assertion of seniority's privilege, Lady Macbeth's manly-hearted ambition, Coriolanus' insistence on unswerving patrician duty and his turning on Rome), the emphasis is clearly elsewhere.[7] The point of Titus's terrible suffering is not to explore questions of human destiny but to provide a means for heightening his character through rhetorical dilation, in the manner of classical declamation.[8] The opening scene displays a series of peremptory decisions on Titus's part that enable successive displays of magnificently expressed resolve, though they are puzzling and even pointless if one tries to understand them morally or politically apart from stoic assumptions:[9] he boasts of his victories in preparing to bury his sons (1.1.70–95); insists on his religious obligation to execute Tamora's son, Alarbus (1.1.121–126); refuses the imperial palliament (186–200); steadfastly maintains that Saturninus be made emperor rather than Bassianus (224–230); piously acknowledges Saturninus's authority (245–253); and stabs his own son, Mutius, to death for supporting Lavinia's marriage to Bassianus rather than Saturninus.[10] Though Titus's suffering begins immediately, when Saturninus betrays him by preferring Tamora to Lavinia, Titus's resolution is undiminished, as he continues to insist that Mutius was disloyal and demonstrates his constancy to the ideals he has upheld by accepting a settlement with Saturninus, who has just deceived him. The multiple reversals of the first scene alone are so striking that they are difficult to explain as anything but an attempt to emphasize Titus's resolution, no matter what happens, and especially its magniloquent expression. "Let us that have our tongues," Titus proposes to his son and brother, "Plot some device of further misery, / To make us wondered at in time to come" (3.1.133–135). The combination of speech ("have our tongues") and being wondered at is in keeping with Titus's greatness. No one speaks as Titus does, and his energy and resolve sweep everyone before him except Saturninus and Tamora, who are treacherous and devious and therefore unpredictable—precisely the opposite of Titus.

As a complement to his magnificence in the first scene, Titus describes himself in images of excess as his sorrow mounts: he is the overflowing Nile (3.1.71); his woes have no limits (219–220); he is the raging sea blown into a storm by Lavinia's sighs (225); he is the earth "overflowed and drowned" by the sea (229). "Andronicus, my noble father," Lucius calls him, "The woefull'st man that ever lived in Rome" (3.1.288–289). Everything about him is excessive—bottomless and unbounded. Titus's self-descriptive imagery not only expresses the greatness of his soul but also prepares for his "overflow" into Latin, when he infers correctly that Lavinia has been raped: *"Magni Dominator poli, / Tam lentus audis scelera, tam lentus vides?"* (4.1.82–83).[11] Though Shakespeare followed Kyd's precedent in *The Spanish Tragedy*, where Hieronomo also breaks into Latin in a moment of severe emotional trauma, the imitation nonetheless shows a deferential awareness of what eloquence required: English yields to Latin, Shakespeare to Seneca, when the great-souled hero is called on to endure his greatest suffering. The classical principle of rhetorical decorum required heightened language to match heroic character, and at this point in Titus's story, English ceased to be adequately decorous.

Intense focus on the tragic hero and his suffering would remain a constant feature in all Shakespeare's tragedies, but *Titus* is the only tragedy Shakespeare wrote in which the focus serves merely to heighten character rhetorically. Titus is not divided against himself, and he learns nothing about himself, because he has nothing to learn. His self-consistency is his most remarkable feature, because it is the proof of his heroic nobility. Whether he demonstrates it in amazing self-control, as in the opening scene, or in his volcano-like explosion into vengeful insanity, he is always greater than any other human being, and his language always conveys his godlike status, even as a mere mortal. Being more than human, he is, in effect, above human judgment—certainly above common judgment. Prompted by Lucius, he construes his execution of Alarbus as an act of piety (1.1.121–126), and his killing of his own children, Mutius and Lavinia, makes sense when understood the same way. Tamora cannot understand why he kills Lavinia (5.3.55), but he has already explained the deed by reference to her shame (46–47): in effect, he restores her honor as his daughter by killing her, as he makes clear by citing the precedent of Virginius (36, 50). This is the same honor that Lavinia herself both expresses and acknowledges when Titus gives her to Saturninus in the play's first scene: "true nobility / Warrants these words in princely courtesy" (1.1.272–273). Mutius' resistance to his father's decision earns him the same fate his sister earns later and for the same reason: his unfilial response has shamed his father, who restores the family honor immediately by killing him: "My sons would never so dishonor me" (1.1.296). Tamora's inability to fathom the cause of Titus' filicide is evidence of her own commonness, and this inability and her shameless sexual duplicity make her a foil in every way to Lavinia and thereby to Titus, whose noble intrepidity she can never hope to understand, let alone to emulate.

ROMEO AND JULIET

Shakespeare seems to have recognized the limitations of giving Seneca an English voice, as he did in Titus, because the next time he tried his hand at tragedy, in *Romeo and Juliet*, he abandoned Seneca entirely, and he put rhetorical self-consciousness to an altogether different purpose. In this play he experimented for the first time in linking comedy and tragedy, and his use of oxymoron not only reflects that experiment but also helps to tie *Romeo and Juliet* specifically to *A Midsummer Night's Dream*, a contemporary comedy in which oxymoron is the characteristic means of expression.[12]

The two plays have much else in common, but perhaps most important is their mutual emphasis on young lovers learning to know themselves in preparation for marriage, because the self-ignorance they overcome is closely tied to self-deception and social division, the hallmarks of Shakespeare's moral suspicion. When we first meet Romeo, he is fruitlessly obsessed with Rosaline, enacting a Petrarchan cliché that Shakespeare satirizes in Lysander's hopeless pursuit of Helena in *A Midsummer Night's Dream*.[13] Lysander declares that his sudden attachment to Helena is entirely reasonable: "The will of man is by his reason swayed, / And reason says you are the worthier maid" (*Midsummer* 2.2.121–122), thus ironically demonstrating his self-deception in traditional moral terms, since his passion (compellingly rendered by means of Puck's ointment as something external to the subject, as in the morality play) has clearly led Lysander's will and reason astray. Romeo makes a similar declaration about Rosaline, ironically appropriating the imagery of love as religion that had become commonplace in Petrarchan verse and rhetorically signaling the reference by speaking in an abbreviated Shakespearean sonnet (a quatrain and a couplet):

> When the devout religion of mine eye
>   Maintains such falsehood, then turn tears to fires;
> And these who, often drowned, could never die,
>   Transparent heretics, be burnt for liars!
> One fairer than my love? The all-seeing sun
> Ne'er saw her match since first the world begun. (*Romeo* 1.2.90–95)

Both Lysander and Romeo make exaggerated and mistaken claims for their devotion, hiding themselves from themselves by means of idealization, in the manner of the young noblemen at the outset of *Love's Labor's Lost*.

Using the same Ovidian imagery Donne uses in "The Good Morrow," Shakespeare has Lysander discover his true love for Hermia at dawn, after a night of confusion and misalignment in the forest. Demetrius simultaneously discovers his true love for Helena: "all the faith, the virtue of my heart, / The object and the pleasure of mine eye, / Is only Helena" (4.1.168–70). Whether he "will forevermore be true to it," as he solemnly declares (175) remains to be seen, of course, but in the brief compass of this play the lovers have undoubtedly reached a stasis that had hitherto eluded them, and Theseus promises that "These couples shall eternally be knit" in the temple with him and Hippolyta (180). Romeo undergoes a similar development when he meets Juliet. He had adamantly rejected Benvolio's assurance that at Capulet's feast he would meet other women who "will make thee think thy swan a crow" (1.2.89), but he has no sooner seen Juliet than he exclaims, "So shows a snowy dove trooping with crows" (1.5.49). Suddenly, but definitively, the object and the pleasure of his eye is only Juliet. "I ne'er saw true beauty till this night," he declares (54), and the Chorus makes clear the difference between his hopeless pining for Rosaline and his new-found love: "Now Romeo is *beloved* and loves again" (2.0.5). Romeo understands this, as he tells Friar Laurence:

> She whom I love now
> Doth grace for grace and love for love allow.
> The other did not so. (2.3.85–87)

Juliet's hope for change in Romeo is thus rewarded. "If thou dost love, pronounce it faithfully," she admonishes him (2.2.94), recognizing his penchant for idealizing artifice ("You kiss by th' book" [1.5.111]) and asking for something more—"but farewell compliment" (2.2.89).[14]

Romeo's change not only makes possible the mutual love described by both him and the Chorus but also, potentially, heals the deepest social division in Verona—the rift between Capulet and Montague. *Romeo and Juliet* are a social and political oxymoron in themselves—the play's only example of opposites coming together across the divisive feud. Friar Laurence consents to marry Romeo and Juliet because he sees that "this alliance may so happy prove / To turn your households' rancor to pure love" (2.3.91–92). Even after Tybalt's death and Romeo's banishment, Friar Laurence continues to hope that their marriage will reconcile the city. He urges Romeo to go to Mantua,

> Where thou shalt live till we can find a time
> To blaze your marriage, reconcile your friends,
> Beg pardon of the Prince, and call thee back
> With twenty hundred thousand times more joy
> Than thou went'st forth in lamentation. (3.3.150–53)

This is not a foolish hope, and it makes clear how deeply dependent on comedy for its effect the tragedy of *Romeo and Juliet* is. Since these two are the presumptive heirs of their respective houses (1.2.14–15 and 1.5.137–38), their marriage indeed holds promise of bringing the feuding families together in a hopeful future, but by the same token, their deaths make the old men's future barren, so the play's final gesture of reconciliation (5.3.296) holds no lasting promise, if only because the patriarchs have no issue of their own to succeed them. The opening Chorus deliberately refers to Capulet's and Montague's "fatal loins"— not "fertile loins" (1.0.5).

In moments of pointed hyperbole, *Romeo and Juliet* between them locate their story in the archetypal story that reaches from the Creation to the Last Judgment. Romeo declares that the sun has never looked on anyone as beautiful as Rosaline, "since first the world begun" (1.2.95). Juliet exclaims that the end of the world has come when she mistakenly infers, as a result of the Nurse's incoherent narrative style, first that Romeo is dead ("Vile earth, to earth resign; end motion here / And thou and Romeo press one heavy bier!" [3.2.59–60]), and then that Tybalt and Romeo have killed each other: "Then, dreadful trumpet, sound the general doom! / For who is living, if these two be gone?" (3.2.67–68). Her situation is not apocalyptic, as she fears, but the allusion helps to identify how this tragedy relates to the divine comedy. In the world this play imagines, the loss of *Romeo and Juliet* has an apocalyptic impact, as if it were indeed the end of all things. "So quick bright things come to confusion," as Lysander says in *A Midsummer Night's Dream* (1.1.149).[15] But as in Shakespearean comedy, so in tragedy: the end of the play is not the end of the world. The loss we experience is enormous, but its meaning remains hidden, in contrast to the revelation of all things in The End, just as the resolution that concludes comedy is not the perfection of a new heaven and earth, but merely a sign of possible perfection in the midst of continuing time. Yet part of the reason the feeling of loss is so powerful at the end of *Romeo and Juliet* is that the terrible deficit emerges from so much promise—the young lovers' demonstrated capacity for change, their ebullient hope, the marriage of true hearts, and the potential for fruitful reconciliation between the feuding families (twice affirmed by the sage friar who marries them). Tragedy consists not only in the loss but also in the promise, whose lack of fulfillment is made more powerful by the promise itself.

Why such things happen is the mystery of human suffering, whose meaning is not revealed in tragedy, because tragedy is not apocalyptic. Certainly *Romeo and Juliet* gives no answer, though it invites speculation along several lines. A sense of inevitability is introduced by the opening Chorus's reference to "star-crossed lovers" (1.0.6), yet nothing compels the sequence of events in the play. Mercutio's death, which, as Susan Snyder points out, is "the death that generates all those that follow," is an accident produced by Romeo's well-intended attempt to part the combatants and stop the fighting.[16] An accident of timing leads to the delay of Friar Laurence's message to Mantua and therefore to Romeo's misunderstanding of what has happened to Juliet and to his untimely return to Verona. Character certainly plays a part in unfolding events, but this is not a tragedy of flawed character. True, the principals are adolescents (Juliet is not yet fourteen [1.3.13]), their judgment is imperfect, and they act impetuously. "Wisely and slow. They stumble that run fast," counsels Friar Laurence (2.3.94). But they mature with astonishing rapidity, and misunderstanding and accident have more to do than impetuosity with the mourning of Verona in the end. As Susan Snyder astutely observes, "There is no villain, only chance and bad timing" (*Comic Matrix*, 66). The feud influences what happens, but it too is not definitive, nor does it impose necessity on events. Old Capulet knows that a Montague has crashed his party on Sunday evening, yet he regards Romeo as "a virtuous and well governed youth" (1.5.69), and he ferociously forbids Tybalt from accosting him (1.5.77–89). "My only love sprung from my only hate," exclaims Juliet oxymoronically, when she discovers Romeo's clan identity (1.5.139), yet her love overcomes inherited hatred, and she risks committing herself to a Montague, defying her father in the process and concealing her commitment (in strong contrast to Ophelia in *Hamlet*), though he is the head of the clan. Overnight, it seems, she acquires the courage, resourcefulness, and independence of Portia, Rosalind, or Imogen.

The point is not only that suffering in *Romeo and Juliet* offers no cause that enables clear moral lessons or cosmic conclusions, but also that the suffering is not justified by the subsequent course of events. It is simply itself, complete in the mysterious chiaroscuro of love and bright promise against a background of death and irrevocable loss—"too sudden, / Too like the lightning, which doth cease to be / Ere one can say it lightens" (2.2.118–20). Capulet looks for meaning in the lovers' death at the end, as he reaches for Montague's hand: they are "the sacrifices of our enmity" (5.3.304), as if their deaths are justified because the feud will die with them. Perhaps it will, but this resolution is far from clear, because the lovers are the only children of their respective fathers, as we noticed, so there will be no issue of these old men's loins to carry on the feud (or anything else) after they die. Even if that were not the case, Capulet's search for meaning in the midst of grief is too reminiscent of Gonzalo's "Beseech you sir, be merry" in the *The Tempest* (2.1.1), and the Prince all but says, "Prithee, peace," as Alonso does to Gonzalo, in bringing us back to the point: "A glooming peace this morning with it brings; / The sun, for sorrow, will not show his head" (*Romeo*, 5.3.305–306). We are to contemplate what we have learned to love and yet have lost—not turn aside from it in a search for compensatory justifications that tragedy cannot, by its very nature, reveal.[17]

When Romeo and Juliet place their story hyperbolically somewhere on the continuum between the Creation and the Last Judgment, they emphasize both its open-endedness and the hiddenness of its meaning. This is important in distinguishing the end of their play from the Apocalypse itself, as I have argued, but it also helps in identifying the tragic quality of their story. We are not called on to judge it as if we were God's spies, but simply to recognize the fragility of human goodness (a response that might be called skeptical) and to respond to this story of human affliction (a response that depends on charity and that might therefore be called faith-ful). This means we are not asked to judge if the lovers' end determines their ultimate end. Their suicides technically damn them by any contemporary standard of Christian judgment, as R. M. Frye pointed out many years ago, but to insist on their eternal damnation is to make their tragedy consist in a perfect revelation of their deaths' meaning and thereby to evade what the play actually requires, that is, to acknowledge the mystery of suffering in the brief lives of two fully imagined young people.[18] At the same time, the story's open-endedness also prevents revelatory judgments about a cruel or meaningless cosmos. This is not The End; it is just an end, and its meaning is not revealed but hidden. All we know is what we have just witnessed, and everything about this play turns our attention back to the bright promise and the mortal frailty of the young lovers. That is what this ending affirms—not their eternal destiny or the pointless destiny of the world in which we find ourselves. We have witnessed events that occurred imaginatively somewhere between the Creation and the Last Judgment and that need to be acknowledged accordingly. This is the tragic equivalent to the tentative resolution that ends Shakespeare's comedies, and in both genres the effect arises from a particular conception of human destiny as only imperfectly revealed before the edge of doom.

The difference between *Titus Andronicus* and *Romeo and Juliet* should now be clear. We are not asked to admire the young lovers because their suffering ennobles them in godlike self-consistency; rather, we are asked to suffer with them and with those who lose them in the world of their play—exactly as the Prince urges in the play's closing lines. This response may be related to the pity that Aristotle said tragedy evokes, though Shakespeare did not know Aristotle's *Poetics*, and Senecan tragedy, which he knew well, evokes admiration for heroic endurance rather than pity.[19] Empathy is one way to identify the response that *Romeo and Juliet* calls forth, though empathy connotes an innovative notion of sentiment among autonomous moral agents that arose for the first time in the nineteenth century and that Elizabethans would probably have a hard time recognizing.[20] All of Shakespeare's contemporaries, however, no matter what their religious affiliation, would have called the response compassion and would have acknowledged its ultimate source in charity. "For as a man feeleth God to himself, so is he to his neighbour," writes William Tyndale, in a succinct statement of how love of neighbor depends on charity, the love of God.[21] When Miranda exclaims that she has suffered with those that she saw suffer, Prospero comments that the shipwreck "touched / The very virtue of compassion in thee" (*The Tempest*, 1.2.5–8, 26–27). Though the age was highly judgmental, everyone nonetheless knew that the love that was the height of Christian virtue required seeing the other as oneself and the other's situation as one's own—however difficult that might be, and however seldom anyone succeeded in doing it. *Romeo and Juliet* calls not for judgment but for entering so fully into the principals' experience that we make it our own and respond accordingly. Though the rhetoric of *Romeo* is no less self-conscious than that of *Titus*, its purpose is not to dilate heroic character but to emphasize the possibility of positive change in human life, even (or especially) when it ends in suffering—a quality expressed in this play in the oxymoronic inscrutability of love in death, light in darkness, bright promise in irrevocable loss, evitable comedy in inevitable tragedy.

As tragedy, this is an important breakthrough; it had no classical precedent but may well have emerged from Shakespeare's continuing reflection on how to enact Christian destiny in dramatic form without claiming to reveal the ways of God in human suffering. Goodness is fragile, because human beings are fallen and redeemable but not yet in a state of eternal perfection—the state initiated by the Four Last Things—and not beyond accident and chance. Since death is the most immediate (and immediately certain) of the Last Things, it is seemingly the ultimate destiny of Shakespeare's tragic principals, without regard to the other three (heaven, hell, and last judgment). While later tragedies than *Romeo* often make us aware of what lies beyond death, none of them is principally concerned with it as the hero's destiny. Their emphasis on present suffering virtually suspends judgment about its meaning, as we have seen in *Romeo and Juliet*. This suspension may well be called skeptical, in that it does not claim to be knowledge, but the skepticism is not conclusively secular, because enigma lies at the heart of Christian affirmation.[22] The focus of Shakespearean tragedy thus complements that of comedy, which imagines life as the proper preparation for death. Looked at this way, the tragedies are more concerned with the effects of both charity and suffering in this life, in light of the Last Things, than with revealing anything about "The undiscovered country from whose bourn / No traveler returns" (*Hamlet*, 3.1.80–81). Though Shakespeare's plays are less concerned than most of his contemporaries were about destiny beyond the grave, it does not follow that the plays either deny that destiny or assert anything about it where the tragic principals themselves are concerned. In other words, the plays do not make revelation itself their concern but rather the effect that eschatological expectation has on the present—the world of the fall, in which the promise of the eschaton is nonetheless present in the virtues of hope, faith, and love. The redemptive promise of these virtues is what makes the tragedies potentially comic, while the definitive hiddenness of tragic meaning in particular lives—which looks so much like a mysterious failure of the very promise we hope for—is precisely what makes them tragic.

In short, Shakespeare's focus on the fallen world remains the same whether a given story ends well for its principals, as in comedy, or badly, as in tragedy. As a breakthrough, what Shakespeare tried in *Romeo and Juliet* was so crucial that he returned to it in later tragedies, yet he waited again for several years after writing *Romeo and Juliet* before writing *Hamlet*, in the meantime penning several of his best comedies. Susan Snyder's formal analysis of *Romeo and Juliet* is helpful in recognizing that Shakespeare "never again returned to the comedy-into-tragedy structure" (*Comic Matrix*, 70). If one thinks in terms of tragic effect, however, rather than tragic structure, the tragedies that A. C. Bradley called "the famous four" can be seen to build on what Shakespeare had done in *Romeo and Juliet*. The difference is that they do not focus on young lovers, and they move beyond the oxymoronic quality of his youthful tragedy to engage more urgent issues in more complex and sophisticated imagined worlds.

HAMLET

The enigma of suffering is central to *Hamlet*, where Shakespeare returned to many of the conventions of Senecan tragedy, as if to explore in his own mind how far he had come from *Titus Andronicus*.[23] It is impossible not to admire Hamlet, and he is undoubtedly the play's most noble character, but his distinctive and complex style does far more than arouse admiration for his steadfast resolution, for he is in fact not always very resolute, as the critical record has long recognized, and at times he chides himself for mere wordiness (2.2.583–88). Moreover, while accident and misunderstanding play their part, as they do in *Romeo and Juliet*, they do so in Hamlet's favor as well as to his detriment. A good example is the "pirate of very warlike appointment" who attacks the ship carrying Hamlet to England (4.6.16). This is the kind of episode one expects to find in romance; something like it in fact reappears in *Pericles*, when pirates seize Marina before Leonine can kill her (*Pericles*, 4.1). Indeed, the whole sea episode in *Hamlet* is fantastic and seems to contribute as much as anything does to Hamlet's ability to let events take their own course without his frenetic and self-blaming effort to control them—an ability he expresses in the confidence that "There is special providence in the fall of a sparrow" (5.2.217–18), alluding to Jesus' description of God's concern and care for creation.[24] No such moment occurs in *Romeo and Juliet*—involving either an accident in their favor or their change of heart because of it. Their change is romantically comic—toward each other in devoted affection. The issues in Hamlet are more serious, and the change in him is more profound.

Nonetheless, his change is comic in its hopefulness and unexpectedness, and it therefore functions to heighten his tragedy by deepening our recognition and understanding of him and our admiration for him—as the young lovers' change does in *Romeo and Juliet*. Maynard Mack identified Hamlet's voyage as an example of a recognizable phase in all of Shakespeare's mature tragedies—the tragic journey, which changes the hero in ways that are quasi-symbolic. Thus, for Hamlet, "After his return, and particularly after what he tells us of his actions while at sea, we are not surprised if he appears, spiritually, a changed man."[25] Howard Felperin acknowledged Mack's point but argued that Hamlet's change (like all the others) is too little and too late, and that it functions therefore to emphasize the bleak world that tragedy imagines: "Shakespeare seems to say there will be no wishful deliverances from a world which remains 'harsh,' in Lear 'tough,' to the bitter end, harsher and tougher than anyone had previously imagined."[26] Felperin is countering the inclination to see tragedy as justifying in the end the suffering we witness (a move he identifies with romance rather than tragedy), but countering this impulse does not require an interpretation of Hamlet's change as mere wish-fulfillment. On the contrary, I would argue that the tragic effect is profound in proportion to the importance of Hamlet's change. The point is not what Hamlet's transformation does or fails to do to make the world better as the play ends or after the play ends, or even how it affects his eternal destiny; the point is what the change makes us hope for and therefore compels us to acknowledge as a loss when the play ends, without in any way diminishing what we have lost.

In this regard, the fact that Hamlet occasionally reverts to his former ways after his change, as Felperin argues, is not evidence of a tragically bleak world but of the fallen world—well short of the apocalypse, as the anonymous priest reminds Laertes (and therefore us) when he asserts that Ophelia's body "should in ground unsanctified been lodged / Till the last trumpet" (5.1.229–30). The priest's phrase establishes in broad terms the context of salvation history for the events of the play, but he draws the wrong conclusion from it. He believes Ophelia's body should lie in unsanctified ground, because "Her death was doubtful" (227), but someone has overruled his liturgical judgment ("great command o'er-sways the order" [228]). He therefore follows the command reluctantly, convinced that he knows Ophelia's destiny ("*doubtful* death" is a euphemistic way for him to assert just the opposite), and that "cha-ritable prayers" for her are inappropriate (230): rather, he says, "shards, flints, and pebbles should be thrown on her" (231). The lines epitomize a definitively judgmental (i.e., all-knowing) response to death in tragedy and clarify its difference from what I am claiming is a charitable response that the play calls for—a response that acknowledges the mys-tery of suffering rather than claiming to comprehend its meaning.

This is the kind of response that Gertrude both articulates and evokes in her rhetorically compelling and compassionate description of Ophelia's death (4.7.167–184), including its implicit acknowledgment of her weakness (179) and fatal passivity (183–184), for charity is not blind. Gertrude in fact shares those faults, but she is nonetheless the most likely source of the "great command" that enables "charitable prayers" to be offered for Ophelia by a grumbling priest. Such moments as this and Hamlet's hopeful change are as much a part of *Hamlet* as the corpse-strewn stage at the end, and while they do not justify what hap-pens, they not only deepen the sense of tragic loss by contrast but also offer something more complex and mysterious than unrelieved bleak-ness. They are the preparation for Horatio's response to Hamlet's death: "Good night, sweet prince, / And flights of angels sing thee to thy rest" (5.2.361–362). Horatio's saying this does not describe its hap-pening, as if Hamlet were a saint in a Baroque altarpiece, nor does it compensate for Horatio's loss and ours; it merely points the way to a response that is neither sentimentally triumphant nor despairing but amazed by affliction and moved by this extraordinary story of it.

OTHELLO

In *Othello* Shakespeare turned again to the comic material of courtship and marriage that he had already treated tragically in *Romeo and Juliet*, but the change of character which I have argued is the essence of comic development occurs retrospectively, remembered compellingly by the principals when they are obliged to defend themselves before the Venetian senate in 2.1, and the play focuses on another change—the undoing of the first—which is unthinkable in *Romeo*, and which heightens the suffering in *Othello* immeasurably. This second change also involves the tragic journey that Maynard Mack identifies, but in *Othello* the journey is, if anything, more nearly symbolic than in *Hamlet*. As several critics have pointed out, Venice and Cyprus are thematic opposites: Venice is contiguous with the mainland, whereas Cyprus is an isolated island; Venice is governed by a Senate that functions effectively in a city at peace, but Cyprus is under martial law with Othello alone in charge; Othello is untroubled by provocation in Venice, while in Cyprus, he is undone; in Venice Desdemona chooses bravely for herself, but in Cyprus events overwhelm and destroy her; in Venice love and marriage originate, whereas in Cyprus marriage degenerates into jealousy, vengeance, and murder; Iago is ineffective in Venice, but in Cyprus his effect is deadly and, until the very end, unerring.[27] John Velz compares this thematic contrast to the contrast in medieval conversion plays that require two symbolic locations, suggesting that *Othello* is "a tragic inversion of the *conversio*, complete with emblematic setting."[28] Iago has long been recognized as a secularized Vice from the medieval morality play, dividing Othello against himself by corrupting his imagination, so that he loses faith in "the divine Desdemona" (2.1.75).[29] She had, in effect, lifted him briefly out of the chaotic and reductive military world that he had endured ever since he was a child and that Iago reconvinces him is all there is.[30]

The emblematic action of *Othello* does not make it an allegory, but it does help to locate the action meaningfully in the same sweep of Christian destiny where nearly all the comedies and several other tragedies are located. This is also the function of Cassio's extraordinary lines when Iago makes him drunk. "Well, God's above all," he declares thickly, "and there be souls must be saved, and there be souls must not be saved" (2.3.97–99). He is using the language of salvation to goad Iago stupidly about their new discrepancy in rank, as Cassio makes clear in hoping to be saved himself (102) and then in asserting that "the lieutenant is to be saved before the ancient" (105–6). The seriousness with which this learned discussion of soteriology is to be taken can be judged from its irreverent context, from the highly charged atmosphere

of military emulation, and from the terrifying threat that Cassio is fool-
ishly ignoring, but the lines are neither gratuitous nor merely ironic.
They locate the action in the fallen world. Suddenly, as if half apolog-
izing for his effrontery, Cassio exclaims, "God forgive us our sins!"
(106–107)—an exclamation not calculated to move Iago, even if, by
some amazing grace, it moves God. Still, Cassio's profane wish echoes
the Lord's prayer ("And forgive us our trespasses, as we forgive them
that trespass against us"[31]), and it therefore evokes the obligation of all
Christians to forgive as they are forgiven and to love their neighbor as
themselves. Whether Cassio says this in such a way as to show that he
believes it is not the point. What is important is that Shakespeare has
him say it.

Cassio's flippant allusions to the salvation of his soul anticipate the
most agonized—and agonizing—speech in the play, when Othello
addresses the dead Desdemona in the sudden awareness that she was
innocent, though he has just killed her because he believed her guilty.
Nothing better expresses his awareness of the second change that happens to him in this play and its deliberate placement in the course of
Christian destiny. Still very much in this world, Othello imagines himself and Desdemona at the Last Judgment: "When we shall meet at
compt, / This look of thine will hurl my soul from heaven, / And fiends
shall snatch at it" (5.2.282–84). In the extremity of his suffering, Othello
invokes the devils to punish him while imagining Desdemona as a soul
in bliss:

> Whip me, ye devils,
> From the possession of this heavenly sight!
> Blow me about in winds! Roast me in sulfur!
> Wash me in steep-down gulfs of liquid fire!
> O Desdemon! Dead, Desdemon! Dead! O! O! (5.2.286–90)

These are undoubtedly expressions of extraordinary anguish, followed
moments later by Othello's suicide, but as in *Romeo and Juliet*, the
tragedy of Othello does not consist in a revelation that he is damned;
it consists in his suffering—imposed on him pointlessly, it seems, by
Iago but also brought on Othello inexplicably by himself. For his suffering is inseparable from the love he encountered for the first time in
Desdemona, because her betrayal of that love (as he mistakenly saw it)
was the reason he killed her, and more important, because he has just
realized—after killing her—that her love was true after all, and there-

fore that everything she meant to him was true as well. The suffering that wills his own damnation is thus mysteriously inseparable from the faith that lifted him lovingly out of himself in the first place. The second does not negate the first; it *depends* on it.

This is an insight that he thought he understood when he exclaimed, "This sorrow's heavenly; / It strikes where it doth love" (5.2.21–22), but that understanding was demonic, induced by the corrupting effect of Iago on Othello's own fear and stoic sense of fate. The terrible irony that wrings Othello's invocation of devils out of him is another revelation, produced by his recognition that his suffering would not be possible if the object of his faith, which he has now destroyed, were not as true and loving as he once believed—and she remains so, even in her death, which he now recognizes, too late, is the death of an innocent. The parallel between Othello's story and mankind's does not work as allegory; it works to make a distinctive kind of tragedy possible—one that depends for its effect not on doubt but on faith, while the response it evokes is not the revelation of knowledge about eternal destiny nor about a bleak, harsh, or tough world before we die; rather, it simply evokes acknowledgment of the complex suffering of a powerfully imagined fellow human being.[32]

MACBETH

This acknowledgment achieves its most explicitly Christian and perhaps its most mysterious treatment in *Macbeth*. Even more than Othello, Macbeth thinks intensely about his salvation—"mine eternal jewel," as he calls it, "Given to the common enemy of man" in his assassination of Duncan (3.1.69–70). Gratuitously murdering a king who had just honored him, Macbeth destroys not only his lord but also his guest and his kinsman (1.7.12–14), thus committing, as several critics have pointed out, the three sins of the ninth circle in Dante's hell.[33] For just one of those sins (betraying one's lord), Dante imagines Brutus, Cassius, and Judas being gnawed forever in the tripartite mouth of Satan. Macbeth's hell is this-worldly ("here, upon this bank and shoal of time" [1.7.6]), as always for Shakespeare's tragic heroes, but his despair derives from a specifically Christian sense of what he does to himself, as Paul Jorgensen has shown, and the background of grace is what makes the suffering of his "deep damnation" (1.7.20) so powerful. This is not the story of a cynical and reductive criminal mind but of an exceptionally conscientious man, fully aware of his alternatives and of what he is doing to himself by rejecting them—yet he rejects them anyway and is afflicted accordingly, but in no surprise at what is happening to him.

Still, the emphasis is on his suffering, not on a triumphalist or vindictive sense of revelatory punishment—though the punishment is both revealing and inevitable, because it is inherent in the deed, as Macbeth acknowledges before he commits the murder (1.7.7–12). His hallucinations, lack of sleep, constant fear, self-deceived hope in the equivocal oracle, even his famously expressed despair (5.3.19–28, 5.5.17–28), all compel us to see what he is doing to himself and how painful the process is to him. Since he is not a disembodied shade, like the souls Dante meets in hell, it is impossible to distance what is happening to him through allegory, symbol, or eschatological insight. His degradation is palpable, and what he degrades is always so close to the surface of his words and actions that it never ceases to be part of them and therefore of him.

Take, for example, Shakespeare's sole use of the unusual verb "gospeled," in the harsh rhetorical questions that Macbeth puts to the men he hires to murder Banquo:

> Do you find
> Your patience so predominant in your nature
> That you can let this go? Are you so gospeled
> To pray for this good man and for his issue,
> Whose heavy hand hath bowed you to the grave
> And beggared yours forever? (3.1.87–92)

The speech is masterful in its appeal to the men's sense of injustice. They are not professional assassins; Macbeth has found someone whom Banquo has oppressed—peasant tenants, presumably—and he plays on their indignation to stiffen their resolve in what he is asking them to do. "Gospeled" alludes to their exposure to Christian teaching—that one should return good for evil, turn the other cheek, forgive as one hopes to be forgiven, love one's neighbor as oneself.[34] Are they, Macbeth demands sardonically, so steeped in Christian ethics that they will return good for evil where Banquo is concerned, even though he participates in a social system that has oppressed and impoverished them and their children—"beggared yours forever?" "We are men, my liege," one of them answers (3.1.92), admitting the force of Macbeth's appeal in a line that presumably means "We are not inhumanly insensible to what Banquo has done to us."

What is striking about this appeal is that it assumes a common affirmation of extraordinary goodness, shared by Macbeth with his interlocutors, though he is a murderer corrupting others to murder. He knows that patience is an eschatological virtue, a sign of the kingdom established by Christ, which will be perfectly revealed at the second coming.[35] This is clear in his linking patience so closely to "gospeled" in his next sentence: patience and charity (the heart of the gospel) are both gifts of grace, signs of divine evitability in human life, evidence of the Holy Ghost. Yet Macbeth affirms all this only in trying to deny it. His words are haunted by his own deeds—as he foresaw before the murder. Where was patience when he killed Duncan? Why did he reverse the gospel admonition to return good for evil by returning evil for good? He refers to Banquo as "this good man" sarcastically, because he wants to reduce Banquo rhetorically to the injustices he has practiced, yet Banquo refused the same temptation to which Macbeth yielded (2.1.6–29), and the phrase "this good man" has a very different meaning for Macbeth in relation to the man *he* murdered, so his own phrase condemns him—as he somehow knows and even half acknowledges in the equivocation of his language.

"We are men, my liege" elicits a meditation by Macbeth on hierarchy—"the valued file"—that ranks men above dogs and some men above others (3.1.93–109). The point of this meditation, he says to his fellow murderers, is that "if you have a station in the file / Not i' the worst rank of manhood," then "I will put that business in your bosoms / Whose execution takes your enemy off" (103–6). But Macbeth cannot escape, in this euphemistic meditation, close ironic echoes of his own thoughts before the murder. Then, Macbeth had resisted his wife's temptation by insisting that "I dare do all that may become a man; / Who dares do more is none" (1.7.47–48). Then, he had asserted, "We will proceed no further in *this business*" (1.7.32). Then, he had recognized "The deep damnation of his [Duncan's] *taking-off*" (1.7.20). Perhaps the ultimate searing irony of Macbeth's own rejected but still remembered goodness is his self-deceived confidence that murdering Banquo will create an apocalyptic end of his suffering—an absolute revelation of meaning in his deed: "Who wear our health but sickly in his life, / Which in his death were perfect" (3.1.108–9). Characters in Shakespearean comedy (Isabella, for example) sometimes imagine that a particular beneficent outcome will amount to "most prosperous perfection"; Macbeth is the only character who hopes for perfection in continuing evil.[36]

Macbeth's suffering would seem to be the least enigmatic of all the suffering in the tragedies, because he so clearly brings it on himself. No accident of chance waylays him; no demonically cunning enemy deceives him (the weird sisters are no Iago); no loved one betrays him; everything that happens to him happens because of a terrible choice he makes and continues to make, with consequences that he cannot avoid, no matter how hard he tries: "They have tied me to a stake. I cannot fly, / But bearlike I must fight the course" (5.7.1–2). Yet our sense of Macbeth's tragedy does not consist in superior moral judgment about his failure, and our unavoidable identification with his suffering makes his tragedy more mysterious, not less. This is the principal difficulty with trying to apply Aristotle's theory of *hamartia* to Shakespearean tragedy: besides the fact that Shakespeare did not know the *Poetics*, the theory of a "tragic flaw" misses the point. These are indeed flawed heroes, but simply to find their flaw (only one?) and to explain what happens to them in light of it is to join the grouchy priest who buries Ophelia, confident that we know what the sufferer deserves, even after death, and anxious to cast the shards, flints, and pebbles of our judgment on him.[37] The horror of Macbeth's suffering—for whatever reason—is what properly moves us, not gratification that he suffers as he deserves. Yet the horror of his suffering can only be apprehended in recognizing the grace that he effaces as he turns away irrevocably from the great animating principle of redemptive hope.[38]

KING LEAR

Of all the mature tragedies, *King Lear* has come to be regarded as the benchmark of bleakness. "Among the tragedies," Howard Felperin notes, "*King Lear* has seemed to many the most scarifying of all."[39] Felperin quotes Samuel Johnson's shocked reaction to reading Shakespeare's play, after having become accustomed to seeing Nahum Tate's optimistic version of it on the stage and having recognized that the chronicle sources agree with Tate, not with Shakespeare. Felperin comments: "In the case of *King Lear* it is history that offers a Hollywood ending, which, to Johnson's bewilderment, Shakespeare rejects as too good to be true. The ending Shakespeare does provide, Johnson is in effect saying, is too true to be good" (111). Felperin is not using "good" esthetically but morally, cued by Johnson's appeal to "the observation of justice" in Tate's version, but not in Shakespeare's. "Poetic justice is the literary equivalent to theodicy," Felperin observes, and he contrasts critics who persist in seeking a theodicy in *Lear* ("who generally admit some sort of Christianity into its universe") with those who "insist on the gratuitousness and 'absurdity' of its suffering." He makes this distinction in order to agree emphatically with the second, "on the grounds that the repudiation of optimistic world views is part of the very structure of Shakespeare's tragedies and central to their tragic effect" (112–13).

I cite Felperin at length, because he wrote at a pivotal juncture in criticism of *King Lear*, and he grasped the issues so clearly. He is right to see a tendency in twentieth-century criticism—traceable principally to A. C. Bradley—to find consolation in the suffering of Shakespeare's tragic heroes—something that justifies it, makes it worthwhile, redeems it, compensates for it.[40] Felperin is also right to see a rejection of that reading, for Lear in particular, beginning with Jan Kott and William Elton.[41] This rejection has in fact become so dominant that calling it "maverick," as Felperin does, now appears almost quaint (113 n. 12). Johnson was certainly right that Shakespeare violated "the faith of the chronicles" in the ending of *King Lear*, and Felperin is right that the yearning for poetic justice produces theodicies to justify the suffering that Shakespeare in fact invented, but it does not follow (and Johnson himself does not say) that admitting "some sort of Christianity into" the universe of *King Lear* necessarily amounts to a justification of Lear's suffering.[42]

On the contrary, I would argue that the suffering of *King Lear* functions the same way suffering functions in other Shakespearean tragedies, and that that function is to emphasize the mystery that these plays require us to recognize, respect, contemplate—in short, to *acknowledge*—without trying to explain, because the meaning of tragic suffering is not revealed but hidden. To acknowledge suffering as enigmatic, however, is not to negate the transcendent goodness with which suffering inexplicably coexists; on the contrary, the enigma depends on that goodness, indeed derives its impact from it, for suffering would simply be expected, even ordinary, rather than mysterious, if it were all we knew in the play. (This comes so close to being its effect in *Titus Andronicus* as to help explain why that play does not "feel" tragic, despite Titus's appalling agony.) Finally, I would urge that the goodness in *King Lear* is no less Christian than the goodness in *Hamlet*, *Othello*, or *Macbeth*, even though the setting of *King Lear* is explicitly pagan. In none of these plays does goodness compensate for suffering, but suffering and death do not negate goodness. The real mystery of Shakespearean tragedy is the mystery of life itself—how goodness and suffering coexist, especially when suffering has the last word.

King Lear is the only tragedy Shakespeare wrote in which he embedded a fully developed comedy of forgiveness, unfolding from the play's first scene to its last, and in no other tragedy (except possibly *Romeo and Juliet*) is it therefore possible to see more clearly how comedy and tragedy are related.[43] From the beginning, Shakespeare contrasts forgiveness with the deference imposed by social hierarchy, because forgiveness is rooted in charity, and charity is not tied to social obligation. In the opening scene, Lear expects his daughters to return what he has conferred on them as king, as parent, and as male, by showing their duty to him publicly, based on their subordinate social roles as his subjects, as his children, and as women. The best description of Cordelia's response in this situation is by Stanley Cavell, who pointed out that the public ceremony enables Lear to evade the very thing he says he seeks, namely, his daughters' love. In public, he can offer his "bribe" in the confident assurance that it will compel his daughters' compliance, because he assumes they want what he is conferring, and because the public context assures that they will neither object to it nor offer real love, which Lear thereby avoids.[44] But his reckoning, Cavell argues, does not include his youngest daughter (whose birth order, incidentally, adds to her social deficit and therefore to what she owes her father):

> Cordelia is alarming precisely because he knows she is offering the real thing, offering something a more opulent third of his kingdom cannot, must not, repay; putting a claim upon him he cannot face. She threatens to expose the necessity for that plan—his terror of being loved, of needing love. (62)

To use different language, Lear is deceiving himself, having fostered a false consciousness based on his social position and expressed in the rhetoric of idealism, which Goneril and Regan know and use perfectly in the public ceremony.[45] They also know, however, that Lear is self-deceived. "Yet he hath ever but slenderly known himself," says Regan later (1.1.296–97), and Goneril chides him in the same terms when he visits her:

> I would you would make use of your good wisdom,
> Whereof I know you are fraught, and put away
> These dispositions which of late transport you
> From what you rightly are. (1.4.217–20)

Cordelia recognizes her father's self-deception as clearly as her sisters—if not more clearly—and her love for him prevents her from responding to the false version of himself that he projects publicly, even if his self-recognition may be more than she can hope for. This is both why he tries to avoid her love (long habituated to social prestige, he has come to love his self-deception more) and why she cannot, in love, pay the social obligation he demands: "Lear is torturing her, claiming her devotion, which she wants to give, but forcing her to help him betray (or not to betray) it, to falsify it publicly" (Cavell, 63). Cordelia refuses to violate what she loves, even at the cost of her own social ruin, and her love is therefore what prevents her from voicing the rhetoric of public adulation, as her sisters do: "What shall Cordelia speak? Love and be silent" (1.1.62).

Her second response, said to herself after Regan's speech, is in keeping with the first (after Goneril's), but it is easily misconstrued:

> Then poor Cordelia!
> And yet not so, since I am sure my love's
> More ponderous than my tongue. (1.1.76–78)

Harry Berger comments that "The speaker of the first line already senses the value of the victim's role," a reading that takes "poor" to imply self-pity.[46] "Poor," however, also connotes literal material poverty, a reading that is clearer in Q1's alternative to line 78: "more *richer* than my tongue."[47] Responding to Lear's bribe, Goneril and Regan both sprinkle their speeches liberally with the language of material value: "dearer," "valued," "rich or rare," "poor," "worth," "precious." Especially striking is Goneril's assertion that she loves her father with "A love that makes breath poor and speech unable" (1.1.60), because she thereby establishes an inverse ratio of love to speech that Cordelia's response implicitly affirms and reflects: "Love and be silent." This

subtext of the sisters' speeches is well understood and in effect explicated by France, when he declares his admiration for Cordelia:

> Fairest Cordelia, that art most rich being poor,
> Most choice, forsaken, and most loved, despised,
> Thee and thy virtues here I seize upon,
> Be it lawful I take up what's cast away. (1.1.254–57)

As he frankly acknowledges, she is literally "dowerless" (260), for he recognizes that she has made herself "poor" in just the way she feared;
nonetheless, France declares that Burgundy cannot "buy this unprized
precious maid of me" (263), echoing Goneril's use of "precious" (74)
but giving it an entirely different evaluation.

Cavell comments that "A reflection of what Cordelia now must feel
is given by one's rush of gratitude toward France, one's almost wild
relief as he speaks his beautiful trust" (65). The moment is straight out
of romance or fairy tale: the youngest child of three, truer and braver
than her siblings, is misunderstood, rejected, and ruined, but suddenly
reprieved and restored by an altogether unexpected intervention. No
other king of France has such a role in Shakespeare's plays, just as no
English victory is sadder or more ominous than the one that defeats the
French invasion in 5.1 and 5.2. But romance has a particular coloring
in *King Lear*. France emphasizes Cordelia's "virtues"—they are what he
"seizes upon" (256)—and her virtues are specifically Christian. "Most
rich being poor" not only carries on the imagery of wealth and poverty
that runs throughout the first scene but also gives it an unmistakably
Christian connotation: "Our Lord Jesus Christ, that he being rich, for
your sakes became poor" (2 Cor 8:9). The biblical echo is the first of
many that attach themselves to Cordelia. Kent describes her as "seeking to give / Losses their remedies" (2.2.172–73), as if that were her
definitive function. "O dear Father, / It is thy business that I go about"
exclaims Cordelia to the absent Lear, in one of the plays' closest biblical echoes (4.4.23–24).[48] An anonymous Gentleman says that "Patience
and sorrow strove / Who should express her goodliest . . . . / Her smiles
and tears / Were like a better way" (4.3.16–19). "There," he adds, "she
shook / The holy water from her heavenly eyes" (30–31).[49] Her own
prayer for her father also links her tears with the beneficent power of
nature, at the same time echoing Kent's allusion to "remedy":

> All blest secrets,
> All you unpublished virtues of the earth,
> Spring with my tears! Be aidant and remediate
> In the good man's distress! (4.4.15–18)[50]

She has forgiven Lear before he asks for her forgiveness, and the anonymous Gentleman again makes the point (speaking to Lear): "Thou hast one daughter / Who redeems nature from the general curse / Which twain have brought her to" (4.6.205–7). "Poor perdu," Cordelia lovingly refers to her father, identifying him as the "lost one" of the parable of the prodigal son in Luke 15, "and wast thou fain, poor Father, / To hovel thee with swine and rogues forlorn / In short and musty straw?" (4.7.36–41).[51]

To acknowledge the origin of these references does not require an allegorical understanding of Cordelia, but they are too persistent and specific to dismiss recognition of them as "the gaudy distractions of Christianizing."[52] Better, I think, to understand them as supplying a particular evaluation for Cordelia's actions (her "virtues," as France refers to them) that links her forgiveness of her father to Shakespeare's comedies of forgiveness, where characters' actions consistently derive from the virtues that animate the divine comedy. As Richard Strier points out, Cordelia's forgiveness of her father enacts the principles of divine grace so perfectly that one can correlate the scene of their reconciliation with George Herbert's "Love (III)"—not because Herbert had *Lear* in mind but because both Shakespeare and Herbert had grace in mind.[53] Kent twice refers to Lear's "shame": "A sovereign shame so elbows him," "burning shame / Detains him from Cordelia" (4.3.43, 47–48). This shame, Cavell points out, expresses itself in an intense desire not to be seen—a desire that motivates Lear's attempt to avoid Cordelia's love both in the play's first scene and in their reconciliation in 4.7.[54] "I cannot look on thee," says Herbert's lyric speaker. "O, look upon me, sir" Cordelia implores Lear (4.7.58), whose response is to try to kneel before her; "My dear, then I will serve," says Herbert's speaker. "You must not kneel," says Cordelia (4.7.60); "you must sit down," says Herbert's Love.

As in Shakespeare's comedies, so in *King Lear*, the restoration of broken relationships depends on the restoration of the self and results in the renewal of community. Lear overcomes his shame when he acknowledges the suffering he has caused Cordelia:

> If you have poison for me I will drink it.
> I know you do not love me, for your sisters
> Have, as I do remember, done me wrong.
> You have some cause, they have not. (4.7.74–77)

Her reply, "No cause, no cause," does not deny what he acknowledges; it simply forgives. His attempt to kneel before her not only accepts his shame for the first time—his felt need to humble himself—but shatters the social decorum on which he had insisted in the play's opening scene. As Ralph Houlbrooke points out, the habit of children kneeling to receive their parents' blessing was deeply ingrained in English family life, both before and after the Reformation. "Potent though the ritual was in conveying an assurance of fundamental love and goodwill, it was even more important in making the child act the role of subject and suppliant."[55] Lear's attempt to kneel before his daughter reverses this social ritual in profound ways, paradoxically restoring Lear to himself by acknowledging his need to ask his daughter's blessing immediately after she, the least of his children, has asked his: "O, look upon me, sir, / And hold your hands in benediction o'er me" (4.7.58–59).

His surprising action is complemented by his no less surprising words, which for the first time in the play transparently, though haltingly, express nothing more than the simplest and plainest truths about himself—no claims of social privilege, no vengeance, no defiance, no self pity, no pretension (he begins by acknowledging his advanced age):

> I am a very foolish fond old man,
> Fourscore and upward, not an hour more or less;
> And, to deal plainly,
> I fear I am not in my perfect mind.
> Methinks I should know you, and know this man,
> Yet I am doubtful; for I am mainly ignorant
> What place this is, and all the skill I have
> Remembers not these garments, nor I know not
> Where I did lodge last night. Do not laugh at me,
> For, as I am a man, I think this lady
> To be my child Cordelia. (4.7.61–71)

For the first time he "deals plainly," as Cordelia had dealt with him in the opening scene ("to plainness honor's bound / When majesty falls to folly," comments Kent [1.1.149–50]); for the first time he recognizes her ("my child, Cordelia"); and for the first time he truly knows himself.

When he explicitly asks her forgiveness, he also describes himself truly: "Pray you, forget and forgive. / I am old and foolish" (89–90).

Shakespeare nowhere imagines a more satisfying and surprising renewal of a relationship, even in the romances, and when we last see Lear and Cordelia alive together, the old king wishes simply to reenact their reconciliation, convinced that he can endure anything in light of it:

> Come, let's away to prison.
> We two alone will sing like birds i' the cage.
> When thou dost ask me blessing, I'll kneel down
> And ask of thee forgiveness. (5.3.8–11)

It is a mark of tragic experience, however, that this transcendent moment is not only their last together but is also the fullest extent of communal renewal in *King Lear*. Kent had revealed himself, through his disguise, to Cordelia, and she had thanked him, fearing that she could not "live and work / To match thy goodness" (4.7.1–3). His reply is thematically rich, recalling the conflict of value in the first scene and what was at stake there: "To be acknowledged, madam is o'erpaid" (4).[56] But the scene in which Cordelia acknowledges Kent is the last time he sees her alive, and when he reveals himself to Lear, after Cordelia's death, the king is too crazed to recognize him.[57] "O my good master!" exclaims Kent, but Lear rejects him: "Prithee, away." Edgar intervenes, "'Tis noble Kent, your friend," but Lear is again beside himself: "A plague upon you, murderers, traitors all!" (5.3.272–74). Like Edmund's repentance, which comes too late (5.3.248–52), Kent's attempt at reconciliation with his master is lost in the chaos of Lear's dying grief, and with that chaos the play ends.

Kent's shock at Cordelia's death is so profound that it elicits his apocalyptic exclamation, "Is this the promised end?" (5.3.268). "Or image of that horror?" rejoins Edgar, both echoing Kent's response and qualifying it at the same time, though Albany fully agrees with Kent: "Fall and cease!" (269). Edgar is in general a less appealing character than Kent, and his inability to agree fully with the old retainer in this case is evidence of it: Edgar did not witness Lear's reconciliation with Cordelia, and Edgar's own reconciliation with his father is more tinged with judgment and even with shame than Cordelia's with Lear.[58] Edgar's assessment of the gods' justice is breathtakingly harsh in the way it understands Gloucester's story (5.3.173–76), and as theology it emphasizes judgment where Cordelia emphasizes grace. Still, Edgar is closer to the truth than Kent in his assessment of Lear's story in the end: this is not indeed the revelation of the Last Judgment but merely an image of that horror, full of hiddenness and impenetrable mystery. As in other Shakespearean tragedies that place their action in the course of Christian destiny between Creation and Judgment, the end of this story is not The End. We are still in the fallen world, where time goes on at the end of every story, no matter what its genre; where suffering seems definitive in tragedy, because it is the last thing we witness; and where someone needs to speak for the community whose life continues, as Edgar finally does, though he appropriately directs our attention back to the events we have witnessed (5.3.329–32), in contrast to Malcolm's closing speech in *Macbeth*.

The function of comedy in *King Lear*, then, is the same as the function of comedy in other Shakespearean tragedies, from *Romeo and Juliet* through *Lear*: to emphasize the suffering of the principals and to invite our recognition of it and our identification with it. Lear's suffering before his reconciliation with Cordelia is "comic" suffering, because it enables him to learn something about himself, a slow and painful process that begins with the rhetorical question: "Who is it that can tell me who I am?" (1.4.227). This question is all-important, because it hints at his fear of being found out in his self-deception, and it initiates a process that is central to the play's comedy of forgiveness. Lear's suffering in the end, however, is different, because it has no explanation and no justification, and we are not asked to reconcile ourselves to it; we are asked simply to see it, acknowledge it, and suffer with it—exactly the response that other Shakespearean tragedies elicit. Cordelia's death shocked Samuel Johnson not because he had an explanation for it, but because he recognized its senselessness, and surely because he, of all critics, understood what she means in her father's life.

To deny that meaning is to turn aside from the play's tragic power, as Tate did when he rewrote Shakespeare's version, and as criticism tends to do both when it looks for a meaning or justification in Lear's dying agony and when it avoids seeing Cordelia's love for what it is. This is why Harry Berger's reading of Cordelia as self-deceived is a partial reading of the play. In his anxiousness to uncover the self-deception that Cordelia ostensibly occludes to the end, Berger himself occludes everything but self-deception, as is clear in his own summary of his comments on Cordelia: "As I argue (chap. 3 above), the reunion scene [in

King Lear] is poignant in part because of Cordelia's moving concern, the love she shows her father in her careful tendance of him" (303). But in his chapter 3, Berger acknowledges concern, love, and careful tendance on Cordelia's part only to emphasize her complicity in her sisters' cause, even when she denies it (46), for this, as Berger explains elsewhere, is her "darker purpose":

> that the thought of Lear's setting his rest on her kind nursery (a heavy phrase! a heavy rest!) must surely be oppressive to her, though she is not likely to admit it to herself; that she would like to break free of the parental bondage, get out from under, though she is not likely to admit that to herself either; that if she could find a way to do it that wouldn't jeopardize her self-respect and her sense of obligation to Lear, she would be likely to take it; and that she does find a way, and does take it. (42)

In other words, if Cordelia's care for her father enacts anything in the way of good faith, it is overwhelmed by the bad faith she exhibits from beginning to end, and *King Lear* is not a tragedy but something like comical satire.

Berger's characterization of his own criticism reveals the force of C. L. Barber's response to Berger, as summarized by Berger himself: "that unless the ironist [Berger] was capable of a minimal level of sympathy for and generosity toward the fictional objects of his criticism, he could not hope to respond adequately to the human claims the characters in the plays make on him."[59] Berger's reply to this critique is that he follows Stanley Cavell in seeking "the common *ethos* informing the behavior of all characters," and that Cavell's argument for the avoidance of love in *King Lear* expresses "the desire of the love it avoids" (51). This accurately summarizes Cavell's reading of *Lear*, but it inadequately explains the bitter and ironic world that Berger's reading uncovers, because Berger's Lear cannot avoid Cordelia's love, if all Cordelia offers is self-deception and self-interest.[60] It seems pertinent to ask whether the one who avoids love in this reading is Lear or the interpreter.

William Elton offers the most learned and sustained defense of *King Lear* as a rejection of Christian hope, but Elton's understanding of Cordelia is not the best part of his argument. Noting her prayer to the "unpublished virtues of the earth" (4.4.16), Elton sees in it only an ironic contrast with Lear's final lament that "She's dead as earth" (5.3.266).[61] This conclusion, however, confuses two experiences that Lear has and that we have with him: the experience of his reconciliation (with

Cordelia and with himself) and the experience of his overwhelming grief at the end. When Cordelia invokes the "blest secrets" of the earth, she asks them to be "aidant and remediate / In the good man's distress" (4.4.15–18), and by any reckoning this prayer is movingly and profoundly answered in the reconciliation of father and daughter. Moreover, its answer contrasts with the gods' responses to prayers in *King Lear* for vindication, vengeance, and justice, which are seldom answered as the beseecher intends.[62] One possible inference is that the gods are more responsive to prayers for the kind of remedy Cordelia offers than to other kinds of prayer, and if that is true, then *King Lear* is far from an atheist tract against Christian hope.[63] To be sure, Cordelia's death robs Lear of hope in the end, denying him any "chance which does redeem all sorrows / That ever I have felt" (5.3.271–72). The end does not negate the hope that precedes it, however; rather, the end derives its devastating power from that hope and makes its impact—both on Lear and on us—in proportion to it. Cordelia's being dead as earth does not mean that the secret powers of the earth did not aid in the remediation of her father. If anything, the impact that her death makes on us depends on that remediation.

Elton's wide reading in theology contemporary with the play inclined him to explain Cordelia as technically deficient to do what she plainly does: "As a pagan antedating Christ, existing under a natural rather than a revealed theology and under a dispensation of nature without grace, Cordelia appears limited to works" (82). She can show human kindness in action, in other words, but she cannot represent grace. Theologically it is true, of course, that no person can save another, even in the dispensation of grace, just as it is true, judging from contemporary theology, that Romeo, Juliet, and Othello are necessarily damned because they commit suicide. It is also theologically true, however, that no one can show the kind of love Cordelia shows apart from grace, no matter what dispensation prevails. The question is whether such observations assist in responding to the tragic effect of these plays. I have argued that the tragedy of *Romeo and Juliet* and of *Othello* does not consist in their damnation; it consists in their suffering, and the same is true of Lear. The play is indeed set in pre-Christian Britain, and Cordelia does not save her father's soul. Nonetheless, their reconciliation is strongly imbued with meaning that derives from the Christian virtues of hope and love, as the allusions surrounding Cordelia make clear, and Lear's tragedy does not amount to his loss of faith in God because his daughter has died; it is inherent in his suffering, which the play invites us to acknowledge, because we have witnessed the transcendent goodness that Cordelia brought to his life—a miracle if ever there was one in Shakespeare. To dismiss this goodness as mere works righteousness is to reduce the tragic suffering in *King Lear* to a theological squabble.[64]

Elton argues not only that Cordelia can do no more than good works for her father but also that whatever good work she does comes to nothing in the end, thus confirming atheist arguments about the vanity of goodness. Cordelia is merely "implying works" when she "exclaims in an analogical *entendre*: 'O dear father! / It is thy business that I go about,'" and "it is a business of unhappy consequence to both" (83). Elton does not explain how an "analogical *entendre*" can imply only works righteousness (if the analogy is with Christ, then it is indubitably to grace), but a more serious problem is that he offers a utilitarian assessment of a story that does not make utilitarian assumptions. A major consequence of Cordelia's going about her father's business is her reunion with him and their reconciliation, neither of which would have happened had Cordelia desisted in seeking to be aidant and remediate to him, and she would not have shown the virtues of hope and love in action if she had desisted; this is what she means when she tells him that "I love Your Majesty / According to my bond, no more nor less" (1.1.92–93). Nor is anything she does for Lear eradicated by her untimely death, given that the virtue she demonstrates is not defined by its outcome.

Nonetheless, her death entails undeniable suffering on her father's part, as it does on the part of any auditor who acknowledges her goodness. That is why Johnson was so shocked by her death that he could not bring himself to reread the end of the play until he had to revise it as an editor. To avoid her love is to perpetuate her father's initial response to her. One can do this through theological hair-splitting, in defense of either a redemptive justification for her death or of ironic hopelessness, both of which miss the point of the tragedy, for the play is not an intellectual treatise in defense of anything, indebted though it is to Christian affirmation for its tragic impact. One can also avoid her love by blaming her, as Harry Berger does, for what happens to her father, but this kind of boundless suspicion also evades the tragedy. Suspicion has its place in

Lear, to be sure, but it is rooted in love and in faith, like the long tradition of moral suspicion that Shakespeare inherited. One might say that Cordelia's resistance to Lear's way of asking for love in the opening scene originates in her suspicion of the false consciousness that his power and prestige enable him to force on her and on everyone else. But her suspicion is based on her love for him and on her faith in the possibility of real love, which, miraculously, he eventually comes to acknowledge.

Lear dies, as Othello does, overwhelmed by distress at the loss of a loved one who has enabled him to "see better," as Kent urges him to do in the first scene (1.1.159). The critical record attests to a need on the part of readers to interpret this distress, explaining it either as somehow redeemed by the love whose loss evokes it or as defining a skeptical negation of everything, including love. What I am suggesting is a different response to Shakespearean tragedy, one that interprets the characters' suffering simply as an appeal that we acknowledge it without trying to divine its meaning. The plays' failure to address what happens to characters after death may be construed as a skeptical affirmation that death is The Last Thing, not just one of Four Last Things. But the plays' silence on that point may also be construed as a way of directing our attention to suffering itself, without assuming that it reveals anything except tragedy. It does not follow that suffering has no explanation; merely that tragedy is not the place for it, for tragedy, again, is not apocalyptic. Love is transformative in Shakespearean tragedy, as even Macbeth recognizes when he destroys the king-becoming graces not only in Duncan but in himself, and the transformative power of love is referred repeatedly in these plays to the Christian story. Those references do not add up to allegory; they simply release us in the fallen world, where goodness is fragile, the future is uncertain, and death is an end but not The End, and they point to a way of responding to tragedy that acknowledges suffering because it acknowledges the love that sees one's neighbor as oneself.

4

HISTORY AND GUILT

And like a scurvy politician
Seem to see the things thou dost not.

King Lear, 4.6.171–72

The most original of the three genres in the First Folio is history, because it has no classical precedent. It derives instead from the narrative of salvation history that in various ways informed the three principal kinds of indigenous English drama by the sixteenth century: the biblical history plays, saints' plays, and morality plays. Shakespearean history thus parallels comedy and tragedy in an exploration of the human situation in the context of Christian destiny. The early histories draw heavily on Shakespeare's religious dramatic heritage in the process of creating a new kind of play that reaches its maturity in the sequence from *Richard II* to *Henry V*, where the influence of medieval religious drama is less evident but no less important. To be sure, the relation of even the early history plays to the master narrative that formed them is complex and ironic: English history as Shakespeare renders it from the outset is not an imitation of salvation history but a contrast to it, even when the plays most clearly show their dramatic origin. In this regard, the history plays emphasize skepticism about human perfectibility more strongly even than tragedy does. But Shakespearean history is never merely secular. That is, his history plays not only derive from but are also informed by a distinctly Christian moral frame of reference, creating implicit expectations for kings and courtiers that they invariably fail to meet.

Precedent for the implied vision of Shakespeare's history plays can be found in the skeptical faith of More and Erasmus early in the sixteenth century. Erasmus was close to kings, but he remained deeply suspicious of them, as his colloquies *A Fish Diet* (1526) and *Charon* (1529) make clear, and he never took service with one, as More did with Henry

97

VIII. In *Praise of Folly*, Erasmus is as hard on kings as he is on pontiffs, prelates, monks, and friars. Kings are easily led astray by flattery, they indulge themselves in luxurious pastimes, sell offices, overtax their subjects, and maintain a hypocritical façade of justice in order to pursue their own interests. In short, a king is typically "a man ignorant of the law, well-nigh an enemy to his people's advantage while intent on his personal convenience, a dedicated voluptuary, a hater of learning, freedom and truth, without a thought for the interests of his country, and measuring everything in terms of his profit and desires."[1] Erasmus rhetorically escapes censure for such candor by putting it in the mouth of Folly.

More's assessment of kings in *Utopia* is no less harsh and rhetorically even more adroit. He assigns his critique to Hythlodaeus, the literally peripatetic philosopher who represents one side in the debate More has with himself in this work about whether an honest and reflective man should take service with a king. This is just what Peter Giles urges Hythlodaeus to do, but the philosopher rejects "servitude to kings," and when Giles corrects "servitude" to "service," Hythlodaeus replies laconically, "The one [*seruias*] is only one syllable less than the other [*seruitiam*]."[2] When character More also urges Hythlodaeus to serve a king, the philosopher offers a more careful two-part answer: kings care only for enhancing their own power and wealth, and they are easily swayed by flatterers who would make the wisdom of an honest advisor appear to be foolish. To illustrate the second point, Hythlodaeus recalls a conversation he had at the table of Cardinal Morton, Lord Chancellor under Henry VII of England, during which the philosopher's trenchant commentary on the sorry state of English society was mocked and derided by a fawning lawyer, a "hanger-on," and a censorious friar. Behind the stalking horse of his fiction, author More thus advances specific observations about the problems, as he saw them, both of contemporary English society and of serving Henry VIII. Though he eventually decided to take the advice of character More regarding royal service, his fate under the king he served suggests that Hythlodaeus was right all along, as Lord Chancellor More must surely have recognized in the end.

The humanist critique of kings is arguably secular, in that it pertains to particular historical circumstances: More thoughtfully analyzes capital punishment for theft and the social consequences of enclosing land for wool production and maintaining local standing armies, for example. But the critique is not merely secular—that is, it does not begin with purely rational presumptions—because it is deeply indebted to the Christian reforming vision of Erasmus and More.[3] In this regard, the humanists offer an illustrative parallel to Shakespeare. His history plays imagine an indelibly secular world, focusing on the actions of those who compete for and wield political power, no matter how often they invoke divine sanction for themselves and in opposition to their competitors. Nonetheless, his realism about politics and history is distinct from that of a writer like Machiavelli, the most important political thinker he might have known. Shakespeare's plays respond suspiciously to politics, as Machiavelli does, because they respond suspiciously to human nature, but suspicion in Shakespeare's plays is limited, because the politicians in his plays are accountable to something more than political self-interest.[4]

CLOAKED COLLUSION IN *2 HENRY VI*

The early history plays offer the strongest evidence that Shakespeare defined a sense of secular history against the conventions of sacred dramatic history, because those conventions are most apparent in the earlier plays, and the contrast is therefore easier to see. Both *1* and *2 Henry VI* include stage devils, for example, and Shakespeare uses this time-honored dramatic device, which had long been a means for imagining the cosmic struggle of good and evil, with full awareness of what it had come to signify in later Tudor drama while at the same time bracketing it apart from the plays' principal action, which involves a struggle to gain political power and hold onto it.[5] The result is an ambivalent treatment of history's cosmic frame: while we are unavoidably aware of it, history seems to go on without reference to it. Important segments of the biblical cycles inform the early histories as well: the false framing and destruction of Humphrey Duke of Gloucester in *2 Henry VI*, 3.1, parallels the passion plays, as Emrys Jones points out, while the beginning of York's rebellion in *3 Henry VI* resembles the beginning of Lucifer's rebellion in all the surviving biblical plays, though York's death in *3 Henry VI*, 1.4, again paradoxically recalls the death of Christ, and the destruction of both York's Rutland and Lancaster's Prince Edward suggests pageants on the slaughter of the innocents in some specific ways.[6] These parallels make a strong emotional impact, but the plays offer no credible way to construe the action as a whole in light of salvation history, so the cumulative effect of particular parallels is to evoke the sacred story in order to provide a contrast with the political history we are called to witness.

Evocations of sacred history do more than ironize the action, however: they provide limits to instrumental thinking about power by pointing to moral thinking about politics of the kind that had infused medieval religious drama since the early fifteenth century.[7] The emergence of social satire in all forms of early drama is due to a critique as particular as anything in More and Erasmus, treating conspicuous consumption, relentlessly destructive competition, and dissimulation in pursuit of power.[8] What I am suggesting about Shakespeare's histories and medieval drama is thus very different from the earliest and most influential attempts to understand Shakespeare's history plays as moral embodiments of Tudor state theory. E. M. W. Tillyard saw a sweep of English history governed by divine providence in the development of events from *1 Henry VI* to *Richard III*, arguing by direct analogy to the providential direction of human events in the biblical history plays.[9] The political chaos of the *Henry VI* plays, Tillyard argued, is to be understood as providential punishment for Henry IV's deposing of Richard II, and since that chaos comes to an end only with the success of a heaven-sent deliverer in *Richard III*, the eight plays together from *Richard II* to *Richard III* constitute "an organic piece of history" that Tillyard called "the Tudor myth" (29), because the deliverer in question is Henry VII, first of the Tudor monarchs. Tillyard understood the Tudor chroniclers' inclination to read English history as a parallel to the providential history of ancient Israel, and he documented it thoroughly, but the parallel does not work for Shakespeare's history plays, as the contrast between his drama of secular history and the drama of sacred history makes clear.[10]

More powerful and subtle than the influence of stage devils in the early histories is the influence of an indigenous English convention for staging the cosmic drama of good and evil—the personified Vice from the morality play.[11] Bernard Spivack pointed to the pervasive effect of the Vice on *Richard III*, arguing that Richard's duplicity, hypocrisy, gleeful cynicism, frankness with the audience, and inevitable comeuppance are all characteristics that derive from decades of English dramatic tradition.[12] Spivack came to his insight as a result of an effort to explain the origin of dramatic character. Citing Coleridge's observation of "motiveless malignity" in characters like Richard, Iago, and Edmund, Spivack argued that they have no humanly comprehensible motive, because they originated as homiletic types, examples of evil per se, and Shakespeare's giving them a particular name and sketchy individuating qualities did not alter their origin or the way they functioned—"a dramatic method that has no relevance to either history or character, imitates neither, and, in fact, abrogates both."[13] By "history" Spivack meant Shakespeare's chronicle sources, but Spivack's focus on character diverted his attention away from the playwright's attempt to render secular history as a continuous contest for political supremacy that overwhelms attempts at reform. Looked at this way, the early histories use the Vice effectively to render "history," and Shakespeare's vision of "history" corresponds with remarkable fidelity to that of Erasmus and More.

Let us consider *2 Henry VI*, for example, because it may be the first history play Shakespeare wrote, and because Spivack looked past it almost entirely in his single-minded focus on Richard.[14] From the first scene of *2 Henry VI*, York behaves not only as Richard's literal father but also as his moral predecessor. York's first long soliloquy, early in the play, is a crucial revelation of ambition and duplicity (*2 Henry VI*, 1.1.212–57), and it recalls self-congratulatory soliloquies from innumerable stage vices while also anticipating his son's first soliloquy in *3 Henry VI* (3.2.124–95). Both echo Tamburlaine in their frank ambition for the "golden" crown, and both rationalize their ambition: York's reason is Henry's unfitness to be king, because he succeeded as a child (*2 Henry VI*, 1.1.243), and because his "bookish rule" renders him incapable of effective governance (257).[15] Richard's soliloquy has often been excised and added to *Richard III* in performance because it seems to offer a plausible psychological reason for Richard's treachery and ambition, but York's soliloquy also offers a plausible reason for action. York's reason, however, is political rather than psychological, and York's soliloquy therefore reveals more clearly than Richard's how Shakespeare turned the morality play into political drama.

When combined with York's second soliloquy (3.1.331–83), the first serves to outline a plot for *2 Henry VI* that focuses in York's plotting to gain the crown.[16] This is a plot, moreover, that Shakespeare created by

imposing a design from the morality play onto material from the chronicles. A probable source of this design is Skelton's *Magnificence*, published
by John Rastell in 1530 and therefore more accessible in the early 1590s
than many manuscript morality plays. In Skelton's play, one of the principal vices, Cloaked Collusion, plots to destroy Magnificence's most
trustworthy advisor, Measure, just as York plots to destroy Humphrey
Duke of Gloucester. Once other vices have begun to undermine
Magnificence's confidence in Measure, Cloaked Collusion reassures
him that he will intervene with the King on his behalf, but he in fact
destroys the King's little remaining confidence in Measure by falsely
confessing to Magnificence that Measure bribed him to speak in his
favor.[17] The result is that the King dismisses Measure from his service,
thus removing his last trustworthy supporter at court, just as Henry dismisses Duke Humphrey.

The importance of Skelton's design to Shakespeare can hardly be
overestimated. It reappeared in one more of the early history plays, and
it stayed with him in several other plays over the course of the next fif-
teen years. In *Richard III*, York's son, Richard of Gloucester, pretends to
support his brother, Clarence, when Clarence falls out of favor with the
King, but Richard really works against Clarence and in fact hires assassins to kill him. In *Two Gentlemen of Verona*, which was written at about
the same time as the early histories, the deceiver is Proteus, who pretends to be Valentine's friend while betraying Valentine to the Duke,
with the result that the Duke banishes Valentine from Milan and thus
eliminates Proteus' most serious rival for the affection of Sylvia.[18] The
pattern influences another comedy in Don John's pretended concern
for his brother's honor in *Much Ado about Nothing*, resulting in Claudio's
rejection of Hero. In his most powerful reiteration of Skelton's design,
Shakespeare recalled the Duke's commendation of Proteus's "honest
care" (*Two Gentlemen*, 3.1.22), when "honest Iago" convinces Othello to
cashier Cassio, while pretending to be Cassio's friend, and then works
even more insidiously to alienate Othello's affections from
Desdemona.[19] Again in *King Lear*, Edmund pretends to have the interest
of his brother, Edgar, at heart, when he is really slandering Edgar to
their father, the Earl of Gloucester, with the consequence that
Gloucester rejects his true son in favor of his false one. Finally, in
Cymbeline, the Queen tells the beleaguered young couple, Posthumus
and Imogen, that she is working on their behalf, though she is actually

working to destroy them. Having developed this pattern in various ways in every genre and in a sequence of very different plays, Shakespeare eventually left it behind, but it is worth noting that its most specifically political application is in the early history plays.

Though Shakespeare changed a great deal of what he read in Hall in order to emphasize York's cloaked collusion in *2 Henry VI*, three examples will suffice to show how consistently the morality play pattern informs the history play's action, and how effectively Shakespeare interprets the pattern in political terms. The first scene of *2 Henry VI* choreographs a complicated ballet of political factions and ambitious rivalry, involving Suffolk, Cardinal Beaufort of Winchester, Somerset, and Buckingham, but Duke Humphrey rises above them all in his disinterested concern for the well-being of the kingdom—a lone reformer in this human jungle.[20] His sole supporters are Salisbury and Warwick, who agree to remain allied

> for the public good,
> In what we can, to bridle and suppress
> The pride of Suffolk and the Cardinal,
> With Somerset's and Buckingham's ambition;
> And, as we may, cherish Duke Humphrey's deeds,
> While they do tend the profit of the land. (1.1.197–202)

The next time these two appear, however, they are in York's company, and he is trying to persuade them that his right to the crown is superior to Henry's (2.2). When he easily succeeds, they swear fealty to York (2.2.63), and he outlines his plan to them in lines that reveal both his awareness that these two are Humphrey's last supporters and York's eagerness to suborn them for his own purpose:

> We thank you, lords. But I am not your king
> Till I be crowned, and that my sword be stained
> With heart-blood of the house of Lancaster;
> And that's not suddenly to be performed,
> But with advice and silent secrecy.
> Do you as I do in these dangerous days:
> Wink at the Duke of Suffolk's insolence,
> At Beaufort's pride, at Somerset's ambition,
> At Buckingham, and all the crew of them,
> Till they have snared the shepherd of the flock,
> That virtuous prince, the good Duke Humphrey.
> 'Tis that they seek, and they in seeking that
> Shall find their deaths, if York can prophesy. (2.2.64–76)

York's acknowledgment that Humphrey, "the shepherd of the flock," is "virtuous" and "good" is a strategy to misdirect the attention of Salisbury and Warwick, because York overheard them admiring Humphrey in the play's first scene. For York's real purpose, as he made clear in his first soliloquy, is to let Humphrey's enemies destroy themselves in the process of destroying the lord protector, whom he regards as expendable under the circumstances. Rhetorically his speech to Warwick and Salisbury is thus a high-wire act of political persuasion. York's use of the revealing word "performed" and his urging "advice and silent secrecy" strongly suggest the Vice, even while his caution to himself earlier to "be still awhile, till time do serve" (1.1.246) emphasizes the temporal arena of political action and anticipates the keen awareness of time that Henry IV and his son share in the later history plays, as we shall see.

A second change that Shakespeare made in his chronicle source also serves to emphasize the political design of York's cloaked collusion as England descends into civil war. The ambition of Humphrey's wife, Eleanor, appears in *2 Henry VI* pretty much as Hall reports it, but Shakespeare invents an elaborate web of intrigue around her arrest for conjuring. A priest, Sir John Hume, acknowledges in soliloquy that he is being paid by Beaufort and Suffolk to spy on Eleanor, even while he is also accepting money from Eleanor to pay a witch for the conjuring, and he is aware (either because someone has told him, or because his own political senses are sufficiently highly developed) that the aim is to bring down Humphrey by bringing down Humphrey's wife (1.2.91–107). Yet Hume never mentions York, even though Shakespeare shows York deeply involved, as he interrupts the diabolical ritual, catches not only the conjurors but Eleanor herself, and congratulates Buckingham in revealing terms: "Lord Buckingham, methinks you watched her well. / A pretty plot, well chosen to build upon" (1.4.56–57). The language of plotting again suggests the Vice, and Shakespeare creates a strong impression that York was intimately involved in the plot from the beginning, if he did not in fact invent it and encourage Suffolk and Beaufort to carry it out in order to destroy Humphrey, as he seems to suggest to Salisbury and Warwick.

As for the third change, Hall records a dispute between "an armorer's servant of London" and his master in a brief paragraph for the year 1446, citing no names, no connection with York, and no reason for the quarrel.[21] Shakespeare names the servant Peter, and the master Thomas Horner, and he invents Horner's service to York. But his most important addition is a cause for the quarrel, for Peter first appears as a petitioner against Horner to Suffolk, accusing Horner of "saying that the Duke of York was rightful heir to the crown" (1.3.28–29). This point makes the incident directly dependent on York's plot and therefore driven by the mainspring of the play's action. Spying an opportunity to weaken or destroy York, Suffolk orders a servant to fetch Horner and assures Peter that "We'll hear of your matter before the King" (1.3.36). Suffolk wastes no time, bringing Peter and Horner before the King in the same scene and slyly threatening York in a hypocritical exclamation: "here is a man accused of treason. / Pray God the Duke of York excuse himself!" (1.3.177–78). York is clearly caught by surprise and unnerved, for the best he can do is to sputter a non-denial denial by turning his wrath on Peter: "Base dunghill villain and mechanical, / I'll have thy head for this thy traitor's speech" (1.3.193–94). The incident thus serves again to suggest the high-risk game that York is playing. While he avoids being destroyed by Peter's revelation, he loses the commission to be regent of France that Humphrey had just recommended (1.3.160–61) and now withdraws: "Let Somerset be regent o'er the French, / Because in York this breeds suspicion" (206–207). Humphrey had not suspected York until Peter charged Horner with saying that York should be king. York's self-interested plotting is thus momentarily checked by Humphrey's political skill in recognizing that Peter's story is not only credible but provides sufficient basis for revoking York's commission in France.

The loss of Humphrey's political skill is Henry's most serious political loss in *2 Henry VI*, because Henry is the genuine item that Richard of Gloucester hypocritically pretends to be in *Richard III*: "too childish-foolish for this world" (1.3.142). The King had earlier removed York carelessly from the French regency in *2 Henry VI* (1.1.63–66), while professing no interest in who had that post: "For my part, noble lords, I care not which; / Or Somerset or York, all's one to me" (1.3.101–2). The King's inattention and nonchalance are politically disastrous and directly anticipate his standing by helplessly when Humphrey's enemies maneuver the former lord protector into a place where he can protect neither the King nor himself (2.3 and 3.1). Shakespeare makes Humphrey's public-spirited skill a foil both to

York's duplicitous plotting and Henry's disastrous naiveté and ineptitude. By the time Horner and Peter have decided the difference between them in a trial by combat, Henry has been forced to dismiss Humphrey, and the King therefore has no one to point out that Peter's unexpected victory vindicates Humphrey's suspicion of York. Henry myopically sees nothing more than the quarrel itself, piously condemning Horner and congratulating Peter:

> Go, take hence that traitor from our sight;
> For by his death we do perceive his guilt,
> And God in justice hath revealed to us
> The truth and innocence of this poor fellow. (2.3.100–3)

Humphrey recognized at once that Peter's claim against Horner implicated York, and after the trial by combat Humphrey would certainly have seen that the traitor who ought to be removed is not the dead Horner but Horner's living master, York. Henry's willful piety, however, makes him incapable of suspicion and therefore yields up both himself and others to the predators who fill the court.

To emphasize Henry's naiveté and Humphrey's important political acumen, Shakespeare introduces a brief episode from Foxe's *Acts and Monuments* as a parallel to the quarrel between Peter and Horner.[22] Henry takes the miracle of Sander Simpcox's supposedly miraculous healing at face value: "Now, God be praised, that to believing souls / Gives light in darkness, comfort in despair!" (2.1.64–65). Humphrey, however, is skeptical of Simpcox—as we noticed in tracing Foxe's influence on this episode in chapter 1—and proves that he is a fraud: "Then, Sander, sit there, the lying'st knave in Christendom" (129–30). Henry's inability to recognize duplicity is his undoing in *2 Henry VI*, and the contrast between his gullibility and Humphrey's incisive suspicion of Simpcox emphasizes Henry's loss of Humphrey when the trial by combat is decided and his even greater loss when York makes his first overt move (5.1), by which time Humphrey is dead.[23] Foxe's comment about Humphrey may well have prompted Shakespeare to include the Simpcox episode: "By this may it be seen how Duke Humphrey had not only an head to discern truth from forged and feigned hypocrisy, but study also and diligence likewise was in him, to reform that which was amiss" (Bullough, 3:128). The qualities that commend Humphrey politically are just the qualities that Henry lacks and therefore sorely needs in someone else if he is to govern effectively.

Consideration of Shakespeare's debt to Skelton in *2 Henry VI* makes clear that divine providence in history is not the point. To be sure, the matter of Horner and Peter is finally decided in a trial by combat that providentially vindicates Peter's initial charge against Horner, as we learn when York outlines his claim to the throne to Salisbury and Warwick (2.2.1–29), and Duke Humphrey shows his political discernment early in this dispute. But Humphrey also shows his insight in the Simpcox case, which involves pious fraud, and which Foxe cites to show "the crafty working of false miracles in the clergy" (Bullough, 3:127)— a comment that recalls the reforming skepticism of Erasmus and More, which gave rise to Protestant skepticism in the first place (above, chapter 1), though Shakespeare uses the Simpcox episode politically rather than satirically. Humphrey is absent by the time Peter is vindicated, so he cannot point out to the pious King the political point of providential vindication—namely, York's ambition—even though Henry stands to gain most by recognizing it, and the reason Humphrey is absent is that King Henry stood by helplessly when malicious enemies dragged the Lord Protector down. If Providence offers a clue in Peter's victory, in other words, Henry fails to act on it, so that history proceeds not as a vindication of religious reformers, as in Foxe, but as a consequence of human failure to recognize a clear instance of divine direction. Moreover, providential direction is no less obfuscated in the matter of what happens ultimately to the vice-like York. To be sure, he suffers a terrible death in *3 Henry VI* 1.4, and his death could be interpreted as a parallel to the edifying deaths of Beaufort and Suffolk in *2 Henry VI* (3.3 and 4.1), but York is tortured psychologically and murdered onstage by Margaret and Clifford. His suffering is so horrible at their hands that sympathy inevitably shifts in his favor, cued by the pity of even one of those who captured him (*3 Henry VI* 1.4.150–51, 169–71) and by York's dying prayer for God's mercy.[24]

Lack of clarity about divine providence in *2 Henry VI* is not, however, a definitive instance of religious doubt on Shakespeare's part, nor does it amount to an endorsement of instrumental reasoning in politics. What we witness is indeed a dispiriting and vicious struggle for power, but the close intertwining of the morality play with political action suggests that more than mere political dominance is at issue, because the preservation of the community is in part the moral responsibility of those who lead it. "What you cannot turn to good you must make as little bad as you can," urges character More in *Utopia*, in effect voicing the reformer's side of the debate in author More's mind.[25] The descent into political chaos in *2 Henry VI* is certainly caused by those who are vicious and self-seeking, like Suffolk, Beaufort, and York, but King Henry also contributes to it by not following character More's advice. Despite his well-intended piety, he repeatedly exhibits willfulness, gullibility, short-sightedness, indecision, and inaction that contribute substantially to the downfall of Humphrey and make Henry at least partially responsible by default for the chaos that follows.[26] "My lords," says Henry to Humphrey's false accusers, "what to your wisdoms seemeth best / Do or undo, as if ourself were here," and shortly thereafter he departs, comparing himself to a helpless cow whose calf is about to be butchered (*2 Henry VI* 3.1.195ff.). As young Clifford is dying in *3 Henry VI*, he blames Henry for his abdication of responsibility, even though Clifford is one of the King's strongest supporters:

> And, Henry, hadst thou swayed as kings should do,
> Or, as thy father and his father did,
> Giving no ground unto the house of York,
> They never then had sprung like summer flies;
> I and ten thousand in this luckless realm
> Had left no mourning widows for our death,
> And thou this day hadst kept thy chair in peace. (2.6.14–20)

Clifford's analysis is political: Henry failed to rule "as kings should do." Importantly, however, Henry's political failure entails more than a loss of Lancastrian hegemony and includes suffering on the part of the innocent—not only the mourning widows Clifford mentions but also an unnamed commoner, forced into the war against his will, who unknowingly kills his father at Towton and another, likewise forced, who unknowingly kills his son (*3 Henry VI* 2.5). For such suffering Henry bears moral as well as political responsibility, though he characteristically does nothing but wring his hands and lament during the carnage at Towton, as he does at court when Humphrey is destroyed. What happens in a vacuum of power created by uncertainty over the succession is imagined in *2* and *3 Henry VI*, but the problem only begins with Henry's minority inheritance; his incompetence perpetuates the power vacuum, his refusal to take timely action makes bad situations worse, and his ineptitude invites moral censure for the reasons Clifford gives.[27]

Shakespeare's adaptation of Skelton's moral play to a play on secu-

lar history therefore offered more than a way to organize masses of
chronicle detail; it also offered a way to imagine moral expectation in
secular history. York's Vice-like plotting to destroy Humphrey is enabled
not only by Eleanor of Gloucester's weak-minded ambition but also by
the King's blameworthy political ineptitude, and the result is a chaos of
"mere oppugnancy" (*Troilus and Cressida* 1.3.111) in which the innocent
suffer, as well as the guilty. Shakespeare's borrowing from *Magnificence*
was no doubt facilitated by the fact that Skelton wrote political satire in
the first place. Cloaked Collusion wears a "cope" in *Magnificence* (601),
which indicates he is a priest, and his closeness to the King inevitably
suggests Cardinal Wolsey, one of Skelton's favorite satirical targets.[28]
Regardless of how one decides the question of particular personal satire
in *Magnificence*, Skelton imagines a king's court, and his rendering of
treachery, false friendship, and factionalism was powerfully affected by
what he saw at the court of Henry VIII. Shakespeare reversed the
process: rather than write a moral play that was influenced by politics,
he wrote a political play that was influenced by moral insight.

3 *HENRY VI* AND THE MORAL LIMITS OF POWER

The political vision of *2 Henry VI* continues in its successor, where the
struggle between the two major factions, Lancaster and York, is played
out with increasingly strident claims to legitimate power that become
increasingly doubtful, because neither side is able to make its claim
good by securing a distinct advantage when the political contest degenerates into a military struggle. A clear indication of Shakespeare's
attempt to render the working of real power is evident in episodes from
the middle of this play onward, where the problem of power *de jure* in
opposition to power *de facto* is rendered with expressive complexity and
without resolution.

In 3.1 two forest keepers confront Henry VI after he has been
defeated at the battle of Towton, and Edward of York, who defeated
him, has declared himself king in Henry's place. The keepers' conversation with Henry directly addresses the question of who is the legitimate
king in such a case: the one who succeeded his father on the throne, or
the one who defeated him in battle? Henry argues that the keepers cannot arrest him, because he is their king and they are his sworn subjects,

but the first keeper objects that they were his subjects only while he was king. Henry replies:

> Why, am I dead? Do I not breathe a man?
> Ah, simple men, you know not what you swear!
> Look, as I blow this feather from my face,
> And as the air blows it to me again,
> Obeying with my wind when I do blow,
> And yielding to another when it blows,
> Commanded always by the greater gust,
> Such is the lightness of you common men.
> But do not break your oaths: for of that sin
> My mild entreaty shall not make you guilty.
> Go where you will, the King shall be commanded;
> And be you kings, command, and I'll obey. (3.1.81–92)

Henry's comment about the "lightness of you common men" is typical of generalizations about commoners collectively in Shakespeare's plays.[29] But the keepers' dilemma is real, and their position represents strict Tudor orthodoxy: subjects must obey whoever is in power, no matter how the monarch acquired power or behaves after gaining it. Henry's yielding to the keepers is just as orthodox, in that he does not want to compel them to violate their oaths to Edward, but his yielding also implicitly admits the realities of power: he is an unarmed man in the forest facing two armed ones, and his inherited legitimacy as king has been strongly challenged by Edward's victory at Towton.

Margaret and Warwick raise the issue again two scenes later (3.3), where the point seems to be the sheer arbitrariness of being a king. Margaret is in France, attempting both to make good on a promise of assistance from King Lewis and to cross Warwick's hope of forging a marriage alliance with the French King, because such an alliance would secure Edward of York on the throne and work powerfully against Lancastrian interests. Arguing with each other openly in the French court, she and Warwick challenge the legitimacy of the other's claimant to the throne, and Lewis finally orders Warwick to declare "even upon thy conscience" his certainty that Edward is "your true king" (113–14). Warwick does not hesitate: "Thereon I pawn my credit and mine honor" (116). Having satisfied himself by this means that York's claim is legitimate, Lewis pointedly tells Margaret:

But if your title to the crown be weak,
As may appear by Edward's good success,
Then 'tis but reason that I be released
From giving aid which late I promisèd. (145–48)

Real power has shifted decisively in York's favor, because Edward has the military advantage ("good success"), and because Warwick has just made an attractive offer, which is clearly more influential with Lewis than a request for aid. Lewis thus obligingly regards Henry's title to the crown as dubious. The defining irony, however, is that the situation is immediately reversed when news arrives that Edward has married Lady Elizabeth Grey. Edward's decision is so politically obtuse and undercuts Warwick so badly that Warwick promptly switches sides, wondering how he could ever have "put Henry from his native right" (190). "Right," for Warwick, has nothing to do with nativity, despite his phrase, and everything to do with effectively maintaining one's power *de facto*. A scene that begins with Warwick's negotiating a marriage alliance between the Yorkist Edward and Lady Bona of France concludes with a marriage alliance between Warwick's daughter and the Lancastrian Edward (241–43).[30]

The problem of legitimate power and power in fact is raised a third time by the actions of Clarence, who switches sides along with Warwick and seals his new allegiance by agreeing to marry Warwick's other daughter (4.1.119–22). On the face of it, Clarence's fate seems to be evidence of divine providence in the early histories, because he perjures himself when he rejoins his brother (5.1.89–91), as Warwick is the first to point out (5.1.106), and this action not only haunts Clarence's guilty dreams in *Richard III* but is also cited by his murderers as justification for their action (*Richard III* 1.4.43–63, 204–10). The Second Murderer is sure that God will exact vengeance against Clarence "for false forswearing. . . . / Thou didst receive the Sacrament to fight / In quarrel of the house of Lancaster" (205–7). Interpreting Clarence's fate as evidence of providence in action is fraught with difficulties, however (divine vengeance is a self-serving and self-confirming reason for a murderer to cite to his prospective victim, for example), and it can easily obscure the point of the parallel with Warwick in Clarence's double betrayal, namely, that power *de jure* requires power *de facto* to be effective.[31] Though Shakespeare shows Clarence doing nothing by himself to alter the military balance, when Clarence rejoins his brother he clearly deals a severe blow to Lancastrian morale, especially given Edward's capture of King Henry (5.1.39–49). Moreover, Shakespeare places Clarence's defection immediately before the decisive military setbacks for Lancaster at Barnet, where Warwick is killed (5.2), and at Tewkesbury, where Margaret and Prince Edward are captured, and the Prince is murdered (5.5). As Shakespeare imagines the baronial wars for the stage, in other words, Clarence's defection initiates a sequence of events more decisive in York's favor than the chronicles recount, making the Yorkists' success seem to depend on Clarence's action. This outcome would not itself seem to have a very compelling providential cause, for why would God favor the side of a perjurer whom God is determined to punish? The "period of tumultuous broils" (5.5.1) seems to arrive at last in *3 Henry VI* not by any discernible intervention of just providence but by Edward's "policy," military aggressiveness (5.4.62–63), and battlefield luck.

As in *2 Henry VI*, however, Shakespeare again suggests limits to instrumental reasoning in *3 Henry VI*, and he does so again by recalling the drama of salvation history in a secular history play. The point of this recall is not that it determines the meaning of the action, but that it provides a contrast against which to recognize moral failure in the quest to obtain and preserve political power. In Shakespeare's history plays, political legitimacy is more than a matter of inheritance, which can be challenged in innumerable ways, as the *Henry VI* plays, *King John*, and *Henry V* make clear. The plays' political realism repeatedly suggests that inheritance needs to be supported by both the demonstration of effective power and by persuasive authority. Henry's failure in exercising power is strongly emphasized in *2 Henry VI*, as we have seen, and his failure continues in *3 Henry VI*, but the emphasis eventually shifts from his incompetence in maintaining political dominance to his success in establishing undoubted religious charisma that gives him unexpected moral authority in the end, even though he remains politically ineffectual. This shift is signaled, moreover, by increasing dependence on medieval dramatic archetypes that again recall the origin of Shakespeare's stagecraft while simultaneously emphasizing the humanist point about the moral responsibility of those who wield power.

In the first two acts of *3 Henry VI*, Henry shows the same ineptitude that he shows throughout *2 Henry VI*. Disputing with York in the first scene of *3 Henry VI*, Henry cannot think what to say in the face of York's claim and admits that his own title is weak (1.1.134). He fears that his followers will desert him (150) and proposes a political compromise: that he be allowed to reign for his lifetime but declare York his successor. This proposal is so self-defeating and incompetent that his followers indeed desert him (170–71), calling him "base, fearful, and despairing" (178), "fainthearted and degnerate" (183), and "unmanly" (186). Only Exeter stands by him, but Exeter has just openly expressed doubt about Henry's legitimacy (148). When Margaret arrives and also denounces Henry's compromise, Henry pleads that York forced him into it (229), an excuse that is weak not only in itself but also in its failure to acknowledge that Henry himself originated a proposal so politically disastrous that no one else would have thought of it. As Margaret points out, the arrangement makes Henry a target and disinherits his son: "Such safety finds / The trembling lamb environèd with wolves" (241–42). Later, when Henry sees the severed head of his archenemy, York, he turns away, conscience-stricken (2.2.5ff.), again expresses guilt about the succession (50), reacts stubbornly and willfully when Clifford urges him to leave the battlefield in order not to hinder the Queen (76), and is interrupted and effectively told to shut up by both Margaret and Clifford in a parley with the enemy (118, 122). Abandoning the battle of Towton, he laments, fantasizes sentimentally, and watches helplessly while two commoners express their grief at killing loved ones unintentionally (2.5).

Beginning in Act 3, however, Henry becomes comparatively less deplorable as an inept politician and more authoritative as a king with saintly qualities—that is, with undisputed moral charisma. When he surrenders to the forest keepers in recognition of their superior power, he also recognizes the genuine dilemma they face: "But do not break your oaths, for of that sin / My mild entreaty shall not make you guilty" (3.1.89–90). In a play that is remarkable for the oaths people make and break with ease, Henry's concern for the loyalty oaths of two commoners in support of his rival deserves attention. His gesture may be politically weak, but seeing the situation from the commoners' point of view and acting accordingly against his own interest suggests a saintly nature, not mere willfulness and gullibility. Henry later shows unquestionable prophetic vision, which Shakespeare presents unambiguously, when the King blesses the young Henry, Earl of Richmond, the future Henry VII, first of the Tudor monarchs:

Come hither, England's hope. (*Lays his hand on his head.*) If secret powers
Suggest but truth to my divining thoughts,
This pretty lad will prove our country's bliss.
His looks are full of peaceful majesty,
His head by nature framed to wear a crown,
His hand to wield a scepter, and himself
Likely in time to bless a regal throne.
Make much of him, my lords, for this is he
Must help you more than you are hurt by me. (4.6.68–76)

The moment obviously serves the Tudor myth, but it also serves to enhance Henry's charisma, despite his political disability.[32]

Henry emphasizes his saintly power again in a more ambiguous context, just before the Yorkists capture him in London. Discussing the military situation with Warwick and Clarence, Henry ineffectually responds to news that Edward of York has returned to England from the continent: "Let's levy men and beat him back again" (4.8.6), for the others ignore him, behaving as if he had not spoken, so his uncharacteristic bellicosity goes nowhere.[33] This sets the context for Henry's confident (though mistaken) assurance that the country will rally behind him in the face of Edward's invasion:

My meed hath got me fame.
I have not stopped mine ears to their demands,
Nor posted off their suits with slow delays.
My pity hath been balm to heal their wounds,
My mildness hath allayed their swelling griefs,
My mercy dried their water-flowing tears.
I have not been desirous of their wealth,
Nor much oppressed them with great subsidies,
Nor forward of revenge, though they much erred.
Then why should they love Edward more than me? (4.8.38–49)

Henry glosses over his political ineptitude by emphasizing his saintly charisma. Increasingly he emerges as a good man, though he remains a hopeless king, in contrast to his able minister, Duke Humphrey, who is public-spirited, honest, and politically savvy. Henry's description of himself mischaracterizes his rule in the past and the present but accurately describes what happened later, when he earned an extraordinary reputation as a miracle-working saint after his death. The contrast is emphasized when the Yorkists break in and capture him, as soon as he has uttered his confident self-assessment.[34]

Shakespeare's strategy in emphasizing Henry's saintliness in the second half of *3 Henry VI* becomes clear when Henry meets his death at the end of the play, for the scene brings together two archetypal figures from medieval drama: the Christlike sufferer and the devil. Just as Henry becomes increasingly pious and appealing as the play progresses, Richard of Gloucester becomes increasingly demonic and threatening—a development that has the effect of emphasizing the moral difference between them. The first hint of Richard's origin is his response to Edward's advice that York break the oath he had sworn to remain loyal to Henry during the king's lifetime, because the end justifies the means: "for a kingdom any oath may be broken" (1.2.16). Speaking to York, Richard at first reacts to Edward's boldly pragmatic advice with apparently pious concern, "No. God forbid Your Grace should be forsworn" (1.2.18), but Richard's reasoning in support of his point is sophistical and designed to rationalize York's perjury:

> An oath is of no moment, being not took
> Before a true and lawful magistrate
> That hath authority over him that swears.
> Henry had none, but did usurp the place.
> Then, seeing 'twas he that made you to depose,
> Your oath, my lord, is vain and frivolous. (1.2.22–24)[35]

Richard agrees with Edward, of course, as he implicitly urges York to violate his oath, but by coloring his advice with apparent moral concern ("God forbid"), he makes an evil choice look like its opposite, thus easing the way for his father and brother to do what he clearly knows they were inclined to do anyway.

Beginning with Richard's remarkable soliloquy in 3.2, his deviousness and treachery become increasingly evident, in direct parallel to Henry's growing saintliness. Gloucester admits that he stands by Edward only for self-serving reasons when Clarence deserts. Both have equally strong motives for deserting their brother, but Gloucester informs us that he remains outwardly loyal, because "My thoughts aim at a further matter; I / Stay not for the love of Edward, but the crown" (4.1.124–25). In the play's most ominous gesture, Gloucester addresses the audience for the third time in the last scene, where Edward's brothers ritually greet his newborn son and heir.[36] Gloucester effectively curses the baby in an aside: "I'll blast his harvest" (5.7.21), and as he

kisses his nephew, he confides: "To say the truth, so Judas kissed his master, / And cried, 'All hail!' whenas he meant all harm" (33–34).

In contrast to Henry's early obtuseness and stubborn myopia, no one
more clearly perceives Richard's devilish nature than Henry, when
Gloucester arrives to kill him. The Lancastrians by this time have grown
accustomed to mocking Richard by identifying his misshapen body as
evidence of his misshapen soul: "Where's that valiant crookback
prodigy, / Dickie your boy," demands Queen Margaret, as she taunts
Richard's father, "that with his grumbling voice / Was wont to cheer his
dad with mutinies?" (1.4.75–77). Margaret uses "prodigy" not to refer
to Richard's precocious talent but to identify his physical deformity as a
divine punishment, also noted by young Clifford when he calls Richard
"foul stigmatic" (*2 Henry VI* 5.1.215).[37] Little wonder, then, that when
Richard arrives to murder Henry in the Tower, Henry addresses him as
devilish:

> Ay, my good lord. My "lord" I should say, rather.
> 'Tis sin to flatter; "good" was little better.
> "Good Gloucester" and "good devil" were alike,
> And both preposterous. Therefore, not "good lord." (5.6.2–5)

Henry refuses to associate "good" with Gloucester, because he views
his visitor oppositionally, as if Gloucester were the devil.[38] That is why
he says that calling either Gloucester or the devil "good" would be
"preposterous," using the word in its literal Latin sense of "back-to-
front," in parallel with common iconography of the devil with a face in
his rear end—apparently the picture that Stephano imagines when he
thinks he has encountered a devilish monster with four human legs and
two heads in *The Tempest*: "His forward voice is now to speak well of his
friend; his backward voice is to utter foul speeches and to detract"
(2.2.91–93). Richard murders Henry just as Henry seems about to
describe a preposterous detail about Richard ("Thou cam'st—"
[5.6.56]) that Richard himself describes later: "I came into the world
with my legs forward" (5.6.71). Preposterousness was characteristic of
the demonic, as Nicholas Rémy points out in his description of witches'
gestures:

> [T]hey love to do everything in a ridiculous and unseemly manner. For
> they turn their backs toward the Demons when they go to worship them,
> and approach them sideways like a crab; when they hold out their hands
> in supplication they turn them downwards; when they converse they

bend their eyes toward the ground; and in other such ways they behave in a manner opposite to that of other men.[39]

Richard of Gloucester indeed behaves "in a manner opposite to that of other men," and his implicit invocation is both preposterous and demonic: "Then, since the heavens have shaped my body so, / Let hell make crook'd my mind to answer it" (5.6.78–79). Henry the saint can see and tell what Richard is, prophesying that many "Shall rue the hour that ever thou wast born" (43) and identifying the "evil signs" that accompanied Richard's birth (44–48).

An obvious reason for Shakespeare to sharpen the contrast between Henry and Richard in *3 Henry VI* was to prepare for *Richard III*, where the successor to Henry VI as Richard's opposite is another morally charismatic figure, Henry Earl of Richmond, whose beneficent reign Henry VI prophesies with "divining thoughts" in *3 Henry VI*. In designing the last two of his early history plays with this contrast in mind, Shakespeare accurately recaptured the origin of the Tudor myth, which included the apotheosis of Henry VI. Henry Tudor helped to secure his dubious inheritance by simultaneously blackening the reputation of the monarch he overthrew, Richard III, and promoting the saintly reputation of the last monarch to bear his own name, around whom a cult of miraculous healing had sprung up during Richard's brief reign.[40] Polydore Vergil's ascription of prophetic power to the last Lancastrian king, noted above, was part of Henry VII's effort to shore up his own strength by promoting the charisma of the king whom some said Richard III had slain with his own hand.[41] Henry VII sought vigorously to have Henry VI canonized, and the effort was continued by Henry VIII, but it came to a sudden end when Henry VIII broke with Rome over the annulment of his marriage to Catherine of Aragon. The last mention of the canonization is in 1528, but even so, Henry VIII "is recorded offering at his [Henry VI's] altar" as late as 10 June 1529, the year of the Reformation Parliament.[42]

The origins of the Tudor myth bring together the political background of the early histories with their place in dramatic history, and both are important indicators of Shakespeare's political thinking when he started writing about English history. Thomas More assisted the Tudor cause by constructing a demonic portrait of the last Yorkist king in his *History of King Richard the Third* (1513), and this portrait became the origin of Shakespeare's Richard, because Shakespeare's source was

Hall, who drew heavily on More's *History* in composing his chronicle. But More likely derived his inspiration from the personified vices of the morality play, especially as treated by the early Tudor court dramatists, Henry Medwall and John Skelton. More's interest in the drama of his day is well documented and was itself dramatized in Shakespeare's generation in the play called *Sir Thomas More*, which Shakespeare may have helped to write. In this play, More is imagined to step impromptu into the part of a missing player in a morality play called *The Marriage of Wit and Wisdom*. In short, when Shakespeare turned to the morality play's personified vices as the model for Richard of Gloucester, he was not combining "history" and drama; he was perpetuating the mode on which "history" had been based in the first place, or in other words, he was following More in offering an interpretation of history that was borrowed from the morality play.

In similar fashion, Shakespeare's way of imagining Henry VI draws in part on the traditional saint's play. Shakespeare's Henry performs no miracles, but he suffers patiently as saints typically do in the plays that celebrate them, and he twice foretells the future accurately and straightforwardly (that is, without equivocation or irony—in contrast to prophecies concerning the deaths of several people in the early histories). Henry foretells not only England's happy future under Henry VII, but also the suffering of the kingdom under the oppression of the man who murders him—"And thus I prophesy" (5.6.37)—whose demonic nature he incisively perceives and describes. "Die, prophet, in thy speech," exclaims Richard (5.6.57), simultaneously illustrating his power over the man and his powerlessness over the future—as if he could prevent what is going to happen by destroying the one who foretells it. Though few saints' plays survive in English, many were performed, and Shakespeare's familiarity with the genre is clear from his adaptation of it in *Pericles*.[43] No record of a play honoring Henry VI has yet been found, but his posthumous miracles were certainly enough to inspire a play, for they gave him a reputation that rivaled Thomas Becket's, as an early printed version of them attests.[44]

In short, Shakespeare drew on traditional drama in *3 Henry VI* in order to emphasize the saintly charisma of Henry VI and thereby to prepare for the moral charisma of Richmond in *Richard III*, but the comparison highlights a difference: Richmond is a master not only of charisma but of real power, as his invasion of England and defeat of Richard III make clear, and he uses these elements of kingship, as the historical Henry VII did, to establish his dubious legitimacy. For obvious reasons, this is a point Shakespeare never has him or anyone else acknowledge, but it is present by its absence in the numerous fruitless debates about legitimate inheritance in the *Henry VI* plays and in the apparent arbitrariness of legitimacy in *3 Henry VI*. More's reforming admonition, noted above, has a bearing on Henry VII's success: "What you cannot turn to good you must make as little bad as you can." Henry VI's inability to make things as little bad as he could defines his failure as a king—including his responsibility for his people's suffering, as Clifford emphasizes—in spite of his undeniable saintliness toward the end of his life. Henry VII's success in ending the baronial wars, by contrast, makes him a better king than Henry VI by More's criterion—better, that is, because he not only legitimates his success with authoritative charismatic appeal but also successfully restores a semblance of political calm.

PLOTS, TIME, AND HISTORY

Though the deep plots of York and his son eventually pall, in Hamlet's phrase (5.2.9), they provide the clearest through-line for events in the *Henry VI* plays and *Richard III*. The way these plays acknowledge their debt to England's indigenous drama of Christian salvation suggests that plotting (as scheming) may have a bearing on plot (as storyline), especially in history plays. "Let us sup betimes," proposes the arch-plotter, Richard of Gloucester, to his fellow political actor, Buckingham, "that afterwards / We may digest our complots in some form" (*Richard III* 3.1.199–200), and the form in question turns out to be the history play. The key component of both schemes and stories about the past is time, because time is required for the unfolding of every kind of plot, and time is essential to secular history as the necessary medium of political action. In this regard, the history play is distinct from comedy, which offers the possibility of restoration, however imperfect and temporary; from tragedy, which imagines the fact of irrevocable loss in ongoing human experience; and from the drama of biblical history, which is defined not by the cause and effect of human action in the continuum of secular time but by God's saving intervention, which defines salvation history in the first place.

In David Kastan's terms, the generic distinctiveness of Shakespeare's history plays derives from "a unique and determinate shape that emerges organically from the playwright's sense of the shape of history itself."[45] A secular sense of history in the history plays emerges in their exclusive focus on political events as an endless temporal quest to acquire and maintain power. Conceiving of time as a secular continuum contrasts with the sense of sacred time in the only other plays about history that Shakespeare knew, the biblical history plays, "where human history is given a dramatic form that emphasizes its providential ordering" by means of God's decisive actions in events: the Creation, the fall of Adam and Eve, Cain's murder of Abel, God's preservation of Noah, and other selected events, culminating in the mission and ministry of Jesus.[46] The drama of sacred history is marked, in other words, by God's unambiguous intervention in events and by discontinuity between events, because what matters in sacred history is not how events relate to each other but how each event relates to God. To distinguish plays that focus on secular history from their sacred predecessors on the English stage therefore requires a different conception of history and a different dramatic form.

In their emphasis on secular history, Shakespeare's histories are even further removed from apocalypse—conceived both as The End and as the complete revelation of meaning—than comedy and tragedy. Both of those forms gesture toward "the promised end" (*King Lear* 5.3.268) in various ways without offering the revelation it promises, and their denouements are therefore partial and imperfect, just as the truth they convey is partial, hidden, and suggestive—dark and enigmatic, as if seen through a distorted lens. History, however, offers nothing but a secular temporal continuum, from start to finish, and the form is therefore insistently and literally open-ended, as Kastan argues, both in meaning and structure. This is the least providential of dramatic shapes, in other words, and the most intently focused on human initiative and action.

The openness of Shakespeare's history plays to the continuum of secular time makes them his least classical genre in their ignoring of Aristotle's specification that a "unified action" must have a distinctive beginning and end.[47] A true beginning in a dramatic action, Aristotle states, is "that which does not necessarily follow on something else, but after it something else naturally is or happens," and by the same token a true ending is "that which naturally follows on something else, either

necessarily or for the most part, but nothing else after it."[48] The biblical history plays fulfill Aristotle's criteria for beginning and ending better than any other play ever written, because they begin with the
Creation and end with the Last Judgment; in other words, they encompass all of human time, and they are definitively revelatory, because
they deal exclusively with acts of God.[49] Relative to this standard, all
other plays are open-ended, and Shakespeare's comedies and tragedies
usually identify their action significantly but indefinitely somewhere
between the Creation and the Apocalypse. Shakespeare's history plays,
however, are uniquely and insistently open-ended because of their focus
on the endless secular contest for political power.

This structural open-endedness marks even the first of them, *1 Henry
VI*, which begins with the funeral of Henry V. Speeches praising the
dead king inform us that he was a famous warrior and a terror to the
French. The formalities are interrupted, however, by quarrelling
between a nobleman and a bishop and by the successive arrival of messengers who report various setbacks suffered by the English fighting in
France. This beginning is deeply embedded in past political events that
are not explained. Why was Henry V fighting in France? How did he
die? Why does a nobleman who is identified in the dialogue simply as
"Gloucester" quarrel so vociferously with a bishop who is unnamed in
the dialogue and identifiable as a cleric only by his costume? What, if
anything, does their quarrel have to do with Henry V's death and the
war in France? Why does the bishop end the first scene by determining
in soliloquy to "steal the king" (1.1.176)? How might one do such a
thing, and what is the bishop's motive for wanting to do it? He seems
determined to seize power (1.1.177), but why would he be? Who is he,
what is he planning, and why? As *1 Henry VI* begins, it seems to assume
that we know a great deal already about what has happened in the life
of the kingdom, because it raises so many questions that it does not
answer. This is not a beginning, in Aristotle's words, that "does not necessarily follow on something else."

This *Henry VI* play ends as contingently as it begins. The Earl of
Suffolk, newly arrived in London from fighting in France, convinces
King Henry to marry a minor French princess, Margaret of Anjou
(introduced as a new character just two scenes earlier), even though her
father is so poor he can afford no dowry. Suffolk tells us, but he does not
tell anyone else—especially the king—that he has himself become infat-

uated with Margaret and has determined to persuade the young king to marry her so that Suffolk can enjoy her as his mistress and influence royal policy through her. The play thus raises several questions at the end that it does not answer. What will be the outcome of Suffolk's bizarre plan? Will Henry indeed be weak enough to fall for it? How will it affect the war in France? How will rivals at the faction-ridden English court respond? The action of *1 Henry VI* ceases with so many questions unanswered that it might more accurately be said to stop rather than end, as Kastan points out (50).

The open-endedness of *1 Henry VI* is characteristic of all Shakespeare's history plays, even of his single Jacobean history play, *Henry VIII*, written some fourteen years after *Henry V*, the last of the series of nine English history plays that he wrote in the 1590s. These plays' political and structural open-endedness, moreover, cannot be explained by the assumption that Shakespeare's audience would have known the history they were watching and therefore needed no exposition to tidy the beginning and no tying up of loose threads at the end. Shakespeare's audience was socially diverse, and most people who saw his plays were unlettered, but among the few who could read, fewer still were well read in English history, which was not taught at any level of contemporary education.[50] Shakespeare learned English history by studying published chronicles, as careful comparisons of his history plays to the chronicles have shown, but the chronicles were expensive books and inaccessible even to most of those who were literate. Shakespeare's attentive use of the chronicles early in his career, before he had accumulated enough wealth to buy copies of his own, almost certainly suggests that he borrowed them from someone else.[51]

Moreover, other plays that Shakespeare derived from the chronicles do not begin and end the same way the history plays do. *King Lear*, for example, begins with a clear exposition of what precedes the first scene, when Gloucester chats with Kent (1.1.1–33). Everything we need to know about the subsequent action is introduced in this brief exchange, whose purpose is clearly to explain what follows in a natural and unobtrusive way: Lear's decision to divide the kingdom, the rivalry of Cornwall and Albany, the illegitimacy of Edmund, and Gloucester's attitude toward his illegitimate son. As for the end of *King Lear*, it is famous for its finality. So shocking is the spectacle of Lear's entry with the dead Cordelia in his arms and his own subsequent death that characters in the play compare what is happening to the Apocalypse, the definitive end of all action, including action in plays (5.3.268–69). This scene does not make the ending of *Lear* literally apocalyptic, but it so trivializes any questions we may have about what follows that they occur only to someone who is determined to try to think of them: Who will reign next? Will Edgar find a wife to carry on Gloucester's line? Will Albany remarry? What will happen to the Duchy of Cornwall? The quasi-apocalyptic closure of *King Lear* clarifies the consistent open-endedness of the history plays by contrast and strongly suggests that the difference is not accidental but indicates the playwright's sense of how to embody the ongoing tensions of secular history in the dramatic form of the history play.[52]

In addition to imitating the continuum of secular history by the way they begin and end, Shakespeare's history plays also emphasize time thematically, as Kastan argues. When Viola invokes time in *Twelfth Night*, she asks, in effect, for patience, and she is rewarded in the end by the resolution of her difficulty: "O Time, thou must untangle this, not I; / It is too hard a knot for me t' untie" (2.2.40–41). In contrast, evo-cations of time in the history plays nearly always reinforce their politi-cal character. The later histories are most brilliant in this regard, but it is apparent from the beginning. In the rose garden scene of *1 Henry VI*, Richard Plantagenet (the future Duke of York) assures Somerset that he could vindicate his attainted father, "Were growing time once ripened to my will" (2.4.99), and he begins his plotting in *2 Henry VI* by caution-ing himself to "be still awhile, till time do serve" (1.1.248), later urging Salisbury and Warwick to bide their time by "winking" at the abuses of power they witness, until those who perpetrate them destroy themselves (2.2.69–76). The political ineptitude of Henry VI is shown in part in *3 Henry VI* by his fantasy during the battle of Towton that he could spend his hours like a homely shepherd, "So minutes, hours, days, months, and years, / Passed over to the end they were created, / Would bring white hairs unto a quiet grave" (2.5.38–40). "If Henry had had his wish to be a shepherd," remarks M. M. Reese pointedly, "he would certainly have lost his sheep."[53] Henry's nemesis, Richard, plots against his brother in anticipation of "the golden time I look for" (3.2.127), and he is constantly hurrying and urging others to hurry, because "the time and case requireth haste" (4.5.18). Time in the history plays is the medium of political struggle, where the destinies of those who compete for power are made and unmade, without regard to eternal verities and with no end in sight.

This way of enacting politics in drama is characteristic not only of the Elizabethan plays about English history but also of *Julius Caesar*, which was first produced in 1599, the same year as *Henry V*. John Velz has described the structure of Julius Caesar as "undular"; a sequence of events created by the succession of powerful men who rise and fall: Pompey, Caesar, Brutus, Cassius, Octavius, and Antony.[54] Shakespeare had exploited this structure before, in the English history plays, where it suggests a struggle for power that is both an end in itself, as in *Julius Caesar*, and politically open-ended. In the Roman history play, too, Shakespeare uses time thematically to reinforce dramatic structure. Cassius dies on his birthday, noting the irony of dying as if he had never lived, as if he were no more than a small eddy in the river of time: "This day I breathèd first. Time is come round, / And where I did begin, there shall I end" (5.3.23–24). Brutus is sorry to hear of Cassius' death and hopes for time in which to bury his friend—"I shall find time, Cassius, I shall find time" (5.3.103)—but events overwhelm him, and he himself dies before the day is out. Invoking fate in *Julius Caesar* is directly analogous to invoking providence in the English history plays: both Cassius and Brutus do it (1.2.139, 3.1.99–101), and both are overtaken in the end by the onrushing course of events. Antony refers to the "tide of times" (3.1.159), and Brutus uses a similar image: "There is a tide in the affairs of men / Which, taken at the flood, leads on to fortune" (4.3.217–18). Using a similar image, Caesar refers disparagingly to commoners in *Antony and Cleopatra*, but actually describes everyone in the history plays (including himself), who "Like to a vagabond flag upon the stream, / Goes to and back, lackeying the varying tide / To rot itself with motion" (1.4.45–47). Caesar's "celerity" in *Antony* is reminiscent of successful kings in the history plays, from Richard III to Henry V: all use time to their political advantage. "Now he weighs time / Even to the utmost grain," says Exeter of Henry V (*Henry V* 2.4.137–38), dismissing Henry's dalliance in the timeless festive world of the tavern when the king was a prince. Time overtakes Henry V too, however, as the heroic political achievements of his play come back, in its closing lines, to the beginning of his son's hapless reign that Shakespeare had depicted in his first history plays.

No matter what Henry V achieves, he ultimately becomes a political eddy in the ongoing river of time and political struggle.

SHAKESPEARE AND MACHIAVELLI

Though the mechanical clock was a medieval invention, time was a discovery of the Renaissance, as Ricardo Quinones argues, and Shakespeare's sense of time as the critical element in political decision-making seems not only to be original with him but is as insightful as anything in the late sixteenth century.[55] It distinguishes his political thinking, for example, from Machiavelli's. To be sure, one can find an occasional passage in Machiavelli that mentions the importance of time in terms similar to those that can be inferred from Shakespeare's history plays. In *Discourses* 1.32, for example, he emphasizes the need for planning, which requires a calculating awareness of the future in relation to the present:

> Whoever is in power, therefore, whether a civil government or a prince, should consider beforehand what sorts of adverse times are likely to come upon him and what men he may need in times of trouble, and then treat them in just the way he thinks he would need to treat them in an emergency of any kind. He who conducts himself otherwise, whether prince or civil government—but especially a prince—and then believes that when the peril is on him he can in a moment regain men with benefits, deceives himself, because he not merely does not make sure of them but even hastens his own ruin.[56]

Such a passage might well be applied to York and his son in contrast to Henry VI, and it is impossible to prove that Shakespeare did not somehow read it (either in a published Italian edition or in one of several manuscript English translations of Machiavelli that circulated in Elizabethan England) and draw from it the insight that consistently motivates the most careful and successful politicians in his plays, from York in *1 Henry VI* to *Henry VIII*.[57]

Before concluding that he did so, however, one needs to weigh Machiavelli's occasional, almost incidental, references to time with his repetitive and deliberate references to fortune.[58] Even a casual reader of Machiavelli cannot miss his insistence that the key to political success lies in the prince's ability to make fortune work for him, rather than against him. Complementing chapter 25 of *The Prince* ("Fortune's Power in Human Affairs and How She Can Be Forestalled") are innumerable other references.[59] Hanna Pitkin's careful study concludes that fortune is to *virtù* in Machiavelli as women are to successful men, as indicated most remarkably in the infamous line that "Fortune is a woman and it is necessary, in order to keep her under, to cuff and maul her."[60] Machiavelli habitually links opportunity with fortune, deifying chance as a secular goddess who submits to the belligerent and the successful while consigning the timid to oblivion. Identifying political success with aggressively seized fortune can be related to the ability to *act in time*, since fortune creates opportunities in time, but Machiavelli does not make that link; he merely emphasizes the importance of fortune.[61]

Shakespeare also refers to fortune, but his conception is different from Machiavelli's, and it is less important in the history plays than time. Occasionally, to be sure, Shakespeare personifies fortune to make a point similar to Machiavelli's. In *King John*, when Philip the Bastard urges John and Lewis to put their quarrel aside for the moment and turn their joint wrath on Angiers, he points out that they can resume their quarrel again after defeating the city:

> Then, in a moment, Fortune shall cull forth
> Out of one side her happy minion,
> To whom in favor she shall give the day,
> And kiss him with a glorious victory. (2.1.387–94)

When Cardinal Wolsey in *Henry VIII* is caught red-handed in a plot against the king, he continues to believe (mistakenly, it turns out) that his luck will hold, and he can succeed yet again, as he has in the past: "yet I know / A way, if it take right, in spite of fortune / Will bring me off again" (3.2.219–21).

More frequently, however, a more stoic sense of fortune appears in Shakespeare, with very different implications from Machiavelli's equation of fortunate success with aggressively seized opportunity. When Warwick captures King Edward in *3 Henry VI*, the king determines to bear the setback bravely: "Though Fortune's malice overthrow my state, / My mind exceeds the compass of her wheel" (4.3.46–47). This sense of fortune, with its allusion to the medieval picture of the goddess Fortune turning a wheel to which people were bound, sometimes rising toward her, sometimes declining away, is more fatalistic than Machiavelli's, though it shares with Machiavelli's idea a cyclical sense of political power and thus contrasts with the linear sense of political timing in Shakespeare's history plays—a sense that is central to his idea that succession is the weakest feature of monarchical government. Nor is King Edward's remark an immature reminiscence in the early histories alone, for it reappears in *Henry V*, the latest of the Elizabethan history plays, and in *Antony and Cleopatra*, as late as 1608.[62]

As with time, then, so with fortune: one cannot prove that Shakespeare did not read Machiavelli and absorb his ideas, but overall the two analyze political success differently, despite their common political realism, and the moral force of Shakespeare's political realism seems more in keeping with More, Erasmus, and medieval religious drama than with Machiavelli.[63] In any case, where his emphasis on time and his interpretation of politics in the continuum of secular history are concerned, Shakespeare may be more innovative than Machiavelli. Fortuna is a Roman goddess, her influence is cyclical (as the image of the wheel indicates), and the necessity to conquer her is part of Machiavelli's medieval political legacy. Time, on the other hand, is a discovery of the Renaissance, as Quinones argues, and the linearity of time is emphasized in the structure of Shakespeare's history plays. As one would expect of a playwright, Shakespeare's insight about history is inseparable from his sense of dramatic form, and understanding his accomplishment as a writer of plays is therefore imperative to understanding him as a thinker. Unlike Machiavelli, who wrote letters, plays, poems, and political treatises, Shakespeare wrote only plays and poems, so we have no critical reflections on which to draw in interpreting him.[64] Shakespeare's writing needs to be understood in its own terms, both generically and historically, and his reflection on secular history makes more sense as an intuitive derivation from the native drama of salvation history than from Italian political theory.

PART II

<u>IDEA</u>

POLITICS

'Tis much when scepters are in children's hands.

1 Henry VI 4.1.192

Woe to that land that's governed by a child!

Richard III 2.3.12

In the first section of this book, I have argued that Shakespeare's sense of genre was shaped most importantly by the master narrative that he and his audience knew best, the narrative of salvation history, in which they located themselves most easily and habitually. His debt to this narrative in comedy, history, and tragedy does not make a spiritual allegory out of it, as Dante, Spenser, and Bunyan all did in various ways, but the evident skepticism in his plays is not demonstrably secular either, because skepticism had become a conceivable part of the narrative itself. What I am calling "skeptical faith" thus informs every dramatic genre Shakespeare attempted in various ways. Shakespearean comedy imagines literal human beings in real situations somewhere between Creation and Judgment, exhibiting intractable weakness but also being surprised by the unexpected and open-ended possibility of renewal and restoration. A web of biblical allusions complements the evident opera-tion of the traditional theological virtues, faith, hope, and love, to allow for unforeseen positive change, though not for perfection.

Shakespeare also alludes to salvation history in *Romeo and Juliet* and Bradley's "famous four" tragedies, but he does so to evoke acknowledg-ment of the mystery of suffering. Shakespeare's tragic worlds are not definitively hopeless, because they neither pretend to complete apoca-lyptic disclosure, any more than comedy does, nor do they deny the operation of the theological virtues in human experience, yet they com-pel us to recognize the real experience of inexplicable loss and its accompanying anguish by identifying with those who endure it. In Shakespeare's most inventive genre, the history plays, salvation history is present as if by default, not only because the biblical history plays were the only plays about history that Shakespeare had for a model, but also because the early histories in particular exhibit specific indebtedness to all forms of medieval religious drama without actually reproducing them. Shakespeare's kings can never definitively claim in their lives the hand of God that influences good and bad kings alike in the biblical history plays, because Shakespeare's kings inhabit a secular world of uncertain political struggle that has no end—no ultimate purpose, that is, beyond the acquiring and maintaining of political power, and no conclusion. All that ties them to their originating story are ironic reminiscences and moral expectation, which is the basis of reform, though no Shakespearean king is a moral reformer. All are ultimately caught up in a competition for power, as More and Erasmus had observed long before, even if some, like Henry VI, John, and Richard II, compete ineptly and unsuccessfully. The irony and uncertainty that seem inherent to kings are evidence both of the secular world and of the doubtful success of human aspiration, while the evident moral concern that kings exhibit, or that is exhibited about them, points to something more than instrumental reasoning in the unceasing struggle for power.

More than Shakespeare's generic sense, however, can be inferred from his plays and poems when it comes to skeptical faith, and one way to go beyond genre is to consider what he wrote in light of several standard philosophical questions, in order to ask what can be said about his thinking in each case—whether skeptical or faithful or both. The most basic of these questions for Shakespeare, I would argue, is the question of religion, which I have addressed by identifying his response to skepticism and faith in a sixteenth-century context and by exploring his implied sense of dramatic genre. In the remaining chapters, I want to turn to five other philosophical questions, two of which, ethics and politics, had been explicitly identified and addressed as separate questions by the sixteenth century, while the others, epistemology, ontology, and esthetics, were not distinguished and named until later. Indeed, as I argue in chapter 7, the indistinct blending of the last three problems in Shakespeare's writing is evidence that in some things he was very much of an age, not for all time, despite Ben Jonson's praise to the contrary.

Where ethics and politics are concerned, Shakespeare inherited a teleological conception from Aristotle, who argued that the purpose of the ethical life is happiness, and that happiness can best be achieved in the kind of polity Aristotle knew in the Greek *poleis*.[1] Ethics, or the study of how human beings achieve their proper end by becoming virtuous, thus serves the purpose of politics. The distinction survives in an attenuated form in *The Faerie Queene*, where Spenser set out to treat the private moral virtues in six books, "as Aristotle hath devised," followed by the public moral virtues in six more, though the distinction broke down immediately in book 1, the "Legend of Holiness," because holiness is represented allegorically by St. George, the patron saint of England, whom Spenser made a distinctly Protestant version of the virtue he represents and therefore an unavoidably political figure for the late sixteenth century.[2] In late Tudor England, ethics had thus become political in a manner Aristotle never envisioned. For Shakespeare, the relationship between ethics and politics is implicit in his way of imagining history as the aspirations and actions of powerful elites, because their aspiration is defined both by power and by moral expectation, and the difference between moral expectation and political action is so wide. Ethics thus logically precedes politics for Shakespeare, as it does for Aristotle and Spenser, but it will be useful here to take up politics first, both to maintain continuity with the preceding chapter about the history plays as a genre and to clarify the continuity in Shakespeare's political vision as it appears in his most mature plays based on English history.

Monarchy, Succession, and Political Realism

Viewed in their late Tudor context, the most striking feature of Shakespeare's history plays is their consistent attention to the problem of monarchical succession, because it is a problem that had troubled the Tudors from the beginning. E. M. W. Tillyard recognized this feature of the plays, but he interpreted it in light of Tudor state theory, creating a closed loop of theoretical historicity that dominated critical commentary for almost fifty years. Tillyard began with what he thought were the neoplatonic assumptions of Shakespeare's political culture: order, degree, hierarchy, and obedience.[3] For Elizabethans, Tillyard argued, God presided over a cosmic scheme, "the Elizabethan world picture," to ensure that its principles were maintained by punishing those who violated them. Since monarchs were at the top of the social and political hierarchy, obedience to monarchs was divinely ordained, and disobedience was punished by divine displeasure, which manifested itself in political turmoil. Political principles were thus moral and theological principles, and Shakespeare's plays embodied those principles by tracing political disorder in the fifteenth century to an original political sin: the overthrow of Richard II by Henry Bolingbroke.

The reaction to Tillyard since the 1980s has been salutary in restoring attention to the way history really works in Shakespeare's history plays, not just the way some of his contemporaries said it ought to work, but the reaction has had the effect of diverting attention away from the history plays as a group and from the problem of monarchical succession that characterizes all of them.[4] New historicism and cultural materialism have neglected the early history plays, and diachronic attention to problems such as containment and subversion has virtually driven synchronic readings from the field.[5] To be sure, in a recent "presentist" argument, Hugh Grady has suggested that monarchical succession preoccupied Shakespeare in *Hamlet* because it obsessed the Essex circle at the end of the 1590s.[6] But Grady reckons without the pervasiveness of monarchical succession as a political problem, both in Tudor history and in Shakespeare's history plays. If Shakespeare's skepticism about politics appears anywhere, it appears in his continuing interest in monarchical succession.

The problem is ubiquitous in the early and later histories; it is the principal issue in *King John*, Shakespeare's other history play written during the reign of Elizabeth; and it is central to *Julius Caesar*, a Roman history from the late 1590s.[7] Political succession was a problem throughout Elizabeth's long reign (1558–1603), because an orderly transfer of power depended on her providing for the royal succession, but she could not decide the issue without in some way compromising her own prerogative, so she refused to name her successor until the very end.[8] Without a stated line of succession, claimed a Commons petition in the Parliament of 1563, in the event of the Queen's death, the kingdom would suffer, starting with "the unspeakable miseries of civil wars" and including many other political problems that Shakespeare imagines in the *Henry VI* plays: "the waste of noble houses, the slaughter of people . . . unsurety of all men's possessions, lives, and estates."[9] The most obvious way for the Queen to secure the future was to marry and produce an heir, but marriage was a more vexed question for a female head of state than for a man, given patriarchal assumptions and the irrepressible competition for power at court. As J. E. Neale points out, marriage for Elizabeth risked her personal independence, no matter whom she married, while marrying a foreign prince would create problems for English political independence as well, and marrying one of her own courtiers would destroy the balance of power that she maintained among the factions at her court.[10] Her sister, Mary Tudor, had handled a foreign marriage badly, and Elizabeth's cousin, Mary Stuart of Scotland, brought her reign to a premature end by an inadvisable marriage with one of her courtiers—though Mary managed to produce a son who in fact became Elizabeth's successor in the process. As long as Elizabeth was of childbearing age, she was under intense pressure to marry, from suitors both at home and abroad and from her own council and parliament, and she almost certainly risked the problems of avoiding marriage because she could see no way to marry without creating greater problems than she faced by remaining single.

Shakespeare was not the first Elizabethan dramatist to think about problems attending uncertain monarchical succession. The play called *Gorboduc*, designed boldly to advise the young Queen about the royal succession, was performed by students of the Inner Temple before the Queen on January 18, 1561, and published the following year, but it was the only play that dared to be so open.[11] Though the political danger of having no successor continued when Elizabeth passed childbearing age, the Queen grew increasingly sensitive on the issue, and parliament ceased to proffer advice on it after 1563 for fear of royal displeasure. The government could not make the problem go away by suppressing discussion of it, however, and "a ragbag collection of outs and malcontents," in Peter Lake's phrase, addressed the succession in various ways.[12] Shakespeare's interest in it is distinct both from dissenters' views and from the heavy-handed official interpretation. His history plays are thus very different from *Gorboduc*'s transparent attempt to advise the Queen about the dangers of uncertain succession, and Tillyard characteristically overstates the case in claiming that "the authors of *Gorboduc* transferred into the dramatic medium and expressed in blank verse most of the ideas about history on which Shakespeare's History Plays were founded."[13] While Shakespeare saw the danger of uncertain political succession as plainly as everyone else, Tillyard was mistaken that Shakespeare's history plays repeat the political truisms of *Gorboduc*, because Shakespeare's plays do much more than remind the Queen of her duty. Their topicality consists in a dispassionate analysis of how power is acquired, maintained, and passed on, but the analysis is displaced onto events in the fifteenth century.[14] The *Henry VI* plays, first produced in the early 1590s, address the issue in their depiction of England destroying itself through factionalism and the instability produced by quarrels over legitimate inheritance that go back to Henry VI's minority succession. Exeter traces the kingdom's instability to Henry's minority succession in *1 Henry VI* 4.1.192, and York's first complaint about the weak Lancastrian king is that he holds the scepter in a "childish fist" (*2 Henry VI* 1.1.243).

This is not to say that Shakespeare modeled any particular character in his history plays on Elizabeth (though Henry V as prince and king is a suggestive possibility[15]), nor that the plays reflect any particular episode in Elizabethan politics. The topicality I am proposing is broader than that, because it involves a political problem that was importantly, though not exclusively, Elizabethan, and that Shakespeare comes back to repeatedly and thoughtfully in the history plays of the 1590s. The first of the Tudors, Henry VII, initially acquired power by overthrowing his predecessor, Richard III, and Shakespeare explores this violent succession in acceptably orthodox terms as providentially arranged while reflecting on it ironically in the see-sawing of power in the *Henry VI* plays (above, chap. 4). The problems in both of the two tetralogies originate in the same problem: the succession of a child. Henry VI succeeded at the age of nine months, and Richard II at the age of nine years. In Shakespeare's depiction, their inheritance as minors compelled both kings to grow up under the influence of powerful relatives, who were reluctant to surrender their power when the child kings came of age, resulting in disruptive conflicts between rival court factions that are played out in both early and late history plays.

The problem was broadly topical, not only because of disputes over the succession to Elizabeth, but also because uncertain succession virtually defined the Tudor regime after the death of Henry VIII. Despite Henry's attempt to provide for an orderly inheritance by act of parliament, his son, Edward VI, obtained the crown in his minority, and both Elizabeth and her sister succeeded to the throne under circumstances that were more unpredictable and dangerous than those surrounding the succession to Elizabeth herself. By the early 1590s, when Shakespeare likely wrote his first history plays, Elizabeth had reigned for over thirty years, but many were alive who could remember the sequence of four monarchs (Henry VIII, Edward VI, Mary, and Elizabeth) over the course of eleven years (1547–1558) at mid-century, when political anxiety and upheaval had been pervasive, and no one could be sure that the civil tumult of the fifteenth century (imagined in the *Henry VI* plays) would not return. Parliamentary concern over the succession in 1563 originated in the conviction that religious civil war would break out if the Queen died, as she very nearly did (of smallpox) in 1562.[16]

Moreover, the Tudors' origin as a dynasty in Henry VII's violent over-throw of a reigning monarch, Richard III, in 1485 could easily prompt a thoughtful observer to recognize that Tudor state doctrine was in part an attempt to secure the Tudors' own doubtful succession.[17] The homily on "Disobedience and Wilful Rebellion," appointed by the crown to be read regularly in churches, has been often cited (by Tillyard among others) as the epitome of Tudor state theory.[18] It argued that a subject might not, under any circumstances, actively resist anointed monarchs, even if they are tyrants, because God permits tyrants to reign in order to punish disobedient subjects, and to resist even a tyrant is therefore to resist God.[19] This is the principle of passive obedience that John of Gaunt appeals to in *Richard II*, though he is convinced of the King's tyranny in ordering the assassination of Gaunt's own brother:

> God's is the quarrel; for God's substitute,
> His deputy anointed in His sight,
> Hath caused his death; the which if wrongfully
> Let heaven revenge, for I may never lift
> An angry arm against His minister. (1.2.37–41)

This kind of argument was designed to strengthen support for the Tudor regime and to prevent violent political opposition, no matter what people might think of any particular Tudor policy or practice.

The monarchist assumptions of Shakespeare's plays partly reveal themselves in a greater regard for charismatic legitimacy than most advocates of democracy are inclined to, but no amount of ceremonial authority is enough to solve the difficulties associated with the transfer of power, as *Richard II* makes particularly clear. Richard not only enjoys the advantages of unambiguous legitimate succession, but he also, in Shakespeare's rendering, has an unusually strong sense of ritual power and mystical influence: he loves ceremony, speaks magnificently, and believes deeply in the awe of majesty. When threatened, he asserts that

> Not all the water in the rough rude sea
> Can wash the balm off from an anointed king;
> The breath of worldly men cannot depose
> The deputy elected by the Lord. (*Richard II* 3.2.54–57)

As Shakespeare imagines it, Richard's problem is that he lacks adequate practical political sense to complement his idealizing conception of himself as king. He is not an innocent whose overthrow reaps a harvest of political turmoil; rather, he inherits political troubles by virtue of his minority succession, and he exercises power arbitrarily in his own behalf—ordering the assassination of political rivals, imposing capricious taxation, seizing a powerful nobleman's estate in his absence. Richard is easily defeated, however, by a more able politician than he is—one who maneuvers the king into surrendering the crown without being able to strike a blow in his own defense. Richard thus parallels Henry VI without any taint of illegitimate succession in his background, but Richard's immaculate succession cannot offset poor political judgment that renders him incapable of overcoming the challenges following his minority inheritance, and he does not survive the resulting political instability. The power of Richard's appeal to his royal aura is undeniable: it is embodied in some of Shakespeare's most moving political rhetoric, and it is not treated ironically except insofar as it exposes Richard's lack of real political skill. In the end, *Richard II* seems equally poised between political idealism (expressed by Richard) and political realism (practiced by both competitors for the throne), but the play leaves no question as to which succeeds in a contest for power. As Richard recognizes with bitter irony: "They well deserve to have / That know the strong'st and surest way to get" (3.3.200–201). This is one way that a dispassionate political skeptic might account for Tudor state theory.

The central difficulty with the Tudor principle of passive obedience is that circumstances in the lives of subjects make the principle very difficult, if not impossible, to interpret and apply, especially amid the chaos of uncertain succession. Shakespeare emphasizes this difficulty in *3 Henry VI*, as we saw in chapter 4, when Henry debates two forest keepers on the subject of their obedience (3.1.80–100). They propose to arrest him, because Edward has deposed him, and though he argues that they are like feathers blown by the wind, he eventually acquiesces, recognizing both their argument and their superior power in the immediate circumstances. The same dilemma faced by the forest keepers in *3 Henry VI* occurs again at a higher social level in *Richard II*. York scolds his nephew, Henry Bolingbroke, for disobeying King Richard's term of banishment (2.3), but once Richard has surrendered his crown to Henry, York is the new king's most fiercely loyal subject, insisting even on the punishment of his own son, Aumerle, for plotting against Henry in the deposed king's interest (5.2 and 5.3). York's vacillation conforms to the Tudor principle of passive obedience that the forest keepers appeal to in *3 Henry VI*, but Shakespeare's skeptical response to the principle is suggested by the fact that in both plays defenders of the principle seem at best excessively meek or weak-minded; at worst, uncritically acquiescent or opportunistic.

Questions of royal charisma aside, Shakespeare presents the problem of monarchical succession as a problem of maintaining political stability by maintaining political dominance from one reign to the next. Henry VI succeeds his father legitimately, but his inability to maintain his power produces challenges based on his grandfather's succession, with resulting infighting, the loss of France, destructive divisiveness at court, and eventual civil war. This gradual slide into political chaos is anatomized carefully in the *Henry VI* plays, and it is reversed only by the effective military intervention of Henry Tudor, Queen Elizabeth's grandfather, who asserts sufficient charismatic authority to offset his violent overthrow of a rival in *Richard III*.

Shakespeare tells the story of Richard II and his two immediate successors in the second tetralogy, which is no less interested in the problem of maintaining political stability across reigns (that is, through transitions of power) than the first. Political tension at the beginning of the play derives from Richard's attempt to secure his succession by eliminating rivals. Though the assassination of Richard's uncle, the Duke of Gloucester, is never definitively resolved, Gloucester's wife privately spells out the king's motive for ordering it (1.2.9–36), and the king's cousin, Henry Bolingbroke, publicly blames the King's deputy in France (1.1), thus coming just short of blaming the King himself. Lacking the determination or opportunity to destroy Bolingbroke as a rival, Richard not only banishes him, thus giving him time and means to gather an invasion force (2.2.278–88), but also adds a credible polit-ical reason for Bolingbroke to resist by seizing the Duchy of Lancaster in his absence. Northumberland reports that Bolingbroke's invasion awaits "The first departing of the King for Ireland" (2.2.290), and Richard obligingly departs, thus presenting Bolingbroke with an oppor-tunity to take the military initiative by invading England when Richard is absent with his army. The result is Richard's deposition and the suc-cession of Henry IV, who deals effectively, if laboriously, with the threats to this own regime, so that he passes the crown in due succession to his son.

Though Henry V thus acquires his place legitimately from his father, the threat of political rivalry does not thereby disappear, and it coa-lesces around the heir of Richard II, the Earl of Mortimer, aided by his brother-in-law, Richard Earl of Cambridge.[20] Very much aware of the challenges to his father's authority, Prince Henry plans to secure his own succession to the throne by seemingly transforming himself from wastrel to responsible ruler (*1 Henry IV* 1.2.189–211), by winning favor with commoners (*1 Henry IV* 2.4.13–14) and by simultaneously astonish-ing everyone at court with his new-found military prowess (*1 Henry IV* 5.4), his ability to turn away from his tavern companions (*2 Henry IV* 5.5), and his piety (*Henry V* 1.1.25–38). The strategy eventually suc-ceeds, though not without serious misunderstanding along the way, as Shakespeare shows in *2 Henry IV*, and Prince Henry completes his plan when he becomes king. His rejection of his tavern companions deci-sively creates the public story of his transformation, and his arrest and execution of a close relative of Richard II's heir, the Earl of Cambridge (*Henry V* 2.2), shows both the king's determination and his ability to cre-ate opportunity—two qualities that Richard II lacked in his competition with Hal's father. When Henry V undertakes the conquest of France, he leaves three quarters of his army in England (*Henry V* 1.2.215), cor-recting Richard's mistake of departing from the kingdom (his patri-mony) with his whole army, and the new king secures his power and succession by effecting a political alliance between England and France in his marriage with the French princess. Significantly, however, Henry cannot guarantee political stability beyond himself, as the final Chorus makes clear in alluding to the succession of the king's son at the end of *Henry V*:

Henry the Sixth, in infant bands crowned King

> Of France and England, did this king succeed;
> Whose state so many had the managing,
>   That they lost France and made his England bleed,
> Which oft our stage hath shown. . . . (Epilogue 9–13)

The second tetralogy thus ends by coming full circle to the first, which begins with the funeral of Henry V, and by making explicit the connection between troubled succession and political instability.

SUCCESSION, TIME, AND HISTORY

Perhaps the key indicator that political succession is central to Shakespeare's thinking in the history plays is his linking it most emphatically to time, rather than legitimacy. This link is made in *Richard II*, when York warns his nephew, King Richard, not to seize the Duchy of Lancaster after the death of John of Gaunt, because doing so would disinherit Henry Bolingbroke, presently Duke of Hereford. York personifies time, where he could personify legitimate inheritance:

> Take Hereford's rights away, and take from Time
> His charters and his customary rights;
> Let not tomorrow then ensue today;
> Be not thyself; for how art thou a king
> But by fair sequence and succession? (2.1.195–99)

"Fair sequence and succession" occurs in time, York points out, and Richard's actions therefore strike at the base of his own succession by violating time. The conjunction seems unexpected, but it fits a pattern in the early history plays of thematic references to time as the matrix of political power, because the powerful act in time—both to seize opportunity and to secure secular ends, which are temporal, not eternal (above, chap. 4).

References to time recur in the later histories and are particularly noticeable in *Richard II*, which explicitly conjoins time and succession in York's admonition to Richard. The culmination of these references is Richard's meditation in Pomfret Castle, just before he is killed. His thinking is prompted by the failure of an overheard musician to maintain a regular beat: "Ha, ha, keep time! How sour sweet music is, / When time is broke and no proportion kept!" (5.5.42–43). Richard characteristically thinks of himself as soon as he hears the music, realizing that he too has failed to "keep time": "I wasted time, and now doth time waste me" (49). Impressed by his own aphorism, he imagines himself in an elaborate conceit as a clock, but he concludes despairingly: "But my time / Runs posting on in Bolingbroke's proud joy, / While I stand fooling here, his jack of the clock" (58–60). Richard perceives the erosion of his power as a misuse of time, but the idea is not his alone. He had started the play in full control of time, ordering varying times of banishment for Mowbray and Bolingbroke, and eliciting Bolingbroke's admiration of his power: "How long a time lies in one little word! . . . / such is the breath of kings" (1.3.213–15). Shakespeare oddly telescopes time in 2.1, moreover, in such a way as to suggest that the initiative has shifted decisively to Bolingbroke, for in the same scene in which we see Gaunt die and Richard seize Lancaster's estates, we also learn that Bolingbroke has already started back from France with an invasion force (2.1.277–88). Though Bolingbroke repeatedly insists that he returns only to reclaim his duchy, Shakespeare's treatment of time in 2.1 suggests that Bolingbroke had planned the invasion long before Richard seized his lands, especially in view of the detail that he is waiting to disembark only because Richard has not yet departed for Ireland (2.1.290). These are strong indications that Bolingbroke seizes the initiative by taking advantage of Richard's mistakes, including the mistake of expropriating Bolingbroke's duchy, because Bolingbroke uses the loss to rationalize his invasion. Using time well is the key to power, in other words, and power is the key to the succession.

Though the conception of time and political action in *Richard II* is thoroughly secular, it is not in Machiavelli, and it appears to be original with Shakespeare.[21] As if to signal its derivation from salvation history, Shakespeare draws the comparison by way of contrast in the Queen's confrontation with York's gardeners (3.4).[22] They speak, in effect, for the playwright, glossing the play's idea of time and political action by speaking of it allegorically in relation to their gardening. "All must be even in our government," muses the gardener, ordering his assistant to "Cut off the heads of too-fast-growing sprays / That look too lofty in our commonwealth" (34–36). The gardener's man wonders, in response, why they must maintain their garden, when "our sea-wallèd garden, the whole land, / Is full of weeds," because its caretaker is less hardworking and effective than the gardeners (43–44). This is not a particularly dark allegory, but in case anyone misses the parallel, the gardener spells it out in terms that anticipate Richard's final meditation on wasting time: it is too bad that "the wasteful King" "had not so trimmed and dressed his land / As we this garden" (55–57). At this point, the Queen, having overheard their conversation, confronts them angrily, berating them, addressing the gardener as "old Adam's likeness, / Set to dress this garden" (72–73), and demanding to know "What Eve, what serpent, hath suggested thee / To make a second fall of cursèd man" in their report that Richard has been deposed (75–76). Her injection of the biblical analogy is a startling contrast to the gardeners' secular allegory, but they are closer to the truth than she is, in that Richard was no innocent in a timeless Eden; he was an ineffective political player, who misused power and time to his own disadvantage, as the gardeners have just acknowledged.

No one learns more ably from Richard's failure than Henry IV's son, who begins his career in Shakespeare's account by promising to redeem "time when men least think I will" (*1 Henry IV* 1.2.211) in securing his succession. This line is his answer to Falstaff's opening inquiry in the scene, "Now, Hal, what time of day is it, lad?" (1.2.1), and Hal's response at that point strongly hints at the "redemption" he promises later, for he asks Falstaff rhetorically, "What a devil hast thou to do with the time of the day?" (5–6), and adds for emphasis, "I see no reason why thou shouldst be so superfluous to demand the time of the day" (10–12). Falstaff lives in a timeless world of endless revelry—a world from which he cannot be removed psychologically, even when he is removed physically, as the Prince discovers when he asks to borrow Falstaff's pistol at the battle of Shrewsbury and finds in the holster a bottle of sack instead of a weapon. "What, is it a time to jest and dally now?" Hal demands, with no suggestion that he finds the situation funny: "*He throws the bottle at him*" (5.3.55, 55SD).

Hal's competition with Hotspur in *1 Henry IV* has long been admired for the way it shows Shakespeare's use of a "foil" character (1.3.209), as he adjusts the two men's historical ages to make them equivalent and emphasizes their competition for honor. Careful attention to what Hal says, however, makes clear that he cares as much about time in this competition as he does about honor, suggesting that he sees honor as acquirable only through the advantageous use of time. Rejecting his father's comparison of him to Richard II, Hal vows to defeat Hotspur, "this same child of honor and renown" (3.2.139):

> I will call him to so strict account
> That he shall render every glory up,
> Yea, even the slightest worship of his time,
> Or I will tear the reckoning from his heart. (3.2.150–52)

Hal's mention of time is unexpected here, but it makes sense in light of the way he sees both Falstaff and Hotspur, neither of whom is able to use time effectively the way Hal does. The first cares nothing for it ("What a devil hast thou to do with the time of the day?") and the other wastes it in wrongheaded and ineffective political action, as Richard II does. The Prince uses a mercantile metaphor in describing Hotspur to Henry IV: "Percy is but my factor, good my lord, / To engross up glorious deeds on my behalf" (147–48), but in describing the same strategy later to Hotspur himself, Hal uses the gardening imagery of *Richard II*, making clear the importance of time in his strategy: "And all the budding honors on thy crest / I'll crop to make a garland for my head" (5.4.72–73). In effect, Hal "farms" Hotspur and profits from the harvest of honor and renown. Hal's strategy makes him the most politically successful of all Shakespeare's kings: he uses time to his advantage in securing his patrimony and his power, and he complements timely action with rhetoric that rivals Richard II's in establishing royal charisma for himself. At the end of *Henry V*, however, the Chorus describes the king's success as limited, and the limitations are those of time: the "small time" Henry V lived (*Henry V,* Epilogue 5) meant that his son was "in infant bands crowned King" (9), and the crisis of succession started all over again, "Which oft our stage hath shown" (13). Even the greatest and most successful king is subject to the same limitation that Hotspur recognizes as he is dying at Hal's hands: "time, that takes survey of all the world, / Must have a stop" (*1 Henry IV* 5.4.82–83). Henry V's untimely death makes his play emphatically open-ended, because the struggle goes on without him, dominated by the continuum of time that he sought, above all things, to control, but that controls him in the end.

HISTORY AND POLITICAL SUSPICION

Shakespeare's secular analysis of political action inevitably invites comparison with Machiavelli's. I have argued that Shakespeare is different from, and possibly more original than, his Italian predecessor in his recognition of time as the medium of politics (above, chap. 4), and I want to urge again that they are different, too, in the quality of political suspicion they convey. For both, to be sure, suspicion is inherent in political realism, which recognizes the difference between what people really do and are in the quest to acquire and maintain political power and what people think they ought to do and be. Bacon regarded this recognition as one of Machiavelli's principal contributions: "So that we are much beholden to Machiavel and others, that write what men do and not what they ought to do."[23] Machiavelli's suspicion of human nature is explicit, along with its relationship to his political thinking: "It is necessary for him who lays out a state and arranges laws for it to presuppose that all men are evil and that they are always going to act according to the wickedness of their spirits whenever they have free scope."[24] This assumption lies behind the observation for which he became most infamous—that it is better for a prince to appear to be good than to be good in fact: "For there is such a difference between how men live and how they ought to live that he who abandons what is done for what ought to be done learns his destruction rather than his preservation, because any man who under all conditions insists on making it his business to be good will surely be destroyed among so many who are not good."[25] In other words, the prince must practice dissimulation in order to avoid defeat at the hands of rivals who cannot be trusted, so that Machiavelli's entire political outlook rests on his suspicion of human nature.

The risk in Machiavellian realism, as Hugh Grady points out, is its reduction of action to instrumentality: "the splitting off of 'values' from 'facts,' the production of technical mentality indifferent to ends, focused only on means" produces a polity of mere appetite and predation of the sort that prevails in *King Lear* after the king's abdication.[26] At the same time Machiavellian "discourse" entered Elizabethan consciousness, Grady argues, Shakespeare recognized the risk of instrumental reasoning and responded to it with the "subjectivity" of Montaigne. While I think Grady is helpful in articulating the limitations of instrumental thinking, I want to suggest a different way of understanding Shakespeare's response to it.

Machiavelli's dim assessment of human nature is not one of his innovations. Even though Machiavelli's assumption is not itself theological, it is consistent with centuries of Christian reflection on original sin, a point about which Catholics and Protestants were in basic agreement. In fact, it is typical of Machiavelli's sardonic rhetoric that he would affirm a theological and moral commonplace but draw a conclusion from it that is surprising, if not shocking, to moral expectation.[27] Characteristically Machiavellian in this respect is Richard's apparently pious response (noted above in chap. 4) to his brother Edward's advice in *3 Henry VI* that York should simply disregard the oath he has taken to uphold Henry VI as king (1.2.18–24). Richard's apparent piety ("God forbid") trumps Edward's crass pragmatism ("For a kingdom any oath may be broken"), but Richard nonetheless offers indubitably instrumental thinking in his appeal to legal principle to rationalize York's perjury. Richard's advice is not only demonic, then, but also politically sophisticated, an effect that again recalls Skelton's moral vision of early Tudor politics.

Richard's instrumental reasoning in *3 Henry VI* is eventually identified explicitly with contemporary notions of its Italianate source, when Richard determines in soliloquy to "set the murderous Machiavel to school" (3.2.193) as he seeks to fulfill his ambition. Richard evokes not only Machiavelli's political realism, however, but also centuries of tradition on the English stage, and this tradition supplies a context for Richard that makes Shakespeare's political realism look very different from Machiavelli's. Richard's success in persuading his father and brothers reproduces the dynamics of temptation in countless earlier plays and anticipates his infamous seduction of Lady Anne in *Richard III*. The staging of temptation is an attempt to render allegorically the process of moral self-deception (above, chap. 1). But it is important for Shakespeare's version of the process that in the traditional course of persuading and corrupting a victim, the tempter is not deceived. In the morality play, *Wisdom*, for example, Satan is not imagined to be deceived himself when he deceives Anima's "mights"; only Anima is, and her self-deception is rendered through her self-division and the corruption of herself by her faculties. To put the allegorical point in abstract terms: though vice deceives the self, vice is not self-deceived. Similarly, in *3 Henry VI* and *Richard III*, Richard is not himself deceived, because he always knows what he wants, why he wants it, and how to get it.[28] He is, however, skilled in deceiving others, and his deception of them requires their deception of themselves—or in other words, they develop a moral false consciousness that what they know to be evil is really good. This is no less true of York and of Richard's brothers in *3 Henry VI* than it is of Lady Anne in *Richard III*. Like Anima in *Wisdom*, those who heed Richard are complicit in their own destruction, because they believe Richard's seductive falsehoods, even though part of them knows better than to do so; their self-division is a way of staging their self-deception.

Recognizing Richard's ability to exploit others' self-deception as he tempts them is important for two reasons. First, it suggests still another kind of moral limit to instrumental political thinking in Shakespeare's history plays. This limit is not new but derived from centuries of moral reflection and its dramatic enactment. "Interiority" was not an innovation in the Renaissance, and Shakespeare did not suddenly discover it in 1595.[29] On the contrary, it was familiar to audiences who had been (and continued to be) fascinated by morality plays, which routinely depicted the interior of the self as exterior to it by means of personification allegory as argued above in chapter 1.[30] This is not to equate the history plays with morality plays; Shakespeare's political realism is a secular departure from sacred history, as I have argued. Rather, I want to emphasize that Shakespeare consistently evoked traditional moral limitations, drawn from his own dramatic tradition, to secular political action, thereby creating in his history plays much more than spectacles of instrumental thinking. In contrast to Grady's argument, Derek Traversi and Donald Wineke have shown that the first tetralogy is just as analyzable in Machiavellian terms as the second, yet neither is a showcase of political pragmatism.[31] Shakespeare's political suspicion is informed by traditional moral insight, which prevents autonomous political realism from emerging in any of his plays.

Second, Shakespeare's reproduction of the familiar dynamics of self-deception from traditional drama shows how compatible pre-Enlightenment thinking is with Paul Ricoeur's idea of suspicion. As noted in chapter 1, Ricoeur argues that postmodern suspicion originates in the doubting of consciousness—a point that fundamentally unites the otherwise disparate thinking of Marx, Freud, and Nietzsche and distinguishes it from the Cartesian rationalism they came to suspect. This innovative postmodern doubt, however, is anticipated by pre-modern reflection on moral self-deception of the kind that informs Shakespeare's plays from the beginning. Where political suspicion and political realism are concerned, the difference between the two tetralogies is not, as Grady claims, that the first is providential and the second is Machiavellian,[32] because political realism is equally evident in both, and both raise suspicions about political claims to providential preference. Rather, the difference is that in the second tetralogy Shakespeare discovered how to internalize the personified allegory of self-deception in those who pursue power—a discovery he owed not to Machiavelli but apparently to his own reflection on dramatic technique.[33] The difference between *Richard III* and *Henry V*, in other words, is that in the process of seeking his own political ends, Henry deceives not only others but also himself. In the second tetralogy, Shakespeare imagines the divided self with no hint of personification, so that the last remnants of allegory— which originated in imagining the individual's moral situation as external to the soul—have disappeared.

Soliloquies, for example, are almost entirely absent in the second tetralogy, and the best-known one—Hal's comment on his role in the tavern in *1 Henry IV* 1.2—is not a revelation of the prince's self but of his political strategy, involving time and the calculated use of Falstaff and Hotspur in securing the prince's patrimony. His self is buried deeper than strategy, so that the description of his strategy is not a transparent revelation of himself but a manifestation of opaque false consciousness that he generates in the process of solidifying his political succession. The ambiguity of Hal's soliloquy is foreign to the self-revelations of Richard in *3 Henry VI* and *Richard III*.[34] Relative to the first tetralogy, the second consistently depicts selves that are opaque, and whose self-deception is inferable only from their context and their actions, because it is explicit neither in action external to them nor in information they divulge about themselves explicitly to us, their privileged auditors.

Bolingbroke in *Richard II* is a good example, for his opacity is remarkable: he has no soliloquy, and he never reveals his motives or his plans to any confidant. Nonetheless, his moral self-deception is inferable from several religious allusions in the play. Consider, by way of contrast, Mowbray's claim to innocence before the trial by combat at Coventry:

> If ever I were traitor,
> My name be blotted from the book of life,
> And I from heaven banished as from hence!
> But what thou art, God, thou, and I do know,

And all too soon, I fear, the King shall rue. (*Richard II* 1.3.201–5)

Swearing on his salvation, Mowbray denies that he is a traitor, perceptively identifies Bolingbroke's dissimulation, and accurately predicts
Bolingbroke's disloyalty to Richard. Mowbray's denial of treachery is
credible, since everything indicates that Mowbray was loyal to Richard,
even to the point of having sworn to assassinate Woodstock, though he
failed to follow through on it (1.1.132–34). His charges regarding
Bolingbroke may be lucky guesses, or they may indicate Mowbray's
political incisiveness, but they hardly serve to undercut his veracity.[35]
Mowbray lends credence to his claim of innocence, and incidentally to
his claim that Bolingbroke is untrustworthy, by not violating the terms
of his banishment, as Bolingbroke does, and by dying after a crusade
"in glorious Christian field" (4.1.93–101), far removed from the power
struggles of English politics. Both Richard and Bolingbroke are more
Machiavellian (i.e., politically opportunistic) than Mowbray in the scene
at Coventry. Richard says he stops the trial by combat because he hopes
to prevent further violence (*Richard II* 1.3.125–38), but if this is true, it
raises the question why he appointed the trial in the first place and
allows it to go as far as it does. A more likely reason for Richard to abort
the trial is that he cannot afford politically to let either combatant win,
and he believes his show of authority in banishing them will establish
his power convincingly—a misjudgment, as Mowbray predicts, and circumstances prove. Mowbray's pious assertion of his innocence at
Coventry thus makes him a foil to the maneuvering politicians around
him: to Richard first of all but also to Bolingbroke, whose real self the
king indeed comes to rue, in Mowbray's phrasing.[36] Bolingbroke is dis-
simulating, in other words, though he never admits it, and his silence on
the subject is what makes him opaque.

Bolingbroke's self-deception about his political ambition is most
strikingly implied in two references he makes to the story of Cain and
Abel—biblical allusions that contrast with Mowbray's oath. In the
play's first scene, Bolingbroke alleges that Mowbray is responsible for
the assassination of Thomas of Woodstock, Duke of Gloucester, and
condemns him indignantly for it:

> That he did plot the duke of Gloucester's death,
> Suggest his soon-believing adversaries,

> And consequently, like a traitor coward,
> Sluiced out his innocent soul through streams of blood—
> Which blood, like sacrificing Abel's, cries
> Even from the tongueless caverns of the earth
> To me for justice and rough chastisement. (1.1.100–6)

Bolingbroke shows an aptitude in these lines for strong political rhetoric—evoking a powerful myth to stigmatize a political rival. By characterizing Mowbray as Cain, Bolingbroke makes the point that Mowbray has violated kinship and therefore deserves the same reprobation as the primeval murderer of a brother. His language accompanies multiple appeals to personal honor, accusations of treachery, and other conventional signs of invoking "anger's privilege" on the part of the nobility.[37]

When Bolingbroke again alludes to Cain and Abel in the play's closing lines, however, he reveals something about himself that casts a different and more serious light on the earlier allusion. The later situation involves Pierce of Exton's presentation of Richard's dead body to the King. Confident that he has done Henry a favor by assassinating Richard, Exton offers the King "thy buried fear" (5.6.31) apparently expecting a reward, but Henry rejects him harshly:

> Though I did wish him dead,
> I hate the murderer, love him murderèd.
> The guilt of conscience take thou for thy labor,
> But neither my good word nor princely favor.
> With Cain go wander through the shades of night,
> And never show thy head by day nor light. (5.6.39–44)

That some part of Henry in fact identifies himself with Cain is evident in his own "guilt of conscience" that imbues his closing lines in the play (5.6.45–52), where he first declares his determination to "make a voyage to the Holy Land / To wash this blood off from my guilty hand"— a determination that seems indebted to Mowbray's death after a crusade (4.1.93–101) and that resurfaces in both *1* and *2 Henry IV*. Henry is indeed an effective politician; he is far more adept than Richard; and Exton believed that he was following Henry's instructions in murdering Richard (5.4.1–10 and 5.6.37). Yet it is impossible to avoid the word *ambivalence* in describing Henry's attitude in the play's closing scene, because he is so deeply divided against himself. Exton perceptively refers to Richard as Henry's "buried fear," but that fear is not removed by Richard's murder; if anything, Henry only buries it deeper, and his rejection of Exton is an attempt to reject part of himself that he can never get rid of—the same part that spoke of Cain earlier in terms of "justice and rough chastisement."[38] Henry's ambivalence demarcates the limits of his instrumental political actions, in that he half recognizes what he should not be doing, and thus anticipates Macbeth's sense of guilt. Though Henry never openly suspects his own consciousness in a soliloquy or aside, the play compels us to suspect it, thereby limiting political realism in moral psychology that Shakespeare inherited, in a less subtle but no less powerful form, from generations of English playwrights before him.

In contrast to Henry's determined evasion of self-knowledge, *Richard II* offers an example of dawning self-awareness that again acquires meaning from the cultural and dramatic tradition in which it appears. Grady argues that Richard's soliloquy in Pomfret Castle reveals "a remarkable (and Montaignean) view of the possibilities of multiple identities within subjectivity," because Richard imagines "in one person many people" (5.5.31).[39] It is not necessary, however, to invoke Montaigne to explain these lines, for Richard is thinking about himself in a manner familiar from centuries of allegory about the self, as he had earlier thought about himself conventionally as a mortal man, subject to death, despite his kingly status (3.2.160–77). He imagines his brain and his soul together begetting various thoughts that "people this world" (i.e., himself [5.5.9]), and he identifies three classes of such thoughts that correspond to recognized social estates: "the better sort, / As thoughts of things divine" (11—the clergy); "Thoughts tending to ambition" (18—the nobility); and "Thoughts tending to content" (23—the commons, whom Shakespeare's kings tend to imagine as more contented than themselves).[40] The thoughts of "the better sort" that occur to Richard at this point are paradoxes from the gospels:

> "Come, little ones,"
And then again,
"It is as hard to come as for a camel
To thread the postern of a small needle's eye." (5.5.14–17)

The thoughts that Richard imagines "ruling" him as the "better sort" at this stage of his life, in other words, are leveling thoughts that make everyone equal before God, no matter what their wealth, social status, or political power.[41] Following this train of thought, Richard comes to a

self-recognition that anticipates the parallel and hard-won insight of
King Lear:

> But whate'er I be,
> Nor I, nor any man that but man is,
> With nothing shall be pleased till he be eased
> With being nothing. (5.5.38–41)

Where knowledge of himself is concerned, Richard is thus in the opposite position from Bolingbroke, and Richard achieves an insight about
his creaturely dependence (that he has been "eased / With being nothing") that Bolingbroke never achieves, despite (or perhaps because of)
Bolingbroke's preoccupation with power, by means of which he
incurred the guilt he attempts to suppress for deposing Richard and
wishing him dead.

The limits of political realism in *Richard II* therefore consist not in
subjectivity per se but in the reality of moral self-deception, with its concomitant potential for self-recognition, which for Richard involves the
recognition that he is not defined by social status and political power:

> Sometimes am I king;
> Then treason makes me wish myself a beggar,
> And so I am. Then crushing penury
> Persuades me I was better when a king;
> Then am I kinged again, and by and by
> Think that I am unkinged by Bolingbroke,
> And straight am nothing. (5.5.32–38)

Like King Robert of Sicily, in the analogue to Lear that Maynard Mack
cites, Richard comes to himself in "crushing penury":

> "What artou?" seide the angel.
>   "Sire, a fol; that wot I wel,
> And more then fol, yif hit may be;
> Kep I non other dignité."[42]

Suspicion of the self is not infinite in Shakespeare's history plays, as it
seems to be in Machiavelli. It is limited by its origin in a moral understanding of self-deception and, in Richard's case, by the possibility of
self-recognition of a particular and traditional kind. The counterpart in
comedy is Duke Senior's affirmation of the rigors of wilderness and
weather, because "these are counselors / That feelingly persuade me

what I am" (*As You Like It* 2.1.10–11). Richard faces only the rigor of political defeat, as Duke Senior once did, but it also has the effect of making him recognize what "man is."

To be sure, Richard's self-recognition has no political utility—that is, it makes no political difference—and because it takes place in a history play, it is therefore pushed aside by the action in a way that self-recognition is not in the comedies and tragedies. Richard's insight occurs at the end of his story, but it is not the end of the play, because time does not come to a stop for him any more than it does for Hotspur or for Henry V. The virtue of Richard's self-recognition is not in what it achieves politically but in itself, because the standard of value in question is not utilitarian; indeed, political effectiveness and self-recognition seem to be mutually exclusive in this play. Richard comes to himself only when he is shorn of power, and Bolingbroke never acquires Richard's insight. Richard's dying words see the world of history (i.e., political struggle) *sub specie aeternitatis*, a perspective that implicitly defines the limits of history in all the history plays: "Mount, mount, my soul! Thy seat is up on high, / Whilst my gross flesh sinks downward, here to die" (5.5.111–12). Machiavelli may hint at a wider perspective, as Bacon suggests in his comment about "what men . . . ought to do," but it is irrelevant to Machiavelli's concern, because knowing what one ought to do has, by definition, no political utility. For Shakespeare, as for Machiavelli, the quest for power requires dissimulation, but in the second tetralogy and in *Julius Caesar*, Shakespeare imagines self-deception as a second and equally compelling consequence of the quest for power.[43]

Henry IV occasionally tries to confront his self-deception, as we noticed, in allusions to undertaking a crusade, which he seems to believe would absolve the guilt he has suppressed for deposing Richard. What prevents his crusade is the pressure of time—"for this cause *awhile* we must neglect / Our holy purpose to Jerusalem" (*1 Henry IV* 1.1.100–1, my emphasis), and postponing the crusade thus has the effect of deepening Henry's deception of himself by making him believe, if only temporarily, that he is as good as his holiest intentions, which are never realized. The pressure of time also prevents his son from stepping off the linear treadmill of history, thereby removing himself from the struggle to maintain political dominance, even though nearly everyone thinks he is taking just that kind of holiday in the tavern. Hal immedi-

ately echoes his father in his first soliloquy: "I will . . . *awhile* uphold /
The unyoked humor of your idleness" (1.2.189–90, my emphasis), making clear that he is in fact "Redeeming time when men least think I will"
(211). His exquisite attention to time is evidence of his commitment to
securing his patrimony, thereby ensuring his political dominance while
deceiving himself about his commitment to anything besides secular
history—especially God, to whom he ascribes his victory in *Henry V*.

Hal's first soliloquy complements his last, in which he conceals himself most successfully from himself. This soliloquy is in *Henry V* (Hal has
no soliloquies in *2 Henry IV*), when the young King turns to God in
prayer on the eve of the battle of Agincourt. Trapped and heavily out-
numbered by the French, Henry prays before one of the most celebrated victories in English history:

> O God of battles, steel my soldiers' hearts;
> Possess them not with fear! Take from them now
> The sense of reckoning, ere th' opposèd numbers
> Pluck their hearts from them. Not today, O Lord,
> O, not today, think not upon the fault
> My father made in compassing the crown!
> I Richard's body have interrèd new,
> And on it have bestowed more contrite tears
> Than from it issued forcèd drops of blood.
> Five hundred poor I have in yearly pay
> Who twice a day their withered hands hold up
> Toward heaven, to pardon blood; and I have built
> Two chantries, where the sad and solemn priests
> Sing still for Richard's soul. More will I do;
> Though all that I can do is nothing worth,
> Since that my penitence comes after all,
> Imploring pardon. (4.1.287–303)

Since virtually every auditor who witnesses this prayer knows the outcome of the battle, it seems to be a self-evident and uncomplicated
example of God answering prayer positively: Shakespeare wrote a
prayer for Henry that the playwright knew would be answered in
Henry's favor.

Several features of the prayer, however, demand that it be regarded
suspiciously, because it is not a revelation of Henry's self before God
but a successful effort at self-evasion and therefore an exercise in self-
deception.[44] The prayer involves four thoughts: (1) Henry asks God to
give his soldiers courage; (2) he asks God to overlook the means by

which Henry's father gained the throne (Henry IV clearly passed on his burden of guilt about the succession to his son); (3) he reminds God of what he has already done for Richard's soul; (4) he promises to do even more but acknowledges that he can never do enough. The move from the first of these thoughts to the second is sudden and surprising, and the connection seems to be the phrase "the sense of reckoning." Referring immediately to the disparity in size between the English and French forces ("reckoning" as enumeration), the phrase also refers to the debt Henry owes God ("reckoning" as accounting of a sum owed).[45] As potential impediments to Henry's success, the prayer thus links the guilt Henry feels about the way his father acquired the throne with his soldiers' possible lack of courage. The guilt Henry feels, moreover, is clearly more serious to him than his soldiers' fear, judging from the amount of time he devotes to each of the two topics in his prayer, and since he nowhere else mentions his guilt, it seems that he is baring his soul before God in a way that he never does elsewhere. (This sense of guilt was deeply buried, for example, when Henry trapped and destroyed Richard Earl of Cambridge, who was Richard II's heir [*Henry V* 2.2].) If we ask what motivates his soul-baring at Agincourt, however, the prayer emerges as more self-deceived than self-knowing, because this part of the prayer is just as clearly linked to victory as the first part. That is, when Henry acknowledges that he is in debt to God but asks God to overlook that debt in the coming battle, the implication is clear: a victory will be the sign that God overlooked the debt. Henry both admits his guilt, then, and withdraws his admission at the same time by bargaining with God not to act in a way that would recognize the guilt, because that recognition would be politically inconvenient for Henry in the present circumstances.

This seems to be one implication of his prayer's closing lines, in which he promises to do even more for Richard's soul and then concedes (with apparent frankness and piety) that "all that I can do is nothing worth, / Since that my penitence comes after all." As Gary Taylor points out, these are ambiguous lines, depending on what the second "all" means: everything Henry has done (to assuage his guilt); everything Henry can still do (to assuage it); or everything his father did (to incur the guilt in the first place).[46] It is important to note that the third possibility can mean something more as well (and it follows logically from what Henry has just been saying): "all" can mean everything Henry V has gained and hopes to gain as king, including the conquest of France. Taken this way, Henry is admitting that as long as he stands to gain from his father's guilty action, he can do nothing to assuage that guilt except "implore pardon." This request too, however, is disingenuous and self-deceived, for Henry again hopes to retain the very thing that he acknowledges, before God, he should not have.[47]

One way of reading Henry's prayer is that it invites skepticism about all prayer. As Stanley Cavell remarks in another context, "the problem with prayers is not that few are answered but that *all* are, one way or the other."[48] Cavell seems to read prayer suspiciously by suggesting that the answer to prayer is in the eye of the beholder—knowledge that a prayer has been answered (or not), in other words, depends on how one interprets the outcome—and the "answer" is therefore not knowledge (the skeptic's primary interest) but something like wish-fulfillment. Cavell's critique applies to Henry, because he prays for God to remove the impediments to his victory, and he gets a resounding victory. But the problem lies in interpreting it any other way. Even the French would have a hard time disbelieving in the success of Henry's prayer, given his amazing success in battle, and Henry would obviously delight in their belief, because it supports his own belief in God's apparent forgetfulness of "the fault / My father made in compassing the crown." The conclusion that the prayer as Shakespeare penned it (knowing the result, of course) functions as a skeptical argument against all prayer seems less certain than that the prayer raises questions about this king's *motivation* in these circumstances. Shakespeare more clearly invites suspicion of Henry's motive in praying than skepticism about prayer per se.

Reinforcing this point is Henry's declaration of what he has done to assuage his guilt for Richard's death. Prayers for the dead were a central point of contention between Catholics and Protestants, and chantries had been banned during the reign of Edward VI in 1547 (the ban was renewed by Edward's sister Elizabeth—still reigning when Shakespeare wrote *Henry V*—after her accession in 1558).[49] Shakespeare could have included this detail for historical effect, of course: Henry V lived and died long before the Reformation, so he knew nothing of the Protestant controversy and in fact was a determined defender of the traditional church against the proto-Protestants called Lollards. But historical effect is not usually the point in Shakespeare's history plays. In fact, this is the only detail in *Henry V* that definitively distinguishes

Henry from a Protestant king of England.[50] Moreover, prayers for the dead invited some of the bitterest attacks against traditional religion in England. Simon Fish's anonymous little book, *A Supplication for the Beggars* (1529) argued sarcastically that the problem of dire poverty in England could be resolved by taking the money lavished on chantries and distributing it among the destitute.[51] Shakespeare perhaps glances at Fish's point in his phrase "five hundred poor," since the number of poor people in England in 1599 (as in 1529) far exceeded 500, and if that is all Henry's chantries are helping, then they are doing only a very little to alleviate poverty, and what little they are doing is designed to enhance Henry's position before God. In short, the vaguely anti-papal detail in Henry's prayer arguably links it with the kind of strategic skepticism that English Protestants used to assail papal authority, and they may well have learned that skepticism from More and Erasmus (above, chap. 1).

The suspicion raised by Henry's prayer is clarified by the thoughts of another Shakespearean king, penned very shortly after *Henry V*. This king is Claudius in *Hamlet* (1599–1601), whose lines function virtually as a commentary on the prayer in *Henry V*, in that both involve guilt about occupying the throne on the part of the current occupant. Paradoxically, however, for a play as fraught with ironic uncertainty as *Hamlet*, Claudius's prayer (or more precisely, his attempt to pray) moves its auditors in the direction of certainty rather than suspicion. Claudius's rhetorical question, "May one be pardoned and retain th' offense?" is the point of contact between the two kings' prayers, and it summarizes Claudius's reasoning in the lines that precede it:

> But O, what form of prayer
> Can serve my turn? "Forgive me my foul murder"?
> That cannot be, since I am still possessed
> Of those effects for which I did the murder:
> My crown, mine own ambition, and my queen. (*Hamlet* 3.3.51–55)

Insofar as Henry V's second "all" (in "More will I do; / Though all that I can do is nothing worth, / Since that my penitence comes after all") means "all I have gained by my father's guilty accession to the throne and my own determination to maintain royal power," Henry V means the same thing Claudius says—that one may not be pardoned as long as one retains the offense.[52] But Claudius says something else that helps to interpret Henry's prayer:

In the corrupted currents of this world
Offense's gilded hand may shove by justice,
And oft 'tis seen the wicked prize itself
Buys out the law. But 'tis not so above.
There is no shuffling, there the action lies
In his true nature, and we ourselves compelled,
Even to the teeth and forehead of our faults,
To give in evidence. (3.3.57–64)

This is a point that Henry V never acknowledges, in his prayer or otherwise: that whereas wealth, status, and power in "this world" may "shove by justice," before God "there is no shuffling."[53] "Shuffling" describes precisely what Henry V does in his prayer, and what defines it is one's recognition that human actions and motives are limited by divine justice—both "above," as Claudius puts it, and at the Last Judgment. "Shuffling," however, is also an excellent way to describe self-deception, and given the political context, it is a fairly precise premodern synonym for Marx's postmodern phrase, "false consciousness."

The searing honesty of Claudius's soliloquy not only contrasts with Henry's self-deceived avoidance of the truth but also ironically provides a surprising point of certainty in *Hamlet*. For Claudius's soliloquy is the only firm evidence in the play that he is guilty of old Hamlet's death: "O, my offense is rank! It smells to heaven, / It hath the primal eldest curse upon 't, / A brother's murder" (3.3.36–38).[54] Hamlet eventually comes to mistrust the ghost (2.2.599–605), and his next recourse (the play-within-the-play) clarifies nothing, despite Hamlet's confidence that it does. He specifically identifies the murderer in *The Murder of Gonzago* as "one Lucianus, nephew to the King" (3.2.242) and therefore directly parallel to Prince Hamlet himself. To everyone who is not privy to the king's guilt (i.e., to everyone but Claudius himself, with the possible exception of Gertrude), Claudius's response to the play would obviously indicate his fear of a coup d'état on the part of his nephew. The weight of apparent evidence against Hamlet is increased by the fact that Claudius nowhere says anything to indicate his suspicion that Hamlet knows about old Hamlet's murder, though Claudius obviously must suspect it after he has seen the play. Since Claudius knows nothing about the ghost, he has no reason to suspect that Hamlet knows about the murder before the staging of *The Murder of Gonzago*. After the play, Claudius says nothing to indicate that he thinks Hamlet knows, presumably because his political fear of Hamlet as a rival is stronger than his fear of Hamlet as one who has somehow found out the truth about the murder. Claudius's infallible political instincts seem to make him aware that he is safest to carry on as if no one else suspects him, even if Hamlet does. Claudius's ordering Rosencrantz and Guildenstern to spy on Hamlet and his abetting Laertes' attempts at vengeance both seem explicable in terms of Claudius's fear of Hamlet as a rival, no matter how old Hamlet died. Claudius possibly fears discovery, as any murderer does, though he never admits his fear, but he certainly fears rivalry, as any ambitious politician must, and he says so repeatedly.

In short, without Claudius's admission of guilt, the principal question in criticism of *Hamlet* would not be why Hamlet delays but whether or not Claudius is guilty. Claudius's obvious statement of his guilt is arguably the most important passage in the play. It is nonpartisan, in that Christians of every persuasion would have assented to it without hesitation. It substantiates the ghost's claim, if not the particulars of the ghost's description.[55] It clarifies Claudius's response to *The Murder of Gonzago* and his earlier aside about his guilty conscience. It helps to vindicate Hamlet's course of action, given the ghost's injunction. It blackens Claudius irrevocably, because it shows him in a moment of absolute candor, considering a radical change in his life, yet unable to give up what he has already gained by murdering his brother, seducing his brother's wife, and covering up his crime so successfully that no one but Hamlet suspects him. Only by relying on an audience's belief in the possibility of repentance can Shakespeare clarify not only Claudius's guilt but the reality of Hamlet's situation as well. At this particular moment in *Hamlet*, faith in the possibility of repentance overwhelms suspicion—at least for us who hear Claudius's thoughts about prayer.

The irony, of course, is that Hamlet hears neither those thoughts nor Claudius's admission that his attempt to pray is ineffectual. Hamlet refrains from killing Claudius in the belief that the kneeling Claudius is repenting, whereas Claudius admits that his attempt to repent is unsuccessful.[56] Hamlet lacks our definitive knowledge of Claudius's guilt, because Hamlet does not hear Claudius's confession. Missing Claudius's admission that his prayer is empty means that Hamlet fails to act because of false confidence that what he sees (an act of repentance) is what he thinks it is. These are all ironies that defeat Hamlet and deepen his tragedy, but Shakespeare gives us knowledge that he withholds from

Hamlet, and our knowledge makes all the difference. Claudius is no skeptic; he is a consummately clever and determined sinner, and Hamlet is right to suspect him from the outset:

> O villain, villain, smiling, damnèd villain!
> My tables—meet it is I set it down
> That one may smile, and smile, and be a villain. (1.5.107–9)

We know with absolute certainty that Hamlet is right to suspect Claudius, however, only because we are granted knowledge that is privy to Claudius and to God alone, and this knowledge, revealed to us by the playwright, definitively reveals Claudius's suspicious duplicity—though to Hamlet that duplicity is impenetrable, however strongly he suspects it. The king's admission is what makes *Hamlet* more than a remarkable esthetic achievement: it makes the play a challenging vision of human uncertainty in a distinctively religious setting that is charged with profound moral seriousness.

That seriousness, moreover, underpins Shakespeare's political thinking even in his most secular plays, where it appears to be least evident. Shakespeare was no less insightful than Machiavelli about the infinite resourcefulness of instrumental thinking, and he embodied that resourcefulness in plays about historical process, which for him, as for Machiavelli, meant political process. Where Shakespeare departs most profoundly from Machiavelli is in his affirmation of moral limitation— not in the political process itself, whose exclusive end is the acquiring and maintaining of political power, but in the human situation that encompasses kings and commoners alike, whether the first are willing to admit it or not. Shakespeare's most successful politicians are the most self-deceived, because self-knowledge comes only with the acknowledgment of human limitations, and politicians, as Machiavelli well knew, need to act as if nothing limits them, least of all moral scruples. Shakespeare knew this too, but his politicians suffer, in ways that Machiavelli's prince never does, because they attempt to deny limitations that their world nonetheless imposes on them.

ETHICS

O hateful Error, Melancholy's child,
Why dost thou show to the apt thoughts of men
The things that are not?

Julius Caesar 5.3.67–69

Oh, that you could turn your eyes toward the napes of your necks and
make but an interior survey of your good selves! Oh, that you could!

Coriolanus 2.1.38–41

For Shakespeare's contemporaries, on both sides of the Catholic/
Protestant divide, questions about ethics were inseparable from religion—not because of a simplified divine-command theory, but because
God was perfect goodness. "Godliness," Hooker asserts, is "the cheifest
top and welpsringe of all true virtues, even as God is of all good
thinges."[1] Addressing the ethical question in Shakespeare's plays is
therefore, in this sense, impossible to address without addressing the
religious question. Shakespeare's drama does not consist of animated
moral abstractions, as in the morality play, but the words and actions of
his imagined characters are morally meaningful, especially when taken
in conjunction with the shape of their story. In the continuum of
Christian destiny between Creation and Last Judgment, characters
understand goodness imperfectly, being deceived or self-deceived or
both, or if they do understand goodness, they fail or refuse to act on it,
as Macbeth does. In the comedies—and sometimes even in the
tragedies—understanding and actions improve, so that self-division,
mistrust, vengeance, and pride give way to self-understanding, trust,
and reconciliation, both for individuals and their communities, in ways
that are recognizably Christian—not because the stories are literally

161

biblical or allegorical, as they were in the religious drama that preceded Shakespeare's, but because characters' words and actions enact distinctive Christian virtues and usually acknowledge their origin in meaningful allusive patterns.

Stoic Ethics

In some plays, however, a different set of ethical expectations is evident, and these plays provide a useful contrast, by default, to those discussed already, especially since virtue in these plays is not as closely tied to religion as Christian virtue is. The medieval distinction between cardinal and theological virtues is helpful here, because Shakespeare consistently identified ancient pre-Christian Rome with stoic ethics, creating an implicit contrast between two sets of ethical assumptions.[2] This contrast is complicated by the fact that stoicism was ambivalently favored in the Renaissance, and that neo-stoicism, as it is called, became a court fashion late in the century; stoic principles therefore affect non-Roman plays as well, as we shall see. Still, one way that Shakespeare distinguishes the Roman world is by imagining characters who live according to the stoic assumption that moral perfection is not only desirable but achievable, and his plays explore the ambiguities of that assumption with increasing subtlety and skepticism.

The simplest and most obvious of these ambiguities is the gap between the philosophical ideal of perfect self-control and the failure to achieve it in fact. Recognition of this gap parallels recognition of the difference between Christian moral affirmation and characters' actions in other plays—a skeptical acknowledgment that is biblical in origin and had been articulated most influentially in the sixteenth century by Erasmus and More. Critique of the stoic quest for self-perfection originated in ancient skepticism and cynicism, and whether Shakespeare knew that critique or not, he imagined it in plays very near the beginning of his career. The comic impetus in *Love's Labor's Lost* derives from the difference between affirmation and practice in "the little academe" proposed by the King of Navarre (1.1.13). Leonato avers in *Much Ado* that "there was never yet philosopher / That could endure the toothache patiently, / However they have writ the style of gods / And made a push at chance and sufferance" (5.1.35–38).

A more complex ambiguity in Shakespeare's exploration of stoic ethics is the conjunction of perfect self-consistency with the assumption that the ability to achieve this state is exclusive to patricians, thus implicitly raising the question whether virtue was determined by oneself or by one's socially defined public role. A commonplace stoic comparison of the wise man to an actor makes this ambiguity clear, for the comparison both emphasizes the need to conform to whatever fortune puts in one's way and raises the possibility that virtue is an act put on for others' benefit and therefore, in effect, determined by them. Cicero urges that we should strive to know ourselves, "else it will seem that actors have more good sense than us. For they do not choose the best plays, but those that are most suited to themselves. . . . If an actor, then, will observe this on the stage, will not a wise man observe it in his life?"[3] Cicero's "we" is clearly not universal; since he contrasts "us" with actors, "wise man" therefore seems to mean "patrician." "But bear it as our Roman actors do," urges Brutus in *Julius Caesar*, "With untired spirits and formal constancy" (2.1227–28).[4]

A related but more subtle ambiguity arguably operates throughout Shakespeare's first Roman play, *Titus Andronicus*, though the play seems to endorse it, rather than call critical attention to it, as *Coriolanus* does.[5] This particular ambiguity involves the tendency of rigorous Senecan self-consistency to become the opposite of itself the more consistently it is pursued.[6] "Turned from a metaphor of spiritual strength into a literal superman," Miles observes, "the Stoic hero becomes a disturbingly ambiguous figure," and he cites Seneca's mad Hercules as an example.[7] Gordon Braden argues that this ambiguity derives from the competitiveness of the Greek and Roman warrior ethos, which became self-competitive and therefore self-destructive when it had no other competitor, as in the empire.[8] "If you want the wise man to be as angry as the atrocity of men's crimes requires, he must not merely be angry, but must go mad with rage," urges Seneca, tellingly attributing an overwhelming competitive passion (righteous indignation to the point of madness) with "the wise man."[9] His comment is an apt description of what happens in *Titus Andronicus*.

Resemblance between Titus and Hercules *furens* thus goes beyond Shakespeare's formal imitation of Senecan tragedy, outlined above in chapter 3. To be sure, Titus's heightened style is an early attempt on Shakespeare's part to achieve an answerable high style, and it therefore

assumes the ancient concept of rhetorical decorum, whereby each subject is treated according to the level of style appropriate to it. But Titus
also manifests what might be described as moral decorum in Cicero,
that is, a standard of stoic virtue that is appropriate to patrician status.[10]
Titus's arresting and magnificent style is thus appropriate to him not
only as the most patrician character but also as the most consistent with
himself, that is, the most morally perfect by stoic expectations. Both
rhetorically and morally, he thus demonstrates perfect decorum. Such a
conjunction of rhetoric and ethics is suggested in Horace's advocacy of
decorum in *Ars Poetica*, as translated by Ben Jonson:

> The comic matter will not be expressed
> In tragic verse; no less Thyestes' feast
> Abhors low numbers and the private strain
> Fit for the sock: each subject should retain
> The place allotted it with decent thews.[11]

Horace distinguishes comedy and tragedy as "low" and "high" genres,
respectively, and he advocates an appropriate selection of subject matter according to genre: common subjects for comedy and noble subjects
for tragedy. This principle helps to explain why Titus, a patrician, is a
"decent" hero for *Titus Andronicus*, a tragedy. Shakespeare seems almost
to have written *Titus* with one eye on this passage in Horace, given the
climactic Thyestean feast in his first tragedy.

   Still, Titus is technically outranked by Saturninus, the emperor, and
this slight departure from rhetorical decorum in Shakespeare's first
tragedy might best be explained by moral decorum, which Horace also
advocates in *Ars Poetica*:

> Or follow fame, thou that dost write, or fain
> Things in themselves agreeing. If again,
> Honored Achilles chance by thee be seized,
> Keep him still active, angry, unappeased;
> Sharp and condemning laws at him should aim,
> Be nought so 'above him but his sword let claim.
> . . . .
> If something strange that never yet was had
> Unto the scene thou bringst and dar'st create
> A mere new person, look he keep his state
> Unto the last, as when he first went forth,
> Still to be like himself, and hold his worth. (170–82)

Horace admonishes poets or playwrights to imagine characters according to their "worth," and his language, as Miles points out, borrows from notions of stoic self-consistency: "Things in themselves agreeing"; "still to be like himself."[12] Self-consistency thus implicitly overrides the more familiar stoic expectation of self-containment, as in Seneca's remark about the wise man going mad with rage, and Horace's example of "Honored Achilles" makes the point well for Shakespeare's Titus: even though "Sharp and condemning laws" might "aim" at him, he remains above them in being "like himself" as a hero without peer, especially in his titanic rage—an expression of himself that bursts the bounds of conventional expectation and shows how much he has in common with Achilles.[13] Titus "keeps his state," in Jonson's phrasing, "unto the last, as when he first went forth." Though his stoic self-consistency thus looks like a failure of self-containment, it is really a form of patrician self-expression that makes him more heroic than the treacherous Saturninus, who, though he technically outranks Titus, allies himself, both politically and through marriage, with Tamora, the anti-Roman barbarian queen and a character more treacherous even than Saturninus, in that she betrays him as well as Titus.[14]

THE RAPE OF LUCRECE

As a character conceived in the stoic vein, Titus has a Roman counterpart in Shakespeare's Lucrece, whose story is invoked several times in *Titus Andronicus* in a way that sheds light both on this play and on *The Rape of Lucrece*.[15] Though the most obvious parallel is between the two rape victims, Lucrece and Lavinia, the most illuminating comparison is between Lucrece and Titus, because of their patrician self-consistency. The gendered Virgilian contrast between unwavering Roman champion and bewitching foreign queen, reproduced precisely in *Titus*, is reversed in *Lucrece*, where the heroine is a constant Roman, and her violator is a wavering intruder—wavering, that is, not in his passionate violation but in his inability to resist pursuing it. Tarquin's self-division is the focus of the extended struggle with himself that Shakespeare describes before the rape: "for himself himself he must forsake" (157); "he himself himself confounds" (160); and his moral false consciousness is evident in the rationalization he invents to excuse his actions

(267–80). Shakespeare describes this division frequently in personification allegory, which is a post-classical influence, derived from Prudentius by way of medieval didactic poetry, the morality play, and Spenser's *The Faerie Queene*:

> Besides, his soul's fair temple is defaced,
> To whose weak ruins muster troops of cares
> To ask the spotted princess how she fares.

> She says her subjects with foul insurrection
> Have battered down her consecrated wall,
> And by their moral fault brought in subjection
> Her immortality . . . . (719–26)

This passage reproduces the central conceit of *The Castle of Perseverance* (1380–1425) and recalls the corruption of Anima in *Wisdom* (1400–1450), but what is at stake in Tarquin's self-division is not the loss of his immortal soul; it is the loss of "his honor" and "his princely name" (599), in which his noble constancy properly consists, as Lucrece emphasizes when she tells him, "Thou art not what thou seem'st" (600).[16] As a rhyme phrase, "foul appetite" in Tarquin is contrasted with "gentle right," that is, with behavior appropriate to a nobleman—one of gentle birth (545–46). He and Collatine, Lucrece's husband, are close friends and comrades-in-arms, their patrician honor valorized by their military accomplishments, as Tarquin makes clear in praising Collatine when he is trying to seduce Lucrece (106–110).[17] What Tarquin gives up, then, when he rapes Lucrece, is precisely what makes Titus heroic, that is, his moral decorum, evident until the rape in Tarquin's noble soldiership and his ability to remain "like himself."

As the chaste Lavinia is the female counterpart to her father in *Titus Andronicus*, acknowledging his "true nobility" and "princely courtesy" when he gives her in marriage to Saturninus (1.1.272–73), so Lucrece is the moral opposite (as well as the gendered opposite) of Tarquin, as her response to the rape makes clear. "She hath lost a dearer thing than life," observes the narrator (687), referring both to her chastity (cf. "Lucrece the chaste" [7]) and to her honor as a patrician Roman wife—the complement to Collatine's honor as a patrician soldier. "Let my good name, that senseless reputation, / For Collatine's dear love be kept unspotted," laments Lucrece after the rape (820–21), hinting at suicide as the only means by which she can regain (or retain) her patrician honor and thus undo what Tarquin has done. Only by ending her life can she remain "like herself"—a familiar stoic paradox. Her suicide is thus highly principled according to stoic assumptions, as her repetition of "resolution" suggests, when she imagines how she will explain her suicide to her husband:[18]

> "Dear lord of that dear jewel I have lost,
> What legacy shall I bequeath to thee?
> My resolution, love, shall be thy boast,
> By whose example thou revenged mayst be.
> . . . .
>
> "My resolution, husband, do thou take;
> Mine honor be the knife's that makes my wound;
> My shame be his that did my fame confound;
>   And all my fame that lived disbursèd be
>   To those that live and think no shame of me." (1191–1204)

Though she lacks Collatine's physical strength, she retains his martial virtues in her suicide—as her repeated contrast of "fame" and "shame" makes clear—declaring her courage, her constancy, and her victory, when she determines to kill herself:

> "Faint not, faint heart, but stoutly say, 'So be it.'
>   Yield to my hand; my hand shall conquer thee.
>   Thou dead, both die, and both shall victors be." (1209–11)

Perhaps the most important evidence of stoic assumptions animating the actions of both Titus and Lucrece is their linking of honor and revenge. When Lucrece rehearses her justification for suicide in her own mind, she emphasizes vengeance, as in the passage quoted above, and she returns to this theme when she requires the beholders of her suicide to swear that they will avenge her (1681–98). She believes that her suicide wreaks vengeance on Tarquin by defeating his purpose in polluting her honor, but vengeance will only be complete when Tarquin has paid for sullying her husband's honor, as well as hers—and even for sullying his own: "Be suddenly revengèd on my foe, / Thine, mine, his own" (1683–84). That Tarquin can be avenged on himself may seem odd, but it makes sense in the competitive terms of stoic ethics, which, as Braden argues, supply the philosophical counterpart to the warrior aristocrat's fame in arms.[19] Since Tarquin defeated his own honor in polluting Lucrece's, Tarquin has become his own enemy, and his enemies therefore paradoxically do him a favor by killing him—in effect, avenging him on himself.[20] Where vengeance is concerned, Titus's grandson

similarly expects Titus merely to kill his persecutors, but Titus has a better idea: "I'll teach thee another course" (4.1.120). Echoing this determination again later, he declares that he "will o'erreach them in their
own devices" (5.2.143), as he proceeds to do in the Thyestean feast he
presents to Tamora. His revenge is just as extraordinary as everything
else about him, proving that he remains like himself to the end, a patrician warrior whose self-consistency makes him a paradoxical model of
stoic sagacity driven mad with titanic rage, as Seneca puts it, by the
atrocity of crimes in a wicked world.

  The Rape of Lucrece and *Titus Andronicus* were both written early in
Shakespeare's career, and they arguably represent the most sympathetic
treatment of stoic ethics in his works. For some reason, his plays became
increasingly critical of stoic assumptions, even as the playwright seems
to have become increasingly knowledgeable about them.[21] In *Love's
Labor's Lost*, he treats four young noblemen satirically, when they take an
oath to live entirely devoid of desire or excess for three years—an oath
they are unable to keep, because they are unable to remain "like themselves" for even a few days, despite their social rank (one of them is a
king). Another early comedy, *The Taming of the Shrew*, begins with a
young gentleman, Tranio, piously determining to study "Virtue and
that part of philosophy / Will I apply that treats of happiness / By
virtue specially to be achieved" (1.1.18–20), while his more knowing servant urges, "Let's be no stoics nor not stocks, I pray" (31)—and the servant's view prevails, though Tranio never acknowledges that it does. I
have argued that Shakespeare discovered a new way to write tragedy in
Romeo and Juliet, drawing on what he had learned in writing comedy and
departing entirely from the Senecan model he had imitated closely in
Titus. Contemporary with *Romeo* is *A Midsummer Night's Dream*, which
parodies early Elizabethan translations of Seneca in the hilarious bom-
bast uttered as "lofty" verse by Bottom, when he offers to "play Ercles
rarely" (1.2.34, 24–25).[22] *Midsummer* seems deliberately to muddle both
moral and rhetorical decorum, and Shakespeare never again showed
such deference to classical expectations as he had in his earlier works.
Duke Theseus may be "like himself"—royal, rational, patriarchal, and
decisive—as he prepares to marry, but he appears in a comedy, where
he rubs shoulders, albeit somewhat stiffly, with common craftsmen, and
Oberon makes clear that Theseus has, in his time, been no less influenced by the fairies than the young lovers are in the action we witness

(2.1.74–80). Far from English deferring to Latin, as in *Titus*, English folklore enjoys a more compelling imaginative place than classical legend in *Midsummer*; Theseus does not believe in the fairies (5.1.2–22), but they have gathered in Athens to bless his marriage bed (5.1.392–401), and they—not the Athenian duke—literally have the last word. Again, where moral decorum is concerned, the "great constancy" that Hippolyta praises has nothing to do with stoic self-consistency but with "the story of the night" in the forest and "minds transfigured so together"—presumably a reference to the change in the young lovers, which parallels the change in *Romeo and Juliet* (above, chap. 3).

JULIUS CAESAR

When Shakespeare returned to Roman subject matter again in *Julius Caesar* (1599), he displayed the ambiguities of stoicism compellingly, in contrast to his practice in *Titus* and *Lucrece*, which take stoic assumptions pretty much at face value. The cobbler who comically identifies himself as "a mender of bad soles" in the first scene appeals to his conscience and declares that when shoes "are in great danger, I recover them" (1.1.13-24). His wordplay on "souls" and his emphasis on the interior life preview the play's focus on the cultivation of virtue by Rome's greatest citizens, who cannot succeed in their task, unlike the cobbler in his, because they have nothing to recover them. Despite their insistent appeals to honor and nobility, and despite Caesar's belief that he remains "constant as the northern star" (3.1.61), each is in fact divided against himself, and all are divided against one another, because their greatest virtue—their determination to remain self-consistent, autonomous, and unaffected by change—is paradoxically the source of their failure. Lucilius bravely impersonates Brutus at the battle of Philippi in order to protect Brutus from Antony's onslaught, but when Antony captures him, Lucilius denies that Brutus has been captured as well, because he is so confident of Brutus's stoic constancy:

> I dare assure thee that no enemy
> Shall ever take alive the noble Brutus.
> The gods defend him from so great a shame!
> When you do find him, or alive or dead,
> He will be found like Brutus, like himself. (5.4.21–25)

Lucilius' point is that the real Brutus, acknowledged by his mortal enemy Antony to be "the noblest Roman of them all" (5.5.68), can never be captured, because he will never surrender his principles, and Lucilius is right. Brutus perfectly embodies the moral decorum that Ben Jonson, translating Horace, urged the poet or playwright to observe in drawing noble character: "Still to be like himself, and hold his worth." "Think not, thou noble Roman," Brutus assures Cassius, "That ever Brutus will go bound to Rome; / He bears too great a mind" (5.1.114–16). Despite some expressed misgivings about suicide (5.1.104–09), Brutus avoids physical capture in the end by killing himself, and Strato echoes Lucilius in praising him: "Brutus only overcame himself" (5.5.56).

Why such noble virtue should be its own worst enemy seems puzzling, if we focus on the virtue in isolation, but Shakespeare imagines it working socially, where its intensely competitive quality becomes apparent, and its inherent aggressiveness eventually becomes the source of its own undoing. When Cassius first approaches Brutus about the conspiracy, he declares that his aim is to enhance Brutus's self-knowledge:

> And since you know you cannot see yourself
> So well as by reflection, I, your glass,
> Will modestly discover to yourself
> That of yourself which you yet know not of. (1.2.67–70)

But Cassius' offer is disingenuous, for it appeals to Brutus's stoic and patrician sense of himself in order to manipulate him into supporting Cassius' plot to destroy Caesar—a plot that can be understood as a defense of republican liberty, as Brutus wants to do, or as an obvious instance of competition between patrician warriors—a possibility Brutus seems unable to conceive. Cassius' lines therefore ironically reveal Brutus's self-deception, because Brutus serves another's purpose when he thinks he most single-mindedly serves his own.[23] Cassius' pride in his success at striking "thus much show of fire from Brutus" (1.2.177) suggests that Cassius has prevailed in his initial competition with Brutus, but not by much, though Brutus does not acknowledge or even seem to realize that Cassius has coopted him.

The outcome is very different in 4.3, when they quarrel in Brutus's tent. From the outset, Brutus uses extraordinary high-mindedness and indomitable self-consistency as formidable weapons to slash at the weak points of Cassius' pragmatism and choler: "from this day forth, / I'll use

you for my mirth, yea, for my laughter, / When you are waspish"
(4.3.49–51). When Cassius yields to Brutus's superior show of self-
control by melodramatically drawing his dagger and ordering Brutus to
kill him (99–107), Brutus also yields ever so slightly: "Be angry when
you will, it shall have scope; / Do what you will, dishonor shall be
humor" (108–109). After a testy reconciliation, Brutus's brief hint of
vulnerability ("I am sick of many griefs" [143]) elicits Cassius' mild
taunt, "Of your philosophy you make no use / If you give place to accidental evils" (144–45), only to be dealt the sharpest blow that Brutus is
capable of in response: "No man knows sorrow better. Portia is dead"
(146).[24] These two continue to have differences of opinion, but Cassius
never again seriously challenges Brutus, who (as Braden says of the stoic
philosopher) "is so far ahead in the competition that he can never be
caught."[25] Brutus establishes the unconquerable superiority of astonish-
ing self-mastery, both as a patrician warrior and as a stoic sage, yet it
does nothing to improve his self-knowledge, because he never realizes
how competitive he is in his determined idealism, nor how easily
Cassius manipulates him by means of it.[26]

Shakespeare had already visited competitive high-mindedness in
Love's Labor's Lost, where it also prevents noblemen from knowing themselves, but his treatment of the problem in *Julius Caesar* is more serious
and sympathetic.[27] The touches of feeling that we see in Brutus, though
he prides himself on perfect rational self-control, are this play's counterpart to the young noblemen's falling in love in the early comedy, but they
are not treated satirically. Though Brutus uses the death of Portia to
establish his superiority over Cassius, as we have just seen, his grief for
his wife is undeniable, and their only scene together shows him strug-
gling with self-control in the face of her expressed concern for him
(2.1).[28] His exclamation, "O ye gods, / Render me worthy of this noble
wife!" uttered in her hearing (303–4), is characteristically condescending
but not designed merely to impress her; it seems to burst from him invol-
untarily. His genuine affection for her is repeated in the tenderness he
shows his page, Lucius, whose musical instrument he carefully removes
when the lad falls asleep, to prevent his breaking it (4.3.272–74). Brutus's
self-control is indeed extraordinary and admirable, but his skill in using
it as a means of dominating others strongly qualifies its goodness,
because he is paradoxically blinded to himself by his own competitive
idealism, so "Virtue itself turns vice, being misapplied," as Friar

Laurence argues (*Romeo and Juliet* 2.3.21), and Brutus arguably lives in desire but without hope, like Dante's virtuous pagans.

Brutus's story is also different from the stories in other Shakespearean tragedies (and indeed from most of the comedies), in the way it is placed on the continuum that stretches from Creation to Last Judgment.[29] Trebonius' frightened allusion to "doomsday" when Caesar dies (3.1.98) is a way of emphasizing that Caesar's death is not apocalyptic. Both the sequence of events and the play's several references to time and history suggest a different destiny that gives the action an "undular structure," in John Velz's phrase.[30] It begins with Pompey's fortunes in decline and Caesar's at their peak; Caesar declines suddenly as the conspirators rise; and they decline with equal suddenness at the battle of Philippi, as Antony and Octavius rise. Moreover, future division between the play's final victors is clear in Octavius' "celerity" (to use Cleopatra's word) and in his peremptory crossing of Antony—actions that not only replay Julius Caesar's military aggression but also anticipate Octavius's eventual triumph in the ongoing political struggle.[31] That triumph was, of course, a commonplace of Augustan imperial mythology, as Shakespeare would have known well from Virgil's impressive treatment of it in the *Aeneid*. This is the destiny that hovers in the background of *Julius Caesar* and generates its undular structure. Its origin is glanced at ironically by Cassius, when he is persuading Brutus to join the conspiracy:

> Ay, as Aeneas, our great ancestor,
> Did from the flames of Troy upon his shoulder
> The old Anchises bear, so from the waves of Tiber
> Did I the tirèd Caesar. And this man
> Is now become a god. (1.2.112–16)

This icon of Roman *pietas* is Virgil's counterpart to Aeneas's shield: from burning Troy he bears the past; in Italy, he is given the future, with Octavius' defeat of Antony as its focus. Yet this all-important myth is evoked in *Julius Caesar* as a rhetorical ploy on Cassius' part, emulously emphasizing his superiority over the supposedly godlike Caesar in order to manipulate Brutus into supporting a revolt that Cassius lacks the courage to lead himself. Moreover, Rome was not, after all, the *urbs aeterna* that Virgil celebrates, for its eventual failure in the fifth century has been known to every reader or viewer of this play from the time it was first written and produced. *Romanitas* in *Julius Caesar* is ironically distanced both from Virgil's idealized heroic virtues on one hand (duty, courage, and *pietas*) and from the *imperium sine fine* on the other that Jove prophesies stirringly at the outset in the *Aeneid* (1.279).

Shakespeare imagined mere emulation, myopia, and misapprehended fate in another classical play, *Troilus and Cressida*, that he wrote shortly after *Julius Caesar*, though the treatment is bitterly satirical. To be sure, the setting is not Rome, and though Hector at one point refers knowingly to the moral philosophy of Aristotle (2.2.166–67), the action is set long before the advent of philosophy, so stoicism is not, strictly speaking, at issue. Still, the play returns to the Trojan fount of Roman destiny, as Cassius briefly does in tempting Brutus, and the Troy we see is remarkably bleak. The failure of vision was part of Shakespeare's conception of Trojan destiny as early as *The Rape of Lucrece*, as Lucrece herself makes clear in addressing a painting of the whole Trojan war:

> Show me the strumpet that began this stir,
> That with my nails her beauty I may tear.
> Thy heat of lust, fond Paris, did incur
> This load of wrath that burning Troy doth bear.
> Thine eye kindled the fire that burneth here,
>> And here in Troy, for trespass of thine eye,
>> The sire, the son, the dame, the daughter die. (1471–77)

The self-destructive competition among warrior aristocrats that creates the undular structure of *Julius Caesar* recalls the destructive competition in the *Henry VI* plays, where Troy is evoked several times.[32] Moreover, the same competition governs the familiar Greek heroes in *Troilus and Cressida*, as if Shakespeare perceived the origins of Roman stoic emulation, as Gordon Braden does, in the Greek warrior ethos.[33] Even Hector, who is the best of heroes, fails to follow his own moral advice in the Trojan council scene (2.2) and dies because he pursues a gaudy trophy: "Most putrefièd core, so fair without" (5.8.1). Though the beginning of the war is recalled and debated by the Trojans (2.2.1–25), only one person foresees its end and thus sees it *in toto*, as Lucrece does, by virtue of hindsight, and that person is Cassandra: "Our firebrand brother Paris burns us all. / . . . Cry, cry! Troy burns, or else let Helen go" (2.2.110–12). The Trojan princes disbelieve Cassandra, however, and their disbelief becomes an emblem of moral myopia ("the error of our eye," as Cressida calls it [5.2.113]) that characterizes everyone in this play. "'Tis our mad sister," remarks Troilus disparagingly, and

Hector simply tells Cassandra to be quiet (2.2.98, 103); otherwise, the council continues as if she had not spoken. Their debate is resolved in the end by the capitulation of moral insight to warrior pride, and it therefore parallels the moral debates in *Julius Caesar*, which are played out in ignorance of a Roman destiny that we see, by virtue of hindsight, though the protagonists do not, just as Lucrece sees a broader picture than everyone in *Troilus and Cressida* except Cassandra.

Shakespeare revisited neo-stoicism occasionally in plays that he wrote before his next Roman tragedy, and he consistently contrasted it, in one way or another, with Christian virtue. Though Hamlet has explicitly Christian reservations about suicide (wishing "that the Everlasting had not fixed / His canon 'gainst self-slaughter" [*Hamlet*, 1.2.131–32]), Horatio threatens to kill himself at once, when he sees Hamlet dying, declaring that he is "more an antique Roman than a Dane" (5.2.343), and he desists only when Hamlet asks him to "Absent thee from felicity awhile, / And in this harsh world draw thy breath in pain / To tell my story" (5.2.349–51).[34] In *Measure for Measure* (1603–1604), Shakespeare equates several characters' stoic confidence in the possibility of self-perfection with a wish for death, and he contrasts it with the possibility for improved self-knowledge, better relationships, and the hope for new life that the play associates with mercy, forgiveness, and charity in explicitly Christian terms.

A similar contrast appears in *Othello*, which is exactly contemporary with *Measure for Measure*. The love and faith that Othello gains in relationship with Desdemona is played out against the background "of most disastrous chances, / Of moving accidents by flood and field" (*Othello* 1.3.136–37) that Othello has learned to endure with magnificent self-control, military skill, and contained aggression that is characteristic of Shakespeare's Roman stoics: "I do agnize / A natural and prompt alacrity / I find in hardness."[35] In love with Desdemona, he discovers a world of trust and feeling that overwhelms the barriers of competitive hyper-vigilance he has erected and maintained since he was a child in a military camp (1.3.85, 134); this is the substance of his "conversion," as argued above in chapter 3. When Iago convinces him that Desdemona has betrayed him, Othello attempts to call up the same resources that enabled him to withstand threats in the past, only to discover that those resources fail him because he has invested himself so deeply in her:

> Had it pleased heaven
> To try me with affliction, had they rained
> All kinds of sores and shames on my bare head,
> Steeped me in poverty to the very lips,
> Given to captivity me and my utmost hopes,
> I should have found in some place of my soul
> A drop of patience. . . .
>
> But there where I have garnered up my heart,
> Where either I must live or bear no life,
> The fountain from the which my current runs
> Or else dries up—to be discarded thence! (4.2.49–62)

Eventually recovering enough of his accustomed self-control to under-take a familiar campaign against a new form of destructive competi-tion, that is, Desdemona herself, he destroys what he thinks is the source of his affliction. He discovers too late, however, that she was not the source after all, and the discovery shows him the ruins of everything he has relied on—both his habitual self-consistency and his newfound con-fidence in trustful love. In this terrible moment, convinced anew of the better world Desdemona had revealed to him and that he has himself destroyed ("one whose hand, / Like the base Indian, threw a pearl away / Richer than all his tribe" [5.2.356–58]), he seems to fall back on the last stoic resource and kills himself. This is a gesture that T. S. Eliot famously mocked: "What Othello seems to me to be doing in making this [his last] speech is cheering himself up."[36] While Eliot was percep-tive about Othello's stoicism, he was too quick to equate it with stoicism in the plays of Shakespeare's contemporaries, such as Chapman and Marston. What Eliot missed in *Othello* is the contrast that makes the play tragic, and to him it therefore seemed merely immoral ("The stoical attitude is the reverse of Christian humility" [9]) and deserving of crit-ical scorn. Though Othello glosses his own suicide with reference to stoic endurance, his death is in fact impulsive—if anything, a conse-quence of his stoic self-consistency having failed him—like the death of Portia in *Julius Caesar,* who in Brutus's own words "fell distract" (4.3.154). The highly principled death of Lucrece is genuinely stoic and admirable but not very moving. With Portia and even more with Othello what we are asked to acknowledge is the overwhelming of stoic principle in unimaginable suffering.

CORIOLANUS

After *Julius Caesar*, Shakespeare returned to Roman material in three plays whose dates cannot be precisely determined: *Antony and Cleopatra*, *Coriolanus*, and *Cymbeline*. For various reasons, they are usually thought to have been composed in the order I have just listed them, with *Cymbeline* possibly as late as 1610, but they could have been written over the span of three years (1606–1608), and since the first and third of them, as listed here, are similar to each other in being significantly different from the other Roman plays, it will be useful to consider *Coriolanus* before *Antony and Cleopatra*.[37] Continuity in Shakespeare's thinking about Rome is evident in his allusions to Coriolanus' story in the first of his Roman plays, *Titus Andronicus*. When Rome turns on Titus, his son Lucius turns to the barbarians and marches on Rome, explicitly comparing himself to Coriolanus in doing so (*Titus Andronicus* 4.4.67–68). Having recognized, with Titus, "That Rome is but a wilderness of tigers" (3.1.54), Lucius addresses the Goths in terms that express the banished Coriolanus' sentiments regarding the Volsci:

> Therefore, great lords, be as your titles witness,
> Imperious, and impatient of your wrongs,
> And wherein Rome hath done you any scath,
> Let him [Saturninus] make treble satisfaction. (5.1.5–8)

His appeal to patrician sentiment, his determination to support Titus's heroic honor in the face of every adversity, his expressed need to compete vengefully with Saturninus—all anticipate Shakespeare's most ambiguous Roman hero.

Yet in spite of these similarities, Titus and Coriolanus are very different, and one of the most important differences is that the latter is more complex and puzzling in his absolute stoic constancy than Shakespeare's first relatively uncritical venture into admirable Roman heroism. Moreover, this difference suggests how far Shakespeare had come in his thinking about stoicism over the course of a decade and a half. Geoffrey Miles emphasizes the ambiguity of Coriolanus' resistance to public pretense, for example, in "this intensely paradoxical play": his self-consistency as a steadfast patrician warrior is the hallmark of stoicism, and it is severely shaken by the failure of both patrician and plebian to acknowledge it as he thinks fit, "his virtue is in fact defined by the opinions of others," and his tragedy consists in his disillusionment when this point becomes clear to him.[38] Coriolanus' self-consistency does not so obviously boil over into its Senecan opposite—Herculean *furor*—as Titus's does, but Coriolanus' refusal to deviate from his patrician sense of himself as an aggressive military champion ("I will not do't, / Lest I surcease to honor mine own truth" [3.2.122–23]) is no less chaotic than Titus's, and Menenius identifies Coriolanus' nobility with his titanic rage (3.2.262–66). Little wonder that the tribunes speak of his mother, who is clearly the source of his identity, as insane—"They say she's mad" (4.2.11); "one that wants her wits" (4.2.46)—and she seems to confirm their judgment in her own rage, climaxing in her famous declaration, "Anger's my meat" (4.2.52). Moreover, Coriolanus compares Volumnia to "the wife of Hercules" (4.1.17), and Menenius compares Coriolanus himself to Hercules, when the Romans fear that their former champion will destroy them (4.6.105). In short, there is plenty to suggest Seneca's mad Hercules in Coriolanus as well as Titus.

Yet no one around Coriolanus can see that his madness is as emblematic as the warriors' myopia in *Troilus and Cressida*. His play is Shakespeare's most critical reflection on Roman stoicism, because the hero's self-destructive habit of being is not only a virtue but also the self-defining virtue of Rome: "I sup upon myself, / And so shall starve with feeding," fulminates Volumnia (4.2.52–53). From the beginning, speaking to the plebian mob, Menenius defines Rome in exclusively patrician terms:

> the Roman state . . . will on
> The way it takes, cracking ten thousand curbs
> Of more strong link asunder than can ever
> Appear in your impediment. (1.1.67–70)

Aggression and constancy (as indomitable intrepidity) are the qualities this assertion ascribes to "the Roman state," and Menenius defines them as exclusively patrician values. He voices the same idea more pithily later in the same scene in contrasting patrician and plebian: "Rome and her rats are at the point of battle" (1.1.161). Menenius is more diplomatic than Coriolanus, but the depth of Rome's self-division is clear in the interchangeability of Menenius' sentiments with Coriolanus', where commoners are concerned. The plebians, of course, see the situation differently: "What is the city but the people?" asks Sicinius rhetorically, and "ALL PLEBIANS" answer obligingly, "True, / The people are the city" (3.1.202–3). Coriolanus, however, naturally agrees with Menenius. He hardly admits that the plebians are Romans:

> I would they were barbarians, as they are,
> Though in Rome littered; not Romans, as they are not,
> Though calved i'th' porch o'th' Capitol. (3.1.243–45)

Defining himself in wholly patrician terms, he defines "Roman" the same way, and whatever is not like him is therefore not Roman. It is hardly surprising that both he and Volumnia wish, at various times, that he could hew down the plebians, as he hews down Rome's enemies (1.1.196-99; 4.2.25–27). Nor is it surprising that Coriolanus' awareness of his unmatchable warrior nobility leads to a conception of himself alone as truly Roman, so that when the city banishes him, he banishes the city (3.3.133).

More is involved in the city's division against itself than perennial divisions of social class, which historically afflicted both the republic and the empire. As that division repeatedly reappears in *Coriolanus*, it mirrors the unbridgeable division in the hero himself, making him in every way an emblem of Rome, though a very different emblem from the one Virgil offers in the *Aeneid*. Coriolanus' first expression of contempt for the plebs reveals his self-deception:

> What's the matter,
> That in these several places of the city
> You cry against the noble Senate, who,
> Under the gods, keep you in awe, which else
> Would feed on one another? (1.1.183–87)

His assertion that the "noble Senate" keeps the commons from mutual predation shows his blindness to other kinds of mutual predation— among patricians, for example, where it is embodied in no one better than in Coriolanus himself; between patrician and plebian, as expressed in Coriolanus' highly prejudiced sentiments; and within Coriolanus himself, who is a prime example of the self-destroying competitive ethos when one competitor so far outstrips his rivals that he turns on himself.[39] To use Volumnia's metaphor, the whole city feeds on itself. The tribune ironically named Junius Brutus is quick to see the point of aristocratic emulation, though Coriolanus cannot see it himself, and though the tribune cannot see his own destructive political ambition:

> Fame, at the which he aims,
> In whom already he's well graced, cannot
> Better be held nor more attained than by
> A place below the first. (1.1.264–67)

The inadequacy of Coriolanus's virtue is evident in the ability of everyone except himself to see it, though no Roman can see how perfectly he represents them all. One of the most trenchant summaries of Coriolanus' weakness is offered early in the play's opening scene by a commoner, not by a patrician:

> I say unto you, what he hath done famously he did it to that end [i.e., being proud]. Though soft-conscienced men can be content to say it was for his country, he did it to please his mother and to be partly proud, which he is, even to the altitude of his virtue. (1.1.35–38)

This is not said in plebian malice, as the Second Citizen suggests accusingly (1.1.33); it is the plain truth, as the subsequent action makes clear. As a commoner's perceptive comment on patricians, the First Citizen's remark is analogous to the cobbler's banter in the first scene of *Julius Caesar.*

Self-destructive warrior emulation is nowhere plainer than in Coriolanus' ambivalent relationship with Aufidius, which is the source of his literal destruction in the end. Unlike Tamora in *Titus Andronicus*, Aufidius is not the fickle barbarian opposite of stoic Roman constancy in *Coriolanus*; he is merely a lesser version of the same thing—Cassius to Coriolanus' Brutus. We hear repeatedly of his defeat at Coriolanus' hands, and his opinion of Coriolanus' heroic deeds is the only opinion that Coriolanus is anxious to learn (3.1.12), because it is offered by the man he perceives to be most like himself and therefore most worthy to evaluate him.[40] The other side of their competitive envy is competitive affection, because each loves to see himself in the other, as becomes clear when Coriolanus flees to Antium. Menenius accurately sees their competitive rivalry but not the other side of it, which is their ambivalent attraction: "He and Aufidius can no more atone / Than violent'st contrariety" (4.6.76–77). This comment also reveals Menenius' failure to understand himself as an emulous patrician whose model of perfection is Coriolanus. The more Coriolanus succeeds, even on the Volscis' behalf, the more Aufidius envies him and determines to destroy him (4.7), even before Coriolanus makes his unexpected accord with Rome. Volumnia fantasizes about a league between Rome and Antium with

Coriolanus dominant: "each in either side / Give the all-hail to thee" (5.3.138–39), but she too is blind to the effects of patrician emulation, even as she manifests them in herself, and she therefore cannot see that neither Aufidius nor Coriolanus can tolerate the other's dominance in the long run. Aufidius defeats Coriolanus unfairly with overwhelming numbers, just as Achilles defeats Hector in *Troilus and Cressida*, but Aufidius knows that "the fall of either / Makes the survivor heir of all" (5.6.17–18), and he rationalizes his cowardice ("a deed whereat valor will weep" [5.6.139]) in the familiar terms of the warrior aristocrat—as vengeance for Coriolanus' dishonoring him (5.6.18–48).

The limitations of Roman destiny are not as plainly complementary to the limitations of Roman character in *Coriolanus* as they are in *Julius Caesar*, because the action in the later play is so clearly focused on the fall of just one hero, rather than a succession of them. Moreover Coriolanus' death preserves Rome, because he is the only warrior great enough to conquer his own city, so the conjunction of stoic self-consistency and Roman destiny is preserved, as in the *Aeneid*. But the preservation is paradoxical and arbitrary and does not bode well for Rome as *urbs aeterna*. When Aufidius eagerly anticipates the destruction of Rome because of his new alliance with Coriolanus (4.5.132–36—echoed by the Third Servingman in 4.5.209–11), the moment is reminiscent of Turnus's determination to destroy the Trojan colonists in Italy before they can gain a foothold and accomplish the gods' design (*Aeneid* 7.469–70, 8.9–17). Virgil intended Turnus's view of the future to be ironic to the *Aeneid*'s first readers, because they knew that Turnus was mistaken, and the same irony marks the predictions of Aufidius and the Third Servingman for anyone who reads *Coriolanus*, because it was written in full knowledge of Rome's well-known rise to dominance and survival until the fifth century CE. Still, Coriolanus is no Turnus (though both are modeled in some sense on Achilles), because Coriolanus so perfectly embodies Roman values, especially Aeneas's stoic constancy, cited by Cassius in *Julius Caesar* as a model by which Caesar fails (1.2.112–16). Moreover, Coriolanus' threat to Rome is a threat to himself, as he discovers when he kneels before his mother. Rome is genuinely at risk because of him, yet neither he nor Aufidius understands that Coriolanus has been produced by Rome's untenable moral ideal, so the fact that the city's destiny hangs by a thread because of Coriolanus is directly relevant to Rome's reputation as the "eternal

city." She is, in effect, her own worst enemy, even at the imagined historical moment when the republic's characteristic institutions are established with the initial appointment of "Five tribunes to defend their
vulgar wisdoms / Of their own choice" (1.1.214–15). Coriolanus' dis-
paraging description makes clear how deeply the division runs between
patrician and plebian. The symmetrical complement to the historical
view of Rome in *Coriolanus* is the republic's coming apart in *Julius Caesar*
because of patrician emulation.[41] Such a vision of Roman history is far
from the Virgilian vision of *fatum*-directed stoic constancy, for what we
see in Coriolanus is a man whose quixotic quest for self-perfecting constancy as the source of honor and preeminence destroys him and very
nearly destroys Rome as well.

ANTONY AND CLEOPATRA

Shakespeare's critical view of Roman destiny is clearest in *Antony and
Cleopatra* and *Cymbeline*, because in these plays he implicitly contrasts it
with Christian destiny, and the sense of value that goes with the contrasting visions of human purpose complements a contrasting set of
ethical assumptions as well. This is not to reduce the infinite variety of
Antony in particular to Christian ethics but simply to urge that the play's
variety is not infinitely ambiguous, because it is defined by the significance of events that wait just off stage, as it were, geographically, historically, and morally.[42] As in *Julius Caesar*, Shakespeare alludes to
Virgil's founding myth of Roman destiny in *Antony and Cleopatra*, only to
reinterpret it. When Antony is planning suicide, in the belief that
Cleopatra has already killed herself, he imagines death as a way to
rejoin her:

> I will o'ertake thee, Cleopatra, and
> Weep for my pardon . . .
> . . . .
> Where souls do couch on flowers, we'll hand in hand,
> And with our sprightly port make the ghosts gaze.
> Dido and her Aeneas shall want troops,
> And all the haunt be ours. (4.14.44–54)

In the *Aeneid*, Dido is Cleopatra's antetype: both are passionate north
African women, who threaten the constancy both of Roman stoic

heroes and of Roman destiny. Shakespeare had exploited this antithesis as early as *Titus Andronicus*, where Tamora is a bewitching barbarian who sexually allures the corrupt Saturninus and uses him in an attempt to destroy the resolute Titus. Maecenas' comment on Antony (clearly expressing Caesar's view) fairly accurately describes Titus's view of Saturninus with Tamora: "th'adulterous Antony, most large / In his abominations . . . / gives his potent regiment to a trull / That noises it against us" (3.6.97–100).

While Antony also sees Dido and Cleopatra as historical parallels, he does so very differently from Virgil.[43] By the time Antony alludes to Dido, his dalliance with Cleopatra has destroyed his Roman dream of power, and his suicide would therefore make sense as a principled stoic act of vengeance on himself, analogous to the vengeance that Lucrece urges Collatine to take against Tarquin because Tarquin has fallen off from himself in raping her. But that is not how Antony defines his action. Rather, he envisions himself in terms similar to Romeo's, after Romeo discovers Juliet dead (or thinks he does)—as a lover whose fidelity is in question because he has not kept pace with his beloved when she hastened her death: "I will o'ertake thee, Cleopatra, and / Weep for my pardon" (4.14.44–45)[44] Antony sees the comparison of Cleoptra with Dido as a loving precedent, not a shameful one, and he even goes so far as to imagine Aeneas with Dido, thus making the Roman progenitor a competitor with Antony in love, not in fighting ability. In contrast, Virgil imagines Aeneas watching sadly but resolutely as Dido turns away from him in rejection (*Aeneid* 6.467–76). A more complete reconception of the Virgilian myth is hard to imagine.

Antony's vision of his destiny as a Roman contrasts not only with Virgil's but also with Caesar's, for Shakespeare imagines Octavius as fully aware of the myth that Virgil would compose for him. Caesar's sense of destiny is sometimes strongly stoic, as when he counsels Octavia after Antony abandons her for Cleopatra:

> Cheer your heart.
> Be you not troubled with the time, which drives
> O'er your content these strong necessities,
> But let determined things to destiny
> Hold unbewailed their way. (3.6.84–88)

For stoics, the point of the good life was to cultivate *apatheia*, or careful control of one's response to external events, because events themselves were deemed to be beyond one's control. In Caesar's formulation, when time drives "strong necessities" over Octavia's "content," Octavia should not bewail "determined things" which she cannot change, but should cheer her heart by controlling her inclination to surrender to sadness about what has happened. After his victory at Actium, however, Caesar appears to believe that he controls destiny, not the other way around, judging from his prediction before the battle of Alexandria:

> The time of universal peace is near.
> Prove this a prosp'rous day, the three-nooked world
> Shall bear the olive freely. (4.6.5–7)

His prediction is premature where the next battle is concerned, because Antony wins it, but Caesar's prediction is right for Rome's future, and it corresponds to the vision of destiny that Virgil imagines for Caesar Augustus in the *Aeneid*.

Just as Antony redefines Virgil's myth of Cleopatra, however, Cleopatra redefines the Virgilian myth of Augustus's *pax Romana*. From the beginning of the last scene, she is certain that Caesar stands less in fortune's eye than he believes he does: " 'Tis paltry to be Caesar; / Not being Fortune, he's but Fortune's knave, / A minister of her will" (5.2.2–4). Just before her death, she imagines Antony from beyond the grave, as he had imagined her in his dying moments: "I hear him mock / The luck of Caesar, which the gods give men / To excuse their after wrath" (5.2.285–87). Cleopatra not only sees destiny as mere luck but also invents a myth of divine retribution, by which the gods keep human success in check by punishing those who enjoy it. The concept has numerous precedents: the medieval wheel of fortune, the ancient Hebraic affirmation of God's historical judgment of nations, even an idea that Shakespeare almost certainly did not know—the ancient Greek sense of balance between *hybris* (human excess) and *dīke* (divinely sanctioned justice). Moments later, applying the asp to her breast, Cleopatra envisions Caesar's political success in even less flattering terms, as she invokes her destroyer, "Oh, couldst thou speak, / That I might hear thee call great Caesar ass / Unpolicied!" (5.2.306–8). Seeking death "after the high Roman fashion" (4.15.92), Cleopatra paradoxically defeats Caesar in the same way Brutus defeats him in *Julius Caesar*—by refusing to let him claim victory. "He words me, girls, he words me, that I should not / Be noble to myself" she insists to her waiting women, after her only meeting with Caesar (5.2.191–92).

Understanding the terms of Roman emulation, she embraces them in the end and thereby defeats him. "Caesar's beguiled," exclaims the First Guard, when he finds her dead (5.2.323), and his exclamation sums up everything about Caesar and the destiny Caesar proclaims. Like other stoic heroes in Shakespeare, Caesar is deceived about his own moral perfectibility no less than he is about the ultimate future of "the three-nooked world." "Kingdoms are clay," Antony declares in the first scene (1.1.37). The words are truer than he knows, both for himself and for the man who defeats him.

The lovers' redefinition of Caesar's mythic success can easily be dismissed as romantic hyperbole and wish fulfillment, but it serves to bring this story into conjunction with another one that reduces Caesar Augustus to a footnote, because he again plays a small part in a broader destiny than the founding of the Roman empire:

> And it came to pass in those days, that there came a commandment from Augustus Caesar, that all the world should be taxed. (This first taxing was made when Cyrenius was governor of Syria.) Therefore went all to be taxed every man to his own city. And Joseph also went up from Galilee out of a city called Nazaret, into Judea, unto the city of David, which is called Bethlehem (because he was of the house and lineage of David). (Luke 2:1-4)

Luke's gospel is the only one that mentions this detail, but it redefines Augustus' story in a way that is analogous to its redefinition in *Antony and Cleopatra*—as a subservient detail in a larger and more important story. Moreover, Shakespeare repeatedly gestures toward this broader context in a series of apocalyptic allusions that run from the first scene of the play to the last.[45] When Antony and Cleopatra first appear, they are wrangling over his fidelity: in response to her assertion that she can "set a bourn" to his love, Antony declares, "Then must thou needs find out new heaven, new earth" (1.1.17), echoing Revelation 21:1, "And I saw a new heaven and a new earth." At the end of the play, the extraordinary vision of Antony that Cleopatra describes to Dolabella just before her suicide (5.2.81–91) similarly draws on the vision of the avenging angel in Revelation 10:1-6.

These details are not allegorical: Antony and Cleopatra are too worldly, too cruel, and too obsessed with themselves to be credibly construed as representatives of Christian virtue.[46] But the biblical allusions do more than dilate the imaginative scope of the lovers. For one thing, the allusions confirm the destiny that subsumes Roman destiny in all the Roman plays—here more explicitly than in earlier ones. Cleopatra's interpretation of Roman destiny as mere "luck" that the gods have granted "to excuse their after wrath" (5.2.286–87) compellingly judges all imperial endeavors, Roman and otherwise, in light of a higher standard. Further, the biblical allusions serve as a reminder, as they do in many other Shakespearean plays, that the end of this play is not The End, as Cleopatra's giving her ladies "leave / To play till doomsday" clearly indicates (5.2.231–32). None of the competing principals in *Antony and Cleopatra* is the alpha and omega of history; that role is reserved for the peasant child born in Bethlehem under "Herod of Jewry," as a consequence of Caesar Augustus' order that all the world should be taxed.[47] Moreover, insofar as the tragedy in this play is not literally apocalyptic, it is enigmatic, like Shakespeare's "pure" tragedies, to use Bradley's term, for a hint of its meaning may be glimpsed in the comparison with Luke's gospel, but that hint is not exhaustive; it is merely suggestive, and it cannot explain away the human loss of "such a mutual pair / And such a twain" as Antony and Cleopatra (1.1.39–40).

Most important, the biblical allusions in *Antony and Cleopatra* provide a way of seeing the play's ethical reversal, which parallels its belittling of Roman imperial destiny. Caesar perfectly represents patrician moral decorum when he deplores Antony's Egyptian depravity:

> Let's grant it is not
> Amiss to tumble on the bed of Ptolemy,
> To give a kingdom for a mirth, to sit
> And keep the turn of tippling with a slave,
> To reel the streets at noon, and stand the buffet
> With knaves that smells of sweat. (1.4.16–21)

In a paralipsis that reveals more about himself than it does about Antony, Caesar condemns Antony's familiar mingling with plebians—"a slave" and "knaves"—even while claiming not to. Even if all this "becomes him," Caesar continues (clearly implying that it does not), "yet must Antony / No way excuse his foils when we do bear / So great weight in his lightness" (1.4.23–25). The real problem in Caesar's view is that Antony's failure of patrician decorum—his failure to be "like himself"—reflects badly on his fellow triumvirs and particularly on Caesar.[48] Caesar thus uses moral superiority, as Brutus does, to trump his rivals, for he simultaneously censures not only Antony but also Lepidus, the third triumvir, who has just been pleading Antony's case.

Caesar's strict belief in his own moral self-perfectibility contrasts not only with Antony's merry dissoluteness but also with the creatural vulnerability that both lovers recognize and affirm in the end. Antony at first seems unable to choose between Rome and Egypt, and his inability suggests a different kind of self-division from Caesar's—more open and less self-deceived, because less inclined to belief in his own perfect self-consistency. When Antony commits suicide, he thinks of himself as "a Roman by a Roman / Valiantly vanquished" (4.15.59–60), yet his motive, as we noticed, is not stoic resolution but his love of Cleopatra, who he thinks is already dead. He evokes Christian paradox, as much as stoic, in his declaration that "with a wound I must be cured" (4.14.78). Furthermore, he wretchedly bungles the deed, so that he is obliged to call on a guard to finish it (4.14.104), and he outlives the attempt long enough to discover that Cleopatra had lied about her death, to register the lie forgivingly, to be carried to Cleopatra's monument, to be hoisted up to her, and to die at last in her arms. While this may be a romantic death, it is hardly the "valiant" one he describes, as Caesar would surely be the first to point out (while somehow claiming not to), yet Antony shows no regret about it, and indeed his reconciliation with Cleopatra seems ample compensation for the awkward mess of his death itself.

Though she determines to die "after the high Roman fashion" (4.15.92), her suicide is, if anything, less stoically decent than his. It begins with a paradox like Antony's that is as Christian as it is stoic: "My desolation does begin to make / A better life" (5.2.1–2), and like him she is deeply vulnerable, though "marble-constant" (5.2.240). She is so overwhelmed by grief when Antony dies that her ladies think she too has died (4.15.72), and she admits her weakness when she recovers:

> No more but e'en a woman, and commanded
> By such poor passion as the maid that milks
> And does the meanest chares. (4.15.78–80)

This is just the kind of weakness that Caesar urges Octavia to suppress (3.6.84–88), and it is the social equivalent to Antony's drinking and boxing with "knaves that smells of sweat," noted disparagingly by Caesar (1.4.21). The difference is that Cleopatra admits it of herself, and her conversation with the Clown who brings her the asp in a basket of figs confirms the point that in her helpless mortality, she is indistinguishable from a rustic commoner: "Those that do die of it do seldom or never recover" (5.2.247–48).

This emphasis on the creatural ordinariness of the lovers is the play's principal contrast with Caesar's insistence on patrician moral perfectionism, but the ironic reversal of social status for Antony and Cleopatra derives from a set of values that are not romantic. We have seen a comparable reversal in *King Lear*, where the model is more clearly Christian. Erich Auerbach pointed out that Augustine learned to embrace what he took to be the subversion of classical rhetorical decorum in Latin translations of the Bible before Jerome's—not high subjects (the gods and heroes) in a high style but the highest subjects (in Augustine's estimation) in a common style, violating rhetorical decorum sacredly in a manner of expression that Augustine called "*sermo humilis*."[49] Augustine argued further that this paradoxical inversion of rhetorical expectation was necessitated by the paradox of the Incarnation—of God becoming human; the divine origin of all things, a peasant baby. Augustine's influence was so great, Auerbach points out, that *sermo humilis* dominated stylistic expectation until the humanist recovery of classical rhetorical standards in the fifteenth and sixteenth centuries. In the history of style, some of the late influence of *sermo humilis* is arguably present in the creatural humbling of the lovers in Antony and Cleopatra, but in the play itself, their humbling seems to be influenced by the originating event for *sermo humilis* that neither they nor Caesar know anything about, though it will happen as a consequence of the three-nooked world bearing the olive freely under Caesar's sole authority after Caesar's defeat of Antony.[50]

Caesar's stoic perfectionism contrasts not only with the defects that make perfection in the lovers but also with Antony's largeness of spirit, referred to three times late in the play as "bounty."[51] Antony falls off from the stoic standard that Caesar professes to admire in him (1.4.56–72)—though Caesar never gives any evidence of testing himself against it—but in his failure Antony seems to discover, as Othello does, a larger and more gracious world (albeit self-indulgent and given to excess in Antony's case), when he falls in love with Cleopatra. True, when he marries Octavia, he admits he has not kept his "square" and promises that "that to come shall be done by th' rule" (2.3.6–7), but the marriage treaty is in fact a political trap that Antony walks into selfdeceivingly, as several characters recognize, and it is arguably a betrayal of what Antony has found with Cleopatra. However one sees his marriage with Octavia, Antony's "square" and "rule" contrast with his "bounty" late in the play. His first gesture in defeat is to urge his soldiers to appropriate a treasure ship that he seems to have reserved for himself—mentioned three times in twenty lines (3.11.4–22). The motif reappears when a soldier reports Antony's reaction to Enobarbus' desertion of him: "Enobarbus, Antony / Hath after thee sent all thy treasure, with / His bounty overplus" (4.6.20–22). Antony's generous response undoes Enobarbus completely:

> O Antony,
> Thou mine of bounty, how wouldst thou have paid
> My better service, when my turpitude
> Thou dost so crown with gold! This blows my heart. (4.6.32–35)

Antony and Cleopatra comes the closest of all the Roman plays before *Cymbeline* to incorporating a comedy of forgiveness, when Enobarbus "repents" (4.9.12) and asks Antony to forgive his treachery: "O Antony, / Nobler than my revolt is infamous, / Forgive me" (4.9.21–23). As in *King Lear*, forgiveness precedes repentance; indeed this play's secular analogue to grace—Antony's "bounty"—is what brings about Enobarbus' repentance. As in the lovers' paradoxical ennobling through humility, Antony's bounty "That grew the more by reaping," in Cleopatra's appreciation of it (5.2.87), seems to borrow its significance from values inaugurated by an event of which Antony is wholly ignorant, because it occurred soon after his death, though his defeat helps in some gracefully mysterious way to bring it about.

CYMBELINE

Having treated the prelude to the reign of Caesar Augustus in *Antony and Cleopatra*, Shakespeare turned to the reign itself in his last Roman play, *Cymbeline*, where the same off-stage event so powerfully influences what happens in a world dominated by Rome that it becomes suffused with Christian value—a marked departure from Shakespeare's consistent identification of ancient Rome with stoicism in earlier plays. *Cymbeline* identifies itself as Roman in a variety of ways, as several critics have pointed out.[52] Alone among all the Roman plays, this one uses the hon-

orific "Augustus" for the first emperor, and it does so five times, definitively identifying the folktale action with a particular historical period.[53]
To reinforce the point, Posthumus alludes to Julius Caesar's invasion of
Britain, thus linking the present action historically with the advent of
Roman influence in its westernmost province (2.4.21–23). One of the
four major plot strands involves Britain's relation to Rome, and of the
four this one comes closest to Shakespeare's chronicle sources—though
not very close, at that.[54] Imogen alludes to Virgil's founding myth, men-
tioning both Aeneas and Sinon (3.4.58–59), and the god of the play is
Jupiter, who presides over the destiny that brings Aeneas from Troy to
Italy in the *Aeneid*, and who appears in a dream vision to Posthumus in
Cymbeline.[55]

Despite these indubitable Roman influences in *Cymbeline*, *Romanitas*
in this play bears scant resemblance to its presence in every other
Roman work Shakespeare wrote. Only one brief scene treats senators
and tribunes in conversation, and in contrast to *Coriolanus*, they work
harmoniously together "to undertake our wars against / The fall'n-off
Britains" (3.7.5–6).[56] As many commentators have pointed out, ancient
Rome in effect becomes an English caricature of Renaissance Italy—a
combination of rhetorical duplicity, hot-tempered competition, and
flashy style. Moreover, some of these traits appear among the British
rather than the Romans—suggesting perhaps the xenophobic fear of
contagion by Italianate behavior in Renaissance England, as Thomas
Olsen argues, but also an exchange of identity between Roman and
Briton that seems self-consciously "modern" (i.e., Jacobean) rather than
ancient.[57]

Most significant, in light of Shakespeare's other Roman plays, is that
the traces of stoicism in *Cymbeline* are also transferred away from Rome
(as they were historically in Jacobean England's courtly affinity for neo-
stoicism), for they appear most prominently in Posthumus. The praise
heaped on him at the outset in the gossip of two anonymous gentlemen
not only proves that he has a remarkable reputation among his peers at
court but also gives the reason for it, testifying to his integrity, his aptitude for learning, his capacity for friendship, and his precocity
(1.1.18–24, 44–54)—all marks of a courtier perfectly educated in the
humanist manner and perfectly responsive to his education. In keeping
with this reputation, he shows his stoic suppression of passion and his
constancy (fidelity) in the first words we hear him speak to Imogen:

Oh, lady, weep no more, lest I give cause
To be suspected of more tenderness
Than doth become a man. I will remain
The loyal'st husband that did e'er plight troth. (1.1.94–97)

Posthumus' similarity to stoics in Shakespeare's other plays, beginning with the young noblemen in *Love's Labor's Lost*, is most striking in his insistent and damaging idealizing, which prevents him from recognizing the gap between his actual experience and the perfection he imagines, both in Imogen and in himself. This gap is especially evident in the memory he describes of Imogen, after his idealized image of her has been easily shattered by Iachimo:

Me of my lawful pleasure she restrained
And prayed me oft forbearance; did it with
A pudency so rosy the sweet view on't
Might well have warmed old Saturn, that I thought her
As chaste as unsunned snow. (2.5.9–13)

This description consists so much of ascribed qualities that it is hard to know what Posthumus is really describing—Imogen's behavior (whatever it was) or his Angelo-like interpretation of her as a woman who aroused his desire by the perfect chastity he imputes to her.

Given Posthumus' idealizing, it is not surprising that he fails to reckon with Iachimo's ability to deceive him, despite Iachimo's warning (1.4.91–94), and with his own ability to deceive himself, expressed in his readiness to accept a wager on Imogen's faithfulness. "My mistress exceeds in goodness the hugeness of your unworthy thinking" (1.5.145–46) is a declaration that says more about Posthumus's readiness to be deceived than it does about Imogen, since his willingness to put her to a test devised and evaluated by Iachimo himself indicates both Posthumus' readiness to trust Iachimo ("credulous fool" he calls himself later [5.5.212]) and his concomitant mistrust of Imogen before the test is even undertaken. Characteristically for those who deceive themselves in Shakespeare, Posthumus' spoken words attesting Imogen's faithfulness state the opposite of what his actions show he really believes. Whatever he learned at court, he seems to have learned little about himself—a weakness he shares with Brutus in *Julius Caesar* (among others), whose idealism is also manipulated by a canny rival without Brutus's being aware of it.

The principal difference between Posthumus and Shakespeare's Roman stoics is that Posthumus benefits symbolically (as nearly everyone in the play does) from the one event that Holinshed associates with the reign of Cymbeline—namely, the birth of Christ.[58] The event is not mentioned in the play, but it hovers off stage, as it does for *Antony and Cleopatra*, and it exerts enormous influence. Its influence is evident, for one thing, in the structure that Shakespeare ascribes to the four plots from various sources that he imagines as the content of Cymbeline's otherwise content-less reign, for each of them follows a pattern of separation, wandering, and reunion that derived ultimately from the morality play.[59] Posthumus is thus separated from Imogen in the marriage plot; Imogen from her father in the family plot; her brothers from their father and their sister in the dynastic plot; and England from Rome in the international plot. The influence of "this gracious season," as Imogen refers to it (5.5.405), is most potent in the motif of forgiveness that makes reunion possible at every level.[60] R. G. Hunter has explored this motif most fully with regard to Posthumus and Imogen,[61] but his account might be supplemented with the point that Posthumus leaves his stoicism behind when he comes to the end of himself, recognizing his deep imperfection, forgiving Imogen (even though he still believes she betrayed him with Iachimo), and asking the gods to forgive him (5.1.1–33). The moral pattern is indubitably Christian and implicitly anti-stoic, though the play's religious references are consistently pagan. Jupiter is, in effect, overruled both historically and ethically by the birth of Jesus, so that the play's densest cluster of biblical allusions occurs in Jupiter's appearance to the Leonati (5.4.30–150), despite their pointed complaint about Jupiter's "adulteries, / Rates and revenges" (5.4.33–34).[62]

Shakespeare reserved a climactic emphasis on the importance of forgiveness for the last scene, which he made a tour de force of comic resolution. After Iachimo's confession, Posthumus briefly reenacts his awareness of his fallibility in a speech full of self-loathing (5.5.211–29) that is reminiscent of Othello's, after Othello also recognizes that he has been duped by another "Italian fiend" into mistrusting and killing his wife (*Othello* 5.2.281–90). Imogen, hearing her husband's confession, steps forward, only to be rejected at first because Posthumus does not recognize her in disguise—a detail that symbolically reenacts his earlier failure and self-deception. Her willingness to forgive him is implicit in her readiness to be reconciled with him, thus resolving the problems of the romantic plot. Their reconciliation produces, in turn, Cymbeline's implicit forgiveness of Imogen for marrying Posthumus against the royal will: "My tears that fall / Prove holy water on thee!" (5.5.271–72).[63] The family plot is thus resolved through forgiveness as well, Cymbeline having at last come to recognize that his Queen was as false as his daughter was true. Resolution in the dynastic plot follows immediately, when Belarius, Guiderius, and Arviragus recognize that Fidele is Imogen, Belarius confesses his vengeful kidnapping of the king's sons twenty years earlier, and Cymbeline, reversing his initially pitiless response (5.5.324–25), implicitly forgives him, using the language of miraculous birth, as he recognizes his long-lost sons: "Oh, what, am I / A mother to the birth of three? Ne'er mother / Rejoiced deliverance more" (5.5.372–74).[64] As in *Antony and Cleopatra*, political success is viewed in diminished terms, compared to the restoration of relationships, as Imogen learns she has been disinherited and instantly declares her love for the newfound brothers who have unintentionally supplanted her (5.5.376–82).

Finally, the international plot is resolved by forgiveness as well—the play's most astonishing and unexpected development.[65] Imogen has no sooner mentioned "this gracious season" than Cymbeline offers mercy to the Roman prisoners he had been about to execute: "All o'erjoyed, / Save those in bonds. Let them be joyful too, / For they shall taste our comfort" (5.5.405–7). Before he has a chance to act on this promise, however, Posthumus forgives Iachimo, explaining that he had spared him earlier, when they fought in the narrow lane (5.5.414–16) and implying that his words formally declare what he has in fact already done: "The power that I have on you is to spare you; / The malice towards you to forgive you. Live, / And deal with others better" (5.5.421–23). This act is what prompts Cymbeline's declaration of general forgiveness, "We'll learn our freeness of a son-in-law! / Pardon's the word to all" (425–26), but Posthumus' forgiveness of Iachimo is important for another reason as well. Had Posthumus killed Iachimo when he had the chance, he would have enacted a vengeance that he felt was his due, but he would thereby have compounded his initial mistake, since Iachimo did not actually do the thing for which Posthumus wanted to kill him. Moreover, the plot could not have unfolded as it does in the last scene, because the unfolding begins when Imogen sees her

ring on Iachimo's finger and asks about it (5.5.104–5). Iachimo therefore has to be present, and her puzzlement is understandable, because
the last time she had seen the ring, it had been on Posthumus' finger,
after she gave it to him (1.1.114). Posthumus' earlier gratuitous decision
to spare Iachimo when they fought ("I had you down and might / Have
made you finish" [5.5.415–16]) thus enables all the other acts of mercy
that characterize the intricate plotting in the play's last scene.
Shakespeare might have plotted differently, of course, but he chose to
do it in a way that emphasizes forgiveness as strongly as possible as the
key to the restoration of human relationships, including the victorious
British king's decision to spare his prisoners and to "submit to Caesar /
And to the Roman empire, promising / To pay our wonted tribute"
(5.5.464–66). As in *Antony and Cleopatra*, the *pax Romana* of Augustus is
superseded by something else, in this case the "peace in earth, and
towards men good will" that the angel in Luke's gospel associates with
the birth of Christ (Luke 2:14).

Perhaps the strongest indication that *Cymbeline* enacts Christian values, rather than stoic ones, is that the joyful resolution points to its ten-
uousness rather than to perfect self-understanding and reconciliation.
As in almost every Shakespearean comedy, the characters we care most
about in this play are capable of improvement, and their change is
imagined in distinctively Christian terms (forgiveness, forbearance,
charity, trust, patience, hope), but they are not perfect, and the reconciliation they achieve does not depend on their self-consistency or their
perfectibility. The clarity of Posthumus' vision is strongly questioned
when he thrusts his wife aside just seconds before he embraces her.
Moments before forgiving his daughter, Cymbeline generalizes misogy-
nistically, "Who is't can read a woman?" (5.5.48) and insists defensively
that "It had been vicious / To have mistrusted" the Queen (66–67),
though Imogen sees through her from the first scene of the play
(1.1.85–86). Cymbeline forgives Belarius because Belarius preserved the
king's sons, but Belarius kidnapped them in the first place, and his reason for doing so is described only by himself in general terms
(3.3.60–68), so his motive remains hidden and doubtful. Cymbeline's
unexpected decision to resume paying tribute to Rome suggests an old
submission for England in the early seventeenth century—a bondage
that Henry VIII and subsequent English monarchs had reversed,
including James VI and I. As we noticed in *The Comedy of Errors*, whose

denouement is also associated with a miraculous birth, the resolution of problems is wonderful, but it is far from perfect. *Cymbeline* releases us into the fallen world, as Shakespeare's plays invariably do, and its refusal to endorse the *pax Romana* without qualification is also, in effect, a refusal to endorse any earthly peace the same way, including that of King James.

In distinguishing pagan and Christian virtue, Shakespeare belongs to a long tradition that begins before Augustine in the fifth century and includes Aquinas, Dante, Erasmus, Calvin, and Milton, who was a child when Shakespeare died. Few writers in this tradition rejected pagan virtue outright; indeed, they usually showed it enormous respect, as Augustine does with Plato, Aquinas with Aristotle, and Milton with virtually the whole classical tradition—philosophical and poetic alike. Calvin was arguably more receptive to stoicism than Shakespeare's plays are: his first publication was a commentary on Seneca's *De clementia* (1532), and his mature theology maintains a fruitful, if sometimes ambivalent, relationship with his early humanism. Ambivalence might well describe Shakespeare's depictions of stoic virtue as well. His portraits of Brutus and Coriolanus in particular are deeply sympathetic, and his reading in Cicero and Plutarch suggests profound fascination with the thinking of the ancients. The attitude that comes through in his writing is not rejection but reservation, and one gains the strongest sense of that attitude through contrast, as in reading his first Roman play, *Titus Andronicus*, together with *Coriolanus* and *Cymbeline*, or *Julius Caesar* with *As You Like It* (both written at almost exactly the same time), or *Antony and Cleopatra* by itself while noting the carefully wrought difference between Caesar and Antony. Even as Shakespeare imagines him, Antony would not make most people's lists of Christian virtue, but Antony's "bounty" is undeniably more charitable than Caesar's calculating aggression, as even Caesar seems to acknowledge (but only after his rival's death), when he describes the dead Cleopatra looking like sleep, "As she would catch another Antony / In her strong toil of grace" (5.2.347–48). Caesar is caught in that toil too, I have argued, though he is not aware of it, and the irony is indicative. Though his power is seemingly uncontested at the end of *Antony and Cleopatra*, it exists for a purpose he cannot imagine, and that purpose paradoxically graces his rival's defeat.

7

ESTHETICS, EPISTEMOLOGY, ONTOLOGY

> I never may believe
> These antique fables nor these fairy toys.

A Midsummer Night's Dream 5.1.2–3

> Love talks with better knowledge, and knowledge with dearer love.

Measure for Measure 3.2.146

For several identifiable reasons, criticism has been boldest in claiming to be able to say something certain about Shakespeare's esthetic thinking. These reasons include the Romantic evaluation of Shakespeare as an inspired genius, the esthetic movement of the late nineteenth and early twentieth centuries, the assumption that Shakespeare was committed to writing poetry and poetic drama above anything else, and most recently, the impact of New Criticism, with its emphasis on autonomous literary artifacts. This line of inquiry has paid rich dividends. Several books have been devoted, in whole or in part, to elucidating Shakespeare's idea of art and of his own art in particular.[1] Everyone now recognizes that Shakespeare frequently drew attention to what he was himself doing as a poet and playwright, from the artful classical imitativeness of *The Comedy of Errors* and *Titus Andronicus* to the discussion of art and nature in *The Winter's Tale* (4.4.79–103) and the image of Prospero as artist in *The Tempest*. Though he left no independent critical comments on the question, he attended to it frequently in his narrative and lyric poetry and his writing for the theater. His staging of plays within plays has attracted particular notice as evidence of esthetic self-consciousness, and thematic analysis of virtually any Shakespearean play as "meta-drama," or a play about making plays, was for a time a small critical growth industry.[2]

Shakespeare's esthetic thinking does not, however, stand by itself, despite critical attention to it as a subject in its own right. It acquires both greater complexity and greater clarity when it is considered in the context of Shakespeare's thinking more broadly. I have argued that the most important category of his intellectual makeup is not esthetic but religious, and I want to urge in this chapter that his way of thinking about art, and about his own art in particular, is closely related to what I am calling skeptical faith. For the esthetic question does not stand alone in Shakespeare's writing; it is seamlessly connected with epistemology, or the nature of knowledge, and ontology, or the nature of being. In the sixteenth century, these three questions had not been separately addressed and identified, as they would be by Enlightenment thinkers, and all were still intimately related to religion. Insofar as any of the three questions can be addressed in Shakespeare's writing, they are bound up with issues concerning liturgy, drama, religious reform, the status of signs, the nature of illusion, the quality of belief, miracles, wonders, devils, and God.

SHAKESPEARE AND SIDNEY

The context to which Shakespeare's sense of his art has usually been referred is Renaissance critical theory, especially as represented by Sidney's *Apology for Poetry*.[3] Sidney's familiarity with Italian humanism made his treatise the most elegant and influential conduit through which Renaissance neoclassicism reached Elizabethan England. Still, *The Comedy of Errors* suggests that Shakespeare may well have learned about neoclassical standards apart from Sidney, because the play perfectly meets those standards despite being staged for the first time earlier than 1595, the year Sidney's *Apology* was published. Moreover, Sidney was acutely conscious of his own political and religious context, as well as that of Italian humanism, and though Shakespeare responded to the same religious and political critique of the theater that Sidney did, Shakespeare regarded the English dramatic heritage more positively than Sidney. In short, comparing Shakespeare's sense of his art to Sidney's critical theory requires consideration of a broader sense of the past than the history of criticism and drama.[4]

Sidney's well-known defense of poetry as fiction, for example, is not only central to his own argument but to Shakespeare's defense of theater as well, and on the face of it, Sidney's assertion that the poet is not tied to imitating nature provides a useful gloss to several passages in Shakespeare. The poet, Sidney says, is "lifted up with the vigor of his own invention," so that he creates "in effect another nature, in making things either better than nature bringeth forth, or, quite anew, forms such as never were in nature" (*Apology*, 156). Theseus seems to echo this view sardonically in *A Midsummer Night's Dream*, when he patronizingly describes the poet as imaginatively bodying forth "the forms of things unknown" (5.1.14–15). Puck is similarly dismissive, asking us at the end of the play to think

> That you have but slumbered here
> While these visions did appear.
> And this weak and idle theme,
> No more yielding but a dream. (5.1.420–23)

In *As You Like It*, Touchstone denies that poetry is a "true thing," "for the truest poetry is the most feigning, and lovers are given to poetry, and what they swear in poetry may be said as lovers they do feign" (3.3.16–20). Prospero recalls Puck's language, drawing an analogy between the masque he has just staged and "The cloud-capped towers, the gorgeous palaces, / The solemn temples, the great globe itself," which he asserts shall all

> dissolve,
> And, like this insubstantial pageant faded,
> Leave not a wrack behind. We are such stuff
> As dreams are made on, and our little life
> Is rounded with a sleep. (*The Tempest* 4.1.152–58)

None of these passages is completely straightforward, but they share an assumption that art is fictive, dreamlike, feigning, fading, illusory— terms that describe all representative art, in contrast to nature, but the art of theater in particular, because of its inherent evanescence.[5]

In thinking about Shakespeare in comparison to Sidney, however, it is important to bear in mind that when Sidney wrote his treatise, he addressed a particular set of problems, for awareness of the same problems illuminates Shakespeare's esthetic comments. Most important, Sidney wrote in response to Stephen Gosson's antitheatrical argument, *The School of Abuse* (1579), which Gosson had dedicated to Sidney, presumably because both were associated with the cause of greater reform in the English church, and Gosson therefore thought he could count on

Sidney's support and patronage.[6] If so, he was mistaken. Sidney indeed identified with the Earl of Leicester's reform-minded party (he was Leicester's nephew and potentially his heir), but Sidney was not as radical as Gosson, as Sidney's robust rebuttal of *The School of Abuse* makes clear.[7] Sidney's assertion that poetry deals in make-believe is a rhetorical feint in his duel with Gosson, for it allows Sidney to respond to Gosson's charge that poets are liars by asserting that the poet's creation of something out of nothing imitates God's creative activity and by conceding that the poet "nothing affirms" in order to assert that the poet also "never lieth" (*Apology*, 184).

Gosson's accusation concerning lying poets belongs to a literal-minded conception of both truth and art that is closely related to arguments concerning reform in the English church. The reason Sidney took Gosson up so sharply is that Gosson's attack could easily be construed as questioning the status quo, which had been decided in the early years of Elizabeth's reign, and Sidney almost certainly did not wish to be identified with that kind of questioning.[8] In the 1560s, when Elizabethan ecclesiastical standards were being formulated, the Queen had very different expectations for Christian worship from those held by religious refugees who flocked back to England from the continent. They assumed that the English church would follow the simplified liturgical model established by continental reformers, but Elizabeth began with almost diametric assumptions, having conformed to the liturgical practices of traditional religion under her sister.[9] The Queen therefore negotiated a difficult compromise with her reform-minded bishops. She wanted all English churches to include candles on the altar, crucifixes with "an image of Christ together with Mary and John," and liturgical vestments.[10] In the end, she compromised with the bishops by not requiring the first two practices, though she retained them in her private chapel for the rest of her life, but she insisted on modified versions of traditional liturgical vestments, and her insistence continued to frustrate more radical reformers throughout her reign.

The Queen's reasoning in the so-called vestment controversy is not as clearly recorded as that of her opposition, but her tolerance for what her opponents called "popish" worship almost certainly indicates some degree of sympathy with the argument that visible signs served as aids to devotion, or in other words, that the truth could be apprehended in part through a perceptible sign, which was acknowledged to be distinct from the thing it signified. Richard Hooker declares "thattire which the minister of God is by order to use at times of divine service" to be an "indifferent" matter, used for "ornament" and "beauty," but it was by no means indifferent in the sacramental sign system that the most radical reformers wanted to eradicate.[11] At least initially, the Queen ordered that priests wear their vestments even when they were not presiding in the liturgy—a measure of how much she affirmed clerical attire as a sign of the sacred office. Retaining vestments, however modified, was thus consistent with a moderate response to the iconoclastic dispute that had first broken out during the reign of Elizabeth's father. In its strongest form, iconoclasm had destroyed much of England's ecclesiastical art during the reign of Edward VI, and the retention of "ornament" for "beauty" in the liturgy conceived of religious devotion differently from those who believed that anything more than the unadorned spoken and written word should be eliminated. The more moderate position is the one that Sidney's defense of poetry implicitly takes in opposition to Gosson. For Sidney's argument that poetry "nothing affirmeth" is more positive than it sounds. It is not equivalent to agnosticism or skepticism: he strongly advocates poetry's morally ameliorative effect, going so far as to assert that the poet "with the force of a divine breath . . . bringeth things forth far surpassing her [nature's] doings," and poetry is therefore evidence in us of "erected wit," that is, the knowledge of God and of moral expectation that "our infected will keepeth us from reaching unto" because of the fall (*Apology*, 157). In short, though Sidney frankly acknowledges poetry to be fictive (thus implicitly yielding a point to Gosson that it is not the truth), he nonetheless asserts that it is an aid to apprehending truth, whose reality he is so far from denying that he simply assumes it, thus making clear his conformity with the principles that underlay the Queen's preference for a modified system of liturgical signs.

Yet for radical reformers, the question could not be decided so easily, for the reason they rejected signs as a means to apprehending truth is that they took signs for "a wicked idol," "monstrous," an "abomination," "wicked and devilish," all terms used by Thomas Becon, who had resided in Strasbourg and Marburg during Mary's reign, and who attacked the traditional liturgy when he returned.[12] Christ wore "such comely apparel as he used daily to wear" when he offered holy communion, Becon complains, but "Ye [popish priests] come unto your

altar as a game-player unto his stage," adorning themselves with various pieces of "costume": surplice, amice, alb, stole, flannel—all declaring what Becon sarcastically calls "a solemn mystery." "Last of all come
on your fool's coat, which called a vestment, lacking nothing but a
cock's comb."[13] The simplified liturgy and attire the reformers advocated was directly related to their conception of a literal biblical truth that
could only be impaired by anything that was imposed between the truth
and those who believed it—a conception underlying their well-known
emphasis on liturgical preaching and the literary plain style. "A sacrament ministered without preaching of the word is but a dumb ceremony," Becon declares, "a glass offered to a blind man, and a tale told
to one that is deaf."[14] As Jonas Barish has pointed out, the reformers'
assumption regarding plain truth also helps to explain their antitheatricalism.[15] Why did the preaching of the Word require "theatrical"
adornment, William Tyndale asked rhetorically in the 1530s: "What
helpeth it that the priest when he goeth to mass disguiseth himself with
a great part of the passion of Christ and playeth out the rest under
silence, with signs and proffers, with nodding, becking and mowing?"
Such "mumming," Tyndale concluded, only served to promote "superstition" rather than the plain truth of the gospel.[16] Tyndale and Becon
were objecting to the Roman mass, but their objection, and their way of
phrasing it, clearly underlies opposition to the reformed English liturgy
in the 1560s and beyond, which paralleled rejection of traditional biblical drama. John Rainolds, professor of Greek at Oxford and a strong
influence on William Gosson, when Gosson was a student at Corpus
Christi, drew the contrast sharply in the 1590s between biblical simplic-
ity and popish theater:

> Whereas the profane and wicked toys of passion plays, plays setting forth
> Christ's passion, procured by popish priests, who, being corrupted from
> the simplicity that is in Christ, as they have transformed the celebrating
> of the sacrament of the Lord's supper into a mass-game, and all other
> parts of the ecclesiastical service into theatrical sights, so instead of
> preaching the word they cause it to be played.[17]

Rainolds' close linking of biblical drama and "the ecclesiastical service"
establishes continuity in resistance to antitheatricalism and "playing" of
all kinds—whether in the liturgy or in the theater itself.

Many Elizabethan bishops who initially opposed the Queen's liturgical preferences eventually conceded, as Hooker does, that vestments

were "adiaphora," or matters of indifference to faith, and they even dismissed reform-minded priests in their dioceses who refused to conform to the modified Elizabethan liturgical style. Still, their determination to eliminate images and candles indicates how strong their initial difference with the Queen was, and how clearly it focused on the ontological status of visible signs. In opposing the Roman view, the English church affirmed that God no longer permitted miracles after the apostolic era, as Shakespeare's Archbishop of Canterbury anachronistically acknowledges in his comment that "miracles are ceased" (*Henry V* 1.1.68), and as Becon suggests in his mockery of vestments as "a solemn mystery," now banished by the plainness of the gospel, but the bishops' resistance to liturgical signs, ornaments, and imagery indicates both the openness of the question and the contentiousness of the English church's eventual compromise.

THEATER AND ECCLESIASTICAL REFORM

Where theater in particular is concerned, the problems were especially vexing, and they help, in part, to account for the ambiguities of late Tudor theater history. Elizabeth's government forbade plays touching on religion and governance of the realm as early as 1559—legislation that eventually led to the demise of the communal biblical history plays but also discouraged the revival of Protestant drama like John Bale's, written at the height of Thomas Cromwell's power and influence during the reign of Henry VIII.[18] Reform-minded ministers and schoolmasters filled the gap with moral plays influenced by humanism, many of them "offered for acting" by traveling groups of actors.[19] The most lasting contribution of these plays was to make the Vice a popular and ubiquitous theatrical fixture, but their popularity faded with the success of permanent commercial theaters near London after 1576. The latter are the real target of Gosson's attack in 1579, for he was not opposed to the strain of humanist moral drama, having contributed plays to it himself, one of which he claims was performed at the Theater.[20] The new commercial theaters were effectively protected by the legislation of 1559, as long as they steered clear of forbidden subjects, though they were opposed by the City of London for a variety of reasons, many of them reflected in Gosson's critique. Since religion was the principal forbidden subject, the 1559 law had the unintended consequence of contributing to secularization of the theater.

Behind this complex and highly politicized development lie struggles with the meaning of signs of the sort that we have seen at issue between Gosson and Sidney—struggles that reflect the English church's compromise. In its most stark terms, as Sarah Beckwith argues, the difference was between those who affirmed a liturgy and theater of acknowledged signs and those who advocated a liturgy of literal truth together with a theater that offered only that truth in disguise (like Bale's or Gosson's), because otherwise theater offered a disguised lie, or a doubling of untruth. But the terms were not necessarily that stark. Sidney, as we have seen, affirmed the fictiveness of "poesy," and thus conceded Gosson's argument that it was a lie, but Sidney defended poesy as a means to truth, despite its fiction; in other words, he defended poesy as a sign system.

While the Elizabethan compromise therefore effectively effaced a culture of sacramental signs, as Beckwith argues, the compromise was still a compromise, and it consequently permitted a broader array of options with correspondingly greater complexity than appeared, say, in the Scottish church. It is difficult to see how the poetry of Edmund Spenser would have been possible had the English church followed its most radical voices. Tolerance of theatricality is a case in point, because it has been cited by critics as a fatal problem for presenting something immaterial that a play purports to be true, such as God, devils, angels, or any of the Four Last Things besides death. "Performance kills belief," writes Stephen Greenblatt, "or rather acknowledging theatricality kills the credibility of the supernatural."[21] Greenblatt is dealing with skeptical Protestant response to exorcism in the late sixteenth century, and exorcism is one of the "solemn mysteries," to use Thomas Becon's phrase, that the English church eventually decided to oppose. Greenblatt's generalization is therefore consistent with the Protestant critique of traditional liturgy and theater as if it were based on disguise rather than confidence in a communally shared sign system. Protestants effected a "transformation of faith into bad faith," in Greenblatt's phrase (113), or to put the same point in different terms: "A theater of epistemological doubt in a signifying language of appearance and reality replaces a theater of acknowledgment that uses the play of presence and absence as its signifying idiom, a presence and absence understood through and achieved by means of the community's availability to and presence to itself."[22]

It is a mistake, however, to extend Greenblatt's generalization to all theater that attempts to stage the immaterial as something material (i.e., visibly performed) in a play. Leanne Groeneveld, for example, makes the same point Greenblatt does about the recourse to theatrical machinery in the Croxton *Play of the Sacrament* from the late fifteenth century:

> The introduction of theatrical spectacle into the church raises the disturbing possibility that theatre is, in fact, already ubiquitous there, where one would least expect and hope to find it. If sophisticated special effects closely or even exactly resemble divine wonders, could not other or all miraculous events be nothing more than impressive theatre?[23]

Groeneveld's point is that staging a miracle makes dramatic fiction inherently untrustworthy, because it deconstructs the very point it tries to make. In support of her point, Groeneveld cites the rood of Boxley as a parallel case. This was a mechanical crucifix that could perform various rudimentary functions, such as moving its eyelids and bowing its head. The mechanism was "exposed" in the initial outburst of iconoclastic reform in 1538, when the rood was used to bolster the case that traditional belief and practice were mere superstition foisted on the ignorant by exploitative and greedy monks—exactly the case that Becon makes against traditional liturgy. Groeneveld cites the rood as suggestive evidence about contemporary response to mechanical miracles, including miracles in plays. This is to read a theater of signs, however, as if it were a theater of disguise. Like the theater of signs, the rood of Boxley was an aid to devotion, and Groeneveld in effect understands traditional drama and its sign system from a rationalistic and radically Protestant point of view.

The distinction between signs and disguise is important in understanding theatricality and skepticism in the sixteenth century and therefore in understanding skepticism and faith. Greenblatt and Groeneveld are right if one considers the impact of Protestantism on traditional drama, but their historical model has a harder time accommodating the skepticism of Erasmus and More, as pointed out in chapter 1. If theatricality destroys belief, then what are we to make of the theatricality that pervades Erasmus's *Exorcism*, which mocks a naïve priest's efforts to exorcise a haunting purgatorial spirit? If Bale learned his skepticism from More and Erasmus, as I suggested earlier, was belief already destroyed before the reformers destroyed it?

I think the answer is "no" for two reasons. First, traditional reformers (i.e., reformers before the reformation) aimed to discover abuses, as they saw them, in faith and practice; they did not aim to change or even challenge the whole sacramental sign system. Evidence of this is Erasmus's conclusion in *Exorcism*. Polus does not expose Faunus as a fraud; he entraps Faunus into exhibiting greed and pride in order to be able to laugh at the resulting spectacle, but he concludes the farcical show he mounted by preserving Faunus's belief system intact, allowing him to think that the spirit he attempted to exorcise had gone to paradise. Nothing in *Exorcism* leads one to question purgatory, ghosts, haunting, or exorcism. It is not even clear from Erasmus's satire how or whether Faunus learned anything, unless the real Faunus was supposed to read Erasmus's colloquy and see himself in the character the satirist invented. If so, then the colloquy is a sign system for Faunus to interpret and learn from, but it is not a means to dismantle everything Faunus and Polus believe together. Additional evidence of the early skeptics' belief is the equal attention their satire pays to kings and clerics. Both are held to the same moral standard, and both are found wanting. The sacramental community was unified in Christ's body, but its unity did not eradicate social class tension or the abuse of wealth and power—if anything, it tended to valorize them by acknowledging them in ritual.[24] To highlight, analyze, and satirize abuses of this kind—whether they pertain to the clergy or the nobility—as More does in *Utopia*, is fundamentally different from Protestant skepticism, which demonized the pope and sanctified the king, as in Bale's *King Johan*, which imagines John as a proto-Protestant martyr to papal ambition and hypocrisy.

The second reason that belief was not destroyed before Protestant reformers destroyed it is that Protestant reformers destroyed belief only in the eyes of traditional believers. In other words, the struggle between traditional belief and Protestantism was not between belief and unbelief but between two systems of belief. Skepticism was used by both sides throughout the sixteenth century as a way of attacking the other. Samuel Harsnett's demolition of exorcistic ritual, cited by Greenblatt as definitive unbelief, belongs to this category. Harsnett was a bishop in the Elizabethan church, and he was an unbeliever (a heretic) only in the eyes of Catholics. To view him as an unbeliever in the vein of Voltaire or David Hume is a simple instance of historical anachronism.

SHAKESPEARE AND THEATRICAL FICTION

The status of real being in theatrical fiction—or what might be called the ontological question in theater—thus lay close to the heart of controversy about signs in the Reformation, and Shakespeare unavoidably addresses it as more than an esthetic question when he addresses the question of truth and fiction in theater. Queen Elizabeth's moderate sympathy with traditional liturgical practice is evident from her stated preferences, as we have seen, and they are preferences that Sidney's *Apology* implicitly endorses with regard to poetry, which he defends as a fiction (or sign) that points to truth beyond itself. In this context, Shakespeare is like Sidney in conceding that drama is an illusory fiction ("the truest poetry is the most feigning," as Touchstone avers [*As You Like It* 3.3.17–18]), while simultaneously affirming that it can be a means to apprehending something true.[25] To Theseus' skeptical rejection of the lovers' story, for example, Hippolyta responds affirmatively:

> But all the story of the night told over,
> And all their minds transfigured so together,
> More witnesseth than fancy's images
> And grows to something of great constancy;
> But, howsoever, strange and admirable.
> (*A Midsummer Night's Dream*, 5.1.23–27)

Fancy's images may be only theatrical illusions (antique fables and fairy toys, in Theseus' phrasing), but they nonetheless witness to something constant—something both faithful and truthful—though its strangeness and admirability indeed make it "more than cool reason ever comprehends," as Theseus has just asserted (5.1.6), and as Bottom attests when he describes his "most rare vision," with its synesthetic allusions to 1 Corinthians 2:9 (4.1.203–14).[26] Describing precisely how signs convey meaning may have been more than anyone could manage in Elizabethan or Jacobean England. At the very least we can say that the rejection of religious signs, in the confident belief that truth was literal, univocal, and transparent, was satisfactory only to a radical minority. The epistemology of *A Midsummer Night's Dream* is a good deal more complex than such a radical view, and Shakespeare's implicit defense of signifying fiction amounts to a subtle but vigorous defense of the theater in the face of attacks like Stephen Gosson's.

In short, the view of illusion that emerges in *Midsummer* is consistent with the consensus reached by church and crown in the 1560s concerning the prescribed value of signs as means to truth, but Shakespeare offers a defense of English drama that is stronger than Sidney's and that understands and sympathizes more fully with long-established indigenous tradition. Sidney has nothing good to say about English drama except *Gorboduc*, which he commends for its Senecan style and the "notable morality which it doth most delightfully teach" (*Apology*, 197). Since the morality in question largely concerns the failure of a king to provide responsibly for his succession, Sidney may be obliquely suggesting his own concern about the Queen's failure in this regard, though this concern was ubiquitous, as we noticed in chapter 5. In any case, Sidney condemns *Gorboduc*, along with other English plays he does not mention, as "defectious in the circumstances," that is, in failing to conform to neoclassical expectations concerning the unities of time and place (*Apology*, 197). He pokes elegant fun at the naïve dramaturgy that requires "the player, when he cometh in" to identify "where he is, or else the tale will not be conceived." What is one minute a garden must next be imagined a rock and then a cave. "While in the meantime two armies fly in, represented with four swords and bucklers, and then what hard heart will not receive it for a pitched field?"[27] Sidney learned his neoclassicism from Italian critics, but its assumption that verisimilitude is necessary for theatrical illusion not only imposes arbitrary limitations, as Samuel Johnson would eventually recognize, but also comports with the literal-mindedness of radical reformers.[28] In his neoclassical critique of native drama, Sidney implicitly concedes another point to Gosson.

Such literal-mindedness is in part what Shakespeare satirizes in the incompetent dramaturgy of the Athenian laborers who stage a play for Duke Theseus. *Pyramus and Thisbe* brilliantly sends up Sidney's assumption (or the assumption he borrowed from the Italians) that theater requires verisimilitude to be credible. The actor playing the lion must explain that he is not a real lion, or the ladies in the audience might be frightened; the casements of the chamber where the play is performed must be left open, so that moonlight can shine on the acting area, or the audience will not believe it is night (3.1.33-54). These are, of course, esthetic concerns, and they arguably respond to neoclassical strictures, as critics have suggested.[29] But they are not merely esthetic concerns. They also bear directly on epistemology (how and what we know from watching a play), and on ontology (whether, and if so how, what we are watching participates in being). The answers suggested by *Midsummer* are not dogmatic, but they undoubtedly go beyond Sidney's defense (which is actually an attack, when it comes to drama), and they are in principle closer to the Queen's position on signs than to the radical reformers'.

Shakespeare's way of setting up the scene with the rude mechanicals in the forest in fact establishes the sign system that undermines their literalism. "Pat, pat," says Quince, "here's a marvelous convenient place for our rehearsal. This green plot shall be our stage, this hawthorn brake our tiring-house, and we will do it in action as we will do it before the Duke" (3.1.2–5). With these brief directions, the actor playing Quince transforms a bare stage into a forest glade, though it had been an urban scene when the play began—precisely the procedure that Sidney condemns, though it was so familiar to Elizabethan audiences that Shakespeare could toy with it effortlessly to create a richly comic effect, as he does in *Two Gentlemen of Verona*, when Launce imagines first one and then another of his shoes to be his father, his hat to be Nan the maid, and himself to be Crab the dog. "No, the dog is himself, and I am the dog—Oh, the dog is me, and I am myself" (2.3.21–22). Launce's hilariously imagined confusion brilliantly makes the point that an audience will accept whatever value the actor ascribes to the objects around him (or indeed to an invisible object): they will become signs for us of whatever he credibly imagines them to be.[30] This is a tribute to the ontology and epistemology of the bare stage, which depends heavily on the actor's art, as the art of mime still does, though without the added advantage of voice. When actors perform "bad acting," we believe them, if they are in fact acting well (amateur actors love to perform *Pyramus and Thisbe*, because they think it gives them license to overact, but their weak performance ironically works against them, as weak performance invariably does), just as we believe the bare stage to be a green plot, even if the actors who are imagining characters who are poor at the craft of acting worry about the possibility of convincing an audience that the moon is shining.[31] We have no trouble believing that the daylit stage is shrouded in night when the actor playing Oberon declares, "Ill met by moonlight, proud Titania" (2.1.60).[32]

The importance of recognizing stage ontology can be illustrated by means of another play within a play: the performance of Falstaff and Prince Henry in the tavern in *1 Henry IV* 2.4. The play they present extempore imagines the Prince's appearance at court before his father, and it therefore allows the performers to speak to each other, as themselves, through roles they assume in the tavern. The Prince is the least disguised of the two, and the roles he assumes are less challenging, for when he plays the Prince, he is obviously playing himself, and when he impersonates the King, he is imagining himself (and asking everyone else to imagine him) in a social and political function (or role) that he will inevitably assume in reality. In both roles, he insults and rejects Falstaff, thus revealing through play his view of their real relationship, as Hal has already made clear in soliloquy (1.2.189–211). Similarly, in both the roles Falstaff plays he defends himself and thus in effect plays himself through the role of king and prince, culminating in the famous line (referring to himself), "banish not him thy Harry's company," repeated verbatim for emphasis (2.4.472–74). The parallel between social roles and theatrical roles makes this scene a touchstone for meta-dramatic critics, who argue that all of Shakespeare's plays are really about making plays, because all of life is role-playing and game-playing.

But metadramatic analysis misses the ontological point. We can see the Prince playing himself through both roles he takes on (the prince and the king) only if we see him as the Prince; if we see him as an actor in reality, we lose the effect. He must establish and maintain his identity in the world of the play, in order for the play he composes and enacts in the tavern to function meaningfully, and in order for us to recognize that he appropriates other forms of drama, such as the morality play, to enhance his power by imagining Falstaff in appropriately damning moral roles—the Vice and the devil. In other words, we need to recognize that Prince Henry casts Falstaff in the role of the Vice before trying to decide whether or not Shakespeare does (that is, whether Falstaff-as-Vice defines his role), because the two issues are distinct: one happens in the ontological world of the play, and the other is a more complicated question of interpreting Falstaff's attitude toward life, his relationship to the Prince, his way of relating to others, his political significance—in short, everything he says and does, not just the social role that Hal wants to define for him. To be sure, mingling commoner and prince—that is, assigning a common actor to play a noble character—has a leveling effect of the sort that Shakespeare punningly acknowledges at the end of *All's Well That Ends Well*: "The king's a beggar now the play is done" (Epilogue 1). But to notice that effect is to move into the ontological reality of "the world" as opposed to "the stage": the play is *done* when we recognize that the king is a beggar, and even that recognition takes a moment to sink in, because the social assertion is so artfully combined with an actor's request for applause.

The ontology of staged action is particularly important in *The Tempest*. Prospero stages a play within a play, as Hal does, but the ontology of Prospero's masque as Shakespeare wrote it is quite different from Hal's extempore play in the tavern. To begin with, the actors in the masque are spirits, as Prospero points out (4.1.148–49). In other words, in the ontological world of the play's sign system, spirits exist, just as fairies exist in *A Midsummer Night's Dream*. Moreover, even though Prospero says he has called the spirits "to enact / My present fancies" (4.1.121–22), the masque is not therefore an expression of its composer's and producer's mind in the same way that Hal's play extempore is an expression of his and Falstaff's minds, because Prospero is not a player in the masque; he does not appear in it. On the other hand, in the world where *The Tempest* was first played (whether at court or at the Globe), the masque was performed by the same actors who performed the play in which the masque appeared, and Prospero's masque was therefore profoundly different from the Jacobean court masques that it imitated.[33] For while the spirits of court masques were indeed performed by the same professional actors who performed the spirits in Prospero's masque, the most important performers in court masques were courtiers, who assumed roles that the presenters of the masque (both the writer and theatrical producer) prepared for them as allegorical representations of their ideal identities.[34] If Shakespeare had allowed Prospero's masque to proceed to a climactic dance in which Ferdinand and Miranda took part, it would be a closer parallel to real court masques, in that their dance would somehow figure their ideal relationship, already anticipated in the truncated masque as we have it. The difference, of course, is that Ferdinand and Miranda were (and are) performed by professional actors, so a culminating dance would parallel the function of Hal and Falstaff in their play extempore, in that

Ferdinand and Miranda would perform themselves through assumed roles in the masque, but a courtiers' dance in *The Tempest* could never achieve the ontological status of the court masque, because the masque required real courtiers to perform roles that revealed their ideal identities, and Ferdinand and Miranda were (and are) actors impersonating courtiers.

Another level of complexity in the ontology and epistemology of Shakespeare's stage never occurs to modern audiences, because the paradigm shift of the Enlightenment achieved clarity and certainty about illusion in particular points that were anything but clear and certain before the eighteenth century. This point concerns stage devils. As Stuart Clark argues, the best thinkers in the sixteenth and seventeenth centuries were unable to establish criteria for discerning "among four categories of extraordinary events: real demonic effects, illusory demonic effects, real non-demonic effects, and illusory non-demonic effects. And among the non-demonic, they had to allow for both the spontaneous workings of nature and those produced by human ingenuity."[35] This particular difficulty in defining a crucial issue in both epistemology and ontology bears importantly on the problem of theater as fiction. A superhuman creature in a play is, for us, a straightforward illusory non-demonic effect, produced by human (i.e., as an actor) ingenuity on one side and ordinary theatrical credulity on the other, but if such effects were difficult to distinguish from "real" demonic effects, then the ontology of stage and world was harder for Shakespeare and his contemporaries to distinguish than it is for us. Moreover, theatrical credulity was almost certainly stronger, and what was to be taken for knowledge was less clear.[36] Several accounts record panic at a performance of Marlowe's *Dr. Faustus* in 1594, because actors and audience alike suddenly became convinced that an extra (non-theatrical) devil had appeared on the stage.[37] The incident illustrates Stuart Clark's point about the pre-Enlightenment difficulty of distinguishing illusory demonic effects from real ones. The devils' ability to deceive, Clark points out, made "demonology as much an exercise in epistemology and ontology as in theology and morality" (166).

This difficulty needs to be kept in mind when considering other immaterial phenomena on the Shakespearean stage, such as spirits, ghosts, fairies, angels, gods, and even witches, as well as words of power, like curses, prophecies, and blasphemy. They are not self-evidently empty signs.[38] Dr. Pinch's exorcism of Antipholus of Ephesus in *The Comedy of Errors* and Feste's exorcism of Malvolio in *Twelfth Night* have been taken as evidence of dogmatic rejection of demonic possession in an Enlightenment vein, but they would seem more likely to be expressions of strategic skepticism in conformity with the English church's expectations, formally codified in the canons of 1604.[39] Both scenes mingle elements from Roman Catholic exorcism and puritan dispossession, suggesting that religious extremes are alike in their recourse to excessive zeal—precisely the position of the English church. Dr. Pinch both refers to "holy prayers" (suggesting the sole recourse that Puritans like John Darrel used in dispossession, because they eschewed Roman ritual), and invokes "all the saints in heaven," which no Puritan would ever do (*The Comedy of Errors* 4.4.55, 57). Maria twice calls Malvolio a "Puritan" (*Twelfth Night* 2.3.139, 146), and Feste exorcises him while disguised in a gown as "Sir Topas the curate" (4.2.2), wishing he "were the first that ever dissembled in such a gown" (4.2.5–6). The vestment and reference to "curate" suggest the Church of England as readily as the Church of Rome, but the latter was more immediately stereotyped as hypocritical in Elizabethan England, so Feste's act would appear to be a sign aimed at Catholic dissent, while at least part of the joke is that a "Puritan" is being dispossessed, since Darrel, the Puritan dispossessor, was garnering considerable charismatic authority at just the time *Twelfth Night* was written.[40]

A merely esthetic analysis is not adequate for the spirits in *The Tempest* either. Art and science were not clearly separated in the early seventeenth century, so Prospero as artist needs to be thought of in comparison to someone like Leonardo da Vinci—painter, poet, architect, inventor, engineer, mystic—rather than almost any artist after the eighteenth century, including Romantic artists, who attempted to recapture a pre-Enlightenment (and even, in some influential cases, a pre-Raphaelite) sense of symbol and metaphor. While Ariel and all his quality therefore undoubtedly contribute to the symbolic world *The Tempest* imagines, they are not merely symbolic. Nothing prevents the inference that *The Tempest* helps to reveal the symbolic order that underlies the apparent chaos of nature that surrounds us. Ariel's name and behavior suggest that he is a spirit of the air and therefore a counterpart to three other kinds of spirit whose influence Prospero acknowledges when he renounces his art: spirits of the earth, fire, and water (5.1.33–57). "Then to the elements / Be free, and fare thou well!" are Prospero's last words to Ariel (5.1.321–22). That the movement of the four elements, however, was due to something alive in them was not merely symbolic in the ontological world of the early seventeenth century; rather, it was literal, it was *scientia*, and it was supported, like the geocentric universe, by the authority of both common sense and classical philosophy. The appearance of an elemental spirit in the ontological world of the play was therefore a carryover from the audience's world, a direct parallel to the appearance of imagined human beings in the play and no more or less illusory than they.

The *scientia* of elemental spirits, however, was not "scientific," that is, no one had thought of testing it, as knowledge, with hypotheses, precise observation, analysis, and calculation. Its imprecision is evident in Ariel's appearance at one point "like a water nymph" (*Tempest* 1.2.319 SD), as if the spirits of the elements are completely interchangeable. Similar imprecision is apparent in William Strachey's account of the shipwreck on which Shakespeare drew in *The Tempest*. Strachey's narrative moves directly from the impossibility of navigating by the stars in a hurricane to

> an apparition of a little round light, like a faint star, trembling, and streaming along with a sparkling blaze, half the height upon the main mast, and shooting sometimes from shroud to shroud, [at]tempting to settle as it were upon any of the four shrouds; and for three or four hours together, or rather more, half the night it kept with us, running sometimes along the mainyard to the very end and then returning.[41]

Neither Strachey nor any of his contemporaries had the language and conceptual apparatus for recognizing and describing discharges of atmospheric electricity.[42] Though he comments patronizingly that "the superstitious seamen make many constructions of this sea-fire," even listing some of them, as if he were a folklorist collecting backwoods aetiological accounts of natural phenomena, it is nonetheless clear from his own account that he had no better explanation of the mysterious light than those he dismisses as superstition: "Be what it will, we laid other foundations of safety or ruin than in the rising or falling of it, could it have served us now miraculously to have taken our height by, it might have stricken amazement, and a reverence in our devotions, according to the due of a miracle."

Strachey's account has long been recognized as an inspiration for Ariel's report of his conduct in *The Tempest*:

> I boarded the King's ship. Now on the beak,
> Now in the waist, the deck, in every cabin,
> I flamed amazement. Sometime I'd divide
> And burn in many places; on the topmast,
> The yards, and bowsprit would I flame distinctly,
> Then meet and join. Jove's lightning, the precursors
> O'th' dreadful thunderclaps, more momentary
> And sight-outrunning were not. The fire and cracks
> Of sulfurous roaring the most mighty Neptune
> Seem to besiege and make his bold waves tremble,
> Yea, his dread trident shake. (1.2.197–207)

At least some part of the power of Shakespeare's language is in its mythologizing of nature: Jove and Neptune are alive and active in the storm. Yet it is not clear that this is *mere* mythologizing—no more than artful language. No one had an explanation for movement of the elements that did not somehow literally animate them, as Strachey does in his attempt to describe the storm: "the glut of water (as if throttling the wind ere while) was no sooner a little emptied and qualified but instantly the winds (as having gotten their mouths now free and at liberty) spake more loud and grew more tumultuous and malignant" (290). Strachey can dismiss the light as a miracle (it would only have been miraculous, he says, if it could have served as a navigational aid), in keeping with the official teaching of the English church regarding the cessation of miracles, but he still has no rational way to account for it, so in a commonly accepted distinction, he seems to admit it as a *mirum* (a wonder) while denying it as a miracle—a distinction with no very clear difference.[43] Similarly, he can attribute violent intention ("throttling") to the water and a desire for freedom to the wind, to which it gives angry voice. The four elements were alive for him and for Shakespeare in a way that they cannot possibly be for us, though no one could say precisely, "scientifically," just what "alive" meant. Ariel is as good an explanation as any (just as the fairies are invoked to explain terrible storms in *A Midsummer Night's Dream* 2.1.81–117), but the explanation clearly misses the mark where science is concerned, even as it exceeds the bounds of art, encroaching wantonly on ontology and epistemology as well, in a way that makes these three philosophical categories impossible to distinguish with the kind of certainty and clarity that came only gradually with the Age of Reason.

What is true for Prospero as "artist" would seem to be true for Shakespeare as well, though we have only his poetry and plays on which to base a conclusion. A strikingly ambiguous detail in *The Tempest* seems to owe much to the play's expansive conception of art. Prospero's speech of renunciation not only implicitly identifies the spirits who serve him with the four natural elements but also draws on Medea's invocation to Night, Hecate, and Earth in Ovid's *Metamorphoses* 7:192–219. Jonathan Bate comments: "The act of imitation here [i.e., Shakespeare's imitating Ovid] implies that all invocations of magical power are in some sense the same . . . and therefore that Prospero and Medea are in some sense the same."[44] In some sense, yes, but what is it? Bate wants to move toward identifying Prospero's power with Medea's witchery, and the principal evidence for doing so is Prospero's claim (echoed from Ovid) that "graves at my command / Have waked their sleepers, oped, and let 'em forth / By my so potent art" (5.1.48–50), because the reversal of death was thought to be God's unique prerogative and therefore beyond the power of benign spirits, who operated within the limits of God's permissive will. For Prospero to have waked the dead must therefore require his recourse to demonic power—precisely the power on which Antichrist draws to raise the dead (or at least to animate zombies) in the Chester *Coming of Antichrist*, though that power is rebuked in the play by God's raising Enock and Helias from the dead.[45] But Prospero's farewell speech to his art is also, "in some sense," Shakespeare's farewell to his art, as interpreters of the play have long recognized. But in what sense? The analogy is not perfect, and it is not allegorical, but raising the dead is "in some sense" true of Shakespeare's plays, if not of Prospero's art, for one of Shakespeare's favorite devices is the return of the dead, from Emilia in *The Comedy of Errors* to Hermione in *The Winter's Tale*.[46] To argue that Prospero must literally be a witch is to oversimplify or disambiguate what he "in some sense" represents, including the artist who created him.[47]

To be sure, Shakespeare's resurrections are different from those in the Chester *Coming of Antichrist* because they are not resurrections in the ontological world of the play. Imagined persons in Shakespeare's play worlds think that someone like Emilia, Hero, Sebastian, Thaisa, Marina, Imogen, or Hermione come to life again, because they thought they were dead, but their thinking so is a mistake (i.e., in the ontological world of the play they think an illusion is true), because the dead characters are, as we say, *only symbolically* dead. Hermione comes the closest to being an exception, because we, as well as most characters in *The Winter's Tale*, think she is dead from the moment a servant announces her death (3.2.145) and Paulina confirms it (3.2.200–3), until the moment "she stirs" and moves to embrace her estranged husband (5.3.103). Shakespeare's concealing of information about Hermione's true state is an instance of tragicomic illusion that may owe something to the dramaturgy of John Fletcher, but one cannot say that Fletcher's dramaturgy is "in some sense" esthetic, because it is merely esthetic— that is, it signifies nothing but its own artfulness—and the same is not true for *The Winter's Tale*. Hermione's resurrection is really (in the ontological world of the play) a decision to reveal herself for the first time in sixteen years in response to the recovery of her long-lost daughter, as she explains:

> For thou shalt hear that I
> Knowing by Paulina that the oracle
> Gave hope thou wast in being, have preserved
> Myself to see the issue. (5.3.126–29)

Shakespeare closely links knowledge with faith, hope, and love in this explanation for Hermione's mysterious reappearance, for her decision to move first toward Leontes and embrace him enacts her forgiveness, with its root in charity, her hope for the future, and her faith in her husband's penitence. These things are all symbolized by Hermione's resurrection, but other verbs than "symbolize" describe them better in the ontological world of the play: "enact," "embody," "live out," even "ethically prove." Hermione's extraordinary troth is also her truth, and it is what we (along with Leontes) must awake our faith to see in the world of the play, which is, of course, "in some sense," only an illusion.

Shakespeare's nonmiraculous miracles are the benign side of a long tradition of stage illusions that he inherited from his own acting tradition, and no one exploited them more brilliantly and more richly than he did. More familiar, and better recognized as meta-theatrical, are malign illusions, especially those associated with the Vice.[48] Evil is powerful when it disguises itself as something else, as the story of the fall had long shown in English drama; in fact, it is so powerful that it can easily make illusion per se appear to be the problem. An example appears in

The Rape of Lucrece, when Lucrece is so overcome with anger and humiliation after her rape that her indignation at the compelling artistic rendition of Sinon's treachery causes her momentarily to lose the distinction between her own world and the ontological world of the painting:

> Here, all enraged, such passion her assails
> That patience is quite beaten from her breast.
> She tears the senseless Sinon with her nails,
> Comparing him to that unhappy guest
> Whose deed hath made herself herself detest.
>   At last she smilingly with this gives o'er:
>   "Fool, fool!" quoth she, "his wounds will not be sore." (1562–68)

Taking the illusion in the painting for reality, she attacks the illusion, only to realize that she cannot make Tarquin suffer by that means. Lucrece lapses momentarily (and utterly forgivably) into iconoclasm, but she rapidly recovers her senses. Shakespeare sets up this brief confusion in a careful description of Sinon's depiction that is fundamentally theatrical. The painter has imagined Sinon so expertly as to reveal no hint of his treachery in the traitor's appearance, giving "the harmless show / An humble gait, calm looks, eyes wailing still" (1507–8) so that no one could detect his deceit.

> But, like a constant and confirmèd devil,
> He entertained a show so seeming just,
> And therein so ensconced his secret evil,
> That jealousy itself could not mistrust
> False-creeping craft and perjury should thrust
>   Into so bright a day such black-faced storms,
>   Or blot with hell-born sin such saintlike forms. (1506–19)

The whole description suggests the actor's art, especially the repetition of "show." Moreover, Shakespeare's use of "devil," "hell-born," and "saintlike" clearly indicate the medieval dramatic tradition on which he is drawing at this point in the narrative, and it is quite distinct from the tradition of Roman stoicism that dominates *Lucrece*, despite stoicism's own inclination to moral self-dramatizing, as pointed out in chapter 6.

As if to prepare for the moment of Lucrece's confusion, when Shakespeare first describes the painting in *Lucrece*, he establishes its ontological world in the same way an actor creates the ontological world of the stage, as illustrated by Launce in *Two Gentlemen of Verona*:

> For much imaginary work was there,
> Conceit deceitful, so compact, so kind,
> That for Achilles' image stood his spear
> Gripped in an armèd hand; himself, behind,
> Was left unseen, save to the eye of mind.
>> A hand, a foot, a face, a leg, a head,
>> Stood for the whole to be imaginèd. (1422–28)

Achilles' spear gripped in an armed hand is enough to evoke the whole warrior in the imagined painting, just as Launce's shoe evokes his mother in his imagined pageant of leave-taking, or "four or five most vile and ragged foils" evoke "the name of Agincourt" in *Henry V* (4.Pro.50, 52).[49] Such an illusion as Achilles' spear in the imagined painting might be described as morally neutral, in contrast to the malign illusion of Sinon that momentarily confuses and enrages Lucrece, because she has just been deceived by Tarquin.

Shakespeare's malign illusions in the theater are famous and often theatrically self-reflective, in keeping with their origin in the Vice of the morality play. It is important, however, that they are not merely theatrical; they are also moral and in at least one case, *Richard III*, they are also powerfully political (see above, chap. 4). When Richard of Gloucester first announces his treacherous ambition to us, the secret auditors of his evil purpose, he compares himself to Ulysses, Sinon, the chameleon, Proteus, and "the murderous Machiavel"—all infamous for their ability to blend in with a background, or even to create a background, that conceals their true identity (*3 Henry VI* 3.2.189–93). Richard's ambition for illegitimate power is unmistakably demonic. He brilliantly and cynically describes himself to a prospective victim, Prince Edward, as if warning him against someone else:

> Sweet Prince, the untainted virtue of your years
> Hath not yet dived into the world's deceit.
> Nor more can you distinguish of a man
> Than of his outward show—which, God he knows,
> Seldom or never jumpeth with the heart. (*Richard III* 3.1.7–11)

Later in his conversation with Prince Edward, again turning confidentially to us, as Iago repeatedly does, Richard identifies the dramatic inspiration for his kind of deception: "Thus, like the formal Vice, Iniquity, / I moralize two meanings in one word" (3.1.82–83). Little wonder that he and Buckingham deliberately "counterfeit the deep tragedian" in deceiving the Lord Mayor and commons with Richard's show of pious reluctance to accept the crown (3.5). Their gleeful deception is not a condemnation of the theater per se but of those who use theatrical illusion for malicious ends, as an honest but fearful scrivener reveals as he talks to himself: "Who is so gross / That cannot see this palpable device? / Yet who's so bold but says he sees it not?" (3.6.10–12). As argued in chapter 1, this kind of analysis is the basis for Shakespearean suspicion.

ILLUSION IN *THE TAMING OF THE SHREW*
AND *MUCH ADO ABOUT NOTHING*

In two comedies, Shakespeare contrasts two different kinds of illusion, as if to make the point that Lucrece recognizes when she comes to her senses after attacking the painted image of Sinon—that signifying fictions are not evil, as some reformers maintained, though they can be put to brilliantly evil purposes; rather, theatrical fiction is neutral in itself and can also be put to benign purposes. *The Taming of the Shrew*, with its Italian setting, begins with a *beffa*, or practical joke, of the kind that Filippo Brunelleschi, the early-fifteenth-century artist, architect, and engineer, is said to have played on a fellow citizen of Florence.[50] Like Brunelleschi's trick on a carpenter, the lord's *beffa* in *Taming* is class-inflected, in that it targets a drunken commoner, Christopher Sly (he describes himself as "by birth a peddler, by education a cardmaker, by transmutation a bearherd, and now by present profession a tinker" [Ind. 2.18–20]), who comes to believe, as the carpenter does, that the identity ascribed to him is real: "Upon my life, I am a lord indeed" (Ind. 2.72). Revealingly, however, he twice calls for a pot of ale when offered sack, the gentleman's drink (Ind. 2.1 and 75), so that his irrepressible appetite as a commoner betrays his belief, imposed by illusion, about a new aristocratic identity.

The Induction to *Taming* technically makes the play itself a play within a play, performed by traveling actors who visit the lord's house, and though the story of the lord's trick on Sly is unfinished in Shakespeare's play, it serves to introduce illusion as a key feature of the two love stories, one of which (the story of Lucentio and Bianca) is based on another kind of Italian theatrical illusion—the "suppose," as Shakespeare encountered it in George Gascoigne's *Supposes*, an English prose adaptation of Ariosto's *I Suppositi*.[51] The Induction thus introduces the theme of illusion that is central to both romantic plots and suggests a contrast between the two courtships, in that one is genuinely transformative, while the other is a mere "suppose."[52] The lord's superficially successful effort to make Sly "forget himself" (Ind. 1.40) anticipates and informs Petruchio's parallel effort with Kate. The most important difference is that Petruchio himself seems to change, unlike the lord in the induction. Starting out as a swaggering gold-digger (1.2.74–75; 2.1.114–37), he learns "reverent care" of Kate (4.1.192), which she acknowledges in her speech of submission (5.2.151), and which he proves by inviting her to kiss him instead of accepting her offer to place her hand beneath his foot (182–84)—the difference between the two gestures both signaling and sealing a new and better stage in their relationship. To be sure, his "care" involves treating Kate with the same perverseness that she treats the rest of the world, thus deceiving her (as the lord deceives Sly) into a new sense of herself and of others. The resulting ambiguity of tone is an indication that Shakespeare only partly resolved the antifeminism that he inherited from folk traditions about taming a wife. Though he eschewed the gross mistreatment of stories such as *The Ballad of the Curst Wife Wrapt in a Morel's Skin* (1550), he was not completely successful in distinguishing the changes in both Kate and Petruchio from crass male dominance.[53] Still, it is clear that the identity Kate acquires goes much deeper than Sly's learned identity. For one thing, what she learns about herself is true, though she had not known it before—namely, that she actually cares about others, as she shows when she goes out of herself to protect the servants whom Petruchio supposedly mistreats (4.1.69–71, 144, 156–57). The self she "forgets" or leaves behind in this process is not independent, self-confident, and assertive; it is codependent, self-loathing, and jealous, because of the way her father and Bianca consistently treat her (details of which Shakespeare adds to Gascoigne). Baptista repeatedly takes Bianca's side against Kate and misinterprets Kate's resulting jealousy, evident in her railing against him:

> She is your treasure, she must have a husband;
> I must dance barefoot on her wedding day,
> And for your love to her lead apes in hell. (2.1.32–34)

Baptista's response is merely to feel sorry for himself: "Was ever gentle-man thus grieved as I?" (2.1.35), wholly ignoring Kate's real grievance. Her father always presents her with an image of herself that she reflects back by striking out at everyone around her. In contrast, Petruchio even-tually learns how to bring out her compassion and charity, which a com-plex fiction (presented as part of the *beffa* played on the fictional Christopher Sly) urges us to accept as her "true" self.

The cooperation between Kate and Petruchio in their mutual trans-formation is signaled in their love of wordplay. Both respond banter-ingly to others as they enter the action separately (1.1.57–58; 1.2.1–17), and when the two first meet, he puns on her name, to which she responds with puns on "move," producing a riff of stichomythia between them (2.1.182ff.). When his verbal facility momentarily over-whelms her in its sexual aggressiveness, she strikes him, and he threat-ens to strike her in return, but she disperses the tension with more puns (2.1.217–23). This moment is the only physical violence between them; he never strikes her, and she strikes him only once in order to recover her briefly lost dignity. Her interest in his linguistic skill is evident in her question, "Where did you study all this goodly speech?" and his reply makes explicit the equality between them that the previous verbal exchange has implicitly established: "It is extempore, from my mother wit" (2.1.259–60). Their mutual love of playfulness reappears in her cooperation with his pretense that the sun is the moon, in his immedi-ate insistence that it is the sun after all, and in her response:

> Then, God be blessed, it is the blessèd sun.
> But sun it is not, when you say it is not,
> And the moon changes even as your mind.
> What you will have it named even that it is,
> And so it shall be so for Katherine. (4.5.18–22)

Wordplay turns to game-playing, when Petruchio insists that Vincentio is a young woman, and Kate greets him accordingly, only to be rebuked playfully by Petruchio for her "mistake," which she gamely retracts with a knowing allusion to their earlier play:

> Pardon, old father, my mistaking eyes,
> That have been so bedazzled with the sun
> That everything I look on seemeth green. (4.5.44–46)

Their ability to cooperate in impromptu wordplay and ludic pretense is the most satisfactory explanation for Kate's speech of submission being a "suppose" that involves exaggeration and facetiousness (5.2.140–83) at the climax of a *beffa* that Kate and Petruchio perform together at the expense of everyone else.[54]

The truth and troth that are enacted in and through the romantic game-playing of Kate and Petruchio are contrasted in the story of Kate's sister, Bianca, whose behavior meets standards of social propriety, though it masks malice, self-centeredness, and social manipulation and therefore amounts, in effect, to a malign illusion—an exploitative suppose. When he first sees her, Lucentio admires her "silence" which he takes to be a sign of "Maid's mild behavior and sobriety" (1.1.70–71). Baptista quickly sides with her, as he always does, apparently induced by her show of weeping, as indicated in Kate's knowing accusation: "A pretty peat! It is best / Put finger in the eye, an she knew why" (1.1.78–79). Bianca's show of piety and dutifulness is clearly designed to impress Baptista:

> Sister, content you in my discontent—
> Sir, to your pleasure humbly I subscribe.
> My books and instruments shall be my company,
> On them to look and practice by myself. (1.1.80–83)

Bianca speaks similarly later, when her hands are tied by Kate (2.1.1–7), and again she wins Baptista's sympathy by weeping as soon as he appears, prompting him to scold Kate. In contrast, Kate weeps only once, from humiliation, when Petruchio fails to show up for their wedding (3.2.26); her display of emotion is not false, and she uses it to manipulate no one. Though briefly sketched in, Bianca's behavior consistently complements her father's to cast Kate in the worst possible light and to provoke her supposedly shrewish behavior. This is the vicious emotional cycle from which Petruchio rescues her, by creating an illusion that brings out her better nature and ultimately changes both of them.

Bianca also cooperates with her lover in creating illusions, as Kate does, but in contrast to Kate, the illusions Bianca and Lucentio fabricate are unnecessary, unproductive, and socially disruptive. Lucentio suggests to his servant, Tranio, that they exchange identities, so as to enable Lucentio to disguise himself as a tutor and thus gain access to the sequestered Bianca (1.1.181–210). This elaborate double disguise, borrowed directly from Gascoigne, is wholly unnecessary, because Baptista welcomes Tranio (pretending to be Lucentio) as Bianca's suitor

(3.2.245–50), thus proving that Lucentio himself would have been so welcomed, rather than his servant. The play also offers no reason why Tranio could not have adopted the tutor's disguise to gain access to Bianca and inform her of Lucentio's interest in her. As a parallel to this false and superfluous illusion, Bianca and Lucentio derive a stilted courtship charade from Ovid (3.1.28–44), in contrast to the extempore and candid bantering of Kate and Petruchio. Lucentio's source is the *Ars Amatoria*, for whose speaker, as Jonathan Bate notes, "language is an instrument of power; like Jupiter, he can get what he wants by means of perjury."[55] Lucentio may think he is getting what he wants, because he has been so impressed by Bianca's show, but he discovers differently in the end.

Having set up an unnecessary disguise, Tranio and Lucentio are compelled to maintain it, persuading a pedant to play Vincentio, as anticipated by the clever servant's earlier rumination, which involves an implicit acknowledgment of Gascoigne's play: "I see no reason but *supposed* Lucentio / Must get a father, called *supposed* Vincentio" (2.1.405–6, my emphasis). This additional suppose obliges Baptista to negotiate Bianca's marriage "with the deceiving father of a deceitful son" (4.4.82–83), and the empty illusion leads to the farcical near arrest of the real Vincentio when he appears, eliciting his bitter exclamation at Tranio, "Thus strangers may be haled and abused. / —O monstrous villain!" (5.1.101–2). Petruchio draws knowing servants into his game with Kate, but he never exploits anyone seriously as Tranio and Lucentio do (provided, of course, that one can regard his treatment of Kate as nonexploitative—an admittedly large provision that the play nonetheless arguably works hard to make credible), and he is indignant when he learns what Lucentio is up to: "Why, this is flat knavery, to take upon you another man's name" (5.1.35–36). Petruchio never plays Lucentio's kind of suppose himself.[56] At the conclusion of the climactic *beffa* that Petruchio and Kate pull off together at everyone else's expense, Bianca reveals what her real nature has been all along—not the dutiful maid whom Lucentio admired at first but a wife who calls duty "foolish" and berates her husband for trusting her: "The more fool you, for laying [wagering] on my duty" (5.1.133).

When Shakespeare returned to the contrast between benign and malicious theatricality and illusion in a later comedy, *Much Ado about Nothing*, he was more successful. *Much Ado* is like *Taming* in using an Italianate plot (Claudio and Hero) as a foil to a plot based on native folk sources (Benedick and Beatrice), involving the same battle of the sexes that lies behind *Taming*. But *Much Ado* eliminates the wife-taming male and more clearly emphasizes a change from suspicion in both skirmishing parties by focusing on trust as the issue that divides them. To be sure, Beatrice at one point addresses the absent Benedick, who she has just discovered to be in love with her: "I will requite thee, / Taming my wild heart to thy loving hand" (3.1.111–12), but this vestige of the taming plot is complex. Benedick himself has nothing to do with the benign illusion that persuades Beatrice that he loves her; in fact, he knows nothing about it, and he has been the object of a parallel *beffa* himself, whose effect was to produce the same change in him that Beatrice undergoes. The result is that *Much Ado* emphasizes both the change and the equality of the two partners more clearly and successfully than *Taming* does.

As if to emphasize the play's distinction between one kind of theatrical fiction and another, Shakespeare includes malicious fictions in *Much Ado*, as well as benign ones, and he makes the authors of the two different kinds of fiction half-brothers. Don Pedro, Prince of Aragon, arranges the charades that clarify the affections of both Benedick and Beatrice, and Don Pedro's half-brother, Don John ("the bastard" [4.1.188, 5.1.187]) arranges two tricks that easily deceive Claudio into believing in Hero's unfaithfulness. Only the plot involving Claudio and Hero, moreover, entails the elaborate social mechanisms that surrounded upper-class marital match-making in Elizabethan society, whereas those mechanisms affect both marital plots in *The Taming of the Shrew*. Don John is able to use Don Pedro's patronal intermediation on Claudio's behalf to make Claudio believe that Hero has lost interest in him (2.1.166–76), and more seriously, Don John impugns Claudio's honor and dependence on the support of aristocratic "friends" by arranging a *beffa* in which Hero seems to make love to Borachio on the night before her wedding.[57] "Give not this rotten orange to your friend," exclaims Claudio angrily, as he hands Hero back to her father, Leonato, during their wedding ceremony (4.1.31), and Don Pedro makes the point clear: "I stand dishonored, that have gone about / To link my dear friend to a common stale" (4.1.63–64). The honor of clans is at stake in the match of Claudio and Hero, just as Claudio seems to be as much in love with Hero's inheritance as with anything else about her, when he inquires whether Leonato has a son (1.1.282–83).[58]

The situation is quite different with Benedick and Beatrice. Though they clearly belong to the same social class, they nonetheless seem to have no family attachments—or at least none that constrains them. Leonato is Beatrice's uncle, and he describes himself as her guardian (2.3.168–69), but she is famously dismissive of paternal oversight, urging Hero to please herself rather than her father in choosing a husband (2.1.49–52). With the helpful prompting of Don Pedro's benign illusions, Benedick and Beatrice choose independently for themselves, rather than at the behest of a patriarchal clan, and their choice is sealed in a crisis of trust, as argued in chapter 1. Moreover, it is preceded by the same trait that marks Kate and Petruchio, namely, love of wordplay that signals their suitability to each other, even though they fail to see it themselves and therefore make sure that "every word stabs" (2.1.237), producing repartee that is funnier, more sophisticated, and more self-revealing than the stichomythia of *The Taming of the Shrew*. Shakespeare seems to have invented this kind of banter as a sign of selves divided between affection and mistrust, though it became a commonplace of comedy after him, and he improved on it immensely in *Much Ado*, after his first discovery of it in *Taming*.

Still another benign illusion deserves mention in *Much Ado*, because it is so central and serves so importantly in the partial resolution of difficulties that arise in both romantic plots. This is the illusion that the friar proposes to Leonato after Claudio has rejected Hero: "Let her awhile be secretly kept in, / And publish it after that she is dead indeed" (4.1.203–4). Shakespeare uses this kind of benign trick in the so-called problem plays as well, *All's Well That Ends Well* and *Measure for Measure*, where its context is more ambiguous but its meaning and effect are similar, though his most esthetically sophisticated treatment of it is in *The Winter's Tale*.[59] In a linguistic vestige of Gascoigne's *Supposes* in *Much Ado*, the friar proposes a "supposition of the lady's death," but he also suggests another range of meanings: "but on this travail look for greater birth" (4.1.238, 213). This description of Hero's symbolic resurrection as a miraculous rebirth is anticipated in the language of Emilia in *The Comedy of Errors* (5.1.401–7) and echoed in the language of Pericles (*Pericles* 5.4.201–2). The friar's understated allusion to the divine comedy helps to valorize Benedick's immediately succeeding declaration of faith in both Beatrice and Hero ("by faith enforced," as he puts it later himself [5.4.8]), which is based in, and expressed simultaneously with, his love of Beatrice. More broadly and more superficially, the friar's *beffa* resolves the difficulties attendant on Claudio's lack of faith by means of a comedy of forgiveness that heals the breach between patriarchal clans as well.[60] The latter reconciliation seems more tenuous than the love of Benedick and Beatrice, just as Bianca and Lucentio reach a less certain agreement than do Kate and Petruchio in *Taming*, and the difference in *Much Ado* would seem to be the social constraints that define Claudio and Hero. The parties to their kind of reconciliation, as Harry Berger astutely observes, "would have to be reborn in a new heaven and earth, a new Messina, before they could enter into a relationship free of the assumptions of their community."[61] As Berger implies, Shakespearean comedy is no more apocalyptic than Shakespearean tragedy, in that neither ends by revealing the New Jerusalem; still, one cannot help feeling that Beatrice and Benedick are closer than Hero and Claudio to something like an earthly paradise.

The *Taming of the Shrew* and *Much Ado about Nothing* show Shakespeare working out an increasingly sophisticated, complex, and self-confident treatment of theatrical fiction as he became more experienced, and the two comedies represent his way of thinking about the problem in his works as a whole. As we saw earlier, the problem of divided selves, the observation of others' performances, and the discerning of truth in illusion are central concerns in his earliest comedies (above, chap. 1). As many critics have noticed, the late romances are particularly rich in self-reflexive allusions to art, from Iachimo's description of a painting or tapestry in Imogen's bedroom, as part of his malign *beffa* at Posthumus' expense (*Cymbeline* 2.4.84–86), to the discussion of art and nature in *The Winter's Tale* (4.4.79–103), with its extraordinary complement in the statue scene (5.3), or the ambiguous magic and benign trickery of Prospero in *The Tempest*, which requires his transformation for its effect, as well as the transformation of those—or at least, of those who are capable of transformation—on whom he plays his artful charade, with reminiscences of Joseph's trick on his brothers in the book of Genesis. Always conceding, as Sidney does, that art is fictional, Shakespeare goes beyond Sidney to insist that the indigenous theater of signs can be as rich a source of art as classical or Italian neoclassical drama. None of his plays deals with fiction as an end in itself nor as inherently evil or good; it may be transformative; it can reveal, and may even participate in, a mysterious world of superhuman reality; it can be a means of knowing, as well as self-revelation. Whatever it is, it is never merely deceptive and never merely an artistic end in itself. While Shakespeare's esthetic thinking is not dogmatic, it is extraordinarily suggestive, and it enters fully into contemporary debate about art, theater, illusion, how we know, and the enigmatic nature of being.

SHAKESPEARE AND THE FRENCH EPISTEMOLOGISTS

the subtle-witted French

1 Henry VI 1.1.25

In view of the link I have suggested in chapter 7 between Shakespeare's esthetics and epistemology, it seems appropriate to consider more specifically his way of thinking about how we know in relation to the epistemological revolution that had its first stirring in the late sixteenth century. The history of modern philosophy is usually said to begin with Descartes, because he established a purely rational foundation for thinking to replace the theological assumptions that had been regarded as necessary in Western philosophy since Augustine. But Descartes, for all his striking originality, did not come out of nowhere, and the context that formed him was very similar to the context in which Shakespeare grew up and pursued his career in the London theater. Influence either way is not the point. Descartes was only ten years old when Shakespeare died, and Descartes's first publication was twenty years later. As for Shakespeare's influence on French philosophy, Descartes does not seem to have read plays, he did not read English, and the impact of Shakespeare on French culture began long after Descartes. Where Shakespeare's thinking is concerned, the point of the comparison is primarily hermeneutical, though it is true that Shakespeare and Descartes shared the same early modern European culture; they lived during the intellectual crisis that eventually emerged from the publication of Sextus Empiricus's *Outlines of Pyrrhonism* in 1562; and they both read Montaigne, in turn a keen reader of Sextus. It might be useful, then, to consider how each thought about knowing in particular.

MONTAIGNE

Let us begin with Montaigne, since he influenced both Descartes and Shakespeare. For over two hundred years, Shakespeare's paraphrase of a passage in Montaigne's essay "Of Cannibals" has been recognized in *The Tempest*, and the reference has given rise to a large and varied bibliography connecting the two.[1] In all that time, however, no one has succeeded in finding another allusion this compelling, and because *The Tempest* is so late, it is impossible to know for certain how early Shakespeare read Montaigne. Undoubtedly they shared a remarkable independence, suppleness, and amplitude of mind, serious doubt about human moral and intellectual capacity, and enough deference to their respective cultures (including their cultures' religious expectations) at least to pass official inspection, but those points of similarity do not prove Shakespeare's indebtedness to Montaigne. In "Of experience," Montaigne remarks that "[i]f our faces were not similar, we could not distinguish man from beast; if they were not dissimilar, we would not distinguish man from man."[2] Taking this point as a cue, I want to urge that although Shakespeare and Montaigne differ from most other writers in the later sixteenth century by virtue of their similarity to each other in ways just mentioned, they also differ from each other.[3]

The point can be illustrated by considering two similarities (not noted by Alice Harmon) that ultimately point to difference. Henry V's prayer on the eve of Agincourt is self-serving and self-deceived, as argued above in chapter 5, and Montaigne's comment on such prayers is striking in its aptness:

> I was just now thinking about where that error of ours comes from, of having recourse to God in all our designs and enterprises, and calling on him in every kind of need and in whatever spot our weakness wants help, without considering whether the occasion is just or unjust, and invoking his name and his power, in whatever condition or action we are involved, however vicious it may be. (*Essays*, I:56, 230)

When Henry prays, he acknowledges that his father wrongfully gained the throne and proposes a bargain with God as a consequence, but the bargain does not make right either Henry IV's wrong or Henry V's victory at Agincourt. Henry thus allows himself to keep what he knows he should not have—a rationalization that Montaigne describes so precisely ("without considering whether the occasion is just or unjust") as to make it seem that Shakespeare wrote the episode with Montaigne in mind. That conclusion, however, is far from certain. For one thing, Harmon's point about common indebtedness needs to be kept in mind. Self-deception in prayer is a problem Jesus addresses in the gospels (Luke 18:9-14, for example), and Christian moralists—including those who wrote drama—had long been aware of it.[4] In the fifteenth-century play, *Mankind*, for example, Titivillus tempts Mankind to pray when he should be working, thus deceiving him into thinking that piety is an excuse for sloth.[5] Moreover, Henry V's self-deception in prayer is integral to a pattern of self-deception on the part of the powerful in Shakespeare's history plays, where it serves to establish an implicit moral limit, even when self-interested political action succeeds (above, chap. 5). Shakespeare's demonstrable awareness of self-deceived power, in other words, complicates the argument for his indebtedness to Montaigne on the point about a king's self-deceived prayer in particular.

Montaigne and Shakespeare also have similar things to say about virtue and vice. In "Of cruelty," Montaigne argues that virtue does not deserve to be called virtue when it suits our nature, but only when we practice it in the face of inclination. Socrates' virtue is hardly worth the name, Montaigne maintains, because Socrates practiced goodness so easily and without constraint. "If virtue can shine only by clashing with opposing appetites," he continues, making his point in a rhetorical question, "shall we then say that it cannot do without the assistance of vice, and that it owes to vice its repute and honor?" (*Essays*, II:11, 308). This passage sounds very like the First Lord's gnomic comment in *All's Well That Ends Well*: "The web of our life is of a mingled yarn, good and ill together. Our virtues would be proud if our faults whipped them not, and our crimes would despair if they were not cherished by our virtues" (4.3.70–73). Again, however, close inspection makes differences evident, despite the similarity. Montaigne's argument is set entirely in the context of classical philosophy. He compares stoic and epicurean conceptions of virtue, and in this case he favors the former (though that is not always his position), specifically quoting or citing Cicero, Seneca, the Roman senator Metellus, and the younger Cato in support of his point.[6]

The First Lord's remark in *All's Well*, on the other hand, makes most sense as a theological comment, as R. M. Frye argues, with its "warning against both pride and despair."[7] The First Lord's point in *All's Well* is not the stoic point that Bertram's true virtue can emerge only in conflict

with vice; rather, it is, first, that Bertram's excessive pride in his inherited nobility needs to be qualified by his recognizing how badly he has
treated Helena. The second part of the First Lord's comment (about
virtue cherishing "crimes") emphasizes grace and the part it plays in
preventing despair, so the comment anticipates the play's end, when
Bertram realizes that the woman he had slept with in Florence was
really his wife and asks her pardon (5.3.309), thus acknowledging his
excessive pride for the first time. Helena prevents his despair by accepting his admission and forgiving him, both in her loving words
(5.3.310–11) and in restoring to him the ring that he had given to her
when he thought she was Diana. This gesture indicates both Helena's
ability to preserve the ring (which clearly symbolizes Bertram's inherited
nobility [3.7.22–25, 4.2.42–45]), when he was prepared to throw it
away, and her literally open-handed attitude toward it: she is not des-
perate for his nobility, nor does she grasp to attain and retain it. In
effect, they share it in the end, by virtue of Helena's resourcefulness and
generosity and by virtue of Bertram's recognition and acknowledgment
of his pridefully self-deceived honor. Bertram is hardly an ideal mate,
and the ending of *All's Well* is more troubled than the end of most
Shakespearean comedies. Still, Bertram appears to learn something in
the course of the play, and Helena arguably "cures" him in a way that
parallels Rosalind's "curing" of Orlando in *As You Like It*, in that Helena
helps Bertram grow up. In addition, she preserves and restores his
nobility (the ring), his manhood (his virility), and his virtue (his ability to
recognize his failure and ask forgiveness for it). In every important way
she thus complements him in a way that no one else in the play does,
and what she does for him makes most sense as a product of ethical
reflection on the divine comedy rather than a comment on stoic ethics,
as in Montaigne's essay.

    Despite many individual similarities between Montaigne and
Shakespeare, a striking overall difference is the way each uses the Bible.
Shakespeare repeatedly acknowledges his Protestant culture (whether
deliberately or not) in an enormous range of biblical references.[8] These
references occur in every play; they involve all the books of the Bible
(including many from the Apocrypha); and they are more than decorative, as I have argued in earlier chapters, because they implicitly situate
the action in the course of human destiny, somewhere between the Fall
and the Last Judgment, and thus assume both a cosmic and moral

framework for what happens. The undeniable focus of Shakespeare's plays on the secular world does not obviate the moral imperative that is inherent in the Christian sense of destiny, even though the plays assert little, if anything, about how divine providence and human choice interact. Even in the history plays, which are insistently secular in their analysis of political action, the framework of moral expectation remains in place, and it clearly derives from humankind's dependence on the story that centuries of Christian reflection had derived from the Bible. To be sure, the definitive connection between human events and the divine that is enacted in communal biblical history plays is absent in Shakespeare's plays, but its absence does not mean that his plays release us in a godless and epistemologically impenetrable world; rather, they release us in the fallen world, where human knowledge is partial, distorted, and self-serving, but where moral insight is not only possible but requisite, and where even change for the better is sometimes possible as well, usually by some evitable earthly grace ("A showing of a heavenly effect in earthly actor," as Lafew's ballad puts it in *All's Well* [2.3.23–24]), though change never amounts to perfection, as the end of *All's Well* makes clear and its ironic title emphasizes. All this, the plays' ubiquitous biblical references help to establish, even though Shakespeare never puts God on stage. Lavatch's elliptical allusion to the gospels in *All's Well* thus applies as aptly to Bertram as the First Lord's comment does: "I am for the house with the narrow gate, which I take to be too little for pomp to enter. Some that humble themselves may, but the many will be too chill and tender, and they'll be for the flowery way that leads to the broad gate and the great fire" (4.5.50–55, alluding to Matt 7:13-14 and Luke 13:24). Insofar as this comment reflects obliquely on Bertram, it is not a definitive description of his eschatological destiny; it is an incisive description of his moral situation in this life.

In contrast, Montaigne's biblical allusions are different in frequency, language, and function. Montaigne cites classical authors far more often than the Bible: as opposed to approximately 1,160 references in Shakespeare (occurring in about 3,500 different places, as estimated from Shaheen's "Index to Shakespeare's Biblical References"), Montaigne has just forty-five biblical citations in all the *Essays* (according to Marianne Meijer's count), in contrast to 500 citations of Plutarch alone, to say nothing of Plato, Aristotle, Seneca, Cicero, Ovid, Horace, Lucretius, and Virgil.[9] Shakespeare also cites many of these classical authorities, of course (or he depends on them, when he doesn't actually cite them), but the number of biblical references in the two writers is still vastly different, and even if the difference is attributed merely to their respective cultures, it still tells us something about the way the two writers thought, judging from what they wrote.[10]

Consider, for example, Shakespeare's clear allusion to a saying of Jesus that we noticed in chapter 2: "You found his mote; the King your mote did see; / But I a beam do find in each of three" (*Love's Labor's Lost*, 4.3.157–58, alluding to Matt 7:3-5). It is worth noting that the concept (though not the imagery) in Jesus' saying has a close parallel in Horace, *Satire* I.iii.25–27: "When you look over your own sins, your eyes are rheumy and daubed with ointment; why, when you view the failings of your friends, are you as keen of sight as an eagle or as a serpent of Epidaurus?"[11] If Shakespeare knew both the biblical and classical sayings, as seems likely, it is clear which one he chose for the allusion in *Love's Labor's Lost*, whereas Montaigne seems unlikely to have made the same choice. Meijer identifies just three quotations from two gospels in all the *Essays*[12] (in contrast to some 800 distinct citations of all four gospels in Shakespeare), and faced with Matthew's gospel and Horace's satires as options, Montaigne would surely prefer his beloved Horace, whom he quotes more than twice as often as he quotes from the entire Bible—or more likely, if he cited one, he would cite the other as a close parallel to the same idea. Moreover, Shakespeare's preference suggests continuity between his thinking in *Love's Labor's Lost* and a long tradition of Christian thinking about the self, as we noticed in chapter 2, whereas Montaigne's preference for classical authors suggests a stronger continuity with classical philosophy, including a general preference for stoicism and Pyrrhonist skepticism.

Where the language of biblical allusions is concerned, it surely makes some difference that all of Shakespeare's quotations are in English (with a tendency to favor the Geneva translation, according to Shaheen[13]), whereas Montaigne quotes the Vulgate about half the time.[14] Quoting Jerome's Latin translation is hardly surprising for a writer whose first language was Latin; indeed Montaigne's use of French translations is more surprising and offers strong evidence of Montaigne's independence of mind, given the Roman church's resistance to vernacular Bibles in the sixteenth century.[15] Still, for whatever reason, the effect of biblical quotations in the two authors is very different by virtue of the way they use the vernacular. Montaigne's Vulgate references tend to align his biblical quotations with his quotations of classical authors in their original languages (which are also translated into English in Frame's edition) and thereby to elevate them for a reader of the *Essays* in French. Shakespeare occasionally quotes a Latin author in the original as well, and the effect is also to elevate speech and thereby the speaker, as we noticed in chapter 4, but his consistent citation of the Bible in English makes it more familiar and integrates it seamlessly into his own language, which is in precisely the same register, as every modern reader of Shakespeare and early translations of the Bible into English immediately recognizes. The effect particularly on early audiences and readers of biblical quotations in Shakespeare and Montaigne was therefore very different.

Most important, biblical quotations in Montaigne and Shakespeare function in quite distinct ways. Whereas Shakespeare uses biblical references to suggest the interaction of Christian destiny and moral expectation, as we have seen, Montaigne consistently uses them as rhetorical *copia*, in just the same way he uses classical citations and often in tandem with them to emphasize the same point. In "Of moderation," for example, Montaigne quotes Horace on "a subtle consideration of philosophy" and then cites "Holy Writ" as another instance (Essays I:30, 146). Though he quotes the Bible in French and Horace in Latin, their impact as parallel rhetorical *sententiae* is still what comes across in the passage.[16] In "Of cruelty," Montaigne cites both Luke's gospel and Ennius (as quoted by Cicero) in Latin in support of the point that "in reality it is little or nothing" to inflict punishment on a corpse, though he advises treating criminals in this way "to keep the people at their duty" (*Essays* II:11, 315). To take another example almost at random, in "Apology for Raymond Sebond," Montaigne cites the gospels on the power of faith and offers a quotation from Quintilian on the power of belief as a parallel (*Essays* II:12, 322). The most sustained demonstration of *copia* in the "Apology" is Montaigne's long list of animal abilities, in order to urge their superiority to human beings (*Essays* II:12, 332–58).[17] Though the passage contains no biblical allusions, it illustrates the habit of mind that governs Montaigne's use of the Bible elsewhere—encyclopedic, moralistic, gnomic, and rationalizing. His evidence from animals is not empirical, for it is seldom based on actual observation but on Montaigne's vast reading, just as his citation of the

Bible is moral but with little or no sense of how Christian ethics depends on and inheres in Christian destiny.[18]

The differences just outlined have a direct bearing on epistemology in Montaigne and Shakespeare, and the point can be illustrated from the one indisputable instance of Shakespeare's indebtedness to Montaigne. In "Of cannibals," Montaigne maintains a consistent stance of ethnographic relativism, beginning with the story of two Greek kings' appreciation for the military order of the supposedly barbaric Romans who had marched to meet them. The implicit point of this brief opening episode is that these Greeks recognized and admired the dignity of barbarians. "Thus should we beware," Montaigne concludes, "of clinging to vulgar opinions, and judge things by reason's way, not by popular say" (*Essays* I:31, 150). He makes clear what he means by "reason" in this case after commending the "simple crude fellow" who described the New World natives to him: "I think there is nothing barbarous and savage in that nation, from what I have been told, except that each man calls barbarism whatever is not his own practice; for indeed it seems we have no other test of truth and reason than the example and pattern of the opinions and customs of the country we live in" (152). Montaigne thus strikingly applies an ancient principle to contemporary European events, for his cultural relativism is indebted to the skepticism of Sextus Empircus, as Montaigne describes it in "Apology for Raymond Sebond."[19] Recognizing the impossibility of both knowing and not knowing definitively, Montaigne avers that Pyrrhonians "lend and accommodate themselves" to "the constitutions of laws and customs" (*Essays* II:12, 374). In other words, they provisionally accept local custom, because they have no grounds for either affirming it or denying it. Montaigne's cultural relativism is so strong that it inevitably raises questions about his frequent affirmations of his own culture's expectations—particularly its religious expectations. Yet these affirmations, as Richard Popkin argues, are complemented, rather than subverted, by Montaigne's skepticism, which is consistent with "a new form of fideism—Catholic Pyrrhonism," enabling the believer to disparage reason, even to the point of complete skepticism, in order to emphasize faith and grace.[20]

Post-colonial criticism in particular has helped to establish widespread acknowledgment of ethnographic relativism in *The Tempest* that certainly resembles—if it does not irrefutably derive from—

Montaigne's essay "Of cannibals." The conflict between Prospero and
Caliban (whose name is an obvious anagram of "canibal") in particular
has come to be understood as more nuanced than it was, say, in Frank
Kermode's edition of *The Tempest*.[21] It is virtually impossible now to see
Caliban, as Kermode did fifty years ago, as a symbol of bestial lust,
rightly suppressed and controlled by the efforts of a divinely enabled
magus. The issues surrounding the quarrel between master and slave
are too complex and too open-ended to make such a reading credible.
Caliban argues his case more compellingly and speaks more lyrically at
times than a symbol of lust should, and Prospero is angrier, more arbitrary, and more vulnerable than Kermode's description of him allows,
though the precise circumstances in which Prospero's quarrel with Caliban originated are impossible to determine with absolute certainty.[22] *The
Tempest* offers a muddle of cultural confusion that is similar to the finely-
tuned irony of the ethnographic standoff represented by Montaigne's
even-handed account ("according to my witnesses") of the New World
natives' first sighting of a man on a horse: "though he had had dealings
with them on several other trips, [he] so horrified them in this posture
that they shot him dead with arrows before they could recognize him"
(*Essays* I:31, 153). The natives may have been ignorant of European
customs, but their weapons were deadly just the same.

If we look at Shakespeare's paraphrase of a passage from "Of cannibals," however, and consider the shape of *The Tempest* as a whole, we
can see differences between Montaigne and Shakespeare that suggest
real differences in their epistemology. Montaigne lists actual characteristics of the New World natives' communal life (at least as reported to
him) in order to assert that Plato's ideal republic was not as good as the
natives' reality: "I am sorry that Lycurgus and Plato did not know of
them," he says, and "I should say to Plato," he continues, as he lists the
characteristics on which Shakespeare drew: "no sort of traffic, no
knowledge of letters, no science of numbers, no name for a magistrate
or for political superiority, no custom of servitude, no riches or poverty,
no contracts, no successions. No partitions, no occupations but leisure
ones, nor care for any but common kinship, no clothes, no agriculture,
no metal, no use of win or wheat" (*Essays* I:31, 153). Shakespeare adapts
this list for a very different purpose in *The Tempest*. It is spoken by
Gonzalo, not as a description of a functioning polity but as a hypothet-
ical possibility and with the apparent intention of offering hope in the

midst of disaster by describing an amazing ideal: "Had I plantation of this isle . . . / And were the king on't, what would I do? . . . / I would by contraries / Execute all things; for no kind of traffic / Would I admit" (*Tempest* 2.1.146–52). In short, Shakespeare paraphrases Montaigne to make Gonzalo talk a little like Plato, while the realism of the scene is not in Gonzalo's description but in the carping of Antonio and Sebastian, who in this case are sometimes right. Gonzalo does indeed, for example, imagine himself as king in a place that he asserts would have "No sovereignty," and Sebastian immediately mocks him for the contradiction (2.1.159). Such even-handedness is characteristic of Shakespeare's dialogue and has encouraged the inference that his thinking is no less Pyrrhonist than Montaigne's: "When they [the Pyrrhonians] say that heavy things go down, they would be very sorry to have anyone take their word for it; and they seek to be contradicted, so as to create doubt and suspension of judgment which is their goal" (*Essays* II:12, 372).

It is not clear, however, that Shakespeare designed *The Tempest* or any other play as a demonstration of Pyrrhonist doubt. Gonzalo is unquestionably an idealist (more like Plato than Montaigne's native Americans), and he is sometimes wrong, as Sebastian points out—but he is sometimes right, as well. He notices, for example, that "Our garments, being, as they were, drenched in the sea, hold notwithstanding their freshness and glosses, being rather new-dyed than stained with salt water" (*Tempest* 2.1.64–67), and in this case his optimism sees the truth, since Ariel had made sure that "On their sustaining garments not a blemish, / But fresher than before" (1.2.219–20). Sebastian's mocking assertion that Gonzalo "doth but mistake the truth totally" (2.1.60) is thus demonstrably false, not merely one of two contrary opinions, and Gonzalo's hopeful assessment of the island—"Here is everything advantageous to life" (2.1.52)—is truer in the long run than Antonio's cynical rejoinder: "True, save means to live" (2.1.53). With Ariel's assistance, Prospero will in fact provide means for Gonzalo and Alonso to live in spite of an assassination plot against them by Antonio and Sebastian, and in the end, Prospero by himself finds means for Antonio and Sebastian to live, despite having justified them traitors and would-be assassins.

While Shakespeare recognizes the claims of opposing cultures, in other words, as Montaigne does, he offers nothing as optimistic as

Montaigne's description of native American sociopolitical relations in contrast to European corruption, and he gives us privileged information about the ship's company, so that we know that some are true, and some are false, and we can say which is which and to what extent. To be sure, Caliban's intimate knowledge of the island (1.2.139–42) and his evident emotional bond with it (3.2.137–45) are suggestive glimpses of unlettered innocence that Prospero's suspicion may have corrupted at some indeterminate time in the past and that the next wave of European immigration degrades beyond all recognition through blatant exploitation and alcohol. Still, we never see Caliban functioning in a community of his own, and Shakespeare displaces Montaigne's description of such a community into the idealistic musing of an ambiguously optimistic European nobleman, which could conceivably be construed as a comment on the optimism of his source.

What *The Tempest* enables us to know is not merely the vanity of ethnocentric reason but the need of everyone in the play, whether highborn or commoner, native American or European, "to be wise hereafter / And seek for grace" (5.1.298–99).[23] This determination is the ultimate mark of Caliban's humanity, and it sets him apart definitively not only from Stephano and Trinculo but also from Antonio and Sebastian, who never come to the same realization. Moreover, Caliban's determination links him and Prospero in their ability to grow and change, for Prospero learns, partly assisted by Ariel, that "the rarer action is / In virtue than in vengeance" (5.1.27–28)—another way to "be wise . . . / And seek for grace." Prospero learns to practice forgiveness, and the actor who plays his part asks us to practice it as well in our response to the play, as the play ends: "As you from crimes would pardoned be, / Let your indulgence set me free" (Epilogue 19–20).

In the early stages of the epistemological revolution, it is not therefore clear that Shakespeare's plays move very far beyond the position of Augustine, who declared that he believed in order that he might understand. Richard Popkin describes this position as fideism, and he identifies Montaigne with it, because Montaigne eschewed reason while affirming faith.[24] But Popkin acknowledges that not everyone defines fideism as broadly as he does,[25] and the lumping together of Augustine, Luther, Calvin, Pascal, and Kierkegaard with Montaigne seems indiscriminate at best, even if it serves a purpose in historical classification.[26] What can be lumped together can also be sorted out, and due attention to differences between Montaigne and Shakespeare indicates that they did not conceive of knowing in the same way, despite their undoubted affinities. Self-recognition, hope for positive change, and charitable acknowledgment of others are all important in Shakespeare's plays, but they derive from the narrative of Christian destiny, not from rational judgment or even from the need to suspend judgment in the interest of equal and opposite choices, as Montaigne frequently seems to conclude.

DESCARTES

What is true for Montaigne is even truer for Descartes: while he and Shakespeare shared many assumptions, differences in the way they thought are no less important than similarities—especially in the way they thought about knowing. Descartes's strategic skepticism is justly famous. Doubting everything except his ability to doubt, which he took self-evidently as equivalent to his ability to think, Descartes worked out a series of proofs based on that single, all-important exception to complete epistemological doubt. These proofs included arguments for God and the soul, "chief among those," as Descartes put it, "that ought to be demonstrated with the aid of philosophy rather than theology."[27] Stanley Cavell sees himself as continuous with the history of skepticism "that begins no later than Descartes and Shakespeare," and Richard Strier has argued more recently that Shakespeare shared Descartes's "skepticism about supernatural intervention and causation" in particular.[28] Shakespeare's interest in Montaigne is often ascribed to their shared skepticism, so it is natural to see Shakespeare and Descartes in the same light as well, especially since both read Montaigne.

In view of what I have argued in this book, however, it will be no surprise that I am skeptical of the skeptical connection between Shakespeare and Descartes. Shakespeare indeed lived during the early years of the epistemological crisis that the translation of Sextus eventually created, but he seems to have been unaware of it as a philosophical development, probably because it was so closely tied to religious controversy throughout his lifetime. Surely a writer with such a keen and absorbent sense of words would not have left "skeptic" and its derivatives out of his writing, had he known or understood them. He was certainly familiar with doubt, and he would have encountered skepticism in Montaigne, but the kind of methodological skepticism that Descartes invented was clearly beyond Shakespeare, as it was beyond virtually everyone else who lived when he did. Descartes is not regarded as an inventive genius in the history of thought for nothing.

Shakespeare was an inventive genius too, of course, and he thought carefully about knowledge, as I have argued, but his way of thinking about it is quite distinct from Descartes's. The standard of proof for Descartes was mathematics, in which he made important break-throughs, and his way of understanding the material world was there-fore mechanical, because mechanical relations were subject to mathematical proof. This was an important insight for the history of science, but Descartes's interpretation of it was radically dualistic, in that he conceived of himself thinking as prior to, distinct from, and more fundamental than himself as a physical (mechanical) being: "And though perhaps (or rather, as I shall soon say, assuredly) I have a body that is very closely joined to me, nevertheless . . . it is certain that I am really distinct from my body, and can exist without it."[29] As Pauline Kiernan has argued, Shakespeare's sense of his art depends on theatri-cal embodiment, and it is no exaggeration to say that he always imag-ines human beings as essentially (though not exclusively) embodied, rather than the reverse, as Descartes does.[30] Indeed, the origin of his doubt about human nature is often rooted in profound suspicion of claims to ethical disembodiment, which he typically interprets as self-deceived, as in *Love's Labor's Lost* and even more trenchantly in *Julius Caesar* and *Coriolanus*. When the hopelessly idealistic lover, Valentine in *Two Gentlemen of Verona*, declines to eat, his servant knows better: "though the chameleon Love can feed on the air, I am one that am nourished by my victuals, and would fain have meat" (2.1.166–68). One of Cleopatra's most important and endearing insights is that she is

> No more but e'en a woman, and commanded
> By such poor passion as the maid that milks
> And does the meanest chares. (*Antony and Cleopatra* 4.15.78–80)

For Shakespeare, the route to self-knowledge lies in part through recog-nition of one's bodily vulnerability, as Lear discovers preeminently, not through disembodied cognition, as for Descartes.

Shakespeare even gave theatrical embodiment to imagined spirits of some sort in the earth, the air, the fire, and the water in *A Midsummer*

Night's Dream and *The Tempest*, as we noticed in chapter 7, so his conception of the natural world (if "conception" is not too cognitive a term for something that seems so compellingly imaginative) is anything but mechanical and moves in the opposite direction from Descartes's thinking. Descartes's positing of "an evil genius, supremely powerful and clever, who has directed his entire effort at deceiving me" is a useful way to clarify the distinction (*Meditations* 16). Descartes's "demon hypothesis" may have been suggested, as Richard Popkin points out, by the trial of a priest called Grandier in 1634, who was accused of using demonic illusion to deceive the nuns in a convent at Loudun.[31] The possibility of demonic illusion raised difficult epistemological issues for the trial, and Descartes may well have been influenced by them, Popkin suggests, in positing demonic deception as his ultimate version of skepticism, especially since his doubt encompasses what seem to be the most basic mathematical certainties: "may I not, in like fashion, be deceived every time I add two and three or count the sides of a square, or perform an even simpler operation, if that can be imagined?" (*Meditations* 15). The demon hypothesis does not, in other words, address the question of whether demons are real, or whether they can really deceive. Its point is that to make thinking the foundation of being provides an incontrovertible epistemological bulwark against demonic deception, because the demon cannot deceive one about one's ability to think, given that thinking is the demon's medium of deception. Having discovered this axiom, Descartes then proceeds to deduce from it the existence of God, the soul, and the external world as perceived by the senses. As Stuart Clark summarizes Descartes' accomplishment, "In one of the most renowned arguments in European philosophy, Descartes (as Pascal and Hume later acknowledged) based his conquest of scepticism on precisely that possibility of total deception that contemporary demonology seemed to hold out."[32]

If Popkin and Clark are right, then Shakespeare and Descartes may be said to begin with similar assumptions, though they come to very different conclusions. Shakespeare certainly understands "th'equivocation of the fiend / That lies like truth," in Macbeth's phrasing (*Macbeth* 5.4.43–44), but Shakespeare posits demonic deception not as a skeptical prelude to rational certainty, as Descartes does, but as part of the framework of a vividly evoked moral world on which the tragic effect of *Macbeth* depends. That the devil is a liar was not news in the seventeenth century, and Macbeth in fact mentions the fiend's equivocation at the very moment he begins to recognize it, when he thinks he sees Birnam Wood moving toward Dunsinane, a prediction the Third Apparition had made to assure him that he had nothing to fear (4.1.92–94). His ambition deceives Macbeth into trusting demonic equivocation, on which he relies as he rejects the king-becoming graces, only to confirm, as he anticipated he would from the outset, that his rest is labor, that the deed cannot be done, and that his life "is a tale / Told by an idiot, full of sound and fury, / Signifying nothing" (5.5.26–28). Paul Jorgensen points out that Macbeth's haunting description of despair echoes *Ecclesiasticus* 20:18: "A man without grace is a foolish tale which is oft told by the mouth of the ignorant," which says a great deal about the tragic impact of his play.[33] For Macbeth's tragedy consists not in his damnation but in the palpable suffering he endures by virtue of a decision he makes—and continues to make—till all his yesterdays have lighted the way to dusty death. The intensity of this suffering is what we are certain of in *Macbeth*—as certain as he had been of it himself before he murdered Duncan, though its impact surprises him and arguably surprises us, because it is the suffering of a murderer. Insofar as certainty inheres in this tragic effect, it is substantially different from the daring hypothesis in Descartes' *Meditations* that forms his basis for rational certainty.

The similarity between Descartes's starting point and Shakespeare's is evident not only in a late play like *Macbeth* but also in an early one like *The Comedy of Errors*. Demonic deception is a conclusion that nearly everyone in Shakespeare's Ephesus reaches readily—too readily, as it turns out. "There's none but witches do inhabit here," exclaims Antipholus of Syracuse (3.2.155), because complete strangers know his name and speak to him as if he should know them. The first explanation that occurs to him is that demons are deceiving everyone: "Sure, these are but imaginary wiles, / And Lapland sorcerers inhabit here" (4.3.10–11). Moreover, others come to the same conclusion. Adriana arranges for Dr. Pinch to exorcise her husband, because he seems not to know her and must therefore be deceived by a devil (4.4). Their conclusions are false, of course, because what is really deceiving them is perfectly natural—the coincidence of two sets of identical twins in the same place at the same time—and the demon hypothesis in this case is therefore superfluous and perverse. The fact of a natural explanation does not, however, rule out the possibility that the demon hypothesis everyone entertains in *The Comedy of Errors* could be right, even if it happens not to be right in this particular case. Shakespeare's plays offer no evidence that he had a more advanced idea about human mental illness than his contemporaries had, and demonic interference was (and continued to be, long after Shakespeare's death) the most common explanation for abnormal thinking and behavior.[34] The obvious joke in *The Comedy of Errors* is that no one is mentally ill (i.e., deceived by a demon); they are merely mistaken. The play is deeply suspicious of human nature, but suspicion is not necessarily equivalent to skepticism, especially where superhuman agency is concerned.[35] Where Shakespeare differs from his contemporaries is in his unusually expansive and imaginative understanding of charity, as I have argued throughout this book, so that he enters more fully into the thinking and feeling of the persons he imagines, including their self-deception and apparent moral weaknesses.

Again, however, despite the similarity of assumptions shared by Shakespeare and Descartes, the conclusions they come to are very far apart. The point of human frailty in *The Comedy of Errors* is not that it provides the skeptical prelude to a philosophical foundation for rational certainty. The play's truth is in its story, which offers a different way of being true from philosophical reasoning, as Sidney argues (above, chap. 7). In *The Comedy of Errors* truth inheres in part in a contrast between the framing narrative, which originates in medieval drama, and the farce of mistaken identity that derives from Plautus. In the Roman play, lack of self-knowledge produces a potentially endless series of hysterical guesses about a perfectly ordinary fact (about this the play raises no doubt)—that two sets of identical twins are in the same town for the first time in many years—and the problem of knowledge is resolved only by the unexpected appearance of Emilia, the one member of the family who is missing from the outset, since she has been sequestered in a local abbey all along. Her surprise reappearance structurally and symbolically anticipates the reappearance of Hermione in *The Winter's Tale*, and connections with the divine comedy are made in both plays ("After so long grief, such nativity!" [*The Comedy of Errors* 5.1.407]; "It is required / You do awake your faith" [*Winter's Tale* 5.3.94–95]). Such references offer less than either dogmatic certainty or rational certainty; they merely assist in establishing a fallen world in the story we are called to witness, together with the possibility of redemptive hope and reconciliation, however imperfectly achieved this side of the eschaton.

PASCAL

The weakness of the case for comparing Shakespeare with Descartes does not mean that the French epistemological tradition offers nothing useful to Shakespeareans. On the contrary, it offers Blaise Pascal. To be sure, of the three French thinkers considered in this chapter, Pascal would seem to be furthest removed from Shakespearean epistemology, because of the chronological gap between them. Born in 1623, the same year the First Folio was published, Pascal was nearly a generation younger than Descartes and therefore even less influenced than Descartes was by the world that had shaped Shakespeare. Though Pascal's family (himself, his father, and two sisters) included Pierre Corneille for a time during their residence in Rouen from 1639 to 1647, Pascal seems to have had little interest in drama, and he almost certainly never heard of an English playwright who had died seven years before Pascal was born, and who was known only in a small part of England.[36] Pascal was a scientist on the modern model—rigorously mathematical and experimental—but he came to regard his principal life's work to be a defense of Christian belief in the face of skepticism and dogmatism. His mathematical ability was evident when he was very young (he invented a calculating machine before he was twenty that was capable of the four arithmetical operations with numbers of up to six figures), and he quickly learned to combine this ability with physical experimentation, by which he proved that a vacuum is possible and went on to prove changes in atmospheric pressure, thus paving the way for the invention of the barometer and altimeter. His scientific commitment not only inclined him to sharp dismissal of ancient authorities on natural knowledge (who maintained that nature abhors a vacuum, for example) but also led him—despite his lifelong devotion to the Roman church—to a subtly satirical debate with the Jesuits that eventually included a critique of papal fallibility in the case of Galileo:

> It was to equally little purpose that you [the Jesuits] obtained against Galileo a decree from Rome, condemning his opinion respecting the

motion of the earth. It will never be proved by such an argument as this
[i.e., a papal decree] that the earth remains stationary; and if it can be
demonstrated by sure observation that it is the earth and not the sun that
revolves, the efforts and arguments of all mankind together will not hinder our planet from revolving, nor hinder themselves from revolving
along with her.[37]

After Augustine, Montaigne was among Pascal's favorite authors, and
Montaigne's most skeptical essay, the "Apology for Raymond Sebond,"
seems to have influenced Pascal more than any other.[38] Pascal met
Descartes, and they shared an interest in mathematics, but Pascal
rejected both Descartes's methodological skepticism and his rationalism: "Descartes useless and uncertain" (S445/L887).[39]

For Shakespeare, the importance of this bundle of apparent contra-
dictions is that it offers an actual historical instance of a seventeenth-
century thinker doing what this book claims Shakespeare did—that is,
imagining the human situation in a framework of faith while acknowledging the challenge of doubt and dependence on grace. The coincidence does not prove that Shakespeare thought like Pascal, but Pascal
proves that it was possible to think like Pascal—to be no less aware of
the *crise pyrrhonienne* than Montaigne and Descartes were, and yet to
affirm thoughtful faith that locates itself between dogmatism on one
hand and skepticism on the other (S142/L110; S164/L131). In short,
Pascal proves the possibility, in the generation just after Shakespeare's
death, of thinking the way I have claimed Shakespeare did, and Pascal
therefore offers a contrary instance to the widely prevailing assumption
that a thoughtful early modern writer's exposure to skepticism and
unbounded suspicion inevitably compelled unqualified assent to them.
Moreover, this position, which I have called skeptical faith, was not new
in the late sixteenth or early seventeenth century, because it can be
traced to Erasmus and More, who translated the Greek skeptic, Lucian,
in the early sixteenth century. To be sure, Shakespeare was very different from Pascal—he was not a rational apologist for the Christian faith,
as Pascal set out to be; he was a poet and playwright, not a scientist; and
his thinking about the natural world in particular seems comparatively
primitive—but Shakespeare brought enormous rhetorical resources,
imagination, and intelligence to the task of writing plays and poetry,
and he was strongly influenced, like Pascal, by the Bible and by a theology that reached beyond scholasticism to reaffirm Augustine.[40]

Where the theory of knowledge in particular is concerned, Shakespeare shares with Pascal the assumption that reason is like every other human faculty, in that it fails without grace. Philosophically Popkin describes this position as fideism, but it encompasses a wide variety of views, and Pascal offers the most sophisticated modern defense of it before Kierkegaard. Pascal follows Montaigne, for example, in emphasizing the weakness of reason, especially in the face of imagination. To make the point that imagination is stronger than reason, Pascal repeats Montaigne's example of a philosopher suspended safely high above the ground who is nonetheless appalled by the height (*Essays* II:12, 449; *Pensées* S78/L44). Shakespeare clearly makes the same point in numerous plays but most strikingly in *A Midsummer Night's Dream*, which dichotomizes reason and imagination thematically in Theseus and Oberon, respectively. To be sure, Shakespeare's evaluation of imagination is more positive than Pascal's, but the point of reason's inferiority is the same, as Theseus himself avers: "in the night, imagining some fear, / How easy is a bush supposed a bear!" (5.1.21–22).

Reason is fooled not only by imagination, for both Shakespeare and Pascal, but also more profoundly by self-deception. This is true in Shakespeare from the beginning, as we noticed in the early comedies and *The Rape of Lucrece*, because it is arguably traceable to his medieval dramatic heritage, where self-deception and self-division were staged by means of personified abstractions. Pascal makes one of his most trenchant comments about self-deception in the process of addressing the salutary benefits of skepticism: "But it is good for the reputation of skepticism that there are so many people in the world who are not skeptics, showing that man is quite capable of the most extravagant opinions, since he is capable of believing that he is not naturally and inevitably weak, and is, on the contrary, naturally wise" (*Pensées* S67/L33). Bottom and Dogberry are delightful illustrations of Pascal's point, but so is Lear, as the Fool tries repeatedly to tell him, and even Macbeth, who persists in a course that he knows to be self-destructive, because he fools himself into believing that he can profit from it. Richard II's gnomic self-realization is an instance of someone—a king, no less—coming out on the other side of the condition Pascal describes:

> But whate'er I be,
> Nor I, nor any man that but man is,

> With nothing shall be pleased till he be eased
> With being nothing. (*Richard II* 5.5.38–41)

Pascal in fact makes a very similar point to Richard's:

> Knowledge is two extremes that meet. The first is the pure, natural igno-
> rance of everyone at birth. The other extreme is reached by great souls
> who run through everything that can be known, only to find that they
> know nothing and to find themselves in the same ignorance from which
> they set out; but this is an erudite ignorance that knows itself. (S117/L83)

Hamlet's ambivalent exclamation about human nature is often cited
as if it were Shakespeare's own view, and it may well be, though it is hard
to imagine a playwright who creates such a variety of endearing persons
not being delighted with human beings himself—even their foibles:

> What a piece of a work is a man! How noble in reason, how infinite in
> faculties, in form and moving how express and admirable, in action how
> like an angel, in apprehension how like a god! The beauty of the world,
> the paragon of animals! And yet, to me, what is this quintessence of dust?
> Man delights not me. (*Hamlet* 2.2.304–10)

Whatever Shakespeare's view may have been, Hamlet's description
finds its place in a tragedy whose most intelligent and sensitive character has little access to crucial truths of the world around him—and we
recognize his ignorance, because the playwright reveals those truths to
us, while hiding them from Hamlet. This discrepancy is a crucial fact of
Shakespearean epistemology and ontology. In any case, Hamlet's
description has a close parallel in Pascal, though Pascal's exclamation is
even more ambivalent—more negative, less admiring:

> What a chimera then is man! What a surprise (*nouveauté*), what a monster,
> what chaos, what a subject of contradiction, what a prodigy! Judge of all
> things, weak (*imbécile*) earthworm; repository of truth, sink of uncertainty
> and error; glory and garbage of the universe! (S164/L131)

The coincidence of views has nothing to do with Pascal's reading of
Shakespeare. Conceivably, it has something to do with both Pascal's
and Shakespeare's reading of Montaigne. Undoubtedly, however, it
points to a similar way of thinking about human nature in the two
writers, and where grace is concerned, this particular coincidence
may well have to do with a shared habit of thinking religiously about
the human condition.

The failure of reason in both Shakespeare and Pascal has the double effect of decentering humankind and of relativizing what we too easily take to be absolute as no more than a habit of custom. For Pascal, Montaigne was no doubt behind these insights, and Montaigne may have influenced Shakespeare's recognition of them as well, though Montaigne's influence on Shakespeare is harder to establish, as we have seen. Drawing on his scientific background, Pascal points both to the frailty of the senses, which tell us that empty spaces exist in nature, and to the folly of the educated, who assert that nature abhors a vacuum (S78/L44). His point is that neither the senses nor education are reliable guides to the truth that genuinely empty spaces exist—empty even of air. "We have many other principles of error," he comments, and he mocks the creature who prides itself on reason (including himself in a humorous aside):

> The mind of this supreme judge of the world is not so independent that it is not liable to be disturbed by the first noise in its vicinity. The din of a cannon is not necessary to hinder its thoughts; it needs only the creaking of a vane or pulley. Do not be surprised if right now it does not reason well: a fly is buzzing in its ears. This is enough to render it incapable of good reflection. If you wish it to be able to reach the truth, chase away the animal holding its reason in check and disturbing that powerful intellect, ruler of towns and kingdoms. Here is a comical god! *Most ridiculous hero*! (S81/L48)

For Pascal, the weakness of reason is directly related to the way political power functions, because it is sustained mostly by custom, force, and popular ignorance, as More and Erasmus had pointed out more than a hundred years earlier:

> The custom of seeing kings accompanied by guards, drums, officers, and all the things that direct the machine to yield respect and fear, makes their faces, when they are sometimes seen alone without these trappings, impress respect and fear in their subjects, because we cannot separate in thought their persons from what usually accompanies them. And the world, which does not know that this effect is the result of custom, believes that it derives from a natural force. From this come these words: *the character of divinity is stamped on his face*, etc. (S59/L25)[41]

> The power of kings is based on reason and on the folly of the people; indeed, much more on folly. The greatest and most important thing in the world has weakness at its foundation, and this foundation is wonderfully

secure, for there is nothing more secure than that the people will be weak. What is based on reason alone is truly ill founded, like esteem for wisdom. (S60/L26)

Pascal's trenchant observations seem to bear out Jonathan Dollimore's point, made over twenty years ago, that skepticism had the effect of decentering humankind and of emphasizing the power of custom, though Dollimore's principal authority is Montaigne.[42] Dollimore's linking of Montaigne with Louis Althusser, however, is misleading—not because the parallels are not credible, but because Dollimore implies that not only Montaigne's thinking but also that of his contemporaries—including Shakespeare—was emergent materialism, anticipating the dialectical materialism of Marx. The example of Pascal is evidence to the contrary, for Pascal explicitly endorses the decentering of humankind and recognizes the power of custom, yet he does so as a believing Christian, not as a materialist. (Dollimore simply ignores Pascal.) What was possible for someone born in 1623 would therefore seem to have been possible for someone born in 1564 as well.

Let us consider a specific example in *King Lear*. Dollimore distinguishes what he calls "the Christian view" of the play from the "essentialist humanist" view, and he argues against both of them: "the Christian view locates man centrally in a providential universe; the humanist view likewise centralises man but now he is in a condition of tragic dislocation: instead of integrating (ultimately) with a teleological design created and sustained by God, man grows to consciousness in a universe which thwarts his deepest needs" (*Radical Tragedy*, 188). Dollimore accurately sees "essentialist humanism" as a secular derivative from Christianity, ultimately traceable to what M. H. Abrams called the "natural supernaturalism" of the Romantics.[43] But Dollimore's description of "the Christian view" is strikingly at odds with Pascal and, I would argue, with the way Christian assumptions operate in *King Lear*.

As argued above in chapter 3, the function of the comedy of forgiveness in *King Lear* is not to affirm divine providence; in fact, the play's ending terrified a Christian moralist like Samuel Johnson, because it seemed to him to have just the opposite effect. Rather, the comedy of forgiveness functions to deepen the mystery of suffering in the end, and the play simply leaves us in the midst of that mystery, as Johnson accurately perceived. Dollimore is right that "insofar as Lear identifies with suffering it is at the point where he is powerless to do anything about it" (192), but Lear's identification with poor Tom involves a critique of self-deceived power, as Lear himself affirms, when he tries to tear off his clothing (*King Lear* 3.4.100–108). His gesture is thus an important stage in affirming the "nothing" that Lear learns to recognize in himself, partly as a consequence of coming face-to-face with the suffering of a destitute madman. "Justice," Dollimore suggests, "is too important to be trusted to empathy" (192)—that is, the empathy Lear learns fails to achieve the only result that matters to Dollimore, namely distributive justice. Such a critique is valuable when it comes to assessing Edgar's claim to be establishing justice, after he has killed Edmund: "the prob-lem of course is that he is making his society supernaturally intelligible at the cost of rendering the concept of divine justice so punitive and 'poetic' as to be, humanly speaking, almost unintelligible" (203). But taking justice of any kind—retributive or distributive—as the bench-mark value in *King Lear* helps little in assessing the end of the play, which repudiates Edgar's view, insofar as the suffering of Lear and Cordelia after their reconciliation is out of all proportion to anything they might be thought to have done to deserve it. Insofar as the play asks us simply to acknowledge their suffering, it eschews explanations and invites something so like compassion that a better word for it is hard to find.[44]

Dollimore is certainly right that the end of Lear is opaque; in this regard, it is like the end of the other "famous four" tragedies, but it does not follow that it is not Christian, for Christian thinking in the Renaissance did not necessarily locate humankind centrally in a prov-idential universe with a knowable teleology sustained by God, as Dollimore asserts. Pascal certainly did not, as we have seen, and indeed for Pascal, opacity itself is key. "That God wanted to be hidden," he notes in *Pensées* S275/L242, "If there were only one religion, God would be overly manifest. If there were martyrs only in our religion that does not explain it is not instructive. Our religion does all this. **Truly you are a hidden God**."[45] As Pascal must have known, this affirmation is another aspect of his thinking that brings him close to the Reformers. One of Luther's tenets (number twenty in the Heidelberg disputation) concerns *Deus Absconditus*, and Luther's point is the very one on which Pascal took issue with Descartes—that God is not accessible to human reason.[46] God is certainly hidden at the end of

King Lear, as God invariably is in Shakespeare's plays, but insofar as the play succeeds in winning our acknowledgment of Lear's pointless suffering, God is not absent.

We do not know whether Shakespeare thought apologetically in the manner of Pascal, because we have nothing but the plays and poems as the record of Shakespeare's thinking. Better, perhaps, that what he thought is hidden in this way, because the record he left welcomes many readers that the author's critical commentary might well exclude. Shakespeare's acknowledgment in *The Winter's Tale* that time stales fresh stories (though he boldly predicts the continuing freshness of his own story [4.1.12–15]) indicates that he was aware of how cultural standards changed over time, as well as across geographical boundaries, and Pascal is a good example. By subsequent critical standards, Pascal's biblical hermeneutic was naïve, rationalistic, and overly literal (he believed, with Rosalind, for example, that the earth was about 6,000 years old).[47] If that kind of thinking were known to lie behind Shakespeare's poems and plays, they might well be less appealing than they have proved to be. My point in turning to Pascal's idea of knowledge is not that Shakespeare should be limited to it, but that it offers a nearly contemporary example of an unusually agile mind finding a way dialectically between dogmatism and skepticism. Shakespeare may have been a materialist, as Dollimore argues, and the materialist hermeneutic has certainly been salutary in shedding new light on what Shakespeare wrote, but with the example of Pascal in mind, the materialist reading makes historical assumptions that are almost as naïve as Pascal's own, for what Dollimore takes to be materialism could as easily be the hiddenness of God.

NOTES

Preface and Acknowledgments

1 On the philosopher's costume, see Julius S. Held, *Rembrandt's Aristotle and Other Rembrandt Studies* (Princeton: Princeton University Press, 1969), 15–16.

2 Despite its suggestive title, Philip Davis's *Shakespeare Thinking* (London: Continuum, 2007) was published too late for me to use in this book. I am grateful to Matthew Fike for bringing it to my attention.

3 James Kennedy and Caroline Simon, *Can Hope Endure? A Historical Case Study in Christian Higher Education* (Grand Rapids: Eerdmans, 2005).

Chapter One

1 Manfred Pfister, "Elizabethan Atheism: Discourse without Subject," *Deutsche Shakespeare Jahrbuch* 127 (1991): 59.

2 Stanley Cavell, *Disowning Knowledge in Six Plays of Shakespeare* (Cambridge: Cambridge University Press, 1987), 35.

3 On Descartes' place in the history of early skepticism, see Richard H. Popkin, *The History of Scepticism from Erasmus to Spinoza* (Berkeley: University of California Press, 1979), 172–92.

4 Shakespeare may not have used "skeptic" and related words because he matured before they became widely known, he did not have a university education, and he did not grow up with aristocrats. According to William Hamlin, the earliest use of "skeptic" in English is by the Scottish scholar and poet, George Buchanan, who at various points in his life tutored both Montaigne and the future King James VI and I (*Tragedy and Scepticism Tragedy in Shakespeare's England* [Basingstoke: Palgrave Macmillan, 2005], 43). Hamlin offers the best summary of early skepticism's reception in England (29–71), pointing out that skeptical ideas were introduced first in the two universities and then, "around the beginning of the 1590s," at the Inns of Court (48), while acknowledging that "Shakespeare may never have seen" *The Sceptick*, a summary of Sextus' main points that is known to have circulated in manuscript in the 1590s (8).

251

5   Robert B. Pierce, "Shakespeare and the Ten Modes of Scepticism," *Shakespeare Survey* 46 (1993): 145–58. The ten modes are spelled out in Montaigne's *Apology for Raymond Sebond*, but Shakespeare is very unlikely to have known Montaigne in the early 1590s, and Pierce does not address the issue of a possible source.

6   Houston Diehl, *Staging Reform, Reforming the Stage* (Ithaca: Cornell University Press, 1997), 28–31.

7   For a model of reading sixteenth-century skepticism in context, see Terence Cave, "Imagining Scepticism in the Sixteenth Century," *Journal of the Institute of Romance Studies* 1 (1992): 193–205.

8   Paul Whitfield White, *Theatre and Reformation: Protestantism, Patronage, and Playing in Tudor England* (Cambridge: Cambridge University Press, 1993), 12–41.

9   *The Colloquies of Erasmus*, trans. Craig R. Thompson (Chicago: University of Chicago Press, 1965), 231.

10 Stephen Greenblatt, *Shakesperaean Negotiations: The Circulation of Social Energy in Renaissance England* (Berkeley: University of California Press, 1988), 113–14.

11 Eamon Duffy, *The Stripping of the Altars: Traditional Religion in England 1400–1580* (New Haven: Yale University Press, 1992).

12 Thomas More, *Translations of Lucian*, ed. Craig R. Thompson (New Haven: Yale University Press, 1974).

13 Christopher Robinson, *Lucian and His Influence* (Chapel Hill: University of North Carolina Press, 1979), 180.

14 Jonson owned a 1530 Latin translation of Lucian and a 1527 edition of Erasmus' *Colloquies*. C. H. Herford and Percy Simpson, ed., *Ben Jonson*, 10 vols. (Oxford: Clarendon, 1952–61), 1:266 and 268.

15 Ben Jonson, *The Devil Is an Ass*, Revels edition, ed. Peter Happé (Manchester University Press, 1994), 5.3.6.

16 Erasmus, *Colloquies*, ed. Thompson, 630.

17 Pope Celestine V (1294) was beatified after his death as a saintly and humble man, but not everyone was impressed. Dante places him in the circle of hell reserved for the opportunists (*Inferno* III) because his indecisiveness and lack of critical judgment resulted in the papacy of Boniface VIII, who reportedly duped and supplanted him, earning a place even lower in hell. Erasmus' wry comment suggests that he evaluated Celestine in about the same way Dante did.

18 Erasmus, *Praise of Folly*, trans. Betty Radice (Harmondsworth: Penguin, 1971), 196. The reference is to 2 Corinthians 11:17. For Folly's stinging attack on "the Supreme Pontiffs," see 178–81. In a letter written in Greek in October, 1518, Erasmus remarks that "*the monarchy of the Roman High*

Priest (as that see now is) is the plague of Christendom." Quoted by James D. Tracy, *The Politics of Erasmus* (Toronto: University of Toronto Press, 1978), 116. Emphasis in the original.

19   "My aim in *Folly* was exactly the same as in other works. Only the presentation was different. In the *Enchiridion* I simply outlined the pattern of Christian life. . . . And in *Folly* I expressed the same ideas as those in the Enchiridion, but in the form of a joke." (*Praise of Folly*, 215).

20   *Querela Pacis*, trans. Betty Radice, in *Collected Works of Erasmus*, vol. 27, *Literary and Educational Writings*, ed. A. H. T. Levi (Toronto: University of Toronto Press, 1986), 304 (my emphasis). *Querela Pacis* reads as if it were an appeal to stop sectarian violence following the Reformation, but it was written in 1516 and in fact appeals to competitive princes who were all adherents of traditional religion.

21   The best reading of these metaphors is by Walter M. Gordon, *Humanist Play and Belief: The Seriocomic Art of Desiderius Erasmus* (Toronto: University of Toronto Press, 1990), especially "The Play of Grace," 155–80.

22   Popkin, *History of Scepticism*, 19. Hamlin identifies an unusual English example of skeptical ideas being used in a Catholic apologetic: Thomas Fitzherbert's *Treatise Concerning Policy and Religion* (1606) (*Tragedy and Scepticism*, 96).

23   Evidence of this "baptism's" success is the fact that Sextus was never placed on the Index (Popkin, 96). In an essay that adds confirming detail to Popkin's analysis of Sextus's initial impact, C. B. Schmidt contrasts the Western church's qualified acceptance of pagan learning—and of Sextus in particular—with the Eastern church's rejection. See C. B. Schmidt, "The Rediscovery of Ancient Skepticism in Modern Times," in *The Skeptical Tradition*, ed. Myles Burnyeat (Berkeley: University of California Press, 1983), 234–35.

24   This point is particularly important in view of the commonly expressed assumption that religious conflict in the sixteenth century immediately bred disbelief. Two relevant examples to the contrary in English are Sir John Davies' *Nosce Teipsum* (1599) and Fulke Greville's *Treatise of Human Learning* (1605), both of which place human ignorance in the context of the fall of man, where Erasmus places it as well. *Nosce Teipsum* draws on Montaigne, among others, in constructing a defense of orthodox Christian belief and the limitations of human knowledge. On Davies' use of Montaigne, see Robert Krueger, ed., *The Poems of Sir John Davies* (Oxford: Clarendon, 1975), 326. Hamlin refers to *Nosce Teipsum* as "a standard paradigm of early modern Britain's appropriation of ancient sceptical thought" (*Tragedy and Scepticism*, 60).

25   "So that our opinion (as *Sextus Empiricus* affirmeth) gives the name of good or ill to every thing. Out of whose works (lately translated into English, for

the benefit of unlearned writers) a man might collect a whole book of this argument." Thomas Nashe, *Works*, ed. Ronald B. McKerrow, rev. F. P. Wilson, 5 vols. (Oxford: Basil Blackwell, 1958), 3:332–33. McKerrow's notes make clear that Nashe himself used the English translation (despite his derisory comment about "unlearned writers"), since his quotations frequently differ from the Latin, sometimes in passages that correspond to other English borrowings from Sextus by writers who presumably had access to the same translation. Contrary to McKerrow's claim, William M. Hamlin has argued persuasively that the translation Nashe used is extant, and Hamlin recently published an edition of it, "A Lost Translation Found? An Edition of *The Sceptick* (c. 1590) Based on Extant Manuscripts [with Text]," *English Literary Renaissance* 31 (2001): 34–51.

26   For evidence that this play belonged to the Chamberlain's Men, see David Kathman, "Reconsidering The *Seven Deadly Sins*," *Early Theatre* 7 (2004): 13–44.

27   "Martinists" refers to Puritans represented by Martin Marprelate, the anonymous satirical attacker of Elizabethan bishops. Nashe may have authored one of the anti-Marprelate tracts himself, *An Almond for a Parrot* (1590). See *Works*, 5:337–76. Nashe's recognition of the Family of Love ("Familists") as an Elizabethan sect has been vindicated by recent historical investigation. See Christopher Marsh, *The Family of Love in English Society, 1550–1630* (Cambridge: Cambridge University Press, 1994). I return to the vestment controversy again in chapter 8, in dealing with Shakespeare's esthetic theory.

28   Popkin points to a parallel example from the other side, published in the same year as Sextus' *Outlines*: Sebastian Castellio's *De arte dubitandi*. Castellio attacks the grounds of Protestant belief, but he begins, in Popkin's words, by asserting that "there are many matters that are not really doubtful, matters that any reasonable person will accept. These, for Castellio, include the existence of God, God's goodness, and the authenticity of Scripture. He offers as evidence the argument from design, and the plausibility of the Scriptural picture of the world" (*History of Scepticism*, 11). Skeptical faith thus characterized both sides of the divide between Catholic and Protestant, and its assumptions, as skepticism, would not have stood up to Enlightenment critique.

29   Popkin, *History of Scepticism*, xviii.

30   Michael Hunter, "The Problem of 'Atheism' in Early Modern England," *Transactions of the Royal Historical Society* 35 (1985): 135–57. The problem Hunter addresses is a large one, but in trying to understand it I have also found useful C. John Sommerville and John Edwards, "Debate: Religious Faith, Doubt and Atheism," *Past and Present* 128 (1990): 152–61; and

Nicholas Davidson, "Christopher Marlowe and Atheism" in *Christopher Marlowe and the English Renaissance*, ed. Darryll Grantley and Peter Roberts (Aldershot: Scolar Press, 1996), 129–47.

31 The critical literature on Shakespeare and Montaigne is vast and inconclusive. At best, Montaigne's influence is likely to have been late: Florio's translation was not published until 1603, and the least disputed reference is in *The Tempest* (1611) 2.1.150–59. I return to Montaigne at greater length in chapter 8.

32 *The Complete Essays of Montaigne*, trans. Donald M. Frame (Stanford: Stanford University Press, 1965), "Apology for Raymond Sebond," 372.

33 *Essays*, "Apology," 374; cf. 380.

34 Popkin, *History of Scepticism*, 96. Popkin refers to Montaigne's thinking as "a new form of fideism—Catholic Pyrrhonism" (43).

35 Paul Ricoeur, "Interpretation as Exercise of Suspicion," in *Freud and Philosophy*, trans. Denis Savage (New Haven: Yale University Press, 1970), 32–36.

36 Ricoeur, 33, emphasis in the original. Ricoeur takes Descartes to be foundational in rational skepticism as confidently as Cavell does, without acknowledging that Descartes is not a skeptic, because he employed skepticism methodologically to arrive at a form of rational dogmatism, as Gail Fine argues in "Descartes and Ancient Skepticism: Reheated Cabbage?" *Philosophical Review* 109 (2000): 195–234. Still, Ricoeur's point about skepticism and consciousness is important, because it highlights the postmodern evasion of conscious rationalism in favor of subconscious self-deception.

37 Herbert Fingarette, *Self-Deception* (London: Routledge & Kegan Paul, 1969), 82–91 (quotation from 85). Writing shortly after Fingarette, but apparently unaware of his analysis, Michael Goldman noticed what he called "the unsounded self" in Shakespeare, borrowing the phrase from *The Rape of Lucrece* and identifying several instances where "the figure of the crowd is used to suggest some sort of varied population inside the body, a throng of multiple possibilities or competing selves" (*Shakespeare and the Energies of Drama* [Princeton: Princeton University Press, 1972], 22). Goldman offers an acute analysis of the word "self" in Shakespeare (Appendix A, 153–58).

38 Mike W. Martin, *Self-Deception and Morality* (Lawrence: University Press of Kansas, 1986), 6–30. Martin's idea of self-acknowledgment may be influenced by Stanley Cavell's argument that where knowledge is impossible for the skeptic, acknowledgment (of oneself and of others) may not only be possible but requisite (Cavell, "Knowing and Acknowledging" in *Must We Mean What We Say?* [Cambridge: Cambridge University Press, 1969],

238–66), especially since Cavell's idea seems to be indebted ultimately to Kant's categorical imperative. Thus Martin: "Full and sincere acknowledgment of others entails knowing or believing what one is saying. But it goes beyond mere cognitive states by being a revelation or open expression of what is known" (*Self-Deception and Morality*, 14). Moreover, Martin recognizes that people often seem most vulnerable to self-deception in the process of uncovering self-deception (11, 37)—an insight that seems to be at work in Malvolio's self-assurance: "I do not now fool myself, to let imagination jade me" (*Twelfth Night* 2.5.160–61). Martin's point also recalls Kant's recognition of how moral agents favor the "dear self" in moral decision-making, and Kant's recognition was indebted, in turn, to his pietist upbringing. See Immanuel Kant, *Grounding for the Metaphysics of Morals*, trans. James W. Ellington (Indianapolis: Hackett, 1981), 20.

39 On this point, see Bernard Spivack, *Shakespeare and the Allegory of Evil* (New York: Columbia University Press, 1958), 78–82. My choice of *Wisdom* to illustrate the point about the divided self is more or less arbitrary; the same point could be made with any number of morality plays and even with a play like the York *Creation and Fall of Man* (early fifteenth century), where Satan's temptation of Eve is closely analogous to the vices' (and the Vice's) temptation of allegorical figures from innumerable plays.

40 Sir John Davies analyzes the fall of Adam and Eve in precisely these terms in the opening lines of *Nosce Teipsum* (1599): "the Spirit of lies" . . . "breathes into their incorrupted breasts / A curious wish, which did corrupt their *will*," and when they act on their wish, they corrupt their reason as well (ll. 14–28).

41 *Apius and Virginia* (1575), ed. R. B. McKerrow (Chiswick Press for the Malone Society, 1911), lines 502–3. I owe this reference to a paper by Alan Dessen, "Staging Ideas and Abstractions: Revisiting Shakespeare's Theatrical Vocabulary," read at the International Shakespeare Conference, 8 August 2006.

42 Nathaniel Woodes, *The Conflict of Conscience*, ed. Herbert Davis and F. P. Wilson, Malone Society Reprints (Oxford University Press, 1952), ll. 1958–59.

43 The First Murderer in *Richard III* tells Clarence, "Come, you deceive yourself," as Clarence indeed does, in believing that Gloucester will rescue him (1.4.245), and the agent of Clarence's self-deception is the Vice-like Richard, who derives directly from the morality play. Shakespeare's most subtle and complex treatment of self-deception is the speaker of the sonnets, and Shakespeare comes close to naming self-deception again in the couplet of Sonnet 4: "For having traffic with thyself alone, / Thou of thyself thy sweet self dost deceive." Sonnet 4 may refer to masturbation, as several critics have recently argued, but that reading offers a limiting account of the sonnet's sense of the self.

44   See above, n. 24. Davies' first section (1–180) asserts the human proneness to self-deception (though without using the phrase), as the following couplet illustrates (again recalling Error in *The Faerie Queene*): "What can we know? Or what can we discerne? / When *Error* chokes the windowes of the mind" (57–58). The second line of Davies' couplet may be a direct allusion to *The Faerie Queene* I.i.18, where Error attempts to choke the Redcrosse Knight.

45   Dyke's book was very popular, going through eleven editions between 1614 and 1642 (four of them by 1616). A French translation in 1634 influenced the much better known maxims on self-deception by La Rochefoucauld.

46   Dyke was educated at Cambridge and read widely, as his citations indicate—ancient and modern, Greek, Latin, English, and Italian (Ambrose, Anacreon, Aquinas, Bernard of Clairvaux, Calvin, Cicero, Chrysostom, Eusebius, John Foxe, Horace, Machiavelli, Martial, Plato, Plautus, Pliny, Seneca, Tertullian)—but his favorite non-biblical authority is Augustine. I consulted Daniel Dyke, *The Mystery of Self-Deceiving: or, A Discourse and Discovery of the Deceitfulness of Man's Heart*. Written by the late faithful Minister of Gods Word Daniel Dyke, Bachelor in Divinitie (London, Printed by William Stansby, 1630).

47   Erasmus, *Colloquies*, ed. Thompson, 235.

48   Richard as a "deep dissimuler" is Tacitean, as Richard Silvester points out in his edition of More's *History of King Richard the Third* (New Haven: Yale University Press, 1963), xciv–xcv, but dissimulation is also a quality of personified vices in contemporary morality plays, and More's description of Richard's character might easily describe Medwall's Pride or Skelton's Cloaked Collusion: "Hee was close and secrete, a deepe dissimuler, lowlye of countynaunce, arrogant of heart, outwardly coumpinable where he inwardely hated, not letting to kisse whome hee thoughte to kyll: dispitious and cruell, nor for euill will always, for ofter for ambicion, and either for the suretie or encrease of his estate" (8).

49   Quoted from *The Geneva Bible, A facsimile of the 1560 edition* (Madison: University of Wisconsin Press, 1969). The Geneva gloss cross-references Luke 6:37 and comments: "he commandeth, not to be curious or malicious to try out, and condemn our neighbour's faults: for hypocrites hide their own faults, and seek not to amend them, but are curious to reprove other men's." Shakespeare alludes to this saying again in *King John* 4.1.90–95 and possibly in *Hamlet* 1.1.116.

50   Patricia Parker, *Shakespeare from the Margins: Language, Culture, Context* (Chicago: University of Chicago Press, 1996), 20–22, 30–32. Parker is unusually attentive to biblical allusions, but she overlooks those in *Love's*

Labor's Lost. Virgil Whitaker notes that the play has almost as many biblical parallels as *The Comedy of Errors, The Taming of the Shrew,* and *Two
Gentlemen of Verona* combined (*Shakespeare's Use of Learning: An Inquiry into the
Growth of His Mind and Art* [San Marino, Calif.: Huntington Library, 1964],
84), and the point is confirmed by Naseeb Shaheen, who adds that "it is
probably safe to conclude that Shakespeare did not borrow any of them
[the play's biblical allusions] from the known analogues" (*Biblical References
in Shakespeare's Plays* [Newark: University of Delaware Press, 1999], 119).

51 Despite its undoubted honesty, the Princess's exclamation is still in striking
decorum with the play's irrepressible rhetorical decorativeness, given the
decisive contrast between her first and last words and their pointed reversal of the natural order of what they represent.

52 See Harry Morris, *Last Things in Shakespeare* (Tallahassee: Florida State
University Press, 1985). My reading of last things in Shakespeare is less
allegorical and totalizing than Morris's, but he offers a thorough review of
the subject.

53 "The Form of Solemnization of Matrimony" from *The Book of Common
Prayer 1559,* ed. John E. Booty (Charlottesville: University Press of Virginia
for the Folger Shakespeare Library, 1976), 292.

54 Lucrece vainly appeals to Tarquin in the name of "common troth" before
he rapes her (*Rape of Lucrece,* 571). Though Shakespeare usually refers
"troth" allusively to Christian ethics, philosophers have recently been
receptive to thinking of love as a virtue without making Christian assumptions. See especially Martha Nussbaum, *Love's Knowledge: Essays on
Philosophy and Literature* (New York: Oxford University Press, 1990), and
more recently Mike Martin, *Love's Virtues* (Lawrence: University of Kansas
Press, 1996): "Faith is not a mere causal prerequisite to love. Indeed, faith
is interwoven with most of love's other defining virtues, each of which
must be exercised on a foundation of trust" (5). Following Stanley Cavell's
lead, Martin includes a chapter in his book on *Othello* (133–48). Caroline
J. Simon comes full circle, as it were, with philosophical reflections on love
and literature based on Christian assumptions, *The Disciplined Heart: Love,
Destiny, and Imagination* (Grand Rapids: Eerdmans, 1997).

55 On this reading of "o'erparted," see Alvin Kernan, *The Playwright as
Magician* (New Haven: Yale University Press, 1979), 72.

56 Geoffrey Miles, *Shakespeare and the Constant Romans* (Oxford: Clarendon,
1996). Miles observes that when Shakespeare's characters use "philosophy" they usually mean stoicism (12–13). Christianity had long been sus-
ceptible to stoic influence, of course, and the highly stoic *Consolation of
Philosophy* by Boethius uses a personified abstraction called "Lady
Philosophy" as its interlocutor with the first-person narrator. Though

Miles does not mention Boethius, the *Consolation* was familiar to medieval Christian poets, and it remained influential in sixteenth-century England; it was translated into English, for example, by Queen Elizabeth I.

57 Parker, *Shakespeare from the Margins*, 56–82.

58 For a fuller argument in support of this effect in *The Comedy of Errors*, see John D. Cox, *Shakespeare and the Dramaturgy of Power* (Princeton: Princeton University Press, 1989), 61–67.

59 This point has been developed particularly well by Barbara Freedman, "Egeon's Debt: Self-Division and Self-Redemption in *The Comedy of Errors*," *English Literary Renaissance* 10 (1980): 360–83.

60 "Wives, submit yourselves unto your husbands, as unto the Lord. For the husband is the wife's head, even as Christ is the head of the Church" (Eph 5:22-23). This admonition is the basis for the promise that the priest asked brides to make in the Elizabethan marriage service: "wilt thou obey [thy wedded husband] and serve him?"

61 He is punning on *respice funem*, "Beware the [hangman's] rope," because Antipholus has beaten him with a rope's end. These and many other eschatological allusions in the play are explicated by Parker, *Shakespeare from the Margins*, 59–75.

62 For comments on the play's overall shape, see Freedman, "Egeon's Debt," 363–64.

63 On this motif, see Parker, *Shakespeare from the Margins*, 71–75.

64 James L. Sanderson, "Patience in *The Comedy of Errors*," *Texas Studies in Literature and Language* 16 (1975): 603–18. Following R. A. Foakes's note, Sanderson identifies one of the play's uses of "patient" ("Nay, 'tis for me to be patient; I am in adversity" [4.4.20–21]) as an echo of Psalm 94:13 ("That thou mayest give him patience in time of adversity") (607).

65 Moreover, this ambivalent quality in Shakespearean comedy is what principally distinguishes it from Dante's *Divine Comedy*. Whereas the latter deals exclusively and literally with a detailed revelation of the Last Things, Shakespearean comedy invariably deals literally with this life but in the enigmatic light of the Last Things.

66 For this effect in *The Comedy of Errors* in particular, see Jonathan V. Crewe, "God or the Good Physician: The Rational Playwright in *The Comedy of Errors*," *Genre* 15 (1982: 203–23.

67 For comments to similar effect about a very late play, see Judith E. Tonning, "'Like This Insubstantial Pageant, Faded': Eschatology and Theatricality in *The Tempest*," *Literature and Theology* 18 (2004): 371–82.

68 Bryan W. Ball, *A Great Expectation: Eschatological Thought in English Protestantism to 1660* (Leiden: E. J. Brill, 1975), 194. See also Philip

Edgcumbe Hughes's chapter on "Sanctification" in *Theology of the English Reformers* (London: Hodder & Stoughton, 1965), esp. 85–87.

69 Edmund Spenser, *The Faerie Queene*, ed. J. C. Smith (Oxford: Clarendon, 1909), 2 vols., I.xii.18 and 41.

70 On the medieval idea of "comedy" as a story in which problems are resolved by the end, see Nevill Coghill, "Comic Form in *Measure for Measure*," *Shakespeare Survey* 8 (1955): 14–27.

71 Stanley Cavell, *The Claim of Reason: Wittgenstein, Skepticism, Morality, and Tragedy* (Oxford: Oxford University Press, 1979), 129–67. For another way of understanding speech-act theory as applied to Shakespeare, see Stanley Fish, "How to Do things with Austin and Searle: Speech-Act Theory and Literary Criticism," in *Is There a Text in This Class?* (Cambridge, Mass.: Harvard University Press, 1980), 197–245.

72 Cavell, *Disowning Knowledge*, 12. Cf. "Most immediately, what philosophy knows as doubt, Othello's violence allegorizes (or recognizes) as some form of jealousy" (7). For summaries of other plays as allegories of skepticism, see 12–13 (*Coriolanus*), 15 (*The Winter's Tale*), and 25 (*Antony and Cleopatra*). For a perceptive analysis of Cavell's hermeneutic, see Gerald L. Bruns, "Stanley Cavell's Shakespeare," *Critical Inquiry* 16 (1990): 612–32.

73 "The Avoidance of Love: A Reading of *King Lear*," in *Disowning Knowledge*, 39–123. This essay has been frequently published separately in other collections.

74 For others, see *Wisdom* 14:22, Isaiah 64:6, Mark 7:21, Romans 1:28-32.

75 Harry Berger, Jr., *Making Trifles of Terrors: Redistributing Complicities in Shakespeare*, ed. Peter Erickson (Stanford: Stanford University Press, 1997), x–xiv.

76 This is an overly simple but I hope not untrue version of Berger's reading of the passage from *All's Well*, which he refers to twice in *Making Trifles* (126–27 and 165–66).

77 This is a problem for William Hamlin as well in *Tragedy and Scepticism*. He wishes to break "the traditional bounds of 'tragedy,'" because "the term, indispensable though it is, perpetually risks the reification of that toward which it gestures, and one of my subsidiary goals is to shake loose the hardened associations that sometimes encrust the concept" (7). The result is that he describes tragedy in relation to skepticism rather than acknowledging aspects of skepticism in tragedy. The only play by Shakespeare to which he devotes a chapter is *Troilus and Cressida*, whose genre is indeed ambiguous, but whose skepticism defines it as tragedy for Hamlin.

78 Compare Berger's reading of Portia in *The Merchant of Venice*, for example (8) with his reading of Edgar in *King Lear* (294–95). The function of these two characters is so important to Berger's analysis that the two plays are hard to distinguish in his criticism.

79 Berger asserts in a note that only an ironic reading of the ending (such as his reading) respects "settled ambivalences of attitude inherent not merely in particular actions or characters, but in the community of the play" (434n. 8), and he finds those ambivalences in the romantic plot of Hero and Claudio.

80 I have reviewed the arguments as they appear in ten books published in the early 2000s in "Was Shakespeare a Christian, and If So, What Kind of Christian Was He?" *Christianity and Literature* 55 (2006): 539–66.

81 "If Shakespeare's plays indicate that he sided with neither papist nor puritan, they also show him striving to resist identification with antipapists and antipuritans" (*Shakespeare's Tribe: Church, Nation, and Theater in Renaissance England* [Chicago: University of Chicago Press, 2002], 50).

82 I develop this point in detail in chapter 8.

83 Alfred Harbage, *As They Liked It: An Essay on Shakespeare and Morality* (New York: Macmillan, 1947). Harbage attends more closely to social ethics than to faith, but his point about the plays reflecting auditors' values back to themselves is true for faith as well.

Chapter Two

1 *Pericles*, the earliest of the romances (1606–1608), was probably written before *Coriolanus* (1608–1610). Howard Felperin includes *Henry VIII* (1613) among the romances, in the most sustained theoretical treatment of that genre, *Shakespearean Romance* (Princeton: Princeton University Press, 1972), 196–210, but *Henry VIII* also recalls the history plays of the 1590s in more than just its title and subject matter.

2 Like *Henry VIII, Two Noble Kinsmen* (1613–1614) is an anomaly in this brief narrative of Shakespeare's writing career: both are later than *The Tempest*, both are of uncertain genre, and Shakespeare shared the authorship of both with someone else, likely John Fletcher. For a useful summary of the issues for both plays, see Lois Potter, ed., *The Two Noble Kinsmen*, The Arden Shakespeare (London: Thomas Nelson, 1997), 1–23; and Gordon McMullan, ed., *Henry VIII (All Is True)*, The Arden Shakespeare (London: Thomson Learning, 2000), 106–20.

3 This does not discount the possibility that his first venture into playwriting was the early history plays, which are inspired as much by Marlowe's *Tamburlaine* as by Senecan tragedy, though they may have launched the genre they represent, which Shakespeare eventually perfected. If these were his first plays, they show his attentiveness to popular taste, as well as to classical strictures, from the outset.

4   Sidney's important treatise was first printed in 1595, but Sidney was killed in 1586 and likely wrote the *Apology* as early as 1583. It shows no awareness of Shakespeare or even of Marlowe, whose *Tamburlaine* was a stunning stage success in the late 1580s, but Shakespeare was clearly aware of the three unities before the publication of Sidney's *Apology*, because he achieved them perfectly in *The Comedy of Errors*. For Sidney on the unities, see *An Apology for Poetry*, ed. G. G. Smith, 2 vols. (Oxford: Clarendon, 1904), 1:196–99.

5   "The First Part of the Sermon of Repentance" in *The Two Books of Homilies*, ed. John Griffiths (London: Oxford University Press, 1859), 533.

6   My point is not that Shakespeare was necessarily influenced by Peele but that what I am claiming about a particular pattern in Shakespearean comedy was vital not just in Elizabethan religious culture but also in the culture of contemporary drama, which included continued productions of morality plays, as well as Peele's play.

7   Inga-Stina Ewbank, "The House of David in Renaissance Drama," *Renaissance Drama* 8 (1965): 3–40.

8   *The Love of King David and Fair Bethsabe*, ed. Elmer Blistein, *Life and Works of George Peele*, 3 vols. (New Haven: Yale University Press, 1952–70), vol. 2, lines 102–5.

9   *The Book of Common Prayer 1559*, ed. John E. Booty (Charlottesville: University Press of Virginia for the Folger Shakespeare Library, 1976), 51, 59 (morning prayer), 61 (evening prayer). The story of the unforgiving servant was read as the gospel on the twenty-second Sunday after Trinity, and the corresponding epistle was Philippians 1:3-11, with its visionary prayer that in the church at Philippi love will "increase yet more and more in knowledge, and in all understanding, that ye may accept the things that are most excellent" (*BCP*, 209). The Collect for that day may well have been designed to assist the dull preacher who did not see the complementary emphases on love and forgiveness in the Epistle and Gospel: "Lord, we beseech thee to keep thy household the Church in continual godliness; that through thy protection it may be free from all adversities, and devoutly given to serve thee in good works, to the glory of thy name; through Jesus Christ our Lord."

10   On Augustine and Hobbes, with regard to both human nature and politics, see Herbert A. Deane, *The Political and Social Ideas of St. Augustine* (New York: Columbia University Press, 1963), 1, 46–47, 50, 56, 59, 117, 144, 234–36.

11   Debora Shuger, *Habits of Thought in the English Renaissance* (Berkeley: University of California Press, 1990), 17–68, quotations from 27–28. For a parallel argument on another theme, see Shuger, "Subversive fathers

and suffering subjects: Shakespeare and Christianity," in *Religion Literature, and Politics in Post-Reformation England, 1540–1688*, ed. Donna B. Hamilton and Richard Strier (Cambridge: Cambridge University Press, 1996), 46–69. Most influential in arguing that Hooker's insistence on hierarchy supplied a parallel—almost a key—to reading Shakespeare was E. M. W. Tillyard, *The Elizabethan World Picture* (London: Chatto & Windus, 1943), a prequel to Tillyard's *Shakespeare's History Plays* (London: Chatto & Windus, 1944). Tillyard influenced Virgil Whitaker (among many others), who made *Troilus and Cressida* central to his narrative of Shakespeare's intellectual development, because "The metaphysics behind" Shakespeare's mature conception of the world "finally comes to explicit statement in Ulysses' speech on degree" (*Shakespeare's Use of Learning: An Inquiry into the Growth of His Mind and Art* [San Marino, Calif.: Huntington Library, 1964], 195). I am proposing a very different account of how Shakespeare's thinking is embodied in his writing.

12 On the polemical context of Hooker's theology, see W. D. J. Cargill Thompson, "The Philosopher of the 'Politic Society': Richard Hooker as a Political Thinker," in *Studies in Richard Hooker*, ed. W. Speed Hill (Cleveland: Case Western Reserve University, 1972), 3–76, and Peter Lake, *Anglicans and Puritans?* (London: Unwin Hyman, 1988), 145–238.

13 R. G. Hunter, *Shakespeare and the Comedy of Forgiveness* (New York: Columbia University Press, 1965). The plays Hunter discusses are *The Two Gentlemen of Verona* (1589–1593), *Much Ado about Nothing* (1598–1600), *All's Well That Ends Well* (1601–1604), *Measure for Measure* (1603–1604), *Cymbeline* (1608–1611), *The Winter's Tale* (1610–1611), and *The Tempest* (1609–1611). Howard Felperin prefers the terms "comedies of atonement or amendment," because "they focus on the romantic rather than the Christian dimension of the plays in question" (*Shakespearean Romance*, 16), but the terms Felperin proposes are no less connotative of Christian theology than "forgiveness," and his dichotomy between generic romance and Christian thinking is based on a narrative of secularization that Felperin assumes without close examinination.

14 While "atone" in this passage seems theologically suggestive, Shakespeare seldom if ever uses the word or its variants in the sense of "redeem" that was available to him in the Geneva Bible (too many references to list, but see Romans 5:11 for an important New Testament example). The word "atonement" was often spelled "at onement" in the sixteenth century, reflecting its primary sense, "to set at one, bring into concord" (*OED* v. I.1), which is how Shakespeare consistently uses it. For examples besides the one in *As You Like It*, see *Richard II* 1.1.202; *Othello* 4.1.231; *Timon of Athens* 5.4.5; *Antony and Cleopatra* 2.2.108; and *Coriolanus* 4.6.76. The sole possible

exception is Parson Evans's eager offer in *The Merry Wives of Windsor*: "I am of the Church, and will be glad to do my benevolence to make atonements and compromises between you" (1.1.28–30), but even here the primary sense of the word is uppermost, as the offered synonym indicates. For comment on this passage, see Patricia Parker, *Shakespeare from the Margins: Language, Culture, Context* (Chicago: University of Chicago Press, 1996), 133–37.

15   Duke Frederick parallels Oliver but is less fully developed. When Oliver says he never loved his brother, Frederick exclaims "More villain thou" (3.1.15), with no acknowledgment of the irony that he has usurped his own brother's place. His exclamation is a clear instance of his own lack of self-knowledge, which is, in turn "cured" (in the metaphor for self-realization that this play repeatedly uses) by "conversion." In other words, Frederick also knows without knowing—recognizes and condemns his own failure in Oliver without acknowledging it in himself.

16   This kind of loving cure effectively responds to Orlando's hopeless longing for a "wise remedy" at the outset (1.1.24; cf. 3.2.359) and contrasts with the "cleansing" guaranteed by Jaques (2.7.58–61), which he asserts is "but good" (63), though even the affable Duke Senior rejects it as so much moral defecation or vomiting (67–69), thus helping to gloss Jaques's name as "jakes" (an outhouse).

17   The intractability of such problems, and the poet's ability to render them incisively, has made Shakespeare's writing answerable to various strains of criticism that emphasize them: feminism (and gender criticism more broadly), post-colonialism, new historicism, cultural materialism. My concern is not to deny or falsify claims based on structural social problems but to suggest that the plays offer something besides those problems as well and therefore cannot be reduced to them.

18   On the play's authorship, see Suzanne Gossett, ed., *Pericles*, The Arden Shakespeare (London: Thomson Learning, 2004), 62–70.

19   This is a brief summary of how T. G. Bishop explicates the incest riddle in *Shakespeare and the Theatre of Wonder* (Cambridge: Cambridge University Press, 1996), 86–101.

20   Jonathan Bate helpfully compares Marina to the classical myth of regeneration embodied in Proserpina, in *Shakespeare and Ovid* (Oxford: Clarendon, 1993), 221–22.

21   The point about the fall has been made by Felperin, *Shakespearean Romance*, 148, and by John Pitcher (who does not refer to Felperin), "The Poet and Taboo: The Riddle of Shakespeare's Pericles," *Essays and Studies* (1982): 15.

22   John Pitcher attributes each of these bouts of melancholy to the incest motif introduced with Antiochus, and I think he is right, though I believe

they are more closely tied to the challenge of self-awareness than Pitcher recognizes. To make his case, Pitcher sees Lysimachus as a symbolic surrogate for Pericles in the brothel at Mytilene ("The Poet and Taboo," 21–25).

23 Destructive male sexuality is both literal and symbolic in the other romances as well, and the motif recurs in a different form even in *Henry VIII*, where the King's dalliance with Ann Bullen results in the sympathetic suffering of Queen Katherine.

24 Expressing a grief similar to Pericles', Lucretius exclaims, after his daughter's death, "If children predecease progenitors, / We are their offspring, and they none of ours" (*The Rape of Lucrece*, 1756–57).

25 I am borrowing Martha Nussbaum's phrase here, though she uses it to describe Greek tragedy, *The Fragility of Goodness: Luck and Ethics in Greek Tragedy and Philosophy* (1986; rev. ed., Cambridge: Cambridge University Press, 2001). I would argue that for Shakespeare goodness is equally fragile in comedy and tragedy, and for much the same reasons in both cases.

26 This point has been made particularly well by Felperin, *Shakespearean Romance*, 162–68.

27 Joel B. Altman, *The Tudor Play of Mind* (Berkeley: University of California Press, 1978), 196–228.

28 Jonathan Bate incisively points out that the movement from academic commitment to erotic love in *Love's Labor's Lost* reverses the movement of Lyly's *Euphues* (*Shakespeare and Ovid*, 33), though I would argue that the young men's turn is fruitless in Shakespeare's play because they learn so little about themselves.

29 Oscar Campbell, *Comicall Satyre and Shakespeare's "Troilus and Cressida"* (San Marino, Calif.: Huntington Library, 1938). More recently, see David M. Bevington, "Shakespeare vs. Jonson on Satire," in *Shakespeare 1971: Proceedings of the World Shakespeare Congress*, ed. Clifford Leech and J. M. R. Margeson (Toronto: University of Toronto Press, 1971), 107–22, and Bevington's comments on the play's historical context in his edition of *Troilus and Cressida*, The Arden Shakespeare (London: Thomas Nelson, 1998), 6–11. William M. Hamlin analyzes the play persuasively in relation to skepticism in *Scepticism and Tragedy in Shakespeare's England* (Basingstoke: Palgrave Macmillan, 2005), 167–83.

30 G. Wilson Knight, "*Measure for Measure* and the Gospels," in *The Wheel of Fire* (London: Methuen, 1949 [1930]), 73–96; Roy Battenhouse, "*Measure for Measure* and the Christian Doctrine of the Atonement," *PMLA* 66 (1946): 1029–59; Nevill Coghill, "Comic Form in *Measure for Measure*," *Shakespeare Survey* 8 (1955): 14–27. See also R. W. Chambers, *Man's Unconquerable Mind* (London: Jonathan Cape, 1939), 277–310.

31 "Problem play" is a phrase originally applied to the drama of Ibsen, and it was first attached to some of Shakespeare's plays by F. S. Boas, who proposed to "borrow a convenient phrase from the theatre of to-day" to describe them (Frederick S. Boas, *Shakspere and His Precedessors* [London: John Murray, 1896], 345). The term stuck, despite its anachronistic origin, and has generated a long bibliography of commentary on Shakespeare's "problem plays."

32 My argument regarding the Duke's fallibility may seem at odds with two recent historical treatments of the Duke as a tribute to the advent of James VI and I: Debora Shuger, *Political Theologies in Shakespeare's England: The Sacred and the State in Measure for Measure* (Basingstoke: Palgrave, 2001), and Peter Lake with Michael Questier, *The Antichrist's Lewd Hat: Protestants, Papists and Players in Post-Reformation England* (New Haven: Yale University Press, 2002), 621–700. I think Shuger's understanding of penitential governance, with its illuminating comparison to South Africa's Truth and Reconciliation Commission, is fully compatible with my suggestion that Shakespearean comedy is informed by Christian principle. Indeed, seeing *Measure for Measure* as a *comedy* is all the more important in light of what its Duke stands for. As for Jacobean flattery in *Measure for Measure*, Lake and Questier argue that it is comically qualified (*The Antichrist's Lewd Hat*, 682–89).

33 I share a demonstrated critical interest in unspoken motivation in *Measure for Measure*, as my emphasis on suspicion makes clear, but my focus is on suspicion in a Renaissance context rather than its nineteenth-century successor. (For an explanation of this difference, see chap. 1 above.) For various readings of the play's hidden motives in psychoanalytic terms, see Richard Wheeler, *Shakespeare's Development and the Problem Comedies: Turn and Counter-Turn* (Berkeley: University of California Press, 1981), 106–20; Carolyn E. Brown, "The Wooing of Duke Vincentio and Isabella of *Measure for Measure*: 'The Image of It Gives [Them] Content,'" *Shakespeare Survey* 22 (1994): 189–219; Alberto Cacicedo, " 'She is fast my wife': Sex, Marriage, and Ducal Authority in *Measure for Measure*," *Shakespeare Studies* 23 (1995): 187–209.

34 The Duke's appointment of Angelo under these circumstances is not, in itself, a Machiavellian political move. To be sure, Norman Holland pointed many years ago to a precedent in Machiavelli for this practice ("*Measure for Measure*: The Duke and the Prince," *Comparative Literature* 11 [1959]: 16–20), but Erasmus offers the same advice in the *Enchiridion*, based on Aristotle's *Politics*, as Felix Raab pointed out, so the practice is not necessarily an indication of political amorality or Machiavellian cunning in *Measure for Measure*. See Raab, *The English Face of Machiavelli* (London: Routledge & Kegan Paul, 1964), 11.

35   Harry Berger takes the Duke's rhetoric literally in these lines and turns it against him, arguing that he deliberately allowed "the mess in Vienna" to develop in order to congratulate himself for cleaning it up, and he is therefore complicit in it and a "moral idiot" (*Making Trifles of Terrors: Redistributing Complicities in Shakespeare* [Stanford: Stanford University Press, 1997], 337). Berger's analysis depends, first of all, on agreeing with the Duke that Vienna is a "mess" (on this point, see n. 38 below), and second, on construing the Duke's semi-confessional expressions of self-blame (he is talking to a friar, after all) as if they were descriptions of a political strategy. Despite the Duke's opening reference to the properties of government (1.1.3), this play is not about politics in the same way the history plays are; it is about the individual's responsibility to God and neighbor at several levels of society. Cf. Debora Shuger's comment that *Measure for Measure* "reflects on the post-Reformation crossover of the sacred from ecclesial to temporal polity, but it is not a history play" (*Political Theologies*, 131).

36   The Duke's inclination to mercy links him to two earlier comic dukes who also set aside harsh laws that they had earlier upheld in order to effect a resolution of difficulties in the end: Solinus in *The Comedy of Errors* (5.1.391) and Theseus in *A Midsummer Night's Dream* (4.1.178). In Solinus' case, the Duke's action also implies forgiveness.

37   Alexander Leggatt sees the secular Duke's disguise as a friar as scandalous for a play set in Catholic Vienna ("Substitution in *Measure for Measure*," *Shakespeare Quarterly* 39 [1988]: 342–59). As R. M. Frye pointed out many years ago, however, the Duke's spiritual assistance of his subjects (even confessing them) would not have troubled Protestants, who affirmed the priesthood of every believer (*Shakespeare and Christian Doctrine* [Princeton: Princeton University Press, 1963], 291). Frye complements Leggat's observation by speculating that the Duke's mendicant disguise may be the reason why a Jesuit censor cut *Measure for Measure* out of a copy of the 1632 Folio that was in the library of the English College in Valladolid. Hilaire Kallendorf has recently pointed out that at least one seventeenth-century Spanish Franciscan was not censored for advocating lay administration of exorcism, and that lay application of other spiritual healing remedies was tolerated in southern Europe during the seventeenth century (*Exorcism and Its Texts* [Toronto: University of Toronto Press, 2003], 176–80), so the degree to which the Duke might have offended Catholics is not clear.

38   "The Viennese mess" is Graham Bradshaw's phrase, *Shakespeare's Scepticism* (Brighton: Harvester, 1987), 166, and it seems to have influenced Harry Berger's references to "the mess in Vienna" (*Making Trifles*, 346, 349). Why these critics are so distressed by the situation as to call it a "mess" is puzzling, since the only crimes Angelo prosecutes in the Duke's absence are

fornication and prostitution. Though the latter involves dark recesses of abuse (associated with Lucio), "social status quo" would still be more accurate (and less moralistic) than "mess," and no ruler, no matter how strict, can prevent every illegal action of every citizen. Bradshaw's attempt to justify "mess" by including murder in the list of crimes the Duke has supposedly winked at is not convincing (169–71). The Provost says Barnardine, "a murderer" (4.2.62), had been accused but not executed, because the Duke thought the case "came not to an undoubtful proof," though Angelo has decided otherwise, and Barnardine has confessed (4.2.133–40). The Provost accepts Angelo's reversal of the Duke's judgment, as he is bound to do, but we are not, since we know how Angelo judges, and Barnardine's confession means nothing. Barnardine says he has been drinking all night in prison (4.3.53–54), and the only consequence is his complete befuddlement, as the Duke recognizes (4.3.67–69)—neither a frame of mind to confess credibly nor murderous rage, as Bradshaw claims (171). In a less ambiguous example of a murderer pleading for mercy with harsh judges, the point of view still favors the perpetrator, not those who judge him. See *Timon of Athens* 3.5, which begins with the First Senator announcing self-importantly (as if he were Angelo) that "Nothing emboldens sin so much as mercy" (3.5.4).

39 Bradshaw argues that the law Claudio violates is not fornication (a victimless crime) but producing a child out of wedlock, thereby creating at least one potential victim (*Shakespeare's Scepticism*, 210–16). The argument is ingenious, but it is based on Mistress Overdone's locution that Claudio is to be executed "for getting Madam Julietta with child" (1.2.70–71), and it appeals to utilitarian standards of social justice rather than to the conception of virtue and vice that dominates *Measure for Measure*. Bradshaw places too much weight on Angelo's two-line argument that he cannot abrogate the law without harming others who might suffer because it was not enforced: "For then I pity those I do not know, / Which a dismissed offense would after gall" (2.2.105–7; Bradshaw, 168). Angelo is not advocating victims' rights; he is advocating deterrence of other violators of the law (who would be "galled" if they broke it), as he has just made clear: "Those many had not dared to do that evil / If the first that did th'edict infringe / Had answered for his deed" (96–98). Moreover, the deadly vindictiveness of his thinking is clear in the next two lines, which Bradshaw does not quote: "And do him right that, answering one foul wrong, / Lives not to act another" (2.2.108–9). Bradshaw's otherwise illuminating comparison of Angelo with Captain Vere in *Billy Budd* (197–99) is thus based on a misreading of Angelo's lines.

40 The Duke's advice to Claudio is sometimes identified as Christian, but its consistent stoicism has been compared to Montaigne's essay, "That to philosophize is to learn to die," which Alice Harmon has shown to be based on a set of stoic commonplaces that Montaigne and Shakespeare would both have known ("How Great Was Shakespeare's Debt to Montaigne?" *PMLA* 57 [1942]: 999–1001). The Duke offers Claudio no hope of any kind, and the argument and imagery of one sentence echo those in Despair's suicidal seduction of the Redcrosse knight in *The Faerie Queene* I.ix.40 and 44: "Thy best of rest is sleep, / And that thou oft provok'st, yet grossly fear'st / Thy death, which is no more" (3.1.17–19). Tellingly, Claudio moves from "I have hope to live" before the Duke's speech (1.3.4) to "To sue to live, I find I seek to die" after it (3.1.42). This death wish anticipates Angelo's in 5.1.477–78. Claudio's echo of the Friar in *Much Ado about Nothing* ("Come lady, die to live" [4.1.253]) is instructive, since the Friar means for Hero to "die" symbolically, whereas the Duke's advice is for Claudio to accept literal death for its own sake. Gordon Braden points out that "the dominant coloration of at least Roman Stoicism is an all but overwhelming longing to be done with it all. . . . *a libido moriendi*." Gordon Braden, *Renaissance Tragedy and the Senecan Tradition: Anger's Privilege* (New Haven: Yale University Press, 1985), 24.

41 Berger helpfully contrasts "the play's dominant Platonico-Puritan ideology of *misosoma*" with another standard "that locates 'corruption' in the failure of community or charity" (*Making Trifles*, 419), and he identifies the Duke with the former and in opposition to the latter. I would argue that the Duke is caught between them, in his own thinking, but that to his credit he inclines more to the second than the first, and that part of the play's interest is in seeing him move definitively from one to the other. For another way of understanding the Duke's opposition to "the Platonic-Puritan system of compulsory virtue and condign punishment," see Shuger, *Political Theologies*, 102–40 (quotation on 133).

42 Knight, *Wheel of Fire*, 89. Cf. Coghill, "Comic Form": "The play bursts into a sudden Paradiso not untouched by hilarity, and I do not see why all the bells in Vienna should not ring, organs peal, *Te Deum* soar, trumpets blow and all the populace dance round the united couples in a general and harmonious happiness" (25). A closer analogue to the Last Judgment in *Measure for Measure* would seem to be Gerard ter Borch's small painting of the Last Judgment, hanging above the grave councilors of Deventer, whose collective portrait they commissioned him to paint in 1667. The portrait is thoroughly this-worldly, but the painting-within-the-painting speaks to issues of judgment, self-knowledge, and relative authority that either the

painter or his subjects (or both) thought somehow relevant to the councilors' secular task.

43 The Duke had earlier boasted of an "ancient skill" in reading "brows," when he accurately saw "honesty and constancy" in the Provost's face (4.2.154–56), so his interpretation of Angelo's face at the end cannot be simply dismissed, but it is not definitive either, since the initiative remains with Angelo, and the play does not show us what he does with it.

44 Lucio's description of Angelo corresponds closely to the Duke's observation, made earlier to Friar Thomas, that

> Lord Angelo is precise
> Stands at a guard with envy, scarce confesses
> That his blood flows or that his appetite
> Is more to bread than stone. (1.3.50–53)

45 The Geneva gloss to this saying in Matthew is pertinent to Angelo: "He commandeth, not to be curious or malicious to try out, and condemn our neighbour's faults: for hypocrites hide their own faults, and seek not to amend them, but are curious to reprove other men's."

46 The compelling circumstances are largely arranged by the resourceful Duke, but in at least one instance the Duke acknowledges "an accident that heaven provides" (4.3.77), which prevents him just in time from violating his own principle that it would be "damnable" to execute an unrepentant prisoner (4.3.64–76). "Heaven" in this case, of course, is the playwright, who thus contrives in yet another way to emphasize the Duke's fallibility and dissimilarity with God.

47 Bradshaw, *Shakespeare's Scepticism*, 189.

48 Harry Berger's trenchant comment is pertinent here: "Part of the fun of Being Bad, as Lucio plays the game, is that one shows oneself to be a wicked villain by pretending to be sanctimonious and accusing another of being the wicked villain one knows oneself to be" (*Making Trifles*, 354). Berger misses the class bias in Lucio's language, however, which suggests that while Lucio may know himself to be Bad, he does not know himself to be Proud. He simply thinks he deserves his status. Pride was one of the oldest and best-conceived personifications in English morality drama.

49 Matthew 19:19; also in Matthew 22:39 and in each of the other synoptic gospels (Mark 12:31 and Luke 10:27). While Augustine often cites this saying as a summary of the "new law," it originates in Leviticus 19:18 and 34 (where the "neighbor" is "the stranger that dwelleth with you"). Shakespeare has Juliet allude to this saying when she answers the Duke's question about her love for Claudio: "Love you the man that wronged you? / Yes, as I love the woman that wronged him" (2.3.25–26). Though the Duke's response to Juliet is misogynistic and moralistic (2.3.29–35), her

avowal of charity in a relationship that is also clearly sexual anticipates the Duke's love for Isabella in the end.

50 Bradshaw's argument that Isabella follows Christian duty in rejecting Claudio misses the point about loving one's neighbor (*Shakespeare's Scepticism*, 203). Bradshaw is certainly right that Christian ethics does not recognize acts of autonomous goodness (202), but that is because good deeds must always be referred to the love of God and neighbor (and they are therefore necessarily heteronymous, in Kant's terms), not because "concern with one's own fate in the next world *must* take precedence over concern with one's own, or anybody else's fate in this world" (203). That is indeed how Isabella responds to Claudio, but she later shows it is a mistake by choosing differently in another difficult situation, as explained below.

51 Some directors of the play have Angelo grab and grope Isabella when he declares he loves her, thus unambiguously motivating her rejection and clarifying his coercive intention from the start, but they thereby close off subtler possibilities that more restrained direction (like Desmond Davis's in 1979 for the BBC) leaves open.

52 Would he have coerced her no matter what answer she gave to "I love you"? That question is impossible to answer, and my point is not to blame Isabella for what Angelo does to her but simply to emphasize the complicated interaction between two people who know themselves so little as these two do.

53 Berger, *Making Trifles*, 363. My understanding of the Duke's proceeding is also at the heart of Debora Shuger's argument for penitential governance in *Political Theologies*.

54 A parallel in this regard between the Duke with Isabella and Rosalind with Orlando in *As You Like It* is distant but nonetheless illuminating.

55 Though I believe Roy Battenhouse is mistaken in reading *Measure for Measure* allegorically, he incisively points to a parallel between the play and one major explanation of the Christian doctrine of atonement, i.e., that God defeated the devil by deceiving him in human form, because the devil had deceived Eve in the form of a serpent ("*Measure for Measure* and the Christian Doctrine of the Atonement," 1041–43). For the use of this idea in medieval religious drama, see John D. Cox, *Shakespeare and the Dramaturgy of Power* (Princeton: Princeton University Press, 1989), 129–31.

56 Since the Duke remains self-important and moralistic to the end, it is easy to reject him as manipulative and voyeuristic in his treatment of Isabella, as Berger does (that is one reason Berger calls him a "moral idiot"), but if we see Isabella changing the Duke over the course of the play, as I have argued, then his motives for assisting Isabella in the way he does are not necessarily exploitative (though they are clearly sexual, as indicated in his proposal of

marriage) but arguably charitable—a loving hope for the best in her, without any guarantee that she will choose it when she faces another crisis.

57 Bradshaw, *Shakespeare's Scepticism*, 188 (Claudio), 193–94 (Juliet).

58 Philip C. McGuire, *Speechless Dialect: Shakespeare's Open Silences* (Berkeley: University of California Press, 1985), 63–96 (quotation on 79).

59 Barton directed the play for the RSC in Stratford-upon-Avon, with Estelle Kohler playing Isabella. Graham Nicholls, *Measure for Measure: Text and Performance* (Basingstoke: Macmillan, 1986), 49, 55–56.

Chapter Three

1 Two other plays from the 1590s are sometimes discussed as tragedies as well: *Richard III* (1592–1594) and *Julius Caesar* (1599). The first is clearly continuous with the *Henry VI* plays, however, as the culmination of a sequence on English history with some obvious Senecan influence, and the genre of the second has been much debated. The editors of the First Folio of 1623 placed it among the tragedies but referred to it variously as the "life and death" (in the table of contents) and the "tragedy" (in the text itself) of Julius Caesar. I would argue that it should more accurately be thought of as a Roman history play rather than a tragedy (see chap. 6 below).

2 Shakespeare also perfected the history play during the 1590s, and my generalization about comedy is not meant to imply that his political ideas played no part in his writing tragedy. For reasons explained below, however, I believe comedy bears the strongest relationship to tragedy in his thinking. I have learned a lot from Susan Snyder's way of making the same point, but we make it differently, *The Comic Matrix of Shakespeare's Tragedies* (Princeton: Princeton University Press, 1979).

3 Northrop Frye generalizes these phases as mythic archetypes, referring them to spring and winter, respectively. See *Anatomy of Criticism* (Princeton: Princeton University Press, 1957), 35–52, and for Shakespeare in particular, *A Natural Perspective: The Development of Shakespearean Comedy and Romance* (New York: Columbia University Press, 1965) and *Fools of Time: Studies in Shakespearean Tragedy* (Toronto: University of Toronto Press, 1967). Frye is most helpful in seeing broad patterns and how Shakespeare's plays fit into them; he is less helpful in understanding Shakespeare in a particular time and place, how he wrote in light of it, and how his writing changed over the course of his career.

4 Here I see comedy differently from Susan Snyder, who argues that "comedy is less at home with 'real experience' . . . than is tragedy," because

comedy focuses on "evitability" rather than its opposite (*Comic Matrix*, 41). Death is certainly more inevitable than anything else in human life, but hope, forgiveness, and reconciliation are no less real in human experience than death, though they are indeed more evitable.

5   As noted in the previous chapter, "the fragility of goodness" is Martha Nussbaum's phrase, used by her to title a book about Greek tragedy, *The Fragility of Goodness: Luck and Ethics in Greek Tragedy and Philosophy* (1986; rev ed., Cambridge: Cambridge University Press, 2001). I am using the phrase not to suggest a link between Greek and Shakespearean tragedy, but to evoke the vision of human destiny that is enacted in both Shakespearean comedy and tragedy.

6   The critical literature on Shakespeare's debt to Seneca is vast, beginning with J. W. Cunliffe, *The Influence of Seneca on Elizabethan Tragedy* (London: Macmillan, 1893), and the extent of Seneca's direct influence has been questioned, even in *Titus Andronicus* (see particularly Howard Baker, *Induction to Tragedy* [University: Louisiana State University Press, 1939], 106–53). For a thorough review of the issues and a strong case for Shakespeare's knowing Seneca, see Robert S. Miola, *Shakespeare and Classical Tragedy: The Influence of Seneca* (Oxford: Clarendon, 1992), 1–32, and for the philosophical influence of Seneca in the later Roman plays, see Geoffrey Miles, *Shakespeare and the Constant Romans* (Oxford: Clarendon, 1996), passim but especially 38–62.

7   Aemilius actually mentions Coriolanus as a precedent for Lucius' march on Rome with the Goths to avenge his father: "Who threats in course of his revenge to do / As much as ever Coriolanus did" (*Titus* 4.4.67–68). For a summary of parallels between the two plays, see Robert S. Miola, *Shakespeare's Rome* (Cambridge: Cambridge University Press, 1983), 204. I take up the similarities again in chapter 6.

8   Eugene M. Waith, *The Pattern of Tragicomedy in Beaumont and Fletcher* (New Haven: Yale University Press, 1952), 86–98.

9   My argument contrasts here with Alan Sommers' argument for a dichotomy of Roman virtue and barbaric evil in the play, " 'Wilderness of Tigers': Structure and Symbolism in *Titus Andronicus*," *Essays in Criticism* 10 (1960): 175–89. While Roman and barbarian are indeed contrasted, the contrast is not between good and evil but between self-suppression and self-indulgence. Lucius, who supposedly restores Roman order at the end, not only allies with the barbarians to defeat Saturninus but also demands the sacrifice of Alarbus at the outset—the originating injustice, in Sommers's view. Lucius proposes this sacrifice in the first place and offers the rationale for it (1.1.96–101), in effect reminding his father piously of the standard they hold in common, and on that reminder Titus acts. In this

speech, Lucius also provides a precedent (1.1.98) for his father's later use of Latin (4.1.82–83)—a heightening of rhetoric on Shakespeare's part in homage to Roman authority.

10 Titus's destruction of Alarbus and Mutius is often held against him, especially in view of Tamora's moving appeal on behalf of her son (1.1.104–20), but Tamora is manifestly duplicitous, in contrast to Titus's single-minded constancy. Moreover, while the immediate model for Titus's sensational filicide was almost certainly Tamburlaine, the *Aeneid* offered powerful literary precedent both for the religious sacrifice of prisoners, which Aeneas himself performs (*Aeneid* 10.517–20 and 11.81–82), and for honorable filicide (*Aeneid* 6.819–23, where Anchises praises Lucius Junius Brutus for ordering the death of his own sons after they plotted the restoration of the Tarquins). Titus's epithet, "Pius," is also Aeneas's (1.1.23; cf. 1.1.64–65). Montaigne quotes the lines just cited from *Aeneid* 10, in making the point that "no nation is innocent of" human sacrifice (*The Complete Essays of Montaigne*, trans. Donald M. Frame [Stanford: Stanford University Press, 1965], "Apology for Raymond Sebond," 387).

11 "Ruler of the mighty universe, are you so slow to hear and see crimes?" (David Bevington's translation). The quotation is slightly altered from Seneca's *Phaedra*. See Miola, *Shakespeare and Classical Tragedy*, 14–15, and Jonathan Bate, ed., *Titus Andronicus*, The Arden Shakespeare (London: Routledge, 1995), 30.

12 On oxymoron in *Romeo and Juliet*, see Harry Levin, "Form and Formality in *Romeo and Juliet*," *Shakespeare Quarterly* 11 (1960): 3–11; and Robert O. Evans, *The Osier Cage: Rhetorical Devices in* Romeo and Juliet (Lexington: University of Kentucky Press, 1966), 18–41; in *A Midsummer Night's Dream*, David Young, *Something of Great Constancy: The Art of "A Midsummer Night's Dream"* (New Haven: Yale University Press, 1966), 64–86, 151–55. Amy J. Riess and George Walton Williams argue that the tragedy was written before the comedy, "'Tragical Mirth': from Romeo to Dream," *Shakespeare Quarterly* 43 (1992): 214–28.

13 Shakespeare revisited this cliché in Silvius's hopeless devotion to Phebe in *As You Like It*, as noted above in chapter 2.

14 Levin, "Form and Formality," 3. Jonathan Bate compares Juliet's lines in 2.2 to their inspiration in Ovid's *Ars Amatoria*, noting the difference between Roman cynicism and "a 'true-love' language that is not dependent on the formalization of an oath" (*Shakespeare and Ovid* [Oxford: Clarendon, 1993], 179).

15 Lysander says this as the conclusion to lines (1.1.144–49) that have a close parallel in *Romeo and Juliet* (2.2.118–20).

16 Snyder, *Comic Matrix*, 59.

17 Turning aside from suffering parallels what Stanley Cavell calls "the avoidance of love" in *King Lear*, though the principle seems to me to apply more broadly: not to recognize, not to acknowledge, the suffering of this character (or of these characters)—including trying to explain it away, to justify it, or to find cosmic meaning in it—is to try to avoid it. See "The Avoidance of Love: A Reading of *King Lear*," in *Disowning Knowledge in Six Plays of Shakespeare* (Cambridge: Cambridge University Press, 1987), 39–123.

18 Roland M. Frye, *Shakespeare and Christian Doctrine* (Princeton: Princeton University Press, 1963), 24–31. A point like this is presumably the basis for Frye's assertion that Shakespeare is a secular playwright. If "secular" means denying complete apocalyptic understanding, then Frye is right, but that denial is also arguably Christian.

19 Judging from what Shakespeare and his contemporaries say about "the function of tragedy," Ekbert Faas cites Shakespeare's ignorance (or ignoring) of Aristotle's formulation and concludes that "The main function of tragedy . . . is to overwhelm with amazement" (*Shakespeare's Poetics* [Cambridge: Cambridge University Press, 1986], 44–47). This conclusion is consistent not only with *Titus Andronicus* but also with what I am suggesting about the impact of suffering in other Shakespearean tragedies.

20 "Empathy" is an early twentieth-century neologism, introduced to translate the German *Einfühlung* in early psychology (*OED*)—a word that was ultimately a product of eighteenth-century sentiment. Deriving an English word from Greek in this case parallels James Strachey's derivation of English neologisms from Greek in translating Freud—"psyche," for example, where Freud used *die Seele*.

21 William Tyndale, *The Parable of the Wicked Mammon* (1527), ed. Thomas Russell, *The Works of the English Reformers*, 3 vols. (London: Ebenezer Palmer, 1831), 1:113. I am grateful to Debora Shuger for this reference.

22 The Elizabethan translation of Paul's image in 1 Corinthians 13:12, "now we see through a glass darkly," translates *ainigmati* or "obscurely, in a riddle" as an affirmation of limited knowledge that requires faith for its fulfillment. I am grateful to Curtis Gruenler for this point.

23 For a recent and judicious reassessment of *Hamlet*'s Senecanism, see Miola, *Shakespeare and Classical Tragedy*, 33–67.

24 Old Adam also alludes to this saying of Jesus in *As You Like It* (2.3.43–45), when he gives his life's savings to Orlando—a charitable gesture that grows directly out of Adam's express confidence in God's care.

25 Maynard Mack, "The Jacobean Shakespeare: Some Observations on the Construction of the Tragedies," in *Jacobean Theatre*, ed. John Russell Brown and Bernard Harris (London: Edward Arnold, 1960), 11–41 (quotation from 35).

26 Howard Felperin, *Shakespearean Romance* (Princeton: Princeton University Press, 1972), 102. Felperin's discussion of "Baconian tragedy" is anticipated by Philip Edwards' distinction between Sidney and Bacon on poetry and illusion, *Shakespeare and the Confines of Art* (London: Methuen, 1968), 1–2.

27 Alvin B. Kernan, " 'Othello': An Introduction," in *Modern Shakespearean Criticism*, ed. Alvin B. Kernan (New York: Harcourt, Brace, & World, 1970), 351–60; Bernard McElroy, *Shakespeare's Mature Tragedies* (Princeton: Princeton University Press, 1973), 91–93.

28 John Velz, "From Jerusalem to Damascus: Bilocal Dramaturgy in Medieval and Shakespearian Conversion Plays," *Comparative Drama* 15 (1981): 311–25 (quotation on 321).

29 On Iago and the Vice, see Bernard Spivack, *Shakespeare and the Allegory of Evil* (New York: Columbia University Press, 1958), 3–59. For a more specialized view that includes an illuminating comparison of Iago with Cloaked Collusion in Skelton's *Magnificence*, see Ann Wierum, " 'Actors' and 'Play Acting' in the Morality Tradition," *Renaissance Drama*, n.s. 3 (1970): 189–214.

30 This is McElroy's view of what Desdemona does for Othello (*Shakespeare's Mature Tragedies*, 125–26).

31 Matthew 6:12; see also Luke 11:4. The prayer was most familiar to Elizabethans from its use in both morning and evening worship. See *The Book of Common Prayer 1559*, ed. John E. Booty (Charlottesville: University Press of Virginia for the Folger Shakespeare Library, 1976), 51, 59 (morning prayer), 61 (evening prayer).

32 Stanley Cavell distinguishes knowledge and acknowledgment, arguing that while knowledge (i.e., absolute certainty, obtained by stated philosophical criteria) is impossible, acknowledgment (i.e., recognizing another human being as a person like oneself) is possible and may even be imperative. See "Knowing and Acknowledging" in *Must We Mean What We Say?* (Cambridge: Cambridge University Press, 1969), 238–66, immediately preceding Cavell's famous essay on *King Lear*. This argument is enabled by a point Cavell considers at length from Wittgenstein, that is, the possibility that the recognition of pain is the basis for certainty about other minds (242–61). Reflection on this point seems to be the basis of Cavell's incisive Shakespearean criticism, which reads the tragedies as allegories of skepticism and of painfully acquired acknowledgment. Cavell's insight about acknowledgment is important, but I would argue that the acknowledgment the tragedies compel on our part for particular characters in their suffering (even if they are "only" imagined characters) is based not on skepticism but on assumed faith, the sister of charity, as the structure of

the plays repeatedly emphasizes. Cavell does not take up the question of whether or how acknowledgment as he conceives of it might relate either to loving one's neighbor as oneself or to Kant's categorical imperative, which Cavell's idea of acknowledgment most closely resembles.

33 Paul Jorgensen, *Our Naked Frailties: Sensational Art and Meaning in* Macbeth (Berkeley: University of California Press, 1971), 56 (acknowledging others who had earlier noted the coincidence of Dante's Caïna and Macbeth's relationship to Duncan).

34 Naseeb Shaheen notes a contrast between Macbeth's rhetorical question to the hired murderers and the blessing that an anonymous Old Man invokes on Ross: "God's benison go with you, and with those / That would make good of bad, and friends of foes!" (2.4.40–41) (*Biblical References in Shakespeare's Plays* [Newark: University of Delaware Press, 1999], 633).

35 This is how Paul interprets patience, in his letter to the Romans: "Neither do we so [rejoice under the hope of the glory of God] only, but also we rejoice in tribulations, knowing that tribulation bringeth forth patience, And patience experience, and experience hope, And hope maketh not ashamed, because the love of God is shed abroad in our hearts by the Holy Ghost, which is given unto us" (Rom 5:3-5). This is not the stoic patience of heroic endurance but the patience that Herbert's speaker learns in "Love (III)" and that Milton acknowledges in Sonnet 19, "When I Consider How My Light Is Spent."

36 A. C. Bradley identified Macbeth's ironic echoes of himself with the theme of equivocation that runs throughout the play, seeing it as a "Sophoclean irony" that is beyond the speakers (*Shakespearean Tragedy* [London: Macmillan, 1904], 339). I would argue, on the contrary, that Macbeth is both aware and unaware of his duplicitous language, because it expresses his self-deception. The appropriate reference is not, therefore, Sophocles, but something much closer to home for Shakespeare—the moral vision of Vice comedy, where "th' equivocation of the fiend" would have been most familiar to him. See Spivack, *Shakespeare and the Allegory of Evil*, 161–75, and John D. Cox, *The Devil and the Sacred in English Drama, 1350–1642* (Cambridge: Cambridge University Press, 2000), 72–76.

37 Aside from a tendency to allegorize the plays, this kind of judgmentalism is the principal difficulty with Roy W. Battenhouse's *Shakespearean Tragedy: Its Art and Its Christian Premises* (Bloomington: Indiana University Press, 1969).

38 This is Macbeth's way of avoiding love—the action that Stanley Cavell argues is central to *King Lear*, as we shall see. Theologically the suffering of Macbeth is identical to the suffering of Milton's Satan, but the difference is that Shakespeare imagines Macbeth in his living humanity, "here, upon this bank and shoal of time," rather than eschatologically, as Milton

imagines Satan (and Dante imagines the shades of hell). Malcolm's part-
ing reference to "this dead butcher and his fiendlike queen" (5.8.70) helps
to clarify the point by contrast. His phrase belongs to the rhetoric of political order, for which Malcolm is now responsible, but it is not an adequate
moral summary of what we have just witnessed; if anything, it serves to
heighten the tragedy by comparison.

39 Felperin, *Shakespearean Romance*, 110.

40 Bradley famously comments that Lear should be titled, "The Redemption
of King Lear" (*Shakespearean Tragedy*, 285). Felperin mentions Maynard
Mack, *King Lear in Our Time* (Berkeley: University of California Press, 1965),
83–117, and Paul A. Jorgensen, *Lear's Self-Discovery* (Berkeley: University of
California Press, 1967). For a summary of this view, complete with references, see R. A. Foakes, *Hamlet Versus Lear: Cultural Politics and Shakespeare's Art*
(Cambridge: Cambridge University Press, 1993), 45–54.

41 Jan Kott, *Shakespeare Our Contemporary*, trans. Boleslaw Taborski (New York:
Doubleday, 1964), and William R. Elton, *King Lear and the Gods* (San Marino:
Huntington Library Press, 1966). Foakes summarizes this view as well
(*Hamlet Versus Lear*, 54–68), particularly noting Barbara Everett's important
article, "The New King Lear," *Critical Quarterly* 2 (1960): 325–39.

42 Writing as a Christian moralist himself, Johnson frankly acknowledges that
"A play in which the wicked prosper and the virtuous miscarry may doubt-
less be good, because it is a just representation of the common events of
human life" (quoted Felperin, *Shakespearean Romance*, 111).

43 Robert G. Hunter, *Shakespeare and the Comedy of Forgiveness* (New York:
Columbia University Press, 1965), does not include *King Lear* as a derivative
of this form, but he easily could have. Again I am indebted to Susan Snyder
in my argument for the complementarity of tragedy and comedy in *King
Lear* in particular (*Comic Matrix*, 137–79). Still, we approach the issues differently: she treats the question formally, including the full range of comic
conventions and structure, addressing religion only as an afterthought
(178–79), while my primary focus in this chapter is how Shakespearean
tragedy deals with the problem of faith and suffering.

44 Cavell, *Disowning Knowledge*, 61–62. "Bribe" is Cavell's word, an idea he
continues in "exchanging," "pay," "bargain," and "return in kind" (61).

45 On Lear's self-deception, see also Harry Berger, *Marking Trifles of Terrors:
Redistributing Complicities in Shakespeare*, ed. Peter Erickson (Stanford: Stanford
University Press, 1997), 32–35. Stephen Greenblatt's comment is appropriate to this situation: "One of the highest achievements of power is to
impose fictions upon the world and one of its supreme pleasures is to
enforce the acceptance of fictions that are known to be fictions" (*Renaissance
Self-Fashioning* [Chicago: University of Chicago Press, 1980], 141).

46 *Making Trifles*, 303. Berger sees Cordelia as self-deceived as well, constru-
    ing her overt piety as a way of competing subconsciously with her sisters
    and her father, because she thereby coerces them into meting "out the
    punishments Lear deserves for having cast her away" and thus shames him
    into acknowledging his guilt so that she can triumph over him in the end.
    I return to this view again below.

47 *The Parallel King Lear 1608–1623*, prepared by Michael Warren (Berkeley
    and Los Angeles: University of California Press, 1989), 4, my emphasis.

48 The young Jesus remonstrates with his parents for retrieving him from
    theological discussions with the elders in the temple: "knew ye not that I
    must go about my father's business?" (Luke 2:49).

49 Among all the Christian allusions associated with Cordelia, this is the only
    one that appears in the 1608 Quarto and not in the 1623 Folio.

50 This is not a pagan or pantheistic prayer. For contemporary theological
    descriptions of the earth's "unpublished virtues," see Elton, *King Lear and
    the Gods*, 81.

51 This reference was noted independently by Roy Battenhouse,
    "Shakespearean Tragedy: A Christian Interpretation," in *Tragic Vision and
    the Christian Faith*, ed. Nathan O. Scott (New York: Association Press, 1957),
    56–98, and Susan Snyder, "King Lear and the Prodigal Son," *Shakespeare
    Quarterly* 17 (1966): 361–69.

52 Cavell, *Disowning Knowledge*, 88.

53 Richard Strier, "Shakespeare and the Skeptics," *Religion and Literature* 32
    (2000): 171–96. Strier refers to grace as "the central theological doctrine
    of the Reformation" (187), but it is also central in pre-Reformation moral-
    ity plays, enacted by characters such as Charity and Mercy in *The Castle of
    Perseverance* (1380–1425), Wisdom in *Wisdom* (1400–1450), Mercy in
    Mankind (1465–1470), Reason and Meekness in Medwall's *Nature* (1496),
    Charity in *Youth* (1513–1514), Pity in *Hickscorner* (1513–1516), and Good
    Hope in Skelton's *Magnificence* (1515–1526). As early as the thirteenth cen-
    tury, Aquinas cites the key text of Reformation theology, Ephesians 2:8-9,
    in rejecting the claim that faith is not "infused by God": "On the contrary,
    It is written: 'By grace you are saved through faith, and that not of your-
    selves . . . that no man may glory . . . for it is the gift of God.' " (*Summa
    Theologica* II–II, Q. 6, Art.1, trans. Dominican Fathers, 3 vols. [New York:
    Benziger Brothers, 1947–1948], 2:1201).

54 Cavell, *Disowning Knowledge*, 49. Strier points out that Q1 uses the imagery of
    sight: "by no means / Will yield *to see* his daughter" (188), my emphasis.

55 Ralph A. Houlbrooke, *The English Family 1450–1700* (London: Longman,
    1984), 145. Volumnia makes the same point, though in a very different
    frame of mind from Lear, when she kneels in supplication to Coriolanus,

"and unproperly / Show duty, as mistaken all this while / Between the child and parent" (*Coriolanus* 5.3.54–56).

56   Cavell, *Disowning Knowledge*, 71n. 9.

57   Snyder, *Comic Matrix*, 150.

58   Cavell, *Disowning Knowledge*, 54–57.

59   Berger, *Making Trifles*, 50. Peter Erickson helpfully summarizes the difference between these two remarkable Shakespeareans at the University of California, Santa Cruz (*Making Trifles*, xxxi–xxxii).

60   "Thus, while the perfomativity of self-representation ensconces Cordelia in the orthopsychic identity she desires and imagines for herself, the performativity of her speech acts continuously structures the dramatic action to ensure both her complicity with her sisters and her ability to remain unaware of it" (Berger, *Making Trifles*, 305).

61   *King Lear and the Gods*, 82.

62   George Walton Williams reexamines Elton's argument in "Petitionary Prayer in *King Lear*," *South Atlantic Quarterly* 85 (1986): 360–73, but he unaccountably omits Cordelia's prayer to the "virtues of the earth."

63   Albany's "The gods defend her" (5.3.261) is often cited as a refutation of the gods as well, because Cordelia dies so senselessly in spite of it. But neither goodness nor the gods depend on the realization of every human hope—or of any particular one.

64   It might also be added that Elton's reasoning seems to apply with equal force to *Pericles*, *Cymbeline*, and *The Winter's Tale*, which his argument would seem to make atheist tracts as well, consigning them to a dispensation of nature without grace, because they also antedate Christ. The consistency across Shakespeare's comedies of forgiveness is what defines the comedy of forgiveness in *King Lear*.

Chapter Four

1   Erasmus, *Praise of Folly*, trans. Betty Radice (Harmondsworth: Penguin, 1971), 115. Just six years after *Praise of Folly*, Erasmus published *On the Education of a Christian Prince*, which describes the ideal that *Folly* assumes: "there stands over [the king] that true King who before long will demand a reckoning of every one of his slightest transgressions, with severity proportionate to the degree of power he held" (*Praise of Folly*, 114).

2   *Utopia*, ed. Edward Surtz and J. H. Hexter (New Haven: Yale University Press, 1965), 55.

3   The Christian bias of sixteenth-century humanism is confirmed by Jonathan Dollimore's critique of it from a materialist point of view in

Radical Tragedy: Religion, Ideology, and Power in the Drama of Shakespeare and His Contemporaries (Chicago: University of Chicago Press, 1984). One does not to have to accept Dollimore's critique to see that he makes an important distinction between humanist and materialist assumptions.

4 Here too the humanists offer a useful parallel. For a comparison of More's thinking in *Utopia* with Machiavelli's, see Gerhard Ritter, *The Corrupting Influence of Power* (London: Tower Bridge, 1952).

5 For a detailed version of this argument, see John D. Cox, *The Devil and the Sacred in English Drama, 1350–1642* (Cambridge: Cambridge University Press, 2000), 140–47.

6 On the death of Duke Humphrey and the passion plays, see Emrys Jones, *The Origins of Shakespeare* (Oxford: Clarendon, 1977), 35–57. Other parallels mentioned here are detailed in John D. Cox, *Shakespeare and the Dramaturgy of Power* (Princeton: Princeton University Press, 1989), 89–97.

7 "Instrumental reasoning" in politics is a phrase Hugh Grady borrows from the Frankfurt School to describe "the splitting off of 'values' from 'facts,' the production of a technical mentality indifferent to ends, focused only on means" in *Shakespeare, Machiavelli, and Montaigne: Power and Subjectivity from Richard II to* Hamlet (Oxford: Oxford University Press, 2002), 61.

8 Cox, *The Devil and the Sacred*, 60–76.

9 E. M. W. Tillyard, *Shakespeare's History Plays* (London: Chatto & Windus, 1944).

10 This is a contrast that Tillyard ignored, and reactions to his interpretation focused principally on his claims for providential direction in the history plays. For critiques of his view of providentialism in the early history plays in particular, see four articles by A. L. French, "Joan of Arc and Henry VI," *English Studies* 29 (1969): 425–29; "Henry VI and the Ghost of Richard II," *English Studies* 29 (1969), *Anglo-American Supplement*, xxvii–xliii; "The World of Richard III," *Shakespeare Studies* 4 (1969): 25–39; and "The Mills of God and Shakespeare's Early History Plays," *English Studies* 55 (1974): 313–24. The early histories have been almost entirely omitted from materialist criticism, which has offered the strongest antiprovidentialist arguments, especially Jonathan Dollimore, *Radical Tragedy: Religion, Ideology, and Power in the Drama of Shakespeare and His Contemporaries* (Chicago: University of Chicago Press, 1984); Alan Sinfield and Jonathan Dollimore, ed., *Political Shakespeare: New Essays in Cultural Materialism* (Ithaca: Cornell University Press, 1985); and Stephen Greenblatt, *Shakespearean Negotiations* (Berkeley: University of California Press, 1988). Perhaps because of this omission in recent criticism, Grady distinguishes the two historical tetralogies in providential terms (*Shakespeare, Machiavelli, and Montaigne*, 44–45).

11 Personified vices appear as early as *The Castle of Perseverance* (1405–1425), but the character designated as "the Vice" was an English innovation of the 1530s and became a staple feature of the Tudor morality play. For comments on the relationship between them, see Cox, *The Devil and the Sacred*, 76–81.

12 Bernard Spivack, *Shakespeare and the Allegory of Evil* (New York: Columbia University Press, 1958), 36, 41, 43–44, 386–407.

13 Spivack, *Shakespeare and the Allegory of Evil*, 24 (citing Coleridge), 388 (quotation on dramatic method).

14 Early versions of the plays called *Henry VI* parts 2 and 3 in the 1623 Folio were published separately in 1594 and 1595, respectively, with *2 Henry VI* titled, *The First Part of the Contention*, whereas *Henry VI* part 1 appeared for the first time in the Folio. For this and other arguments that *1 Henry VI* is a later play (a "prequel" to the other two), see Edward Burns, ed., *King Henry VI Part 1*, The Arden Shakespeare (London: Thomson Learning, 2000), 69–73.

15 Shakespeare repeatedly comes back to Henry's minority succession in *2 Henry VI*. Duke Humphrey mentions it before York does (1.1.91–92), and Henry himself refers to it again in 4.9.3–4. This is a point of specifically political analysis with broad topical application in the 1590s, as we shall see in chapter 5.

16 Tillyard noticed the personification allegory in Salisbury's speech in *2 Henry VI* 1.1.178–202, and he used it to read the whole play as a morality play, with "the Realm, Respublica" as the main character (in the manner of Udall's *Respublica* [1553]), opposed by Buckingham and Somerset as "two allegorical characters, Pride and Ambition, the bane of the realm" (*Shakespeare's History Plays*, 178). Buckingham and Somerset seem, however, to be tools of York, as pointed out below.

17 John Skelton, *Magnificence*, ed. Paula Neuss (Manchester: Manchester University Press for the Revels Plays, 1980), lines 1630–68. Cloaked Collusion enters the play boasting in soliloquy that "Double-dealing and I be all one; / Crafting and hafting contrived is by me" (696–97).

18 Aside from *Two Gentlemen*, Shakespeare's only allusion to Proteus, the changeable god of the sea, is when Richard of Gloucester determines to "Change shapes with Proteus for advantages" (*3 Henry VI* 3.2.192).

19 Ann Wierum compares Iago in some detail to Cloaked Collusion in "'Actors' and 'Play Acting' in the Morality Tradition," *Renaissance Drama*, n.s. 3 (1970): 189–214.

20 For detailed thematic analysis of *2 Henry VI*, including the opening scene, see Edward I. Berry, *Patterns of Decay: Shakespeare's Early Histories* (Charlottesville: University Press of Virginia, 1975), 29–52.

21 Geoffrey Bullough, ed., *Narrative and Dramatic Sources of Shakespeare*, 8 vols. (New York: Columbia University Press, 1957–1975), 3:105.

22 Bullough, *Narrative and Dramatic Sources*, 3:126–28. Emrys Jones reads the episode as suggesting Humphrey's own ambition and arrogance (*Origins of Shakespeare*, 175–78), but Jones's suggestion does not negate Humphrey's political acumen in the scene as a foil to Henry's naiveté.

23 The ability to discern duplicity is important to reformers as various as Dante and Milton and arguably underlies the satire of pious credulity that appears in Erasmus' colloquy, *Exorcism*, as noted above in chapter 1.

24 Though Shakespeare does not make York's suffering Christlike, the scene includes elements from pageants on the buffeting and scourging of Christ in the biblical plays, and Holinshed says that "they kneeled down afore him (as the Jews did unto Christ) in scorn" and mocked him (Bullough, *Narrative and Dramatic Sources*, 3:210). A. L. French is particularly good on the ambiguities of providential death in the early histories, "Mills of God," 314–17.

25 *Utopia*, ed. Surtz and Hexter, 101.

26 David L. Frey overstates the case in asserting that Shakespeare presents Henry "as completely good, innocent, and free from moral blame" (*The First Tetralogy, Shakespeare's Scrutiny of the Tudor Myth: A Dramatic Exploration of Divine Providence* [The Hague: Mouton, 1976], 2). Contributing to political chaos by default is a real moral problem in the early histories, though a complex one. Frey's view was anticipated by Harold Goddard, *The Meaning of Shakespeare* (Chicago: University of Chicago Press, 1951), 30–32, and by Michael Manheim, *The Weak King Dilemma in the Shakespearean History Play* (Syracuse, N.Y.: Syracuse University Press, 1973), 76–115.

27 This summary of Shakespeare's play corresponds with a modern historian's summary of the problems facing Henry's canonization as a saint in the early sixteenth century, despite its being strongly pressed in Rome by the first two Tudor monarchs: "Decisions he took, and the courses of action he initiated and approved, on earth, had produced less good than evil." Bertram Wolffe, *Henry VI* (London: Eyre Methuen, 1981), 356. Henry's lack of political skill is comparable in some ways to Richard II's, another Shakespearean king who succeeds in his minority and fails to deal effectively with the inevitable aftermath. If nothing else, the comparison helps to make clear that Richard's downfall is political rather than the providential beginning of decades of English woe, as Tillyard claimed. See A. L. French, "Who Deposed Richard the Second?" *Essays in Criticism* 17 (1967): 411–33.

28 Neuss, ed., *Magnificence*, 31–42.

29 Anne Barton argues that the first shift in this position is late in Shakespeare's career, in *Coriolanus* (1608), where assembled commoners

speak for the first time as intelligent individuals, "Livy, Machiavelli, and Shakespeare's 'Coriolanus,'" *Shakespeare Survey* 38 (1985): 115–29.

30   Shakespeare invented Warwick's reputation as a kingmaker. It is not in the chronicles, but it appears first in *2 Henry VI* 2.2.78–79, and it reappears many times in *3 Henry VI* (1.1.45–49; 2.1.151–56, 192–97; 2.6.103–5; 3.3.47–48; etc.). For suggestions that frequent invented acknowledgments of Warwick's influence are the most important of several deliberate topical allusions to Shakespeare's native county, see Randall Martin and John D. Cox, "Who Is 'Somerville' in *3 Henry VI?*" *Shakespeare Quarterly* 51 (2000): 332–52.

31   On the making and breaking of oaths in the *Henry VI* plays, see French, "Mills of God," 318–21.

32   Henry's prophecy was reported originally by Polydore Vergil, who wrote at the height of the dead king's saintly reputation around the turn of the sixteenth century, but Hall recounts the prophecy without his usual skeptical remarks concerning alleged miracles from before the Reformation. Hall's version is quoted in full in the note to this passage in *Henry VI Part 3*, ed. John D. Cox and Eric Rasmussen, The Arden Shakespeare (London: Thomson Learning, 2001), 321. See also Bullough, *Narrative and Dramatic Sources*, 3:195. David Frey sees skepticism in the change from the Octavo's "Heavenly powers" in Henry's invocation to the Folio's "secret powers" (*The First Tetralogy*, 64).

33   Samuel Johnson thought this line expressed "a spirit of war so unsuitable to the character of Henry" that an editor should ascribe it to Warwick instead (*Johnson on Shakespeare*, ed. Arthur Sherbo and Bernard H. Bronson [1968], vols. 7 and 8 of *The Yale Edition of the Works of Samuel Johnson* [New Haven: Yale University Press, 1958–1990], 8:608), but the fact that Clarence and Warwick continue the conversation as if Henry hasn't spoken is itself a way of characterizing Henry.

34   For details about Henry's saintly reputation and a judicious assessment of them, see Wolffe, *Henry VI*, 3–21.

35   Michael Hattaway points out that Samuel Johnson objected strongly to Richard's sophistry on moral grounds: "The obligation of an oath is here eluded by very despicable sophistry. A lawful magistrate alone has the power to exact an oath, but the oath derives no part of its force from the magistrate. The plea against the obligation of an oath obliging to maintain an usurper, taken from the unlawfulness of the oath itself in the foregoing play, was rational and just" (*3 Henry VI* [Cambridge: Cambridge University Press, 1993], 1.2.22–25n). Tom McAlindon agrees with Johnson not only about this particular sophistry but also other examples of foreswearing, so that, for him, the whole first tetralogy is governed by

moral idealism, as it is for Tillyard, rather than political realism ("Swearing and Forswearing in Shakespeare's Histories: The Playwright as Contra-Machiavel," *Review of English Studies* 51 [2000]: 208–29).

36 Richard's aside before the gates of York may also count as an audience aside, insofar as it reinforces his other ambitious disclosures: "But when the fox hath once got in his nose, / He'll soon find means to make the body follow" (4.7.25–26). In the immediate context, however, this particular aside seems to be meant for Edward, because it refers primarily to his duplicity, rather than Richard's.

37 A precise parallel to Margaret's "prodigy" is Oberon's blessing of the marriage beds in *A Midsummer Night's Dream*:

> Never mole, harelip, nor scar,
> Nor mark prodigious, such as are
> Despisèd in nativity,
> Shall upon their children be. (5.1.406–9)

38 On "oppositional thinking" in demonology, see Stuart Clark, *Thinking with Demons: The Idea of Witchcraft in Early Modern Europe* (Oxford: Clarendon, 1997), 31–93.

39 Quoted Clark, *Thinking with Demons*, 14.

40 Henry VII's claim was weak on both sides: paternally it lay through his grandmother, the widow of Henry V, Katherine of Valois, whose second husband was Owen Tudor, Henry's grandfather. On his mother's side, Henry's claim to the throne was ultimately through John of Gaunt by Catherine Swynford, Gaunt's third wife and former mistress. As a usurper, Henry faced constant threats throughout his reign from a series of pretenders, from Lambert Simnel in 1487 through Perkin Warbeck in the 1490s to the Earl of Suffolk, Richard III's heir, whom Henry eventually managed to imprison only in 1506, three years before his own death. For a useful summary, see S. B. Chrimes, *Henry VII* (Berkeley: University of California Press, 1972), 68–94.

41 An account dated eleven years after Henry's murder (that is, in July, 1482, during the reign of Edward IV) holds Richard responsible for it as the highest-ranking nobleman in the Tower at the time, but the first claim that Richard did the deed himself was written in 1496—almost ten years into the reign of Henry VII and twenty-five years after Henry died (Wolffe, *Henry VI*, 347). Thomas More's preference for the later version was part of his attempt to vindicate Henry VII by blackening the reputation of Richard III.

42 Wolffe, *Henry VI*, 354.

43 Clifford Davidson has collected and annotated a list of well over 100 titles of English saints' plays, all now lost, in "Saint Plays and Pageants of Medieval Britain," *Early Drama, Art, and Music Newsletter* 22 (1999): 11–37.

44 M. R. James, ed., *Henry the Sixth: A Reprint of John Blacman's Memoir* (Cambridge: Cambridge University Press, 1919). Blacman's book, published in 1510, incidentally offers evidence of the early Tudor effort to canonize Henry VI.

45 David Scott Kastan, *Shakespeare and the Shapes of Time* (Hanover: University Press of New England, 1982), 41.

46 Kastan, *Shapes of Time*, 41.

47 Kastan, *Shapes of Time*, 26.

48 Aristotle, *Poetics*, trans. Gerald F. Else (Ann Arbor: University of Michigan Press, 1973), 30.

49 The mystery plays' omission of the present (moving, as they do, directly from the ascension of Christ to the Last Judgment) is a decorous acknowledgment that revelation is complete only in biblical history, not in secular events.

50 John Roe asserts, without explanation, that Shakespeare's audience "all knew" the history behind the history plays, "though some in more complexity than others" (*Shakespeare and Machiavelli* [Cambridge: D. S. Brewer, 2002], 35). Later, in the same vein, he asserts that "the audience knew the sources and could appreciate how and with what economy Shakespeare was using them" (39). What we know of Shakespeare's audience makes such assertions unlikely.

51 Charles Forker, "How Did Shakespeare Come By His Books?" *Shakespeare Yearbook* 14 (2004): 109–20.

52 What I mean by political open-endedness is that the beginning and end raise but do not answer specifically political questions about who has moved, or will move, to acquire or maintain power in the kingdom, and why. Questions implicitly left open in other genres, by contrast, focus on ethical and psychological issues—especially commitments to relationships, ethical choices, individual change, and personal suffering and loss.

53 M. M. Reese, *The Cease of Majesty: A Study of Shakespeare's History Plays* (New York: St. Martin's, 1962), 200.

54 John Velz, "Undular Structure in *Julius Caesar*," *Modern Language Review* 66 (1971): 21–30.

55 Ricardo J. Quinones, *The Renaissance Discovery of Time* (Cambridge, Mass.: Harvard University Press, 1972). On Shakespeare's history plays, see 290–360. Frederick Turner sees no relation between time and history, in that he omits the history plays entirely in *Shakespeare and the Nature of Time: Moral and Philosophical Themes in Some Plays and Poems by William Shakespeare* (Oxford: Clarendon, 1971).

56 Machiavelli, *Chief Works and Others*, trans. Allan Gilbert, 3 vols. (Durham, North Carolina: Duke University Press, 1965), 1:264.

57 Machiavelli may well have influenced Shakespeare's secular thinking about power in general, but his specific influence in the plays has yet to be demonstrated, as N. W. Bawcutt argues in "Did Shakespeare Read Machiavelli?" an unpublished paper presented in a seminar on Shakespeare and Machiavelli at the World Shakespeare Congress in Valencia, 2001. I am grateful for Nigel Bawcutt's comments on an earlier version of this chapter that was presented in the same seminar. Hugh Grady effectively summarizes Bawcutt's position: "Shakespeare was never 'a Machiavellian' in any straightforward sense—in fact, there is no direct evidence that he ever read a page of Machiavelli's works" (*Shakespeare, Machiavelli, and Montaigne*, 20).

58 Robert Orr discusses both time and fortune in "The Time Motif in Machiavelli," in *Machiavelli and the Nature of Political Thought*, ed. Martin Fleisher (London: Croom Helm, 1973), 185–208. Orr's explication of time in Machiavelli (188–97) is very close to Shakespeare's conception of "acting in time" in the history plays, but Machiavelli does not address the issue of time directly, as Orr acknowledges (187), in contrast to fortune, to which he refers insistently and ubiquitously. At the very least, to say that Shakespeare ignored Machiavelli's explicit idea of fortune and somehow divined his implicit idea of time is to say that Shakespeare thought differently from Machiavelli.

59 Among many others, see particularly *Discourses*, 2.29, 2.30, and 3.37.

60 The quotation is from *The Prince*, chapter 25 (*Chief Works*, ed. Gilbert, 1:92). See Hanna Fenichel Pitkin, *Fortune Is a Woman: Gender and Politics in the Thought of Niccolò Machiavelli* (Berkeley: University of California Press, 1984), 138–69.

61 J. G. A. Pocock infers a link between fortune and time in Machiavelli, but he does not attribute it to Machiavelli, i.e., he cites no statement of Machiavelli's in support of it. See *The Machiavellian Moment* (Princeton: Princeton University Press, 1975), 178.

62 See *Henry V* 3.6.27–29, *As You Like It* 1.2.30–31, and *Antony and Cleopatra* 4.15.46.

63 This point can be illustrated from a frequently cited parallel between *Measure for Measure* and Machiavelli's *The Prince*, chapter 7, where Machiavelli commends Cesare Borgia for putting a cruel substitute in charge of cleaning up Romagna and then executing the man (*Chief Works*, ed. Gilbert, 1:31). The episode is cited as more or less conclusive by Harry V. Jaffa, in John Alvis and Thomas G. West, eds., *Shakespeare as Political Thinker* (Durham, North Carolina: Carolina Academic Press, 1981), 188–89; by Allan Bloom, *Love and Friendship* (New York: Simon & Schuster, 1993), 330; by Steven Marx, *Shakespeare and the Bible* (Oxford: Oxford

University Press, 2000), 101; and by Tim Spiekerman, *Shakespeare's Political Realism* (Albany: State University of New York Press, 2001), 25. As Norman Holland argues, however, if Shakespeare was indebted to this episode, he could more easily have read it in Gentillet's *Contra-Machiavel* than in Machiavelli, whose works were not published in English during Shakespeare's lifetime ("*Measure for Measure*: The Duke and the Prince," *Comparative Literature* 11 [1959]: 16–20.). Most damaging to the claim for Machiavelli's influence on *Measure for Measure*, however, is Felix Raab's observation that the principle Machiavelli commends Cesare Borgia for following in Romagna had also been recommended by Erasmus in *Enchiridion*, following Aristotle's *Politics* (Felix Raab, *The English Face of Machiavelli* [London: Routledge & Kegan Paul, 1964], 11).

64   Shakespeare comes closest to a critical comment on narrative openness in referring elliptically to his narrative poem, *The Rape of Lucrece* (1594), as a "Pamphlet without beginning" (in the dedication to Southampton). *Lucrece* also begins abruptly, as the history plays do.

Chapter 5

1   Aristotle, *Nichomachean Ethics* 1094a1–1094b10, trans. Martin Ostwald (Indianapolis: Bobbs-Merrill, 1968), 4–5. Ostwald notes that "politikē is the science of the city-state, the *polis*, and its members, not merely in our narrow 'political' sense of the word but also in the sense that a civilized existence is, according to Plato and Aristotle, only possible in the *polis*" (4n. 8).

2   Spenser outlines his plan in "A Letter of the Authors to Sir Walter Raleigh," in *Poetical Works of Edmund Spenser*, ed. J. C. Smith, 3 vols. (Oxford: Clarendon, 1909), 2:485–87.

3   E. M. W. Tillyard, *Shakespeare's History Plays* (London: Chatto & Windus, 1944). Tillyard published the more widely read *Elizabethan World Picture* in 1943 (also by Chatto & Windus) as a precursor to the longer book.

4   Graham Bradshaw points out that there were two "great assaults" on Tillyard, an immediate one and another beginning in the 1980s, in *Misrepresentations: Shakespeare and the Materialists* (Ithaca: Cornell University Press, 1993), 1–8.

5   The most famous and influential New Historicist essay on the history plays (arguing that they contain their own subversion) is by Stephen Greenblatt, "Invisible Bullets," *Shakespearean Negotiations* (Berkeley: University of California Press, 1988), 21–65. Greenblatt also has the best New Historicist essay on the early histories, but it treats only Jack Cade's rebel-

lion in *2 Henry VI*, and then almost as an afterthought, "Murdering Peasants: Status, Genre, and the Representation of Rebellion," *Learning to Curse: Essays in Early Modern Culture* (New York: Routledge, 1990), 99–130.

6   Hugh Grady, *Shakespeare, Machiavelli, and Montaigne: Power and Subjectivity from Richard II to Hamlet* (Oxford: Oxford University Press, 2002), 247–48. On Shakespeare's putative affinity with the Essex circle, see 30–38, and on succession as a central problem in *1* and *2 Henry IV*, see 133. Grady does not recognize succession as an issue in the first tetralogy; he never mentions *King John*; and he does not explain why Shakespeare's "Machiavellian moment" waited until 1595, when Kyd had already depicted "prevalent Machiavellian deception within a royal court" in *The Spanish Tragedy* in the late 1580s (245).

7   Shakespeare's only English history play in which succession is not the ultimate source of political instability is *Henry VIII*, written in 1613, during the reign of Elizabeth's successor, James VI and I, who had several legitimate children and who therefore caused no anxiety about who would reign after him.

8   David M. Bevington, *Tudor Drama and Politics: A Critical Approach to Topical Meaning* (Cambridge, Mass.: Harvard University Press, 1968), 141–42.

9   J. E. Neale, *Elizabeth I and Her Parliaments*, 2 vols., *1559–1581* and *1584–1601* (New York: St. Martin's, 1958), 1.106. Neale devotes three chapters to negotiations concerning the succession in the parliaments of 1563 and 1566 (1.101–13, 129–64).

10 J. E. Neale, *Queen Elizabeth* (London: Jonathan Cape, 1934), 32–53, 68–81, 97–110.

11 Bevington, *Tudor Drama and Politics*, 143–46.

12 Peter Lake, "From *Leicester his Commonwealth* to *Sejanus his Fall*: Ben Jonson and the politics of Roman (Catholic) virtue," in *Catholics and the "Protestant Nation,"* ed. Ethan Shagan (Manchester: Manchester University Press, 2005), 128–61 (quotation on 129). The Puritan Peter Wentworth drafted a tract in 1587 and broached the question too boldly in the Parliament of 1593, earning a place in the Tower for his outspokenness, where he remained until his death in 1596 (Neale, *Queen Elizabeth I and Her Parliaments*, 2.251–66). Catholic opinion was published surreptitiously in a tract called "Leceister's Commonwealth" (1584), long thought to be by the Jesuit Robert Persons, and in another that Persons wrote, called *Conference about the Next Succession to the Crown of England* (1594). For comment, see Bevington, *Tudor Drama and Politics*, 11, 19, 22, 232, 237, and more recently, Victor Houliston, "The Hare and the Drum: Robert Persons's writings on the English succession, 1593–96," *Renaissance Studies* 14 (2000): 235–50.

13 *Shakespeare's History Plays*, 98
14 The cool distance implied by "dispassionate" inevitably suggests skepticism, and the suggestion is exactly right for Shakespeare's history plays. The distance involved, however, is from partisan passion, not from faith per se, which the plays manifest in multiple but understated ways (as opposed to religious unbelief), as argued here and in chapter 4.
15 See "The Elizabethan Hal" in John D. Cox, *Shakespeare and the Dramaturgy of Power* (Princeton: Princeton University Press, 1989), 104–27.
16 Neale, *Queen Elizabeth I and Her Parliaments*, 1.101.
17 For details of Henry VII's weak claim to the throne and the problems it caused, see chapter 4 above, n. 40.
18 This sermon was first published in 1571, when Shakespeare was seven years old, and portions of it were read on nine Sundays of every year thereafter throughout Elizabeth's reign. Alfred Hart, *Shakespeare and the Homilies* (Melbourne: Melbourne University Press, 1934), 23. For Tillyard's discussion of it, see Shakespeare's *History Plays*, 65–70. One of Tillyard's sharpest critics, Jonathan Dollimore, acknowledges the importance of the homilies, though he interprets them, as I do, as means of maintaining Tudor state power. See *Radical Tragedy: Religion, Ideology and Power in the Drama of Shakespeare and His Contemporaries* (Chicago: University of Chicago Press, 1984), 83–84.
19 This point is traceable to Calvin. See *Luther and Calvin on Secular Authority*, ed. Harro Höpel (Cambridge: Cambridge University Press, 1991), 74–77.
20 Cambridge is arrested and sentenced to death in *Henry V* (2.2.176–81), but Shakespeare had depicted Mortimer as still alive in Henry VI's reign and able to pass the claim on to Cambridge's son, Richard Plantagenet, later Duke of York (*1 Henry VI* 2.5), who becomes the focus of opposition to Henry VI (above, chap. 4). *Henry V* omits a detail that Mortimer mentions in *1 Henry VI*, that Cambridge had "levied an army" in Mortimer's behalf (2.5.88).
21 The point is made above in chapter 4. It is worth noting that succession is also an issue for which Shakespeare was unlikely to have been indebted to Machiavelli, because Machiavelli pays little or no attention to it. He acknowledges in passing that hereditary power gives a ruler an advantage (*The Prince*, chaps. 2 and 19), but this is not one of his keener political insights, and while he recognizes that hereditary rulers can be bad, he never focuses on the transition of monarchical power as a problem in itself, as Shakespeare consistently does.
22 Kastan, *Shakespeare and the Shapes of Time*, 51.
23 *The Advancement of Learning*, ed. Brian Vickers, Francis Bacon (Oxford: Oxford University Press, 1996), 254.

24 *Discourses* 1.3, in Machiavelli, *Chief Works and Others*, trans. Allan Gilbert, 3
    vols. (Durham, N.C.: Duke University Press, 1965), 1:201.

25 *The Prince*, chap. 15 (Gilbert, ed., *Chief Works*, 1:57–58). This argument
    goes back to Plato, who puts it in the mouth of Thrasymachus in *The
    Republic* (336b–342e), as a position for Socrates to refute. Machiavelli's
    straightforward endorsement of the argument therefore seems sardonic.

26 Grady, *Shakespeare, Machiavelli, and Montaigne*, 61.

27 Victoria Kahn argues that Machiavelli's contemporaries responded to his
    political advice ambivalently because of his duplicitous rhetoric: on one
    hand, they loathed him as a "Machiavel"; on the other, they devoured his
    technical advice and applied it expertly. In England this was happening as
    early as the middle of the reign of Henry VIII. Victoria Kahn, *Machiavellian
    Rhetoric from the Counter-Reformation to Milton* (Princeton: Princeton University
    Press, 1994), 135–41 (for the reference to Henry VIII).

28 Ultimately, of course, it is possible to see both Richard and Satan as self-
    deceived, because in the long run both misjudge what they can achieve by
    guile. In the long run, in other words, guile is self-deceived, an insight that
    contributes to the common medieval dramatic motif of the "guiler
    beguiled." In the act of seducing others, however, neither is deceived
    about what he thinks he is doing, in contrast to those whom they seduce.

29 Hugh Grady follows Katherine Eisaman Maus in claiming that interiority
    was innovative, *Inwardness and Theater in the English Renaissance* (Chicago:
    University of Chicago Press, 1995). I would argue for a different source for
    "inwardness" from the one Maus puts forward, however. She traces it to
    religious conflict in the Reformation, on the grounds that that conflict
    required one to hide what one really believed from what political authori-
    ties required one to believe. Recognition of a distinct interior reality, how-
    ever, is arguably as old as the Hebrew Bible, ("God seeth not as man seeth:
    for man looketh on the outward appearance, but the Lord beholdeth the
    heart" [1 Sam 16.7; see also Job 10:4, Prov 15:11, Isa 55:8-9, Jer 11:20,
    17:10, 20:12]), and it is ubiquitous in medieval thinking.

30 "Externalizing the Internal" is the title of the first half of a paper read by
    Alan Dessen at the International Shakespeare Conference on 8 August
    2006, "Staging Ideas and Abstractions: Revisiting Shakespeare's
    Theatrical Vocabulary," including several examples from morality plays.

31 Derek Traversi, "Shakespeare and Machiavelli: Some Thoughts on
    Shakespeare's Early History Plays," *Jadavpur University English Essays and
    Studies* 3 (1980): 18–31; Donald R. Wineke, "The Relevance of Machiavelli
    to Shakespeare: A Discussion of *1 Henry VI*," *Clio* 13 (1983): 17–36.

32 Grady, *Shakespeare, Machiavelli, and Montaigne*, 44–45.

33 Robert Ellrodt argues that Montaigne made the difference in Shakespeare's thinking about the self, and that self-consciousness does not appear before *Hamlet* and *Macbeth*, "Self-Consciousness in Montaigne and Shakespeare," *Shakespeare Survey* 28 (1975): 37–50. Ellrodt's observations about the shift from allegorical "objectivity" about the self to "spontaneous forms of self-awareness" (46) are helpful, but self-division and self-deception are already evident in two early comedies (above, chap. 1), which seem to owe very little, if anything, to Montaigne while frequently acknowledging their debt to the divine comedy.

34 For appreciative comments about the ambiguity of Hal's soliloquy, see Grady, *Shakespeare, Machiavelli, and Montaigne*, 162–64 and 169–74. For a reading of the soliloquy, on the other hand, as manifesting "a pure Machiavellian spirit of calculation," see John Roe, *Shakespeare and Machiavelli* (Cambridge: D. S. Brewer, 2002), 70–71.

35 "Such is the logic of this aspect of Machiavellian rhetoric, however, that we cannot be certain of Mowbray's veracity: we can as easily say of a speech like this that it creates excellent deception as that it rings true and has choric suggestiveness" (Grady, *Shakespeare, Machiavelli, and Montaigne*, 71).

36 An illuminating contrast to Mowbray's oath in *Richard II* is the Earl of Warwick oath on his salvation in *2 Henry VI* 3.2.153–57, whose function is clearly to intimidate a rival. In other words, a politician's religious oath is more clearly Machiavellian in the earlier play than in the later one. For comments on Warwick's oath, see Cox, *Shakespeare and the Dramaturgy of Power*, 90–91.

37 Grady overstates the case in claiming that one of the two combatants in this scene "has to be lying, and it is of the essence of the epistemology of this understated play that the audience can never be certain which one is" (*Shakespeare, Machiavelli, and Montaigne*, 68). This claim invites the deconstructive observation that both could be lying, and both could be telling the (partial) truth, as political rivals routinely do.

38 A similar ambiguity—or more properly, ambivalence—is evident in Duke Frederick's censorious exclamation to Oliver in *As You Like It* 3.1.15 (above, chap. 2, n. 15).

39 Grady, *Shakespeare, Machiavelli, and Montaigne*, 101.

40 See, e.g., *3 Henry VI* 2.5.21–54, *2 Henry IV* 3.1.4–31, 4.5.23–28; and *Henry V* 4.1.257–282.

41 The Geneva Bible's gloss to Matthew 19:24 ("It is easier for a camel") is, "What hindrance men have by riches."

42 Maynard Mack, *King Lear in Our Time* (Berkeley: University of California Press, 1965), 50–51. The quotation is from *King Robert of Sicily*, ed. W. H.

French and C. B. Hale, *Middle English Metrical Romances*, 2 vols. (New York: Russell & Russell, 1964), ll. 389–92.

43 On self-deception in *Julius Caesar*, see Geoffrey Miles, *Shakespeare and the Constant Romans* (Oxford: Clarendon, 1996), 123–48; David Daniell, ed., *Julius Caesar*, The Arden Shakespeare (London: Thomas Nelson, 1998), 57–58; Robin Headlam Wells, "Julius Caesar, Machiavelli, and the Uses of History," *Shakespeare Survey* 55 (2002), 209–18. For a contrary view, see Roe, *Shakespeare and Machiavelli*, 141–42.

44 Despite this assertion, I agree with Graham Bradshaw that identifying Henry as "hypocritical" is reductive (*Misrepresentations*, 84–85). The term obviously applies to Richard III's histrionics ("I thank my God for my humility," for example [*Richard III* 2.1.73]), but it is too blunt for the apparent sincerity of Henry V and his father—as indeed it would be if applied to virtually any real Renaissance monarch, including Elizabeth I.

45 Williams has just used "reckoning" in the second sense, in his debate with King Henry (who is in disguise) on the king's responsibility for the death and injury of his men (4.1.135). See also *1 Henry IV* 1.2.48 and 3.2.152, where a similar wordplay appears on "reckoning."

46 Gary Taylor, ed., *Henry V* (Oxford: Oxford University Press, 1982), 295–301. Taylor argues that none of these alternatives is clear or satisfactory, and he therefore emends "all" to "ill," but the chief value of his long note is to show that three meanings of "all" are indeed present in Henry's lines, and that the emendation is therefore unnecessary, because the confused phrasing makes more sense as a revelation of Henry's suspicious special pleading than it does as a mistake on the part of the playwright or compositor.

47 Whether the heirs of Henry IV should return the kingdom to Richard II's heir is fruitlessly debated when Henry V's son is on the throne in the *Henry VI* plays. The point is not that Henry V absolutely should give up his kingdom; the point is that he *feels guilty* about keeping it (as his son still does in *3 Henry VI*: "I know what to say; my title's weak" [1.1.134]), but he keeps it anyway—and indeed expands it by claiming France as well.

48 Stanley Cavell, *Disowning Knowledge in Six Plays of Shakespeare* (Cambridge: Cambridge University Press, 1987), 80.

49 The contention over prayers for the dead is central to Stephen Greenblatt's *Hamlet in Purgatory* (Princeton: Princeton University Press, 2001). Greenblatt also reads Henry V's prayer as an attempt to bargain with God (21–22), as does Vickie Sullivan, "Princes to Act: Henry V as the Machiavellian Prince of Appearance," in *Shakespeare's Political Pageant: Essays in Literature and Politics*, ed. Joseph Alulis and Vickie Sullivan (Lanham: Rowman & Littlefield, 1996), 125–51.

50   This point has been argued by Cox, *Shakespeare and the Dramaturgy of Power*, 104–27.
51   Greenblatt, *Hamlet in Purgatory*, 10–46.
52   The instructions that introduce the Elizabethan communion liturgy repeatedly emphasize the need for a penitent not only to declare his "naughty life" publicly but also to recompense "the parties whom he hath done wrong unto, or at the least declare himself to be in full purpose so to do, as soon as he conveniently may" (*The Book of Common Prayer 1559*, ed. John E. Booty [Washington, D.C.: Folger Shakespeare Library, 1976], 247).
53   As Maus remarks, "God's immediate, superhuman knowledge of the hidden interior of persons is one of the primary qualities for which he is admired and feared by many early modern Christians" (*Inwardness and Theater*, 10). I would emend Maus's statement only by deleting the qualifier, "early modern Christians," since the divine quality she describes is not an invention of Renaissance Christians but is as old as the Hebrew scriptures (see above, n. 29).
54   Claudius's earlier aside is sometimes cited as evidence as well:

>   O 'tis too true!
> How smart a lash that speech doth give my conscience!
> The harlot's cheek, beautied with plastering art,
> Is not more ugly to the thing that helps it
> Than is my deed to my most painted word.
> O heavy burden! (3.1.49–55)

What these lines prove, however, is that Claudius has a guilty conscience, and without the later admission, one could argue that what he feels guilty about is his "o'erhasty marriage," as Gertrude guiltily calls it (2.2.57).
55   W. W. Greg argued that the manner of old Hamlet's death is a figment of young Hamlet's imagination, "Hamlet's Hallucination," *MLR* 12 (1917): 393–421; and his argument prompted John Dover Wilson's influential response, *What Happens in* Hamlet (Cambridge: Cambridge University Press, 1951). Cavell has recently revived and defended Greg's reading on Freudian grounds (*Disowning Knowledge*, 180–82).
56   Hamlet refrains, of course, because he hopes to see Claudius damned, not because he hopes for Claudius's repentance, and Hamlet's frame of mind is therefore suspicious as well, but it has no bearing on what he thinks he knows on the basis of what he sees.

Chapter Six

1   *The Folger Library Edition of the Works of Richard Hooker*, ed. W. Speed Hill, 7 vols. (Cambridge, Mass.: Harvard University Press, 1977), *Of The Laws of Ecclesiastical Polity*, Fifth Book, 2:17.

2   I owe this point in broad terms to J. L. Simmons, *Shakespeare's Pagan World* (Charlottesville: University Press of Virginia, 1973), but for him the distinction has to do with providentialism in Christian history, whereas I believe Shakespeare's English history plays are more continuous with the Roman plays than Simmons allows, for reasons made clear in chapters 4 and 5, and that the real distinction in the Roman plays is ethical. Simmons based his assumption on J. Leeds Barroll's essay, "Shakespeare and Roman History," *Modern Language Review* 53 (1958): 327–43; and Barroll in turn drew heavily on E. M. W. Tillyard's book, *Shakespeare's History Plays* (London: Chatto & Windus, 1944).

3   Cicero, *On Duties*, ed. M. T. Griffin and E. M. Atkins (Cambridge: Cambridge University Press, 1991), 44–45. Geoffrey Miles argues that *De officiis*, an Elizabethan school text, was a major influence on Shakespeare's idea of the Romans, *Shakespeare and the Constant Romans* (Oxford: Clarendon, 1996), 18. Miles makes the point about the ambiguity of the stoics' theatrical comparison in a chapter called "Cicero and the Roman Actors," 18–37.

4   Brutus is a prime example of this contradiction in action, as Geoffrey Miles points out (*Shakespeare and the Constant Romans*, 123–48).

5   *Titus Andronicus* has usually been regarded as an early anomaly, distinct from the Roman plays based on Plutarch that came later. Two critics in the same year first argued that all of Shakespeare's Roman works deserve to be considered together: Robert S. Miola, *Shakespeare's Rome* (Cambridge: Cambridge University Press, 1983), and Michael Platt, *Rome and Romans according to Shakespeare* (Lanham, Md.: University Press of America, 1983). They set a precedent for more recent examples, such as Charles Wells, *The Wide Arch: Roman Values in Shakespeare* (New York: St. Martins, 1992), and Coppélia Kahn, *Roman Shakespeare: Warriors, Wounds, and Women* (London: Routledge, 1997).

6   This chapter was complete when I encountered Jan H. Blits's newly published *Spirit, Soul and City: Shakespeare's Coriolanus* (Lanham, Md.: Lexington Books, 2006), which argues the same point for *Coriolanus* (45, 172), though without linking it to *Titus*.

7   *Shakespeare and the Constant Romans*, 60.

8   Gordon Braden, *Renaissance Tragedy and the Senecan Tradition: Anger's Privilege* (New Haven: Yale University Press, 1985), 5–27.

9   Seneca, *Minor Dialogues and On Clemency*, trans. Aubrey Steward (London: George Bell and Sons, 1889), Dialogue IV.9 (84). Cited by Braden, *Renaissance Tragedy*, 22.

10 On this point in *De officiis*, see Miles, *Shakespeare and the Constant Romans*, 30–37.

11 "Horace His Art of Poetry," in *Ben Jonson*, ed. C. H. Herford and Percy and Evelyn Simpson, 11 vols. (Oxford: Clarendon, 1925–52), 8:311, ll. 121–25. Jonson here uses "thews" to mean "traits" or "attributes," and he knew that "decent" and "decorous" have the same Latin root.

12 Miles, *Shakespeare and the Constant Romans*, 31n. 22. Miles traces this conception of decorous self-consistency to Cicero's *De officiis*, thus emphasizing a different Ciceronian source from those cited as anti-stoic, such as *De finibus* and *Paradoxa Stoicorum*, by Marvin L. Vawter, " 'Division 'tween Our Souls': Shakespeare's Stoic Brutus," *Shakespeare Studies* 7 (1974): 173–95.

13 Braden's comments on *thymos* in Plato's ethical scheme are helpful in understanding both Achilles' and Titus's anger and competitiveness and their appeal to neo-stoics in the Renaissance (*Renaissance Tragedy*, 10–13). Blits makes a similar point in *Soul, Spirit and City* (2–3), without acknowledging Braden. Jonathan Bate points to another Horatian text in *Titus* that reinforces the hero's implacable self-possession: the verse inscribed on the arrows he gives to Chiron and Demetrius is from Horace's ode, "Integer vitae," which "claims that if one is armed with integrity one can roam in the Sabine wood and the wolf will flee from you." Jonathan Bate, *Shakespeare and Ovid* (Oxford: Clarendon, 1993), 109. Titus's integrity derives from his patrician self-consistency.

14 The contrast between Roman and barbarian in Titus has less to do with precise stoic teaching than with the potent influence of Virgil's *Aeneid*, perhaps the single most important embodiment of a generalized stoic *Romanitas*, especially for subsequent poets. The *Aeneid* provides warrant both for Titus's religious sacrifice of prisoners and for his honorable execution of his children (above, chap. 3), and Virgil's influence is even more pronounced in the stark contrast between the steadfast Roman hero and a passionately fickle barbarian queen, a contrast Shakespeare revisited many years later in *Antony and Cleopatra*.

15 For references to Lucrece, see *Titus* 2.1.108–109 (Aaron), 3.1.296–98 (Lucius), 4.1.64–65 (Titus), 4.1.90–92 (Marcus). Miola comments that "the rape of Lucrece functions as a deep source for *Titus Andronicus*," and he outlines several parallels (*Shakespeare's Rome*, 58–59).

16 To be sure, where the soul is concerned, Shakespeare is not entirely consistent in Lucrece. When Lucrece contemplates suicide, she worries about "pollution" in Christian terms, not stoic—or at least not Senecan terms

(1156–76). In the end, however, the stoic conception clearly prevails in Lucrece's suicide, as the narrator makes clear (1723–36). It is worth noting however, that even the stoic defense of suicide was not entirely consistent (see J. M. Rist, *Stoic Philosophy* [Cambridge: Cambridge University Press, 1966], 233–55), and in *Biathanatos* Donne attempted a complex and paradoxical defense of suicide in Christian terms in the early seventeenth century.

17 Honor occasionally takes on a distinctly Elizabethan hew in *Lucrece*, as when Tarquin reasons with himself that the rape will create "an eyesore in my golden coat [i.e., coat of arms]; / Some loathsome dash the herald will contrive / To cipher me how fondly I did dote" (205–7). The poem undoubtedly speaks to its immediate context in complex ways (it is dedicated to an ambitious young nobleman at Elizabeth's court, after all), but aside from the rising fashion of neo-stoicism, they do not bear directly on its ethical assumptions, which are my present concern.

18 "Resolution" is used in precisely the same sense when a Messenger brings grisly tokens of torturous betrayal from Saturninus to Titus and declares, "Thy grief their sports, thy resolution mocked" (*Titus* 3.1.238).

19 Braden, *Renaissance Tragedy*, 23.

20 A similar paradox is uttered by Cassius in *Julius Caesar*, even though he is a self-declared Epicurean, when he remarks that "Cassius from bondage will deliver Cassius" if Caesar is crowned king (1.3.90).

21 Plutarch helped to make the difference in the three plays based on his work, *Julius Caesar*, *Antony and Cleopatra*, and *Coriolanus*, but Shakespeare had begun to qualify his admiration for classical heroic value long before 1599, when *Julius Caesar* was likely written.

22 As David Young points out, the passage closely parodies Jaspar Heywood's translation of *Hercules Furens*, one of Seneca's most influential plays, *Something of Great Constancy: The Art of "A Midsummer Night's Dream"* (New Haven: Yale University Press, 1966), 35–37.

23 Cassius' argument in 1.2.67–70 uses the imagery John Davies uses in *Nosce Teipsum* 105–110, addressing the issue of self-deception:

> Is it because the mind is like the eye,
> (Through which it gathers knowledge by degrees)
> Whose rays reflect not, but spread outwardly,
> Not seeing itself, when other things it sees?
>
> No doubtless, for the mind can backward cast
> Upon herself her understanding light.

The Poems of Sir John Davies, ed. Robert Kruger (Oxford: Clarendon, 1975), who suggests that Davies may have influenced the passage in *Julius Caesar* (331).

24 Having revealed Portia's death to Cassius, Brutus acts as if he has not heard of it when Messala enters to inform him (4.3.170ff.). Geoffrey Miles' explanation of this apparent crux deserves to be quoted: "I see it . . . as central to Shakespeare's portrayal of constancy: as a genuinely noble ideal which nevertheless rests on unnatural suppression of feeling and on 'artful' presence, both directed toward satisfying the opinions of others" (*Shakespeare and the Constant Romans*, 143). I would add only that the "art" involved contributes even more emphatically to Brutus's psychological and moral defeat of Cassius, as Cassius makes clear: "I have as much of this in art as you, / But yet my nature could not bear it so" (193–94).

25 Braden, *Renaissance Tragedy*, 23.

26 On the failure of self-knowledge in *Julius Caesar*, see especially Miles, *Shakespeare and the Constant Romans*, 123–48.

27 In this respect, I think Vawter, " 'Division 'tween Our Souls,' " overstates the case in a moralistic analysis of self-deception. In the same vein, see John Anson, "*Julius Caesar*: The Politics of the Hardened Heart," *Shakespeare Studies* 2 (1966): 11–33. Before Miles, the most suggestive comments on the ambiguity of Roman stoic constancy in Shakespeare are by R. J. Kaufmann and Clifford J. Ronan, "Shakespeare's *Julius Caesar*: An Apollonian and Comparative Reading," *Comparative Drama* 4 (1970): 18–51.

28 Cf. Miles: "Those patricians who, unlike Antony, hold to the Roman code of rationality are in fact more strongly influenced by feelings than they are prepared to acknowledge" (*Shakespeare and the Constant Romans*, 131). For Miles, the play is "almost Freudian" in its impression of repressed emotion welling up unintentionally (132). I would refer this suspicious self-division to Shakespeare's inherited moral tradition, rather than to Freud, as argued above in chapter 1.

29 The best reading of biblical allusions in *Julius Caesar* is by Harold Fisch, *The Biblical Presence in Shakespeare, Milton, and Blake* (Oxford: Clarendon, 1999), 3–34, which focuses on blood imagery and brings the play's pervasive stoicism into conjunction with Ezekiel 11:19 (echoed in 36:26), "I will take the stony heart out of their bodies, and will give them an heart of flesh."

30 John Velz, "Undular Structure in *Julius Caesar*," *Modern Language Review* 66 (1971): 21–30.

31 Octavius makes his timely presence felt immediately after Caesar's assassination, when one of his servants enters (3.1.277SD), and again just after Antony's oration (3.2.261SD). Octavius' ominous "crossing" of Antony in 5.1.1–20 is no less designed to challenge his ally for supremacy than is Brutus's crossing of Cassius in 4.3.

32 *1 Henry VI* 2.3.20, 5.5.103–6; *2 Henry VI* 1.4.18, 3.2.116–18, 5.1.100; *3 Henry VI* 2.1.51–52, 2.2.146–48, 2.5.120, 3.2.188–90, 4.2.19–21, 4.8.25.

33 Braden, *Renaissance Tragedy*: "Roman political history in general recapitu-
lates the Greek experience, from city-state and republic to empire and
monarchy, and in so doing it is animated by something like Greek heroic
values; but they operate at a higher pitch of abstraction and efficiency, and
take the story one step farther. Combative selfhood in Rome has almost
from the start a clearer sort of official sanction" (13).

34 On stoicism in *Hamlet*, see Baker, *The Dignity of Man*, 302, and Hiram
Haydn, *The Counter-Renaissance* (New York: Scribner, 1950) 628–36.
Clifford Ronan points out that suicide as a mark (not always well under-
stood) of the distinctly "other" was the most common identification for
"Roman-ness" in English Renaissance drama, *"Antike Roman": Power
Symbology and the Roman Play in Early Modern England, 1585–1635* (Athens:
University of Georgia Press, 1995), 87–107.

35 On Othello's stoicism, see Bernard McElroy, *Shakespeare's Mature Tragedies*
(Princeton: Princeton University Press, 1973), 112–13, 120–26. Though
McElroy does not refer to stoicism, his analysis of Othello's allusions to fate
and destiny strongly suggest stoic ideas, and the analysis is original with
McElroy.

36 T. S. Eliot, *Shakespeare and the Stoicism of Seneca* (London: Oxford University
Press for the Shakespeare Association, 1927), 7–8. The essay has been
reprinted in more accessible collections of Eliot's criticism.

37 Geoffrey Miles treats the plays in the order I am proposing as well, but for
different reasons. He sees the three Plutarchan plays as "a kind of triptych
on the theme of constancy," with "Brutus embodying the virtue of constancy, Antony its defect, inconstancy, and Coriolanus its excess, wilful
obstinacy" (*Shakespeare and the Constant Romans*, 110–11). This is an illuminating approach, but it leaves other Roman works out of account, and its
precise focus does not reckon with evident reservations about stoicism
more generally in Shakespeare's plays.

38 Miles, *Shakespeare and the Constant Romans*, 149, 155.

39 To illustrate this ethos, Braden cites Plutarch's observation about "Julius
Caesar's feeling of being in unsatisfiable competition with himself, 'as if he
were another man,' and being driven while at the peak of what would
seem unsurpassable success" (*Renaissance Tragedy*, 14).

40 His anxiousness for Aufidius' opinion of him underscores Miles's point that
Coriolanus is, ironically, defined by others' views. Though he frequently dis-
dains praise, because he does not believe anyone other than Aufidius is worthy to judge him (see 1.5.16; 1.9.13–15, 37–38, 49–52; 2.2.68–70, 75–7,
148–51; etc.), his inability to remain indifferent to the commons' refusal to
acknowledge him allows them to define him. Stanley Fish aptly remarks,
"His reluctance to make a request and his inability to accept praise have a

single source in a desire for total independence," but Fish does not add that the desire is impossible to satisfy. "How To Do Things with Austin and Searle: Speech-Act Theory and Literary Criticism," *Is There a Text in This Class?* (Cambridge, Mass.: Harvard University Press, 1980), 210.

41 This sense of Roman history almost certainly came to Shakespeare from reading Plutarch. Though he had already grasped the central points of Senecan stoicism in *Titus Andronicus*, that play wantonly combines barbarians with the *imperium* in a way that suggests timeless and impressionistic *"Romanitas"* rather than any kind of historical destiny.

42 The most influential description of the play as essentially ambiguous is by Janet Adelman, *The Common Liar: An Essay on* Antony and Cleopatra (New Haven: Yale University Press, 1973), especially 102–21.

43 For fuller comments on this difference, see Adelman, *Common Liar*, 68–78. Jonathan Bate reads Shakespeare's difference from Virgil against the background of Ovid in particular (*Shakespeare and Ovid*, 211–14).

44 Cf. "Ah, dear Juliet . . . / . . . I will stay with thee / And never from this palace of dim night / Depart again" (*Romeo and Juliet* 5.3.101–8).

45 Ethel Seaton, "*Antony and Cleopatra* and the Book of Revelation," *Review of English Studies* 22 (1946): 219–24. "The undertones of Revelation, like sunken bells under the tide, sound through the surge and swell of the poetry" (222). Importantly, the undertones Seaton hears consistently occur in poetry associated with Antony and Cleopatra, not with Caesar.

46 Adelman points out that the play has attracted allegorical Christian readings, and that they are often mutually exclusive (*Common Liar*, 193n. 15). She mentions in particular S. L. Bethel, *Shakespeare and the Popular Tradition* (London: Staples, 1944), 116–32; and John F. Danby, *Poets on Fortune's Hill* (London: Faber & Faber, 1952), 128–51.

47 Herod is mentioned five times in *Antony*—five times as often as in any other play by Shakespeare (cf. 1.2.29–30, 3.3.3 and 4, 3.6.75, 4.6.14). Naseeb Shaheen sorts out these references, clarifies the historical distinctions between one Herod and another, and asserts that in one case, "Shakespeare's Source was North's text, not Scripture" (*Biblical References in Shakespeare's Plays* [Newark: University of Delaware Press, 1999], 649). However, when Charmian begs the soothsayer to foresee her having "a child at fifty, to whom Herod of Jewry may do homage" (2.2.29–30), or when Cleopatra declares imperiously, "That Herod's head / I'll have" (3.3.4–5), no one in Shakespeare's audience seems likely to have doubted that they were allusions to the Bible, even if North is technically the source in one case.

48 For a careful and detailed exposition of Caesar's moral duplicity and self-deception, see J. Leeds Barroll, "The Characterization of Octavius,"

Shakespeare Studies 6 (1970): 231–88. As Barroll points out, Caesar resembles no other Shakespearean character more closely than Angelo in *Measure for Measure*.

49   Erich Auerbach, "*Sermo Humilis*," in *Literary Language and Its Public in Late Latin Antiquity and in the Middle Ages*, trans. Ralph Manheim (New York: Pantheon Books, 1965), 25–66.

50   Harold Fisch also discusses *sermo humilis* in *Antony and Cleopatra* (*Biblical Presence*, 58–59).

51   See 4.6.22, 4.6.33, and 5.2.85. Shakespeare pointedly contrasts Antony's bounty with Caesar's, when Proculeius urges Cleopatra not to "abuse my master's [Caesar's] bounty by / Th' undoing of yourself" (5.2.42–43).

52   Hugh Richmond, "Shakespeare's Roman Trilogy: The Climax in *Cymbeline*," *Studies in the Literary Imagination* 5 (1972): 129–39; David M. Bergeron, "*Cymbeline*: Shakespeare's Last Roman Play," *Shakespeare Quarterly* 31 (1980): 31–41; Miola, *Shakespeare's Rome*, 206–35.

53   "Augustus" is used by four different characters in four scenes: 2.4.1, 3.1.1, 3.1.62, 3.5.101, and 5.5.83.

54   Britain's refusal to pay the tribute it owes to Rome comes from Holinshed, who is unclear about whether the refusal occurred during Cymbeline's reign or that of his son, Guiderius. See *Narrative and Dramatic Sources of Shakespeare*, ed. Geoffrey Bullough, 8 vols. (New York: Columbia University Press, 1957–1975), 8:43–46.

55   Jupiter is mentioned more times in *Cymbeline* than in all the other Roman plays put together, and *Cymbeline* contains Jupiter's only theophany. The fullest explication of the Virgilian myth in *Cymbeline* is by Patricia Parker, "Romance and Empire: Anachronistic *Cymbeline*," in *Unfolded Tales: Essay on Renaissance Romance*, ed. George M. Logan and Gorgon Teskey (Ithaca: Cornell University Press, 1989), 189–207.

56   The scene is so brief and superfluous that it is often cut in performance. It prominently features the perennial social class distinctions in ancient Rome: a senator calls on the tribunes to levy troops from "the gentry" (7), since "the common men" are already mustered in Gaul (2–3). Yet the tribunes are virtually mute and remarkably compliant: "We will discharge our duty" (16). The imagined situation seems more reminiscent of mustering local militias in Jacobean England than of anything in ancient Rome.

57   Thomas G. Olsen, "Iachimo's 'Drug-Damn'd Italy' and the Problem of British National Character in *Cymbeline*," *Shakespeare Yearbook* 10 (1999): 168–96.

58   Bullough, *Narrative and Dramatic Sources*, 8:43. The point and its significance were first mentioned by Northrop Frye in his important essay for Shakespearean comedy, "The Argument of Comedy," *English Institute*

Essays 1948 (New York: Columbia University Press, 1949), 58–73 (allusion on 72), and J. P. Brockbank elaborated on it in "History and Histrionics in *Cymbeline*," *Shakespeare Survey* 11 (1958): 42–49, but its fullest development remains Robin Moffett's essay, "*Cymbeline* and the Nativity," *Shakespeare Quarterly* 13 (1962), 207–18.

59   On the derivation of this structural pattern from the morality plays, see David M. Bevington, *From Mankind to Marlowe: Growth of Structure in the Popular Drama of Tudor England* (Cambridge, Mass.: Harvard University Press, 1962), 190–98. For the influence of medieval drama more generally on *Cymbeline*, see Howard Felperin, *Shakespearean Romance* (Princeton: Princeton University Press, 1972), 177–96, and for another specific morality play influence (the satire of preoccupation with fashionable clothing), see John Scott Colley, "Disguise and New Guise in *Cymbeline*," *Shakespeare Studies* 7 (1974): 233–52. For detailed analysis of the motif Colley traces to medieval drama, see John D. Cox, *The Devil and the Sacred in English Drama, 1350–1642* (Cambridge: Cambridge University Press, 2000), 61–68.

60   Moffet, "*Cymbeline* and the Nativity," notes the coincidence of language between Imogen's phrase, "this gracious season," and Marcellus' description of Christmas as "that season . . . so hallowed and gracious" in *Hamlet* 1.1.164–70 (215).

61   R. G. Hunter, *Shakespeare and the Comedy of Forgiveness* (New York: Columbia University Press, 1965), 159–76.

62   Similarly, Milton would claim that "The [pagan] oracles are dumb," because they have been superseded by the Word made flesh in "On the Morning of Christ's Nativity." The interpretation of the pagan gods in Christian terms was at least as old as Augustine for Shakespeare and as new as Spenser, though in the early seventeenth century it still awaited its most impressive literary treatment in the poetry of Milton. On the biblical allusions in the scene with Jupiter, see Shaheen, *Biblical Allusions in Shakespeare's Plays*, 712–14.

63   The imagery of tears as holy water, and implicitly as a symbol of grace, is also used of Cordelia in *King Lear* 4.3.30–33.

64   Shakespeare similarly uses the imagery of miraculous birth at moments of climactic reunion in *The Comedy of Errors* 5.1.401–07, and *Pericles* 5.1.200.

65   Of the four plots, this one is most responsive to the play's Jacobean context and seems most strongly influenced by it. See Emrys Jones, "Stuart *Cymbeline*," *Essays in Criticism* 11 (1961): 89–95; and Leah Marcus, *Puzzling Shakespeare: Local Reading and Its Discontents* (Berkeley: University of California Press, 1988), 109–59.

Chapter Seven

1　Among others, see Anne Righter [Barton], *Shakespeare and the Idea of the Play* (London: Chatto & Windus, 1962); David Young, *Something of Great Constancy: The Art of "A Midsummer Night's Dream"* (New Haven: Yale University Press, 1966); Philip Edwards, *Shakespeare and the Confines of Art* (London: Methuen, 1968); Michael Goldman, *Shakespeare and the Energies of Drama* (Princeton: Princeton University Press, 1972); David Young, *The Heart's Forest: A Study of Shakespeare's Pastoral Plays* (New Haven: Yale University Press, 1972); Robert Egan, *Drama within Drama: Shakespeare's Sense of His Art in* King Lear, The Winter's Tale, *and* The Tempest (New York: Columbia University Press, 1975); Alvin B. Kernan, *The Playwright as Magician: Shakespeare's Image of the Poet in the English Public Theater* (New Haven: Yale University Press, 1979); Ekbert Faas, *Shakespeare's Poetics* (Cambridge: Cambridge University Press, 1986); Pauline Kiernan, *Shakespeare's Theory of Drama* (Cambridge: Cambridge University Press, 1996).

2　The term seems to have originated with Lionel Abel, *Metatheatre: A New View of Dramatic Form* (New York: Hill & Wang, 1963), but its variant "metadrama" was made popular by James Calderwood in *Shakespearean Metadrama* (Minneapolis: University of Minnesota Press, 1971), *Metadrama in Shakespeare's Henriad:* Richard II *to* Henry V (Berkeley: University of California Press, 1979), and *To Be or Not To Be: Negation and Metadrama in* Hamlet (New York: Columbia University Press, 1983). Richard Fly noted the principal reason why this vein of interpretation was eventually abandoned: "Under the disenchanted gaze of the metadramatic critic, all of the plays may lose their distinctive generic features and become 'metaphors for art'" ("The Evolution of Shakespearean Metadrama: Abel, Burckhardt, and Calderwood," *Comparative Drama* 20 [1986]: 124–39 [quotation from 134]). A later example, Judd D. Hubert's *Metatheater: The Example of Shakespeare* (Lincoln: University of Nebraska Press, 1991), is both more formalist and more deconstructive than Calderwood.

3　Sir Philip Sidney, *An Apology for Poetry*, ed. G. G. Smith, 2 vols. (Oxford: Clarendon, 1904), 1:148–207. Among many critical discussions of Shakespeare and Sidney are Edwards, *Shakespeare and the Confines of Art*, 1–2; Howard Felperin, *Shakespearean Romance* (Princeton: Princeton University Press, 1972), 3–54; Richard Henze, *"A Midsummer Night's Dream*: Analogous Image," *Shakespeare Studies* 7 (1974): 115–23; Faas, *Shakespeare's Poetics*, 20–24; Kiernan, *Shakespeare's Theory of Drama*, 6–20.

4　For a thorough discussion of the doctrinal issues involved, see Andrew D. Weiner, *Sir Philip Sidney and the Poetics of Protestantism* (Minneapolis:

University of Minnesota Press, 1978), 3–50. What I hope to add to
Weiner's account is a fuller sense of religion and theater in particular.

5   Recognizing that poetry and theater alike have a tenuous hold on reality,
    as Shakespeare describes them, helps to correct the impression that he sin-
    gles out theater alone for this kind of critique, as Kernan argues, *The
    Playwright as Magician*, 132–33, 151.

6   Arthur F. Kinney, *Markets of Bawdrie: The Dramatic Criticism of Stephen Gosson*
    (Salzburg: Institut für Englische Sprache und Literatur, 1974), 15–16,
    43–51.

7   Sidney never mentions Gosson, to be sure, but Sidney's defensive stance,
    his repeated appeal to Protestant assumptions, and his sarcasm aimed at
    those who attack poetry make his essay an unmistakable companion piece
    to Gosson's. Kinney summarizes the commentary on Sidney's *Apology* as a
    response to Gosson (44–45). Weiner acknowledges Gosson incidentally
    and focuses on Sidney's differences with an earlier defender of poetry,
    George Gascoigne (*Sidney*, 28–32).

8   Kinney notes how close Gosson and Sidney were on the issue of reform
    and remarks that "Sidney's initial annoyance is therefore a little difficult to
    explain" (*Markets of Bawdrie*, 46), but his annoyance surely points to differ-
    ences between reformers.

9   On Elizabeth's conformity under Mary, see J. E. Neale, *Queen Elizabeth*
    (London: Jonathan Cape, 1934), 40–43. On her continuing preference for
    traditional liturgical practices, see Patrick Collinson, *Elizabethans* (London:
    Hambledon & London, 2003), 108–15.

10 The controversy over candles on the altar indicates that they provided
    more than atmosphere. For their traditional liturgical significance, see
    Eamon Duffy, *The Stripping of the Altars: Traditional Religion in England
    c1400–c1580* (New Haven: Yale University Press, 1992), 15–22, 281, 330,
    361–62. The quotation is from William P. Haugaard, *Elizabeth and the
    English Reformation* (Cambridge: Cambridge University Press, 1968), 190.
    For Thomas Nashe's defense of the English church's position on vestments
    against puritan attack in the 1590s, see above, chap. 1.

11 *The Folger Library Edition of the Works of Richard Hooker*, ed. W. Speed Hill, 7
    vols. (Cambridge, Mass.: Harvard University Press, 1977), *Of The Laws of
    Ecclesiastical Polity*, Fifth Book, 2:123. Elizabethan theologians such as
    William Whitaker and Henry Bullinger spelled out the position on visible
    signs, as Weiner points out in arguing that Sidney was influenced by it
    (*Sidney*, 42–43), and their primary motive was to distinguish a moderate
    Protestant position on the body and blood of Christ from the Catholic
    position.

12 Thomas Becon, *The Displaying of the Popish Mass* in *Prayers and Other Pieces of Thomas Becon*, ed. John Ayre for the Parker Society (Cambridge: Cambridge University Press, 1844), 252–53.

13 Becon, *Displaying*, 259.

14 Becon, *Displaying*, 255. On the Protestant plain style, see John King, *English Reformation Literature: The Tudor Origins of the Protestant Tradition* (Princeton: Princeton University Press, 1982). Weiner points out that Gascoigne explicitly defends poetry against literal interpretation, thus providing a precedent for Sidney (*Sidney*, 31).

15 Jonas Barish, *The Antitheatrical Prejudice* (Berkeley: University of California Press, 1981), 80–131.

16 Quoted by Colin Rice, *Ungodly Delights: Puritan Opposition to the Theatre 1576–1633* (Genova: Edizioni dell'Orso, 1997), 17.

17 Quoted from Rainolds' *Overthrow of Stage Plays* (published in 1629, but written much earlier) by Rice, *Ungodly Delights*, 15. On Rainolds and Gosson, see Kinney, *Markets of Bawdrie*, 10–11. William M. Hamlin points out that Gosson learned academic skepticism from Rainolds (*Tragedy and Scepticism in Shakespeare's England* [Basingstoke: Palgrave Macmillan, 2005], 45), and both teacher and pupil in this case conform to a sixteenth-century pattern, noted in chapter 1 above, of using skepticism to promote reform and attack one's opponents in religious controversy. While Gosson learned his skepticism at university, the precedents for his use of it include Foxe, Becon, Bale, and Tyndale and ultimately Erasmus and More.

18 The legislation of 1559 is transcribed by E. K. Chambers, *The Elizabethan Stage*, 4 vols. (Oxford: Clarendon, 1923), 4:264–66, and summarized by Rice, *Ungodly Delights*, 13. On the decline of communal biblical history plays, see Harold C. Gardiner, *Mysteries' End: An Investigation of the Last Days of the Medieval Religious Stage* (New Haven: Yale University Press, 1946), and more recently Sarah Beckwith, *Signifying God: Social Relation and Symbolic Act in the York Corpus Christi Plays* (Chicago: University of Chicago Press, 2001), who persuasively distinguishes a traditional theater of "signs" from a reformed theater of "disguises" (121–57). For Cromwell's encouragement of antipapal drama, see Paul Whitfield White, *Theatre and Reformation: Protestantism, Patronage, and Playing in Tudor England* (Cambridge: Cambridge University Press, 1993), 12–41.

19 David M. Bevington, *From Mankind to Marlowe: Growth of Structure in the Popular Drama of Tudor England* (Cambridge, Mass.: Harvard University Press, 1962).

20 Kinney, *Markets of Bawdrie*, 13–14.

21 *Shakespearean Negotiations: The Circulation of Social Energy in Renaissance England* (Berkeley: University of California Press, 1988), 109.

22   Beckwith, *Signifying God*, 152.
23   Leanne Groeneveld, "Christ as Image in the Croxton Play of the Sacrament," *Research Opportunities in Renaissance Drama* 40 (2001): 190.
24   The classic description of this acknowledgment in the Corpus Christi procession is by Mervyn James, "Ritual, Drama and Social Body in the Late Medieval English Town," *Past and Present* 98 (1983): 3–29.. Beckwith discusses the way economic differences manifest themselves in the York plays in *Signifying God*, 59–71.
25   For reasons outlined below, I think Pauline Kiernan overstates the case in asserting that "Shakespeare's drama claims only the status of fiction. All it can do, and wants to do, is lie" (*Shakespeare's Theory of Drama*, 160). Sidney and Shakespeare both affirm that art is inherently fictive, but that is not the same as asserting that it is merely fictive. Contrast Alvin Kernan's remark that a Shakespearean play asserts its "ability to reveal by means of indirections the reality of the world, ranging from the factual to the metaphysical, and to change human lives by the power with which it presents these truths" (*The Playwright as Magician*, 150).
26   Stephen Greenblatt brings something like the radical reformers' literal mindedness to Bottom's "vision" in reading it as merely "the joke of a decisively secular dramatist, a writer who deftly turned the dream of the sacred into popular entertainment" in *Will in the World: How Shakespeare Became Shakespeare* (New York: W. W. Norton, 2004), 36. For a richer, more nuanced, and more historically informed reading, see R. Chris Hassel, *Faith and Folly in Shakespeare's Romantic Comedies* (Athens: University of Georgia Press, 1980), 53–58.
27   Sidney, *Apology*, 197. Sidney's sardonic description of popular dramaturgy may well owe something to Gosson's sarcastic description of "players that come to the scaffold with drum and trumpet to proffer skirmish, and when they have sounded alarum, off go the pieces to encounter a shadow or conquer a paper monster" (*School of Abuse*, ed. Kinney, *Markets of Bawdrie*, 78), but Gosson did not find an elegant Italian source for his literalistic conception of theater.
28   On Sidney's debt to the Italians, see Faas, *Shakespeare's Poetics*, 56–58. Johnson's important critique of neoclassical verisimilitude appears in his defense of Shakespeare. See *Johnson on Shakespeare*, ed. Arthur Sherbo, vols. 7 and 8 in *The Yale Edition of the Works of Samuel Johnson* (New Haven: Yale University Press, 1968), 7:74–81.
29   Young, *Something of Great Constancy*, 42–45; Kiernan, *Shakespeare's Theory of Drama*, 109–13.
30   The scene is discussed briefly by Keir Elam, *The Semiotics of Theatre and Drama* (London: Methuen, 1980), 14; Bert O. States, *Great Reckonings in Little Rooms:*

On the Phenomenology of Theater (Berkeley: University of California Press, 1985), 32–36; and Beckwith, *Signifying God*, 63. I am principally indebted to Jerzy Limon's analysis of it, however, "Shakespeare the Semiotician, or, How to create something out of aery nothing," an unpublished paper read at the International Shakespeare Conference, Stratford-upon-Avon, July 26, 2004. I am grateful to Jerzy Limon for sending me a copy of his paper.

31   I think Pauline Kiernan oversimplifies stage ontology in describing this scene: "Quince and company are rehearsing in a green plot, which they are pretending is a stage" (*Shakespeare's Theory of Drama*, 112). More accurately, actors are performing on a bare stage, which they pretend to be a green plot, which for purposes of an imagined rehearsal the persons they are impersonating pretend to be a stage. Contrary to Sidney's assertion, an audience easily follows the actors' multiple illusions—easily sees the truth the playwright wants to convey through them, though the truth is complex and therefore not easy to describe apart from the performance, which, if well done, is effortlessly clear.

32   To be sure, it takes more than Oberon's line to make moonlight shine imaginatively on a daylit stage. The scene has been set through exquisite lyric poetry in the exchange between Puck and an anonymous fairy (2.1.1–17) and in several references to "night" (Young, *Something of Great Constancy*, 74–86). Pauline Kiernan's emphasis on theatrical embodiment as the key to Shakespeare's theory of drama is important, but it understates the function of dramatic language. However much Shakespeare depended on talented actors, they were not mimes, and their effective vocalization of the lines he wrote for them was just as dependent on embodiment (volume, articulation, accent, pace, pause, pitch, feeling, occasional singing) and just as important as their inventive bodily actions in creating theatrical illusion.

33   On Shakespeare's imitation of the Jacobean masque, see Glynne Wickham, "Masque and Anti-masque in *The Tempest*," *Essays and Studies* 28 (1975): 1–14. Pauline Kiernan's dismissal of Prospero's masque confuses the difference between *The Tempest* and the masque by asserting that "these actors were spirits before the masque began" (*Shakespeare's Theory of Drama*, 85). In the Jacobean court masque, professional actors played spirits, as they do in Shakespeare's; in other words, the spirits were actors before the masque began, and in the socially charged world of the theater, they remain actors throughout it.

34   This point has been made brilliantly by Stephen Orgel, *The Jonsonian Masque* (Cambridge, Mass.: Harvard University Press, 1965), 19–36.

35   Stuart Clark, *Thinking with Demons: The Idea of Witchcraft in Early Modern Europe* (Oxford: Clarendon, 1997), 167.

36 I have argued this point for several plays that stage devils in the early seventeenth century in *The Devil and the Sacred in English Drama, 1350–1642* (Cambridge: Cambridge University Press, 2000), 150–87.

37 E. K. Chambers, *The Elizabethan Stage*, 4 vols. (Oxford: Clarendon, 1923), 3:423–24, and Eric Rasmussen, "*The Black Book* and the Date of *Doctor Faustus*," *Notes and Queries* 235, n.s. 37 (1990): 168–70.

38 I think Jonathan Bate oversimplifies in asserting that Hymen's appearance in *As You Like It* "is more performance than theophany: the god is meant to be seen as an actor, for Rosalind is orchestrating the script" (*Shakespeare and Ovid* [Oxford: Clarendon, 1993], 161). This analysis raises serious ontological questions, for Hymen is obviously an actor in Shakespeare's play, but how do we know he is one in Rosalind's? Rosalind is orchestrating a script with people who exist ontologically in the world of Rosalind as real people, not as actors (except for Rosalind herself, of course, because she is disguised as Ganymede). Why would Hymen not be a parallel instance?

39 On rejection of exorcism in Shakespeare, see Greenblatt, *Shakespearean Negotiations*, 94–128, and Richard Strier, "Shakespeare and the Skeptics," *Religion and Literature* 32 (2000): 171–96. The Enlightenment view, a form of negative dogmatism, is stronger but also narrower than the openness that typically accompanies the supernatural in Shakespeare and that differs again from the positive dogmatism that characterizes historicist interpretations like John Dover Wilson's in *What Happens in* Hamlet (Cambridge: Cambridge University Press, 1935).

40 Brownlow, *Shakespeare, Harsnett, and the Devils of Denham*, 53–61.

41 William Strachey, *A True Repertory of the Wrack and Redemption of Sir Thomas Gates, Knight*, in *The Tempest*, ed. Virginia Mason Vaughan and Alden T. Vaughan, The Arden Shakespeare (London: Thomas Nelson, 1999), 292.

42 Even as late as 1851, when Herman Melville published *Moby Dick*, the manifestation of storm-induced static electricity was still sufficiently awe-inspiring that he could treat its flaming amazement in quasi-mystical terms, which he mingled with a matter-of-fact description of lightning rods aboard a Nantucket whaler in yet another instance of that novel's repeated insistence on both hard-headed rationality and credulous imagination (chap. 119, "The Candles").

43 On the acceptance of this distinction in demonology, see Clark, *Thinking with Demons*, 165.

44 Bate, *Shakespeare and Ovid*, 9.

45 Of course, all resurrections in the Chester play—whether enabled by Antichrist or by God—were performed by actors who only feigned to die

and come to life again, but to object to the "real" resurrections in the play, because they are just as feigned as the false ones, is to misconstrue the ontological world of a theater of signs and, in effect, to repeat the literalism of reformers who exposed and destroyed the rood of Boxley as a mere mechanism. Acknowledging that the misuse of drama is a concern of the Chester cycle, David Mills remarks that the *Antichrist* play "can be read as a warning of how readily illusion can become delusion when it is divorced from moral function." *Staging the Chester Cycle* (Leeds: University of Leeds School of English, 1985), 11.

46 For a similar point about Prospero's claim to resurrection, see Greenblatt, *Will in the World*, 375–76. An unpublished paper by Sarah Beckwith, "Shakespeare's Resurrections," read at the meeting of the Shakespeare Association of America, 2006, is the best treatment of the subject I know of, and I am grateful to her for a copy of her paper.

47 Shakespeare's ambiguous mingling of his own voice with that of Prospero has a precedent in the Chorus of Time in *The Winter's Tale*, 4.1, where the first person singular starts out being only Time, then becomes both Time and Shakespeare, then, briefly, Shakespeare alone ("And remember well / I mentioned a son o' the King's, which Florizel / I now name to you"), and finally, again, Time alone. For comment on this effect in Time's speech, see Young, *Heart's Forest*, 140–45.

48 Anne Barton points out that the Vice was the means by which the metaphor of the world as a stage made its way onto the stage itself, *Shakespeare and the Idea of the Play*, 68.

49 The spear gripped with an armed hand in *Lucrece* is also a visual rendering of Shakespeare's name, as Patrick Cheney points out in "Shakespeare's Counter-Laureate Authorship: The Spear of Achilles," a paper read at the meeting of the Shakespeare Association of America in Bermuda, April 2005. With Cheney's argument in mind, nothing prevents this stanza in *The Rape of Lucrece* from being a covert symbolic signature of the artist who really created the imagined painting of Troy's demise, along with reflections about its status as art and illusion. Looked at this way, the painting in Lucrece anticipates Julio Romano's statue in *The Winter's Tale*. I am grateful to Patrick Cheney for sending me a copy of his paper in advance of its publication.

50 Ross King, *Brunelleschi's Dome* (London: Chatto & Windus, 2000), 78–82. King compares the trick to *A Midsummer Night's Dream* (80), but it applies with equal or greater relevance to the Induction of *Taming*.

51 Geoffrey Bullough, *Narrative and Dramatic Sources of Shakespeare*, 8 vols. (New York: Columbia University Press, 1957–1975), 1:65–68, 111–58.

52   For more on this contrast, see David Daniell, "The Good Marriage of Katherine and Petruchio," *Shakespeare Survey* 37 (1984): 23–31. For insightful comments about Ovidian metamorphosis as a point of thematic continuity in *Taming*, see Bate, *Shakespeare and Ovid*, 118–31.

53   The ballad is mentioned by Bullough, *Narrative and Dramatic Sources*, 2:63.

54   Daniell, "Good Marriage," 30–31. Bate reads Kate's exchange with Vincentio helpfully against the background of Ovid's Salmacis and Hermaphroditus (*Shakespeare and Ovid*, 122–24), but he sees the episode as unique rather than representative, and he therefore neglects the game-playing in Kate's speech of supposed submission.

55   Bate, *Shakespeare and Ovid*, 179.

56   Petruchio is consistently associated with openness and candor, as in his refusal to meet social expectation for fine clothing (3.2.117–20) and his complementary abuse of Kate's tailor (4.3.165–79), in contrast to Lucentio's constant recourse to deceiving others in elaborate disguise.

57   This use of "friend" contrasts strongly with the same word as Benedick and Beatrice use it of each other when they first acknowledge their mutual affection (4.1.255 ff.).

58   Leonato confirms that Hero is his sole heir after the masked ball (2.1.288–89), and he repeats it after the families' reconciliation at the end (5.1.284), reinforcing his social conventionality and incidentally that of Claudio and Hero as well. In this and other ways—especially his massive self-centeredness (4.1.120–43)—Leonato is like Baptista in *The Taming of the Shrew*.

59   For suggestions that this kind of trick has deep theological roots, as well as parallels in popular and Italian dramaturgy, see chapter 2 above, n. 55.

60   R. G. Hunter, *Shakespeare and the Comedy of Forgiveness* (New York: Columbia University Press, 1965), 85–105.

61   Harry Berger Jr., *Making Trifles of Terrors: Redistributing Complicities in Shakespeare*, ed. Peter Erickson (Stanford: Stanford University Press, 1997), 24.

Chapter Eight

1   Edward Capell first noticed the parallel, in *Notes and Various Readings to Shakespeare*, 4 vols. (London: Printed for Edward and Charles Dilly, 1774), 4:63. A judicious summary of scholarship on Shakespeare and Montaigne appears in Alice Harmon's essay, "How Great Was Shakespeare's Debt to Montaigne?" *PMLA* 57 (1942): 988–1008. Much fine and illuminating interpretive work has been published since then, but Harmon's argument remains fundamentally sound: "Those who have attempted to show that

Shakespeare's borrowing from Montaigne was extensive have failed to take sufficient account of the wide currency in the Renaissance of ideas common to the two writers" (989). William M. Hamlin notes Shakespeare's possible debt to Florio's translation of Montaigne for particular English words, and then adds, in a rare example of special pleading, "And he may well have encountered three other terms that Florio introduced into English, terms specifically derived from the sceptical lexicon: 'Pyrrhonisme,' 'Ataraxie' and 'Pyrrhonize'" (*Tragedy and Scepticism in Shakespeare's England* [Basingstoke: Palgrave Macmillan, 2005], 61). Speculation about the words that Shakespeare may have seen without actually using is endless and unpersuasive.

2   *The Complete Essays of Montaigne*, trans. Donald M. Frame (Stanford: Stanford University Press, 1965), 819. Cited hereafter as "*Essays*" with the traditional designation of book and essay by Roman and Arabic numerals, respectively, and the page number in Frame's edition.

3   Hugh Grady suggests a particular point of similarity between the two: "The works of Niccolò Machiavelli, or their widely disseminated ideas, constituted an intellectual crisis for both Montaigne and Shakespeare that was one of the starting points of their meditations on modern subjectivity" (*Shakespeare, Machiavelli, and Montaigne: Power and Subjectivity from Richard II to Hamlet* [Oxford: Oxford University Press, 2002], 57). A claim that writers in the past suffered an intellectual crisis that was unacknowledged by the writers themselves can neither be falsified nor substantiated; one simply has to take it on faith.

4   In an imagined letter by "Mary, Mother of Jesus," Erasmus mocks self-interested prayer in terms very similar to Montaigne's critique. *The Colloquies of Erasmus*, trans. Craig R. Thompson (Chicago: University of Chicago Press, 1965), 289–91. Erasmus later defended the colloquy in which the letter appears as an attack on Reformation iconoclasm, but he did not retract his criticism of self-interested prayer (*Colloquies*, 631).

5   *Medieval Drama*, ed. David M. Bevington (Boston: Houghton Mifflin, 1975), *Mankind*, lines 549–64.

6   Elsewhere, in a demonstration of intellectual agility, Montaigne is as dubious as Shakespeare is in the Roman plays about the self-derived virtue of stoicism. See *Essays* II:12, 361, for example.

7   Roland Mushat Frye, *Shakespeare and Christian Doctrine* (Princeton: Princeton University Press, 1963), 256–61 (quotation on 260). Frye cites Luther and Hooker, but the need to avoid both pride and despair was not a Reformation discovery, as Frye implies; it animates many fifteenth-century morality plays and is spectacularly enacted in the story of Lucifer's fall in the biblical history plays.

8   Naseeb Shaheen, *Biblical References in Shakespeare's Plays* (Newark: University
     of Delaware Press, 1999). It is remarkable, as Steven Marx points out, that
     despite the evident permeation of Shakespeare's imagination by the Bible,
     no one has studied how he uses it, *Shakespeare and the Bible* (Oxford: Oxford
     University Press, 2000), 2. While I have learned much from Marx's effort
     to fill this gap, I do not find his way of construing the two texts in light of
     each other to be persuasive. Comparing *The Tempest* to Genesis, for exam-
     ple, because both begin in chaos, and *The Tempest* is the first play in the
     Folio (Marx, 15) is not insightful but merely arbitrary. The subject still
     awaits the same kind of insight that Jonathan Bate brings to a related task
     in *Shakespeare and Ovid* (Oxford: Clarendon, 1993).
9   Marianne S. Meijer, "Montaigne et la Bible," *Bulletin de la Société des amis de
     Montaigne* 20 (1976): 23–57. The count is approximate, as Meijer points
     out, because of the difficulty of determining with precision what a citation
     consists of (23). In any case, her count is more generous than Donald
     Frame's, whose index lists just thirty-seven biblical citations, of which only
     thirty are actual quotations.
10   William Hamlin notes that Montaigne "stresses human frailty incessantly
     yet rarely yokes it with Original Sin" (*Tragedy and Scepticism*, 125).
11   Horace, *Satires, Epistles, Ars Poetica*, trans. H. Rushton Fairclough. Loeb
     Classical Library (Cambridge, Mass.: Harvard University Press, 1939),
     34–35.
12   Meijer, "Montaigne et la Bible," 54–55.
13   Shaheen, *Biblical References*, 38–48. In a strong dissent from Shaheen,
     David Beauregard argues that Shakespeare preferred the Rheims transla-
     tion, rather than Geneva, "Shakespeare and the Bible," *Religion and the Arts*
     5 (2001): 317–30. But Beauregard's argument depends on the assumption
     that Shakespeare was a recusant who would have risked using a banned
     edition out of pious devotion to the Roman church. To reduce the risk,
     Beauregard argues, Shakespeare likely used the "perfect cover" of William
     Fulke's "confutation" of Rheims, because it includes the Rheims New
     Testament in a "safe" edition (324). This elaborate explanation would
     seem to make Beauregard's hypothesis of Shakespeare's recusancy unnec-
     essary rather than convincing.
14   Meijer, "Montaigne et la Bible," 24. In Frame's edition of the *Essays*, his
     translation of all Montaigne's biblical references into English misrepre-
     sents the presence of the vernacular in the original.
15   Apparently in conformity to the church's expectation, Montaigne inveighs
     against vernacular translations of the Bible in *Essays* I:56, 232, though his
     implication that the original language of the Bible was Latin (when he and
     every other educated reader knew better) seems ironically to undercut his

conformist point: "The Jews, the Mohammedans, and almost all others have espoused, and revere, the language in which their mysteries were originally conceived; and any alteration or change in them is forbidden, not without reason."

16 Montaigne could have easily cited this biblical quotation in Latin, for the Vulgate form of Romans 12:3, which appears here, was one of many sayings, both classical and biblical, that were carved into the rafters of his library.

17 The argument from animal abilities is borrowed directly from Sextus Empiricus' *Outlines of Skepticism*, though Montaigne adds many examples of his own.

18 This is not to say that the *Essays* lack a sense of Christian destiny and ethics, but that their mutual dependence is not the function of Montaigne's biblical quotations, as it generally is for Shakespeare's.

19 On Montaigne's debt to Sextus, see Richard H. Popkin, *The History of Scepticism from Erasmus to Spinoza* (Berkeley: University of California Press, 1979), 42–65, and Hamlin, *Tragedy and Scepticism*, 60–71.

20 Popkin, *History of Scepticism*, 43. Popkin acknowledges that his own view is "that, at best, Montaigne was probably mildly religious. His attitude appears to be more that of indifference or unexcited acceptance, without any serious religious experience or involvement" (55).

21 Frank Kermode, ed., *The Tempest*, The Arden Shakespeare (London: Methuen, 1954).

22 I have argued in detail elsewhere that *The Tempest* conceals exactly what Caliban did—and when he did it—to earn Prospero's enduring indignation by emphasizing a profound misunderstanding between them: "Recovering Something Christian about *The Tempest*," *Christianity and Literature* 50 (2000): 31–51, esp. 32–35, 40–45.

23 For helpful comment on these lines, see William M. Hamlin, *The Image of America in Montaigne, Spenser, and Shakespeare* (New York: St. Martin's, 1995), 117–18.

24 Popkin, *History of Scepticism*, 43–46. William Hamlin points out that Montaigne could not have used the "imbecility of reason to justify a leap of faith" if he had been a true Pyrrhonist; then Hamlin adds, "But it is by no means clear that Montaigne could have been a true Pyrrhonist. It is by no means clear that anyone can—or that the term is even coherent" (*Tragedy and Scepticism*, 65).

25 Popkin, *History of Scepticism*, xx–xxi.

26 A subtler development of Popkin's point is offered by Terence Penelhum, "Skepticism and Fideism," *The Skeptical Tradition*, ed. Myles Burnyeat (Berkeley: University of California Press, 1983), 287–318. Penelhum also

overstates his case, however. His conclusion, for example, that "the theologies of groundlessness and paradox have a Skeptic ancestry" (297) reckons without a long tradition of their ancestry in mysticism, long before the advent of Pyrrhonist skepticism in the sixteenth century.

27 René Descartes, *Meditations on First Philosophy*, trans. Donald A. Cress, 3rd ed. (Indianapolis: Hackett Publishing, 1993), 1.

28 Stanley Cavell, *Disowning Knowledge in Six Plays of Shakespeare* (Cambridge: Cambridge University Press, 1987), 35; Richard Strier, "Shakespeare and the Skeptics," *Religion and Literature* 32 (2000): 171–96 (quotation from 171). William Hamlin points out that Descartes's use of skepticism only as a method to achieve rational certainty actually makes him "less remarkable for his doubt than for the edifice of certainty his doubt enables him to build" (*Tragedy and Scepticism*, 145).

29 *Meditations*, 51. The quotation is from Meditation Six, "Concerning the Existence of Material Things, and the Real Distinction between Mind and Body," but Descartes had already anticipated this argument in his axiomatic recognition of himself as a thinking being in Mediation One: "I am therefore precisely nothing but a thinking being . . . . I am not that concatenation of members we call the human body" (19).

30 Pauline Kiernan, *Shakespeare's Theory of Drama* (Cambridge: Cambridge University Press, 1996). I use "essentially" unabashedly here, despite recent doubt that materialist criticism has cast on its applicability to Shakespeare. Jonathan Bate also challenges the materialists on this point, quoting Vives on the essence of human nature remaining unchanged (*Shakespeare and Ovid*, 6). Even though Bate's point is that Shakespeare seems more drawn to Ovid's notion of essential change than to Vives's static conception, embodiment is still essential to Ovid's vision of metamorphosis, which always involves transposition from one kind of body to another. Even in the closing lines of *The Metamorphoses*, where Ovid imagines the apotheosis of Augustus, he describes the emperor mounting to heaven and listening to the prayers of mortals.

31 Popkin, *History of Scepticism*, 180–81. Stuart Clark elaborates on Popkin's suggestion in *Thinking with Demons: The Idea of Witchcraft in Early Modern Europe* (Oxford: Clarendon, 1997), 174–75.

32 Clark, *Thinking with Demons*, 175.

33 Paul Jorgensen, *Our Naked Frailties: Sensational Art and Meaning in Macbeth* (Berkely: University of California Press, 1971), 153.

34 On the persistence of this view and its gradual change, see Michael MacDonald, "Religion, Social Change, and Psychological Healing in England, 1600–1800," in *The Church and Healing*, ed. W. L. Sheils (Oxford: Blackwell, 1982), 101–25.

35 On the difference between "supernatural" and "superhuman," see Clark, *Thinking with Demons*, 167–72. I think Richard Strier is right when he asserts that "*The Comedy of Errors* has an extraordinarily dark view of human intellectual capacity," but he states more than the evidence warrants when he asserts that "the play is startling in its skepticism about supernatural powers" ("Shakespeare and the Skeptics," 172–73, 174).

36 Pascal quotes a dramatist just once in the *Pensées*, and Corneille is the dramatist he quotes. See *Pensées*, ed. and trans. Roger Ariew (Indianapolis: Hackett, 2005), S32/L413. The *Pensées* are cited here in the customary fashion, with the "S" number referring to the edition of Philippe Sellier (Paris: Mercure, 1976), and "L" referring to the edition of Louis Lafuma in *Oeuvres complètes* (Paris: Edition du Seuil, 1963).

37 Blaise Pascal, *Pensées and The Provincial Letters* (New York: Modern Library, 1941), 615. Pascal conducted his debate with the Jesuits anonymously in a series of eighteen letters written over a period of two years (1656–1657). The quotation is from the eighteenth and last of the *Provincial Letters*. Given this kind of critique, it is not clear that Pascal refers indubitably in S443/L881 to the Roman Church, rather than to the City of God: "It is impossible for those who love God with all their heart to fail to recognize the Church; so evident is it."

38 Bernard Croquette, *Pascal et Mongaigne: Étude des réminiscences des essays dans l'oeuvre de Pascal* (Geneva: Droz, 1974).

39 Pascal also mentions Descartes in S118/L84 and S462/L553. In S164/L131, he seems to allude to the "demon hypothesis" of Descartes's *Meditations* in asserting that only faith (i.e., not reason, as Descartes had argued) offers certainty "as to whether man was created by a good God, by an evil demon, or by chance, so depending on our origin, it is doubtful whether these principles given to us are true, false, or uncertain."

40 Though Pascal eschewed Protestant heresies, he was profoundly influenced by the Augustinianism of the Jansenists of Port Royal, whom he defended against the Jesuits in *Provincial Letters* (a battle Pascal won, though the Jesuits won the war against the Jansenists), and his theology of grace is more closely tied to predestination than post-Tridentine theology was, because of Augustine's influence. For a helpful introduction, see Michael Moriarty, "Grace and religious belief in Pascal" in *The Cambridge Companion to Pascal*, ed. Nicholas Hammond (Cambridge: University of Cambridge Press, 2003), 144–161. On Pascal's knowledge and use of the Bible, which he eventually learned virtually by heart in its entirety, see André Gounelle, *La Bible selon Pascal* (Paris: Presses universitaires de France, 1970).

41 Not surprisingly, for a scientist and inventor, Pascal uses *la machine* in the *Pensées* more frequently and more complexly than Shakespeare uses

"machine." Shakespeare's one certain reference is Hamlet's designation of his body as a "machine" in a letter to Ophelia (2.2.124), which has no direct counterpart in the *Pensées*, but Pascal uses *la machine* to refer to the state apparatus, in the quotation above; in S118/L84 (entitled "Descartes"), he uses the word to refer to the whole sensible world; and in S617/L741, he refers to his mechanical calculator. Significantly, he also uses *la machine* to refer to the idea for which he is best known—his famous cosmic wager (S39/L5, S41/L7, S45/L11, S680/L418).

42   Jonathan Dollimore, *Radical Tragedy: Religion, Ideology and Power in the Drama of Shakespeare and His Contemporaries* (Brighton: Harvester, 1985), 17–19, 269–71. The whole of Dollimore's part III is called "Man Decentred" (153–246).

43   M. H. Abrams, *Natural Supernaturalism: Tradition and Revolution in Romantic Literature* (New York: Norton, 1971).

44   Dollimore's "empathy" is a twentieth-century neologism, as we noticed in chapter 3 n. 20 above. He uses "empathy" twice and "empathise" once in two pages (192–93).

45   The text in boldface is Isaiah 45:15, quoted by Pascal from the Vulgate: "*Vere tu es Deus absconditus.*"

46   John McDade SJ argues that Pascal's conception differs from Luther's, in that for Pascal the hiddenness of God "culminates, neither in the Incarnation nor the crucifixion, as in the Lutheran tradition, but in the Eucharist"; still, the two writers agree that the incarnation and crucifixion are key parts of the story, as Paul suggests in 1 Corinthians 1:25–29. See John McDade SJ, "Divine Disclosure and Concealment in Bach, Pascal and Levinas," *New Blackfriars* 85 (2004): 121–32 (quotation on 122).

47   David Wetsel, "Pascal and holy writ," in *The Cambridge Companion to Pascal*, ed. Nicholas Hammond (Cambridge: University of Cambridge Press, 2003), 162–81. Rosalind asserts that "The poor world is almost six thousand years old" (*As You Like It* 4.1.88–89), and Shakespeare probably thought it was as well, since all of his contemporaries did, but without his testimony one way or the other, we are free to indulge our assumption of his transcendent genius by imagining that he was more enlightened than the character he created.

WORKS CITED

Primary

Apius and Virginia. 1575. Edited by R. B. McKerrow. Chiswick Press for the Malone Society, 1911.

Aquinas. *Summa Theologica*. Translated by Dominican Fathers. 3 vols. New York: Benziger Brothers, 1947–1948.

Aristotle. *Nichomachean Ethics*. Translated by Martin Ostwald. Indianapolis: Bobbs-Merrill, 1962.

———. *Poetics*. Translated by Gerald F. Else. Ann Arbor: University of Michigan Press, 1973.

Bacon, Francis. *The Advancement of Learning. Francis Bacon: The Major Works*. Edited by Brian Vickers. Oxford: Oxford University Press, 1996.

Becon, Thomas. *The Displaying of the Popish Mass. Prayers and Other Pieces of Thomas Becon*. Edited by John Ayre for the Parker Society. Cambridge: Cambridge University Press, 1844.

Blackman, John. *Henry the Sixth: A Reprint of John Blacman's Memoir*. Edited by M. R. James. Cambridge: Cambridge University Press, 1919.

Bullough, Geoffrey, ed. *Narrative and Dramatic Sources of Shakespeare*. 8 vols. New York: Columbia University Press, 1957–1975.

Calvin, John. "On Civil Government." *Luther and Calvin on Secular Authority*. Edited by Harro Höpel. Cambridge: Cambridge University Press, 1991. 47–86.

Cicero. *De officiis*. Translated by Walter Miller. Loeb Classical Library. Cambridge, Mass.: Harvard University Press, 1947.

———. *On Duties*. Edited by M. T. Griffin and E. M. Atkins. Cambridge: Cambridge University Press, 1991.

Davies, John. *The Poems of Sir John Davies*. Edited by Robert Krueger. Oxford: Clarendon, 1975.

Descartes, René. *Meditations on First Philosophy*. Translated by Donald A. Cress. 3rd ed. Indianapolis: Hackett, 1993.

Dyke, Daniel. *The Mystery of Self-Deceiving: or, A Discourse and Discovery of the Deceitfulness of Man's Heart. Written by the late faithful Minister of Gods Word Daniel Dyke, Bachelor in Divinities*. London: Printed by William Stansby, 1630.

Erasmus. *The Colloquies of Erasmus*. Translated by Craig R. Thompson. Chicago: University of Chicago Press, 1965.

———. *Praise of Folly*. Translated by Betty Radice. Harmondsworth: Penguin, 1971.

——— *Querela Pacis*. In *The Collected Works of Erasmus*. Vol. 27. *Literary and Educational Writings*. Edited by A. H. T. Levi. Translated by Betty Radice. Toronto: University of Toronto Press, 1986.

"The First Part of the Sermon of Repentance." *The Two Books of Homilies*. Edited by John Griffiths. London: Oxford University Press, 1859.

The Geneva Bible. A facsimile of the 1560 edition. Madison: University of Wisconsin Press, 1969.

Hooker, Richard. *The Folger Library Edition of the Works of Richard Hooker*. Edited by W. Speed Hill. 7 vols. Cambridge, Mass.: Harvard University Press, 1977.

Horace. *Satires, Epistles, Ars Poetica*. Translated by H. Rushton Fairclough. Loeb Classical Library. Cambridge, Mass.: Harvard University Press, 1939.

Jonson, Ben. *The Devil Is an Ass*. Edited by Peter Happé. Revels edition. Manchester: Manchester University Press, 1994.

———. *Ben Jonson*. Edited by C. H. Herford and Percy and Evelyn Simpson. 11 vols. Oxford: Clarendon, 1925–1952.

Kant, Immanuel. *Grounding for the Metaphysics of Morals*. Translated by James W. Ellington. Indianapolis: Hackett, 1981.

King Robert of Sicily. *Middle English Metrical Romances*. Edited by W. H. French and C. B. Hale. 2 vols. New York: Russell & Russell, 1964.

Machiavelli, Niccolò. *Chief Works and Others*. Translated by Allan Gilbert. 3 vols. Durham, N.C.: Duke University Press, 1965.

Medieval Drama. Edited by David M. Bevington. Boston: Houghton Mifflin, 1975.

Montaigne, Michel de. *The Complete Essays of Montaigne*. Translated by Donald M. Frame. Stanford: Stanford University Press, 1965.

More, Sir Thomas. *History of King Richard the Third*. Edited by Richard Silvester. New Haven: Yale University Press, 1963.

———. *Translations of Lucian*. Edited by Craig R. Thompson. New Haven: Yale University Press, 1974.

———. *Utopia*. Edited by Edward Surtz and J. H. Hexter. New Haven: Yale University Press, 1965.

Nashe, Thomas. *Works*. Edited by Ronald B. McKerrow. Revised by F. P. Wilson. 5 vols. Oxford: Basil Blackwell, 1958.

Pascal, Blaise. *Pensées*. Edited by and Translated by Roger Ariew. Indianapolis: Hackett, 2005.

———. *Pensées and The Provincial Letters*. New York: Modern Library, 1941.

Peele, George. *The Love of King David and Fair Bethsabe*. Edited by Elmer Blistein. *Life and Works of George Peele*. 3 vols. New Haven: Yale University Press, 1952–1970.

Seneca. *Minor Dialogues and On Clemency*. Translated by Aubrey Steward. London: George Bell & Sons, 1889.

Shakespeare, William. *Complete Works*. Edited by David M. Bevington. 5th ed. New York: Pearson Longman, 2004.

———. *3 Henry VI*. Edited by Michael Hattaway. Cambridge: Cambridge University Press, 1993.

———. *Edward III*. Edited by Fred Lapides. New York: Garland, 1980.

———. *Henry V*. Edited by Gary Taylor. Oxford: Oxford University Press, 1982.

———. *Julius Caesar*. Edited by David Daniell. The Arden Shakespeare. London: Thomas Nelson, 1998.

———. *King Henry VI Part 1*. Edited by Edward Burns. The Arden Shakespeare. London: Thomson Learning, 2000.

———. *King Henry VI Part 3*. Edited by John D. Cox and Eric Rasmussen. The Arden Shakespeare. London: Thomson Learning, 2001.

———. *The Parallel King Lear 1608–1623*. Prepared by Michael Warren. Berkeley: University of California Press, 1989.

———. *Pericles*. Edited by Suzanne Gossett. The Arden Shakespeare. London: Thomson Learning, 2004.

———. *The Tempest*. Edited by Frank Kermode. The Arden Shakespeare. London: Methuen, 1954.

———. *The Tempest*. Edited by Virginia Mason Vaughan and Alden T. Vaughan. The Arden Shakespeare. London: Thomas Nelson, 1999.

———. *Titus Andronicus*. The Arden Shakespeare. Edited by Jonathan Bate. London and New York: Routledge, 1995.

———. *Troilus and Cressida*. Edited by David M. Bevington. The Arden Shakespeare. London: Thomas Nelson, 1998.

Shakespeare, William, and John Fletcher. *King Henry VIII (All Is True)*. Edited by Gordon McMullan. The Arden Shakespeare. London: Thomson Learning, 2000.

Sidney, Sir Philip. *An Apology for Poetry. Elizabethan Critical Essays*. Edited by G. G. Smith. 2 vols. Oxford: Clarendon, 1904.

Spenser, Edmund. *The Faerie Queene*. Edited by J. C. Smith. 2 vols. Oxford: Clarendon, 1909.

Tyndale, William *The Parable of the Wicked Mammon*. 1527. *The Works of the English Reformers*. Edited by Thomas Russell. 3 vols. London: Ebenezer Palmer, 1831.

Secondary

Abel, Lionel. *Metatheatre: A New View of Dramatic Form*. New York: Hill & Wang, 1963.

Abrams, M. H. *Natural Supernaturalism: Tradition and Revolution in Romantic Literature*. New York: Norton, 1971.

Adelman, Janet. *The Common Liar: An Essay on* Antony and Cleopatra. New Haven: Yale University Press, 1973.

Altman, Joel B. *The Tudor Play of Mind*. Berkeley & Los Angeles: University of California Press, 1978.

Anson, John. *"Julius Caesar:* The Politics of the Hardened Heart." *Shakespeare Studies* 2 (1966): 11–33.

Auerbach, Erich. *"Sermo Humilis." Literary Language and Its Public in Late Latin Antiquity and in the Middle Ages*. Translated by Ralph Manheim. New York: Pantheon Books, 1965.

Baker, Howard. *Induction to Tragedy*. University: Louisiana State University Press, 1939.

Ball, Bryan W. *A Great Expectation: Eschatological Thought in English Protestantism to 1660*. Leiden: E. J. Brill, 1975.

Barish, Jonas. *The Antitheatrical Prejudice*. Berkeley: University of California Press, 1981.

Barroll, J. Leeds. "Shakespeare and Roman History." *Modern Language Review* 53 (1958): 327–43.

———. "The Characterization of Octavius." *Shakespeare Studies* 6 (1970): 231–88.

Barton, Anne. "Livy, Machiavelli, and Shakespeare's Coriolanus." *Shakespeare Survey* 38 (1985): 115–29.

Bate, Jonathan. *Shakespeare and Ovid*. Oxford: Clarendon, 1993.

Battenhouse, Roy W. *"Measure for Measure* and the Christian Doctrine of the Atonement." *PMLA* 66 (1946): 1029–59.

———. "Shakespearean Tragedy: A Christian Interpretation." *Tragic Vision and the Christian Faith*. Edited by Nathan O. Scott. New York: Association Press, 1957. 56–98.

———. *Shakespearean Tragedy: Its Art and Its Christian Premises*. Bloomington: Indiana University Press, 1969.

Bawcutt, N. W. "Did Shakespeare Read Machiavelli?" Paper presented at the World Shakespeare Congress. Valencia, April 2001.

Beauregard, David. "Shakespeare and the Bible." *Religion and the Arts* 5 (2001): 317–30.

Beckwith, Sarah. "Shakespeare's Resurrections." Paper presented at the meeting of the Shakespeare Association of America. Philadelphia, April 2006.

———. *Signifying God: Social Relation and Symbolic Act in the York Corpus Christi Plays.* Chicago: University of Chicago Press, 2001.

Berger, Harry. *Making Trifles of Terrors: Redistributing Complicities in Shakespeare.* Edited by Peter Erickson. Stanford: Stanford University Press, 1997.

Bergeron, David M. "*Cymbeline*: Shakespeare's Last Roman Play." *Shakespeare Quarterly* 31 (1980): 31–41.

Berry, Edward I. *Patterns of Decay: Shakespeare's Early Histories.* Charlottesville: University Press of Virginia, 1975.

Bethel, S. L. *Shakespeare and the Popular Tradition.* London: Staples, 1944.

Bevington, David M. *From Mankind to Marlowe: Growth of Structure in the Popular Drama of Tudor England.* Cambridge, Mass.: Harvard University Press, 1962.

———. "Shakespeare vs. Jonson on Satire." In *Shakespeare 1971: Proceedings of the World Shakespeare Congress.* Edited by Clifford Leech and J. M. R. Margeson. Toronto: University of Toronto Press, 1971. 107–22.

———. *Tudor Drama and Politics: A Critical Approach to Topical Meaning.* Cambridge, Mass.: Harvard University Press, 1968.

Bishop, T. G. *Shakespeare and the Theatre of Wonder.* Cambridge: Cambridge University Press, 1996.

Blits, Jan H. *Spirit, Soul and City: Shakespeare's Coriolanus.* Lanham, Md.: Lexington Books, 2006.

Bloom, Allan. *Love and Friendship.* New York: Simon & Schuster, 1993.

Boas, Frederick S. *Shakspere and His Predecessors.* London: John Murray, 1896.

Braden, Gordon. *Renaissance Tragedy and the Senecan Tradition: Anger's Privilege.* New Haven: Yale University Press, 1985.

Bradley, A. C. *Shakespearean Tragedy.* London: Macmillan, 1904.

Bradshaw, Graham. *Misrepresentations: Shakespeare and the Materialists.* Ithaca, New York: Cornell University Press, 1993.

———. *Shakespeare's Scepticism.* Brighton: Harvester, 1987.

Brockbank, J. P. "History and Histrionics in *Cymbeline*." *Shakespeare Survey* 11 (1958): 42–49.

Brown, Carolyn E. "The Wooing of Duke Vincentio and Isabella of *Measure for Measure*: 'The Image of It Gives [Them] Content.' " *Shakespeare Survey* 22 (1994): 189–219.

Bruns, Gerald L. "Stanley Cavell's Shakespeare." *Critical Inquiry* 16 (1990): 612–32.

Cacicedo, Alberto. " 'She is Fast my Wife': Sex, Marriage, and Ducal Authority in *Measure for Measure*." *Shakespeare Studies* 23 (1995): 187–209.

Calderwood, James. *Metadrama in Shakespeare's Henriad:* Richard II *to* Henry V. Berkeley: University of California Press, 1979.

———. *Shakespearean Metadrama.* Minneapolis: University of Minnesota Press, 1971.

Calderwood, James. *To Be or Not To Be: Negation and Metadrama in* Hamlet. New York: Columbia University Press, 1983.

Campbell, Oscar. *Comicall Satyre and Shakespeare's "Troilus and Cressida"*. San Marino, Calif.: Huntington Library, 1938.

Capell, Edward. *Notes and Various Readings to Shakespeare*. 4 vols. London: Printed for Edward and Charles Dilly, 1774.

Cave, Terence. "Imagining Scepticism in the Sixteenth Century." *Journal of the Institute of Romance Studies* 1 (1992): 193–205.

Cavell, Stanley. *The Claim of Reason: Wittgenstein, Skepticism, Morality, and Tragedy*. Oxford: Oxford University Press, 1979.

———. *Disowning Knowledge in Six Plays of Shakespeare*. Cambridge: Cambridge University Press, 1987.

———. *"Knowing and Acknowledging." Must We Mean What We Say?* Cambridge: Cambridge University Press, 1969. 238–66.

Chambers, E. K. *The Elizabethan Stage*. 4 vols. Oxford: Clarendon, 1923.

Chambers, R. W. *Man's Unconquerable Mind*. London: Jonathan Cape, 1939.

Cheney, Patrick. "Shakespeare's Counter-Laureate Authorship: The Spear of Achilles." Paper presented at the meeting of the Shakespeare Association of America. Bermuda, April 2005.

Chrimes, S. B. *Henry VII*. Berkeley: University of California Press, 1972.

Clark, Stuart. *Thinking with Demons: The Idea of Witchcraft in Early Modern Europe*. Oxford: Clarendon, 1997.

Coghill, Nevill. "Comic Form in *Measure for Measure*." *Shakespeare Survey* 8 (1955): 14–27.

Colley, John Scott. "Disguise and New Guise in *Cymbeline*." *Shakespeare Studies* 7 (1974): 233–52.

Collinson, Patrick. *Elizabethans*. London: Hambledon & London, 2003.

Cox, John D. *The Devil and the Sacred in English Drama, 1350–1642*. Cambridge: Cambridge University Press, 2000.

———. "Recovering Something Christian about *The Tempest*." *Christianity and Literature* 50 (2000): 31–51.

———. *Shakespeare and the Dramaturgy of Power*. Princeton: Princeton University Press, 1989.

———. "Was Shakespeare a Christian, and If So, What Kind of Christian Was He?" *Christianity and Literature* 55 (2006): 539–66.

Crewe, Jonathan V. "God or the Good Physician: The Rational Playwright in *The Comedy of Errors*." *Genre* 15 (1982): 203–23.

Croquette, Bernard. *Pascal et Mongaigne: Étude des réminiscences des essays dans l'oeuvre de Pascal*. Geneva: Droz, 1974.

Cunliffe, J. W. *The Influence of Seneca on Elizabethan Tragedy*. London: Macmillan, 1893.

Danby, John F. *Poets on Fortune's Hill.* London: Faber & Faber, 1952.

Daniell, David. "The Good Marriage of Katherine and Petruchio." *Shakespeare Survey* 37 (1984): 23–31.

Davidson, Clifford. "Saint Plays and Pageants of Medieval Britain." *Early Drama, Art, and Music Newsletter* 22 (1999): 11–37.

Davidson, Nicholas. "Christopher Marlowe and Atheism." In *Christopher Marlowe and the English Renaissance.* Edited by Darryll Grantley and Peter Roberts. Aldershot: Scolar Press, 1996. 129–47.

Deane, Herbert A. *The Political and Social Ideas of St. Augustine.* New York: Columbia University Press, 1963.

Dessen, Alan. "Staging Ideas and Abstractions: Revisiting Shakespeare's Theatrical Vocabulary." Paper presented at the International Shakespeare Conference. Stratford-upon-Avon, 2006.

Diehl, Houston. *Staging Reform, Reforming the Stage.* Ithaca: Cornell University Press, 1997.

Dollimore, Jonathan. *Radical Tragedy: Religion, Ideology and Power in the Drama of Shakespeare and His Contemporaries.* Chicago: University of Chicago Press, 1984.

Duffy, Eamon. *The Stripping of the Altars: Traditional Religion in England 1400–1580.* New Haven: Yale University Press, 1992.

Edwards, Philip. *Shakespeare and the Confines of Art.* London: Methuen, 1968.

Egan, Robert. *Drama within Drama: Shakespeare's Sense of His Art in* King Lear, The Winter's Tale, *and* The Tempest. New York: Columbia University Press, 1975.

Elam, Keir. *The Semiotics of Theatre and Drama.* London: Methuen, 1980.

Eliot, T. S. *Shakespeare and the Stoicism of Seneca.* London: Oxford University Press for the Shakespeare Association, 1927.

Ellrodt, Robert. "Self-Consciousness in Montaigne and Shakespeare." *Shakespeare Survey* 28 (1975): 37–50.

Elton, William R. *King Lear and the Gods.* San Marino: Huntington Library, 1966.

Evans, Robert O. *The Osier Cage: Rhetorical Devices in* Romeo and Juliet. Lexington: University of Kentucky Press, 1966.

Everett, Barbara. "The New *King Lear.*" *Critical Quarterly* 2 (1960): 325–39.

Ewbank, Inga-Stina. "The House of David in Renaissance Drama." *Renaissance Drama* 8 (1965): 3–40.

Faas, Ekbert. *Shakespeare's Poetics.* Cambridge: Cambridge University Press, 1986.

Felperin, Howard. *Shakespearean Romance.* Princeton: Princeton University Press, 1972.

Fine, Gail. "Descartes and Ancient Skepticism: Reheated Cabbage?" *Philosophical Review* 109 (2000): 195–234.

Fingarette, Herbert. *Self-Deception*. London: Routledge & Kegan Paul, 1969.

Fisch, Harold. *The Biblical Presence in Shakespeare, Milton, and Blake*. Oxford: Clarendon, 1999.

Fish, Stanley. "How To Do Things with Austin and Searle: Speech-Act Theory and Literary Criticism." In *Is There a Text in This Class?* Cambridge, Mass.: Harvard University Press, 1980. 197–245.

Fly, Richard. "The Evolution of Shakespearean Metadrama: Abel, Burckhardt, and Calderwood." *Comparative Drama* 20 (1986): 124–39.

Foakes, R. A. *Hamlet Versus Lear: Cultural Politics and Shakespeare's Art*. Cambridge: Cambridge University Press, 1993.

Forker, Charles. "How Did Shakespeare Come By His Books?" *Shakespeare Yearbook* 14 (2004): 109–20.

Freedman, Barbara. "Egeon's Debt: Self-Division and Self-Redemption in *The Comedy of Errors*." *English Literary Renaissance* 10 (1980): 360–83.

French, A. L. "Henry VI and the Ghost of Richard II." *English Studies* 50 (1969): Anglo-American Supplement, xxvii–xliii.

———. "Joan of Arc and Henry VI." *English Studies* 29 (1969): 425–29.

———. "The Mills of God and Shakespeare's Early History Plays." *English Studies* 55 (1974): 313–24.

———. "Who Deposed Richard the Second?" *Essays in Criticism* 17 (1967): 411–33.

———. "The World of Richard III." *Shakespeare Studies* 4 (1969): 25–39.

Frey, David L. *The First Tetralogy, Shakespeare's Scrutiny of the Tudor Myth: A Dramatic Exploration of Divine Providence*. The Hague: Mouton, 1976.

Frye, Northrop. *Anatomy of Criticism*. Princeton: Princeton University Press, 1957.

———. "The Argument of Comedy." In *English Institute Essays 1948*. New York: Columbia University Press, 1949. 58–73.

———. *Fools of Time: Studies in Shakespearean Tragedy*. Toronto: University of Toronto Press, 1967.

———. *A Natural Perspective: The Development of Shakespearean Comedy and Romance*. New York: Columbia University Press, 1965.

Frye, Roland Mushat. *Shakespeare and Christian Doctrine*. Princeton: Princeton University Press, 1963.

Gardiner, Harold C. *Mysteries' End: An Investigation of the Last Days of the Medieval Religious Stage*. New Haven: Yale University Press, 1946.

Goddard, Harold. *The Meaning of Shakespeare*. Chicago: University of Chicago Press, 1951.

Goldman, Michael. *Shakespeare and the Energies of Drama*. Princeton: Princeton University Press, 1972.

Gordon, Walter M. *Humanist Play and Belief: The Seriocomic Art of Desiderius Erasmus*. Toronto: University of Toronto Press, 1990.

Gounelle, André. *La Bible selon Pascal.* Paris: Presses universitaires de France, 1970.

Grady, Hugh. *Shakespeare, Machiavelli, and Montaigne: Power and Subjectivity from* Richard II *to* Hamlet. Oxford: Oxford University Press, 2002.

Greenblatt, Stephen. *Hamlet in Purgatory.* Princeton: Princeton University Press, 2001.

———. "Invisible Bullets." In *Shakespearean Negotiations: The Circulation of Social Energy in Renaissance England.* Berkeley: University of California Press, 1988. 21–65.

———. "Murdering Peasants: Status, Genre, and the Representation of Rebellion." In *Learning to Curse: Essays in Early Modern Culture.* London: Routledge, 1990. 99–130.

———. *Renaissance Self-Fashioning.* Chicago: University of Chicago Press, 1980.

———. *Will in the World: How Shakespeare Became Shakespeare.* New York: W. W. Norton, 2004.

Greg, W. W. "Hamlet's Hallucination." *Modern Language Review* 12 (1917): 393–421.

Groeneveld, Leanne. "Christ as Image in the Croxton Play of the Sacrament." *Research Opportunities in Renaissance Drama* 40 (2001): 190.

Hamlin, William M. *The Image of America in Montaigne, Spenser, and Shakespeare.* New York: St. Martin's, 1995.

———. "A Lost Translation Found? An Edition of *The Sceptick.* c. 1590. Based on Extant Manuscripts [with Text]." *English Literary Renaissance* 31 (2001): 34–51.

———. *Tragedy and Scepticism in Shakespeare's England.* Basingstoke: Palgrave Macmillan, 2005.

Harbage, Alfred. *As They Liked It: An Essay on Shakespeare and Morality.* New York: Macmillan, 1947.

Harmon, Alice. "How Great Was Shakespeare's Debt to Montaigne?" *PMLA* 57 (1942): 988–1008.

Hart, Alfred. *Shakespeare and the Homilies.* Melbourne: Melbourne University Press, 1934.

Hassel, R. Chris. *Faith and Folly in Shakespeare's Romantic Comedies.* Athens: University of Georgia Press, 1980.

Hattaway, Michael. "Swearing and Forswearing in Shakespeare's Histories: The Playwright as Contra-Machiavel." *Review of English Studies* (2000): 208–29.

Haugaard, William P. *Elizabeth and the English Reformation.* Cambridge: Cambridge University Press, 1968.

Haydn, Hiram. *The Counter-Renaissance.* New York: Scribner, 1950.

Held, Julius S. *Rembrandt's Aristotle and Other Rembrandt Studies.* Princeton: Princeton University Press, 1969.

Henze, Richard. "*A Midsummer Night's Dream*: Analogous Image." Shakespeare Studies 7 (1974): 115–23.

Holland, Norman. "*Measure for Measure*: The Duke and the Prince." *Comparative Literature* 11 (1959): 16–20.

Houlbrooke, Ralph A. *The English Family 1450–1700*. London: Longman, 1984.

Houliston, Victor. "The Hare and the Drum: Robert Persons's Writings on the English Succession, 1593–96." *Renaissance Studies* 14 (2000): 235–50.

Hubert, Judd D. *Metatheater: The Example of Shakespeare*. Lincoln: University of Nebraska Press, 1991.

Hughes, Philip Edgcumbe. *Theology of the English Reformers*. London: Hodder and Stoughton, 1965.

Hunter, Michael. "The Problem of 'Atheism' in Early Modern England." *Transactions of the Royal Historical Society* 35 (1985): 135–57.

Hunter, R. G. *Shakespeare and the Comedy of Forgiveness*. New York: Columbia University Press, 1965.

James, Mervyn. "Ritual, Drama and Social Body in the Late Medieval English Town." *Past and Present* 98 (1983): 3–29.

Johnson, Samuel. *Johnson on Shakespeare*. Edited by Arthur Sherbo and Bernard H. Bronson (1968). Vols. 7 and 8 of *The Yale Edition of the Works of Samuel Johnson*. New Haven: Yale University Press, 1958–1990.

Jones, Emrys. *The Origins of Shakespeare*. Oxford: Clarendon, 1977.

Jorgensen, Paul A. *Lear's Self-Discovery*. Berkeley: University of California Press, 1967.

———. *Our Naked Frailties: Sensational Art and Meaning in* Macbeth. Berkeley: University of California Press, 1971.

Kahn, Coppélia. *Roman Shakespeare: Warriors, Wounds, and Women*. London: Routledge, 1997.

Kahn, Victoria. *Machiavellian Rhetoric from the Counter-Reformation to Milton*. Princeton: Princeton University Press, 1994.

Kallendorf, Hilaire. *Exorcism and Its Texts*. Toronto: University of Toronto Press, 2003.

Kastan, David Scott. *Shakespeare and the Shapes of Time*. Hanover: University Press of New England, 1982.

Kathman, David. "Reconsidering *The Seven Deadly Sins*." *Early Theatre* 7 (2004): 13–44.

Kaufmann, R. J., and Clifford J. Ronan. "Shakespeare's *Julius Caesar*: An Apollonian and Comparative Reading." *Comparative Drama* 4 (1970): 18–51.

Kernan, Alvin B. "*Othello*: An Introduction." In *Modern Shakespearean Criticism*. Edited by Alvin B. Kernan. New York: Harcourt, Brace & World, 1970. 351–60.

———. *The Playwright as Magician: Shakespeare's Image of the Poet in the English Public Theater.* New Haven: Yale University Press, 1979.

Kiernan, Pauline. *Shakespeare's Theory of Drama.* Cambridge: Cambridge University Press, 1996.

King, John. *English Reformation Literature: The Tudor Origins of the Protestant Tradition.* Princeton: Princeton University Press, 1982.

King, Ross. *Brunelleschi's Dome.* London: Chatto & Windus, 2000.

Kinney, Arthur F. *Markets of Bawdrie: The Dramatic Criticism of Stephen Gosson.* Salzburg: Institut für Englische Sprache und Literatur, 1974.

Knapp, Jeffrey. *Shakespeare's Tribe: Church, Nation, and Theater in Renaissance England.* Chicago: University of Chicago Press, 2002.

Knight, G. Wilson. "*Measure for Measure* and the Gospels." Chapter 4 in *The Wheel of Fire.* London: Methuen, 1949 [1930]. 73–96.

Kott, Jan. *Shakespeare Our Contemporary.* Translated by Boleslaw Taborski. New York: Doubleday, 1964.

Lake, Peter. *Anglicans and Puritans?* London: Unwin Hyman, 1988.

———. "From Leicester His Commonwealth to Sejanus His Fall: Ben Jonson and the Politics of Roman (Catholic) Virtue." In *Catholics and the "Protestant Nation."* Edited by Ethan Shagan. Manchester: Manchester University Press, 2005. 128–61.

Lake, Peter, and Michael Questier. *The Antichrist's Lewd Hat: Protestants, Papists and Players in Post-Reformation England.* New Haven: Yale University Press, 2002.

Leggatt, Alexander. "Substitution in *Measure for Measure.*" *Shakespeare Quarterly* 39 (1988): 342–59.

Levin, Harry. "Form and Formality in *Romeo and Juliet.*" *Shakespeare Quarterly* 11 (1960): 3–11.

Limon, Jerzy. "Shakespeare the Semiotician, or, How to Create Something out of Aery Nothing." Paper read at the International Shakespeare Conference. Stratford-upon-Avon, July 26, 2004.

MacDonald, Michael. "Religion, Social Change, and Psychological Healing in England, 1600–1800." In *The Church and Healing.* Edited by W. L. Sheils. Oxford: Blackwell, 1982. 101–25.

Mack, Maynard. "The Jacobean Shakespeare: Some Observations on the Construction of the Tragedies." In *Jacobean Theatre.* Edited by John Russell Brown and Bernard Harris. London: Edward Arnold, 1960. 11–41.

———. *King Lear in Our Time.* Berkeley: University of California Press, 1965.

Manheim, Michael. *The Weak King Dilemma in the Shakespearean History Play.* Syracuse, N.Y.: Syracuse University Press, 1973.

Marcus, Leah. *Puzzling Shakespeare: Local Reading and Its Discontents.* Berkeley: University of California Press, 1988.

Marsh, Christopher. *The Family of Love in English Society, 1550–1630.* Cambridge: Cambridge University Press, 1994.

Martin, Mike W. *Love's Virtues.* Lawrence: University of Kansas Press, 1996.

———. *Self-Deception and Morality.* Lawrence: University Press of Kansas, 1986.

Martin, Randall, and John D. Cox. "Who Is 'Somerville' in *3 Henry VI?*" *Shakespeare Quarterly* 51(2000): 332–52.

Marx, Steven. *Shakespeare and the Bible.* Oxford: Oxford University Press, 2000.

Maus, Katharine Eisaman. *Inwardness and Theater in the English Renaissance.* Chicago: University of Chicago Press, 1995.

McAlindon, Tom. "Swearing and Forswearing in Shakespeare's Histories: The Playwright as Contra-Machiavel." *Review of English Studies* 51 (2000): 208–29.

McDade, John, SJ. "Divine Disclosure and Concealment in Bach, Pascal and Levinas." *New Blackfriars* 85 (2004): 121–32.

McElroy, Bernard. *Shakespeare's Mature Tragedies.* Princeton: Princeton University Press, 1973.

McGuire, Philip C. *Speechless Dialect: Shakespeare's Open Silences.* Berkeley: University of California Press, 1985.

Meijer, Marianne S. "Montaigne et la Bible." *Bulletin de la Société des amis de Montaigne* 20 (1976): 23–57.

Miles, Geoffrey. *Shakespeare and the Constant Romans.* Oxford: Clarendon, 1996.

Mills, David. *Staging the Chester Cycle.* Leeds: University of Leeds School of English, 1985.

Miola, Robert S. *Shakespeare and Classical Tragedy: The Influence of Seneca.* Oxford: Clarendon, 1992.

———. *Shakespeare's Rome.* Cambridge: Cambridge University Press, 1983.

Moffett, Robin. "*Cymbeline* and the Nativity." *Shakespeare Quarterly* 13 (1962): 207–18.

Moriarty, Michael. "Grace and Religious Belief in Pascal." In *The Cambridge Companion to Pascal.* Edited by Nicholas Hammond. Cambridge: University of Cambridge Press, 2003. 144–61.

Morris, Harry. *Last Things in Shakespeare.* Tallahassee: Florida State University Press, 1985.

Neale, J. E. *Elizabeth I and Her Parliaments.* 2 vols. 1559–1581 and 1584–1601. New York: St. Martin's, 1958.

———. *Queen Elizabeth.* London: Jonathan Cape, 1934.

Nicholls, Graham. *Measure for Measure: Text and Performance.* Basingstoke: Macmillan, 1986.

Nussbaum, Martha. *The Fragility of Goodness: Luck and Ethics in Greek Tragedy and Philosophy.* 2nd ed. Cambridge: Cambridge University Press, 2001.

———. *Love's Knowledge: Essays on Philosophy and Literature.* New York: Oxford University Press, 1990.

Olsen, Thomas G. "Iachimo's 'Drug-Damn'd Italy' and the Problem of British National Character in *Cymbeline*." *Shakespeare Yearbook* 10 (1999): 168–96.

Orgel, Stephen. *The Jonsonian Masque*. Cambridge, Mass.: Harvard University Press, 1965.

Orr, Robert. "The Time Motif in Machiavelli." In *Machiavelli and the Nature of Political Thought*. Edited by Martin Fleisher. London: Croom Helm, 1973. 185–208.

Parker, Patricia. "Romance and Empire: Anachronistic *Cymbeline*." In *Unfolded Tales: Essays on Renaissance Romance*. Edited by George M. Logan and Gorgon Teskey. Ithaca: Cornell University Press, 1989. 189–207.

———. *Shakespeare from the Margins: Language, Culture, Context*. Chicago: University of Chicago Press, 1996.

Penelhum, Terence. "Skepticism and Fideism." In *The Skeptical Tradition*. Edited by Myles Burnyeat. Berkeley: University of California Press, 1983. 287–318.

Pfister, Manfred. "Elizabethan Atheism: Discourse without Subject." *Deutsche Shakespeare Jahrbuch* 127 (1991): 59–81.

Pierce, Robert B. "Shakespeare and the Ten Modes of Scepticism." *Shakespeare Survey* 46 (1993): 145–58.

Pitcher, John. "The Poet and Taboo: The Riddle of Shakespeare's *Pericles*." *Essays and Studies* 35 (1982): 14–29.

Pitkin, Hanna Fenichel. *Fortune Is a Woman: Gender and Politics in the Thought of Niccolò Machiavelli*. Berkeley: University of California Press, 1984.

Platt, Michael. *Rome and Romans According to Shakespeare*. Lanham, Md.: University Press of America, 1983.

Pocock, J. G. A. *The Machiavellian Moment*. Princeton: Princeton University Press, 1975.

Popkin, Richard H. *The History of Scepticism from Erasmus to Spinoza*. Berkeley: University of California Press, 1979.

Quinones, Ricardo J. *The Renaissance Discovery of Time*. Cambridge, Mass.: Harvard University Press, 1972.

Raab, Felix. *The English Face of Machiavelli*. London: Routledge & Kegan Paul, 1964.

Rasmussen, Eric. "*The Black Book* and the Date of *Doctor Faustus*." *Notes and Queries* 235, n.s. 37 (1990): 168–70.

Reese, M. M. *The Cease of Majesty: A Study of Shakespeare's History Plays*. New York: St. Martin's, 1962.

Rice, Colin. *Ungodly Delights: Puritan Opposition to the Theatre 1576–1633*. Genova: Edizioni dell'Orso, 1997.

Richmond, Hugh. "Shakespeare's Roman Trilogy: The Climax in *Cymbeline*." *Studies in the Literary Imagination* 5 (1972): 129–39.

Ricoeur, Paul. "Interpretation as Exercise of Suspicion." In *Freud and Philosophy*. Translated by Denis Savage. New Haven: Yale University Press, 1970. 31–36.

Riess, Amy J., and George Walton Williams. "'Tragical Mirth': from *Romeo* to *Dream*." *Shakespeare Quarterly* 43 (1992): 214–28.

Righter [Barton], Anne. *Shakespeare and the Idea of the Play*. London: Chatto & Windus, 1962.

Rist, J. M. *Stoic Philosophy*. Cambridge: Cambridge University Press, 1966.

Ritter, Gerhard. *The Corrupting Influence of Power*. London: Tower Bridge, 1952.

Robinson, Christopher. *Lucian and His Influence*. Chapel Hill: University of North Carolina Press, 1979.

Roe, John. *Shakespeare and Machiavelli*. Cambridge: D. S. Brewer, 2002.

Ronan, Clifford. *"Antike Roman": Power Symbology and the Roman Play in Early Modern England, 1585–1635*. Athens: University of Georgia Press, 1995.

Sanderson, James L. "Patience in *The Comedy of Errors*." *Texas Studies in Literature and Language* 16 (1975): 603–18.

Schmidt, C. B. "The Rediscovery of Ancient Skepticism in Modern Times." In *The Skeptical Tradition*. Edited by Myles Burnyeat. Berkeley: University of California Press, 1983. 225–51.

Seaton, Ethel. "*Antony and Cleopatra* and the Book of Revelation." *Review of English Studies* 22 (1946): 219–24.

Shaheen, Naseeb. *Biblical References in Shakespeare's Plays*. Newark: University of Delaware Press, 1999.

Shuger, Debora. *Habits of Thought in the English Renaissance*. Berkeley: University of California Press, 1990.

———. *Political Theologies in Shakespeare's England: The Sacred and the State in Measure for Measure*. Basingstoke: Palgrave, 2001.

———. "Subversive Fathers and Suffering Subjects: Shakespeare and Christianity." In *Religion Literature, and Politics in Post-Reformation England, 1540–1688*. Edited by Donna B. Hamilton and Richard Strier. Cambridge: Cambridge University Press, 1996. 46–69.

Simmons, J. L. *Shakespeare's Pagan World*. Charlottesville: University Press of Virginia, 1973.

Simon, Caroline J. *The Disciplined Heart: Love, Destiny, and Imagination*. Grand Rapids: Eerdmans, 1997.

Sinfield, Alan, and Jonathan Dollimore, eds. *Political Shakespeare: New Essays in Cultural Materialism*. Ithaca: Cornell University Press, 1985.

Skelton, John. *Magnificence*. Edited by Paula Neuss. Revel Plays. Manchester: Manchester University Press, 1980.

Snyder, Susan. *The Comic Matrix of Shakespeare's Tragedies*. Princeton: Princeton University Press, 1979.

———. "*King Lear* and the Prodigal Son." *Shakespeare Quarterly* 17 (1966): 361–69.

Sommers, Alan. "'Wilderness of Tigers': Structure and Symbolism in *Titus Andronicus.*" *Essays in Criticism* 10 (1960): 250–74.

Sommerville, C. John, and John Edwards. "Debate: Religious Faith, Doubt and Atheism." *Past and Present* 128 (1990): 152–61.

Spiekerman, Tim. *Shakespeare's Political Realism.* Albany: State University of New York Press, 2001.

Spivack, Bernard. *Shakespeare and the Allegory of Evil.* New York: Columbia University Press, 1958.

States, Bert O. *Great Reckonings in Little Rooms: On the Phenomenology of Theater.* Berkeley: University of California Press, 1985.

Strier, Richard. "Shakespeare and the Skeptics." *Religion and Literature* 32 (2000): 171–96.

Sullivan, Vickie. "Princes to Act: Henry V as the Machiavellian Prince of Appearance." In *Shakespeare's Political Pageant: Essays in Literature and Politics.* Edited by Joseph Alulis and Vickie Sullivan. Lanham, Md.: Rowman & Littlefield, 1996. 125–51.

Thompson, W. D. J. Cargill. "The Philosopher of the 'Politic Society': Richard Hooker as a Political Thinker." In *Studies in Richard Hooker.* Edited by W. Speed Hill. Cleveland: Case Western Reserve University, 1972. 3–76.

Tillyard, E. M. W. *The Elizabethan World Picture.* London: Chatto & Windus, 1943.

———. *Shakespeare's History Plays.* London: Chatto & Windus, 1944.

Tonning, Judith E. "'Like This Insubstantial Pageant, Faded': Eschatology and Theatricality in *The Tempest.*" *Literature and Theology* 18 (2004): 371–82.

Tracy, James D. *The Politics of Erasmus.* Toronto: University of Toronto Press, 1978.

Traversi, Derek. "Shakespeare and Machiavelli: Some Thoughts on Shakespeare's Early History Plays." *Jadavpur University English Essays and Studies* 3 (1980): 18–31.

Turner, Frederick. *Shakespeare and the Nature of Time: Moral and Philosophical Themes in Some Plays and Poems by William Shakespeare.* Oxford: Clarendon, 1971.

Vawter, Marvin L. "'Division 'tween Our Souls': Shakespeare's Stoic Brutus." *Shakespeare Studies* 7 (1974): 173–95.

Velz, John. "From Jerusalem to Damascus: Bilocal Dramaturgy in Medieval and Shakespearian Conversion Plays." *Comparative Drama* 15 (1981): 311–25.

———. "Undular Structure in *Julius Caesar.*" *Modern Language Review* 66 (1971): 21–30.

Waith, Eugene M. *The Pattern of Tragicomedy in Beaumont and Fletcher.* New Haven: Yale University Press, 1952.

Weiner, Andrew D. *Sir Philip Sidney and the Poetics of Protestantism.* Minneapolis: University of Minnesota Press, 1978.

Wells, Charles. *The Wide Arch: Roman Values in Shakespeare.* New York: St. Martins, 1992.

Wells, Robin Headlam. "*Julius Caesar*, Machiavelli, and the Uses of History." *Shakespeare Survey* 55 (2002): 209–18.

Wetsel, David. "Pascal and Holy Writ." In *The Cambridge Companion to Pascal.* Edited by Nicholas Hammond. Cambridge: University of Cambridge Press, 2003. 162–81.

Whitaker, Virgil. *Shakespeare's Use of Learning: An Inquiry into the Growth of His Mind and Art.* San Marino, Calif.: Huntington Library, 1964.

White, Paul Whitfield. *Theatre and Reformation: Protestantism, Patronage, and Playing in Tudor England.* Cambridge: Cambridge University Press, 1993.

Wickham, Glynne. "Masque and Anti-masque in *The Tempest*." *Essays and Studies* 28 (1975): 1–14.

Wierum, Ann. "'Actors' and 'Play Acting' in the Morality Tradition." *Renaissance Drama*, n.s. 3 (1970): 189–214.

Williams, George Walton. "Petitionary Prayer in King Lear." *South Atlantic Quarterly* 85 (1986): 360–73.

Wilson, John Dover. *What Happens in* Hamlet. Cambridge: Cambridge University Press, 1935.

Wineke, Donald R. "The Relevance of Machiavelli to Shakespeare: A Discussion of *1 Henry VI*." *Clio* 13 (1983): 17–36.

Wolffe, Bertram. *Henry VI.* London: Eyre Methuen, 1981.

Woodes, Nathaniel. *The Conflict of Conscience.* Edited by Herbert Davis and F. P. Wilson. Malone Society Reprints. Oxford: Oxford University Press, 1952.

Young, David. *The Heart's Forest: A Study of Shakespeare's Pastoral Plays.* New Haven: Yale University Press, 1972.

———. *Something of Great Constancy: The Art of "A Midsummer Night's Dream."* New Haven: Yale University Press, 1966.

INDEX

and politics in Shakespeare's plays, 133, 147

and religion, in sixteenth century, 161

of revenge in Rape of Lucrece, 167

of revenge in Titus Andronicus, 167, 176

and secular history, 109

and self-deception in *As You Like It*, 264n. 16

of self-deception in *Henry V*, 154

and self-deception in *1 Henry IV*, 153

and self-deception in *Richard II*, 148

and self-deception in temptation, 146

and Shakespearean suspicion, 69

and Shakespeare's political realism, 127

ethics, Christian

and charity in *As You Like It*, 40

and Claudius' attempt to pray in *Hamlet*, 157

in *Comedy of Errors*, 20, 22, 23, 24

and "conversion" in *As You Like It*, 39

in *Cymbeline*, 193

and early humanist critique of kings, 97

in *Faerie Queene*, 24

and forgiveness, in *Cymbeline*, 191

in *Hamlet*, 76

and instrumental thinking in politics, 146

in *King Lear*, 88, 94

in *Love's Labor's Lost*, 16, 18

in *Macbeth*, 82

in *Measure for Measure*, 51, 55, 57, 60, 271n. 50

and patience in *Comedy of Errors*, 23

and patience in *Macbeth*, 83

in *Pericles*, 47

and reversal in *Antony and Cleopatra*, 185

and salvation history, 22, 23, 24, 25, 34, 60, 62, 66, 78, 80, 161, 172, 181, 187, 191

and salvation history, in history plays, 97

and self-deception in *Henry V*, 154

and self-knowledge in *Richard II*, 151

and Shakespeare's history plays, 100

and suspicion in comedy, 34–39

and suspicion in *King Lear*, 96

and suspicion in the gospels, 37

and the morality play Vice, 100

and the theological virtues in comedy, 131

ethics, stoic, 162–65

ambiguity of, in *Coriolanus*, 176

ambiguity of, in *Julius Caesar*, 169

ambiguity of, in Shakespeare, 162, 176

in *Antony and Cleopatra*, 182

in *Coriolanus*, 176

in *Cymbeline*, 189

T. S. Eliot on, 175

in *Julius Caesar*, 170

in *Love's Labor's Lost*, 16

in *Measure for Measure*, 52, 269n. 40

Montaigne on, 311n. 6

in *Othello*, 174

and patrician competition, 170

in *Rape of Lucrece*, 165

and self-deception in *Antony and Cleopatra*, 184

and self-deception in *Coriolanus*, 178

and self-deception in *Julius Caesar*, 171

and self-deception, in *Love's Labor's Lost*, 16

in *Titus Andronicus*, 67, 163

Every Man out of His Humor (Jonson), 49

friar's illusion in, 224
illusion in, 223
wordplay in, 224

Nashe, Thomas, 8, 254n. 25
Neale, J. E., 135, 289n. 9
Nussbaum, Martha, 273n. 5

Olsen, Thomas, 189
ontology
  and esthetics and epistemology in
    Shakespeare's writing, 196
  and esthetics and epistemology in
    The Tempest, 213
  Lucrece's confusion about, 216
  rendered esthetically in *Rape of
    Lucrece*, 216
  and resurrection in Shakespeare,
    214
  and stage devils, 210
  stage, and theatrical signs, 205
  theatrical, in *1 Henry IV*, 208
  theatrical, in *Midsummer Night's
    Dream*, 207
  theatrical, in *Rape of Lucrece*, 216
  theatrical, in *The Tempest*, 209, 212
  theatrical, in *Two Gentlemen of
    Verona*, 207
Orr, Robert, 287n. 58
Othello (Shakespeare), 78–81
  Christian destiny in, 79
  mystery of suffering in, 81
  stoicism in, 174
  tragedy depends on comedy in, 81
  Venice and Cyprus symbolic
    locations in, 79
Ovid. *See also* Bate, Jonathan
  Ars Amatoria, 222
  Metamorphoses, 214

Parker, Patricia, 17, 20, 22, 301n. 55

Pascal, Blaise, 243–50
  and Augustine, 315n. 40
  his debate with the Jesuits, 315n. 37
  on Descartes, 315n. 39
  his epistemology based on faith,
    245
  on God's hiddenness, 249
  and *Hamlet*, 246
  "la machine" in the *Pensées*,
    315–16n. 41
  follows Montaigne on the weak-
    ness of reason, 245
  on reason and custom, 247
  and *Richard II*, 245–46
  on self-deception, 245
  his similarity to Shakespeare, 244
  and skeptical faith, 244
Penelhum, Terence, 313-14n. 26
Pericles (Shakespeare), 42–47
  and *Comedy of Errors*, 44
  framed by verbal paradoxes, 43
  self-division in, 43, 45
  self-knowledge in, 47
Persons, Robert, SJ, 289n. 12
Pierce, Robert, 2
Pitcher, John, 264n. 22
Pitkin, Hanna, 126
Play of the Sacrament (from Croxton),
  203
politics. *See also* monarchical succession
  and ethics, Aristotle on, 133,
    288n. 1
  and ethics, in *Faerie Queene*, 133
  and the ethics of self-deception in
    Henry V, 154
  and ethics, in Shakespeare's plays,
    133
  and instrumental thinking, 145
  and minority succession in
    Shakespeare's histories, 136

his political suspicion different
  from Machiavelli's, 99
his similarity to Pascal, 244
his use of "atone," 40, 263n. 14
on the weakness of reason, 245
prefers gospel reference to one in
  Horace, 232
Shuger, Debora, 38, 262-63n. 11,
  266n. 32, 267n. 35
Sidney, Sir Philip, 35
  his assessment of contemporary
    English drama, 206
  and Elizabethan esthetics, 201
  his esthetics and moral affirmation,
    199
  his response to Stephen Gosson,
    197, 304n. 7, 306n. 27
  and Shakespeare's defense of fic-
    tion, 196
  on unities of time and place, 206,
    262n. 4
Simmons, J. L., 295n. 2
Simon, Caroline J. 258n. 54
Sir Thomas More (Munday and others),
  118
Skelton, John, 14, 118
skepticism
  John Bale and, 3
  Stanley Cavell on, 1, 238
  and *crise pyrrhonienne*, 8, 244
  Descartes and, 1, 8, 238
  distinguished from suspicion, 10,
    242
  and exorcism, 4, 211
  faith and, in Pascal's thinking, 244
  faith and, in sixteenth century, 7
  Foxe and, 2
  history play and, 97
  humanist, 3
  and Lucian, 3
  Montaigne and, 9, 234

Nashe and, 8
Robert Pierce on, 2
Protestant, contrasted with traditional faith, 204
and Protestant belief, 204
religious controversy and, 7
Sextus Empiricus' ten modes of, 2
Shakespeare's, 131
in sixteenth century, 1–9
and suspicion, 26
and tragedy, 75
Snyder, Susan, 72, 76, 272-73n.4,
  277n. 43
Sommers, Alan, 273n. 9
Spanish Tragedy, The (Kyd), 68
Spenser, Edmund. *See also Faerie Queene*
  and Elizabethan esthetic of signs,
    202
Spivack, Bernard, 100
stoicism
  in *Antony and Cleopatra*, 182
  and competition in *Julius Caesar*,
    170
  in *Coriolanus*, 176
  in *Cymbeline*, 189
  and ethical ambiguity in
    Coriolanus, 176
  and ethical ambiguity in *Julius
    Caesar*, 169
  and ethical ambiguity in
    Shakespeare, 162
  and ethics, 162–65
  in *Hamlet*, 174, 299n. 34
  and imperfect self-control, 162
  in *Measure for Measure*, 52
  in *Othello*, 174, 299n. 35
  and pagan Rome, 162
  and patrician virtue in *Coriolanus*,
    177
  patrician bias of, 163
  in Renaissance, 162